For Priscilla —
from
Fr. Ron Lawson

D1383645

"LET ME BE A LIGHT"

The Faith Journey of
Father Ron Lawson

Richard L. Rotelli

With an Afterword by Father Ron

ISBN 978-0-7414-6021-9

Printed in the United States of America

Published February 2013

INFINITY PUBLISHING
1094 New DeHaven Street, Suite 100
West Conshohocken, PA 19428-2713
Toll-free (877) BUY BOOK
Local Phone (610) 941-9999
Fax (610) 941-9959
Info@buybooksontheweb.com
www.buybooksontheweb.com

This book is dedicated to all those who hear the call to a Religious life, then follow that call, no matter how convoluted the path may be.

CONTENTS

CONTENTS

PROLOGUE

I first became aware of some of the fascinating life that Father Ron Lawson has led when he suddenly appeared at the 11 AM Mass at St. Mary Parish in Chelmsford, Massachusetts in late November 2008. My wife, Pat, and I have been parishioners there since we first moved to Chelmsford in 1959, and have seen a large number of priests and deacons come and go over those years. But this newcomer was different. He was our new Senior Priest in Residence; but that is not what caught my attention. He had been sitting off to the side of the altar all during Mass, and at its conclusion he arose, and using a cane for support and balance, walked with obvious difficulty up to the lectern and said, "You are probably wondering who this young fellow up here is." And then, with a strong and deeply resonant voice and, without referring to any notes, he proceeded to give a fascinating overview of his background. As he spoke, his twinkling blue eyes seemed to be making contact with the entire congregation, or at least those in the first several pews. But his words reached the entire captivated audience. He held me spellbound. When he had completed his brief background narrative and walked away to a nice round of welcoming applause, I leaned over to Pat and said, "That's my next book!"

Several years earlier, I had written a book that captured the lives of two amazing men: one was a paralyzed ex-cowboy, named Floyd Walser who became a well-known artist in my hometown of Framingham, Massachusetts in spite of having the use of only his right arm and hand. The other was my father, Richie, who was mechanically gifted and had made an enormous difference in Floyd's life. The book, *A Creative Odyssey: the Story of Floyd and Richie*, took much more time and effort for me to write than I had

1

anticipated. Many people have enjoyed reading that true account and many have asked me when or if I planned to write another. My stock answer was always along the lines of "Never!" It simply was too much effort. As one of several publicity venues for that book, I was interviewed for Local Access TV here in Chelmsford. As the TV cameras recorded the dialog, I was asked by Sandy Donovan, the producer and host of the show, called *Faith Connections*, if I planned to write another book. For the first time, my response to that question was, "Well, if I get an inspiration, I might just do that." The very next Sunday I had my inspiration as Father Ron spoke from his heart at our church.

After thinking about the possible challenge that might be ahead of me if I were to undertake such an effort, and without understanding the full scope of the task at that time, I made telephone contact with Father Ron. I introduced myself as a parishioner, nearly his age who had been moved by his introductory remarks at the end of the Mass and who had written a biographical book. I suggested that I would very much like to document his life story. He indicated that he had been thinking for quite a while about making that happen, but in spite of the fact that he had gathered a prestigious amount of background material, had made no real progress toward achieving that goal. I explained that I had written one book that had been a hit with a large local audience. It got excellent reviews. I had made several presentations about it, in person, on radio and on TV, enjoying every minute of those opportunities to bring that inspiring true story to the attention of a wider readership.

I brought him *A Creative Odyssey* to read so that he would be able to get a feeling for my writing style and suggested that if he liked what he read, then I would enjoy the challenge of capturing his story. After about a week, Father Ron called me to say that he had very much enjoyed my book, making the comment that he would loved to have known both Floyd and Richie. He went on to say, "I'd like to go with you."

So from the few minutes when our new priest gave a snapshot of his basic story, to my work with him to describe his marvelous background and right up to the conclusion of this book, I have been constantly captivated by the faith journey he has traveled. It also became obvious to me why he has made so many great friends from all over the world. Enjoy the narrative. It's all true!

Richard L. Rotelli

CHAPTER 1

THE EPISODE OF LIGHT
DECEMBER 1959

The Christmas holidays are always special, no matter where you happen to be. But for 2nd Lieutenant Ron Lawson and a few of his closest friends, the late December days in Bavaria in 1959 were nearly perfect. Ron was a US Army Intelligence Corps officer, who had graduated from Middlebury College in his home state of Vermont in 1956 with a commission as a 2nd lieutenant in Military Intelligence. He was now being further groomed for a year, to work in the field of counter-espionage, or as some would call it, "spy-catching", and would soon attain the rank of 1st lieutenant. He knew that his superiors had a special assignment in mind for him, but they had not yet revealed just where that would be. He was sure that it would be exciting and no doubt would rely heavily on his language skills. He was also quite sure that the expert rank he had earned at the pistol range would come into play. As he thought about where his future assignment might take him, he felt confident that he wasn't being trained so thoroughly in the German language if that country was not to be his destination.

He had majored in Russian at Middlebury and was serious about his Reserve Officer Training Corps (ROTC) studies, enjoying the drills and role-playing exercises. He had a solid, muscular build and loved the outdoors, especially when he could enjoy the winter sports of skiing and ice hockey. Perhaps his most unique feature was his electric blue eyes. When they focused on the person he would be talking to at the time, that person knew that Ron was not simply listening to what was being said, but that he was committing all of his attention to his audience. People often found themselves telling him much more about themselves than they had planned to. It was almost as though he could somehow touch the other person's soul, or at least connect with them on a deeply personal level. Of course there were many times when he would simply be part of a gang having fun at whatever activity was happening. During those times, his clear blue eyes were simply part of what made him a handsome young man.

He had been sent by the Army in June 1959, to the unique village of Oberammergau in Bavaria to spend a year in an Army Intelligence dual language course specializing in Polish and German. This would facilitate his ability to translate to and from those languages should the need arise. He suspected that the Army knew that such a need would indeed arise once he got into his special assignment, wherever that may be. He was stationed at "O'Gau", as the GIs nicknamed it, in what was known as Hawkins Barracks. From an early age, Ron found languages to be relatively easy to learn, including French, which was often spoken by many folks in the vicinity of his hometown. The exception to this affinity for languages was the notoriously difficult Russian he struggled with in college. When he recalled having to stand up in front of the class and read aloud Leo Tolstoy's *War and Peace*, reading it in Russian, he was happy that was in the past.

This was his first time in Europe and he was told in advance that the high elevation of Oberammergau would be something that could take about a week to adjust to. He did find that to be true, but it in no way diminished his enthusiasm for the beauty of that charming place. That municipality, at nearly the southern border of Germany, is famous for several reasons, but probably most notably for its Passion Play, the story of Christ's last supper and crucifixion. In the year 1634 the residents of that village vowed that if God would spare them from the horrible effects of the bubonic plague that was ravaging the areas all around them, then they would perform a Passion Play every 10 years. This promise has been carried out and the play is performed in years that end in a zero. Many of the people of the tiny village take part in the performance which usually includes over 2000 singers, actors and instrumentalists plus technicians; the entire cast and crew all being residents of that magical place.

Now, at the end of December 1959 just after he had turned 25, he was joined by a few of his compatriots from Hawkins Barracks in the quaint village of Kitzbühel, Austria, a few hours east of Bavaria's Oberammergau. The big attraction for this youthful, athletic group was the fabulous skiing to be had on the mountain known as the Kitzbüheler Horn in this "Pearl of the Alps". This was a break from their assigned duties and had been anticipated for weeks.

So now, here on these spectacular ski slopes with some of his best pals, all of them in their mid-twenties, the focus was on who could outdo whom on the powdery course, as they made run after run on the many excellent trails. The weather had been perfect the entire time since the group had arrived in Austria. The crisp, clean mountain air and the almost painfully beautiful views in all directions only added to the thrill. Rounding out the fun of it all was their enjoyment of the warmth of the fireplaces, hearty sandwiches and an occasional brew in the various inns they all migrated to in the village after each day of kicking up plumes of snow powder and occasionally wiping out big-time.

The many difficult, winding and often narrow ski trails called for attention to technique as well as caution to avoid accidentally careening out of control down an expert trail. That could quickly take away the fun and result in spending the remaining time around a fireplace wearing any of a variety of casts. All in Ron's group were adventurous and yet cautious enough on the slopes to avoid any serious injury. Each year, the famed Hahnenkamm downhill world cup ski race was held on this mountain, but none of his skiers participated in that excitement. However, they did ski its trails once at nighttime with full moonlight. But most of the time, Ron did not really care for nighttime skiing since the shadows made for a potentially dangerous adventure.

Getting up to any one of the starting points on a particular trail was made easy with the use of a variety of lifts: rope tows for the lower slopes, Poma lifts (on which one sat and was dragged up the incline; that is, once one mastered the technique of how to actually get safely on and off this device; easy when you know how, but takes some practice) as well as enclosed lifts in the style of a gondola. In one memorable ride in one of these enclosed lifts, Ron noticed a beautiful young skier about his age, with blue-green eyes, riding along with him. She had a movie star aura about her. She did indeed have a brief movie career later in the mid-sixties. It turned out that she was the former Princess Soraya, the ex-empress of the Shah of Iran. Not even a single word was exchanged between the two of them, but the ride close to the woman whose life story is like something from a novel, was remarkable, nonetheless. Later, his buddies couldn't believe that he didn't at least try to strike up a conversation with that beauty. It wasn't every day that he could expect to be in such close proximity to such a woman. He wasn't sure himself just why he was so tongue-tied, but resolved to do better next time - - if there were to be a next time.

Ron, who grew up active in his Methodist faith, had been very involved in the Methodist Youth Group and was its president in his senior year of high school. He particularly enjoyed the social aspects of the group. He had several Catholic friends back then and accompanied them to Mass on one Christmas Eve. But he never really gave a lot of thought to spirituality as such at that time. However, there were several recent faith-filled experiences that began to affect him deeply: none more than the following episode.

It was Christmas Eve, 1959 and he and his friends had finished another fun-packed day on the ski slopes of the Kitzbüheler Horn. They all walked down into the village as dusk approached on a day that was so cold that the powdery snow crunched underfoot. Ron spotted a unique building and he noticed that the sign on its front door proclaimed *Kapelle*, which he knew instantly meant Chapel in German. He told his buddies that he would meet up with them in a bit, but wanted to explore the Chapel. They continued on their way as he walked nearer. He stopped in front of the massive door and pulled on its large, ornate handle. It immediately yielded to him.

He was not prepared for the sight that greeted him. The room was literally ablaze with light. It hurt his eyes after just having been out in the twilight. Once his eyes adapted, the sight took his breath away. The light was coming from hundreds of candles. He realized that he was in a memorial chapel since these brightly burning candles were each directly in front of and below framed photographs affixed to the wall. The youthful faces in the photos were all of young men of the village who had made the supreme sacrifice in World War II. The candles were burning as prayer offerings in their memory. He was deeply moved to realize that all those burning candles represented so much love. These young men were still being thought about and prayed for after all the years since that war.

He stood there, transfixed by the scene he had just stumbled upon. On impulse, he reached for a nearby wick used for lighting the candles and lit it from one of the burning ones. He found an unlit candle and touched the flame to it. He dropped to his knees on the cold stone floor and said out loud, "God, let me be a light!" He remained in this chapel for several thoughtful minutes and realized that this was for him a deeply spiritual moment. It was the first step in the realization that he was being called to a deeper faith. He really didn't understand why the words escaped his mouth, but was to appreciate their meaning in later years. His life was changing.

CHAPTER 2

THE EARLY DAYS

Montpelier, as the capital city of Vermont has the distinction of being the smallest capital city of the entire 50 states. Long-time residents could not be prouder of their city than if it were measured by any other standard. With a long traditional history of farming, natives often happily labeled themselves as n^{th} generation Vermonters, where the larger the numerical value of "n" the more bragging rights one could claim.

Montpelier in the 21st century is a vital, charming community and in 2004 was named among the top ten places to do business in the country. Its colleges and top-notch local school system are all well known for their quality.

It was into this small city (population of just under 8,000 at the time) that Ronald Curtis Lawson was born on December 21, 1934 (a 7th generation Vermonter) the second son of Sidney and Ruth (Russell) Lawson. Ronald, or Ronnie as he would be called, had a brother, Milan, (pronounced My-Lin) who was a year and a half older. Just close enough in age to ensure plenty of good-natured sibling rivalry as they grew through their early years. As it turned out, Ronnie and Milan were really the best of buddies and shared many made-up adventures and kid's games even if they often got into mischief. They remained good friends as they matured and went their separate ways. However, one minor incident points out that boys will be boys. With Ronnie still young enough that he was not yet fully released from his crib to a regular bed, his big brother had been teasing him just a little too long. It was sort of fun for a while, but it eventually got on Ronnie's nerves. Spotting a small toy tomahawk, he whacked Milan over the head with it. Of course Milan wailed and cried and ran around shouting that Ronnie had tried to scalp him, and for no good reason. The tomahawk disappeared and was never seen again. The next day the boys were back to being best pals even if Mom and Dad were left wondering if they had gotten the whole story. (It should be noted here, that although this little episode tended, for years, to be repeated endlessly and laughed over by the various adults in the extended family, neither Ron nor Milan retained any memory of the event.)

Ronnie and Milan   Ronnie and Sidney, Jr.

As a sort of a tag-along, younger brother (and last child), Sidney, Jr., showed up a little over five years after Ronnie was born. He was just enough younger so that he usually palled around with a different group of kids as each of the brothers went through the process of growing to adulthood. Once however, when Ronnie was about six, he thought that he could provide a nice fingernail trimming for little Sid. He had seen adults carefully trimming their nails and he had his own trimmed by Mom when needed. Spotting a razor blade on the

11

kitchen counter, he decided that it would make an ideal tool for a first-class nail trim, even if nobody else had ever thought of such a technique. By the time Mom came running to see why Sid was crying so loudly, a couple of his fingertips were bleeding while Ronnie sheepishly held the bloody razor blade. She was horrified that her sweet son could possibly take it into his head to do something like that. The danger of doing such a dangerous thing was carefully explained to Ronnie but the household never again left razor blades where inquisitive kids could reach them. In spite of (maybe because of) incidents like these, the three brothers were about as close as any brothers could be. They all felt comfortable as a family and knew they were loved by Mom and Dad.

Mom. Dad. Ronnie. Milan   Sidney, Jr. with Mom

There really was very little punishment or spanking doled out by the parents in this normally happy household, but one time, Ronnie and Milan were both taken across their Dad's knee and were simultaneously gently spanked for some now long forgotten misdeed or mischief for which they were both culpable. Chances are that Dad was the one who felt the worst for the discipline but the very young boys promised that they would follow the rules from then on.

The only other memorable punishment for a probably relatively serious infraction was the episode of the canoe paddle. Hanging over the kitchen pantry door was a souvenir canoe paddle. Mom used to threaten the boys with it whenever they acted up in their youthful exuberance. Usually a verbal threat from her suggesting that it would be used was enough to calm things down. But, again for an unremembered misdeed (probably relatively serious by their household's standards), the paddle actually was taken down from its mount and with a stern warning from his Mom, was gently swung at the general vicinity Ronnie's rear end. His reaction was pure athleticism as he jumped aside. The paddle hit the doorjamb, causing a small crack to form in the souvenir. He couldn't tell if his mother was more upset with herself that she had cracked the paddle or had actually intended to use it on her second son, even if the swing was a soft one. He promised to shape up.

It was always a lot of fun for Milan and Ronnie, who sometimes seemed by their pals to be joined at the hip, to role play; acting out the cowboy hero's actions at the movies they would see. Movies in the late '30s and early '40s were an inexpensive and entertaining way to spend an afternoon when they were given permission to actually go and spend the admission price of ten cents each from their allowances. Usually, as soon as they, along with their cousin, Raymond, got home from the matinee, they would re-enact the movie excitement in the back yards of their houses. They would use piles of granite dust as their mountains and their youthful imaginations would keep them (and any bystanders) entertained until suppertime when all would scatter for home. Their backyards were the locations of granite sheds for the Montpelier granite businesses. These sheds were where workers would grind slabs of the hard stone harvested from nearby quarries for industrial and commercial uses. The dust from all that activity would be dumped behind the sheds to be hauled away later. There always seemed to be plenty of mountain-making material available. Later, during the war the sheds were all locked and empty since the workers had all been called off to join the service. The only activity around some of the sheds was at those a bit further away and close to railroad tracks. Hobos would jump off parked trains and sit around, hidden by the sheds, and drink beer. When the train began moving again and they had to jump back on or have to wait for another, they would toss the beer bottles away. Ronnie and his pals used to really get a kick out of collecting as many beer bottles as they could and redeeming them at the local package store for pennies.

Raymond's mom, Mae St. John who was Ronnie's mother's sister, was a significant part of his and his brothers' lives. Aunt Mae and her family lived nearby and were a constant part of the lives of the brothers Lawson. They really loved Aunt Mae for her constant good nature and smiling welcomes every time they showed up at her place. The fact that she was an outstanding pastry cook who was always whipping up some mighty fine pies, cakes, doughnuts and all manner of delightful sweet treats made it all that much easier to think the world of her. Milan and Ronnie would be playing one of their many fun games in the area between home and Aunt Mae's when they would shortly make their way over to call on Raymond. Their delightful aunt would invariably greet them with an invitation to sample a newly baked goodie. They never refused. She would very often take the boys to the Saturday afternoon movies that she seemed to enjoy almost as much as they did. On the occasions when Ronnie's parents needed a baby sitter for their kids, Aunt Mae was the obvious choice as she delighted her charges with a never-ending supply of fun things to do. As the boys got older and needed a chaperone for certain special events, again it was Aunt Mae to the rescue. Ronnie never saw her sad; true to her big-hearted nature, she was always smiling.

The boys' father had joined the Montpelier Fire Department in 1930 and was named Fire Chief in 1937. At that time he was the youngest Fire Chief in all of New England. He had as many as 30 firemen (sometimes more) under his command at various times. They covered two shifts to provide maximum fire protection for the city. There were fire alarm bells installed in the Lawson home and the household was often interrupted at meal times or in the middle of the night when the Chief was abruptly summoned to duty. Over the years, Chief Lawson was involved in many dramatic and often dangerous fire situations. During one particularly stubborn blaze he was exposed to phosgene gas and inhaled it. Initially he thought he was smelling newly mown hay or green corn, a characteristic odor of low levels of phosgene gas, but once the concentration built, the smell was strong and unpleasant. There is little doubt that the poisonous gas in his lungs led to emphysema, most likely hastened by the many cigarettes he enjoyed. He eventually retired from the Fire Department after 42 years of loyal, dedicated service.

Fire Chief Sidney Lawson, 1939

Ronnie's dad always had the use of the fire Chief's car in case of a fire emergency while he was off duty, so that exciting-looking vehicle was often parked at the Lawson household. The kids thought it was pretty special to be the ones who had such a brightly painted red car on their property. Most people in those days in Montpelier, including the Chief, walked everywhere for whatever was needed. He eventually, in 1950 or so, purchased a car to make getting around easier. Since he was a smoker, his inquisitive and imaginative young sons were fascinated by his cigarettes and how much pleasure he seemed to get from deeply inhaling and blowing out clouds of smoke. It was therefore not too surprising that one day when the older brothers were just about of elementary school age, Milan snitched two of his Dad's cigarettes and a book of matches, and with Ronnie practically in lock step, dashed down to the far side of one of the granite sheds to experiment. The seven and eight year-old had no real idea at all of how to smoke a cigarette, but Milan managed to get one lit. Not only did he not inhale, but he actually blew through it causing the lit end to fly right onto Ronnie's eyelid. They stashed the cigarettes and matches for trial another day and both agreed to tell their Mom that the sore spot on Ronnie's eyelid was caused by his clumsily tripping and landing on a rock. She bought the story, or at least they thought she did.

The boys were simply not allowed to stay indoors unless the weather was impossible. Ronnie and Milan loved to use their imaginations when playing with the gang of kids in their neighborhood. Cops and robbers, cowboys and Indians and other games that they made up as they went along had them chasing through the woods that covered nearly all of the local area. When Ronnie and Milan were about ages eight and nine, they built a little cabin in the woods. Although it lacked any real similarity to an actual shed, with barely enough headroom in there for them to stand up straight, they were proud of their handiwork. They also found that it was a great place to squirrel away some of Dad's cigarettes.

One day, little three year-old Sidney, Jr. along with his playmate, Carol, got into the structure his big brothers had built and soon found the stash of cigarettes, but unfortunately also found the book of matches. Before long the little five-by-five shed was ablaze. Mom Lawson spotted the fire in the little structure almost as soon as it began and quickly called the Fire Department. With sirens wailing and red lights flashing, the firemen were on the scene in no time, ladder truck and all. The fire in the shed was engulfing the only way out, so little Sidney and Carol were really trapped inside. The strong, but calm voice of the first fireman at the shed instructed the kids to step back and keep away from the door. They did as they were told and in seconds, the fireman's axe came smashing through the burning door. Their hero, bending to clear the interior, grabbed up both kids and carried them out to safety. The area around the shed was heavily covered with dry leaves and other flammable material, some of which was beginning to burn. The fire was quickly extinguished, but it took quite a while for Chief Lawson to cool down when he heard about it. He was more than a little embarrassed about having a fire at his own home, especially once the source was discovered. When the Chief was told that his youngest child and a little friend had been in serious danger in that fire, he heaped praise upon his firemen and hugged the kids as he delivered a stern lecture about never playing with matches. When he figured out how matches got into the shed in the first place, he had a serious and loud discussion with his oldest two. He also reminded himself about being sure to keep things like matches and cigarettes out of reach of inquisitive youngsters. The punishment for this transgression, although it must have been harsh, is long forgotten.

The school for the Lawson boys was Union School in Montpelier. Not only was it new, having been built in 1939, but it was also designed to be bombproof. All the students, from Kindergarten through eighth grade responded with reasonable attention to instructions whenever there was a drill, by moving out into the corridor and standing on their assigned marble square.

Shortly after the United States got into the war in 1941, a local teenage girl came into Ronnie's First Grade classroom and gave a talk about what had happened to her family while they had been vacationing in Rome in December of that "infamous" year. They were gathered together at the Coliseum and simply because they were Americans, they were placed under arrest. After several harrowing phone calls and a few days when they were concerned for their safety, the family was allowed to return home. A few weeks later, a classmate of Ronnie's who was from Hawaii and had been there with her family when the Japanese attacked Pearl Harbor, described the awful bombing. The entire classroom was silent as she tearfully described the carnage and how close her family came to not surviving. Fortunately her family was quickly evacuated back to their native Vermont.

Ronnie, Sidney, Jr. and Milan
1944

During World War II, the boys spent their summers, along with about five other cousins, on the extended family's farm in Woodbury, about 20 miles (32 km) north. Their Dad felt the call to duty and had enlisted in the Navy in April of 1943. He had to get special permission from the Selective Service System to enlist since he was, at that time over the normally accepted age of 35. He became a Navy medical corpsman, Hospital Apprentice 1st Class, and was stationed at the Naval Hospital in San Diego. He served there in that capacity until shortly after the war was over and was discharged near the end of October 1945. His sons were very proud of their Dad's service and Ronnie was convinced that one day he would join the Navy too. He followed the action in the war by listening carefully to what his elementary school teachers had to say about it and from the newsreels shown at the local movie theatres between the feature films. Once his Dad was in the service he would frequently ask his fourth grade teacher, Mrs. Laramee, whose husband was in the South Pacific, for regular reports on what she knew to be happening.

In spite of the fact that their Dad was away and serving his country in the war, the boys really enjoyed their summers at the Woodbury, Vermont farmhouse. This was where their great-grandmother (Dora Tompkins Lawson) lived along with her widowed daughter Theresa Ainsworth (Ronnie's great aunt) and her grandson, Gerald. The intriguing farmhouse had been built in 1818 by Ronnie's great-great-great grandfather, Daniel Lawson, Sr. Ronnie never knew his paternal grandparents since both of them had died before he was born. His father was orphaned at age 16 and had been sent to live with his aunt and uncle, who also had a farm in Woodbury. But his great-grandmother's place was pure delight. It was up on a mountainside and overlooked a picturesque lake known as Nelson Pond. There was great fishing and swimming to be had in this small pond whenever they could get supervised walks down the steep pasture hillside to get to it.

The boys loved working with the cows and horses and the other farm animals and enjoyed generally being useful. They really loved one little horse in particular and came up with a clever name for it that made the diminutive animal practically a member of the household. He was called "Lawnie". The farm was not equipped with electricity at that time, and running water was only available from a spring-fed faucet in the kitchen. Bathroom breaks were kept short since the sole facility for such a need was the 3-holer outhouse located in the unheated back chamber.

Ronnie and Milan with Lawnie

Part of the fun of working and living in such a place, was sleeping in the beds with large down comforters that you could bury yourself in. Other things in the house that really captured Ronnie's imagination were the large wood-burning cast iron stove in the kitchen, used for heat and cooking; his great-grandfather Freeman Lawson's big old rocking chair; and the old tub. Maybe mostly the tub. It was right there in the kitchen, made of copper and (at least to a kid) was huge. It was short at one end and higher at the other. This was the tub that everyone in the family for several generations had used to take a bath. The water was heated in a pot on the stove and generally was not emptied from the tub until all the planned baths were taken. Ronnie tried not to get too dirty, but eventually a bath was needed. He always made sure it was a quick one.

Other curious things that captured the kids' attention as they explored the farmhouse were the large barrel in the upstairs antechamber, and the perpetually cool cellar. The large barrel was full of homemade maple sugar, a sweet-toothed boy's delight. They were told that it was normally off-limits, since it was the main source of sugar for the farm. The cool (sometimes even cold) cellar had been blasted out of the stone ledge that surrounded the property in order to build the house. That had resulted in a natural refrigeration, or at least a very cold walk-in storage space where some foods could be safely kept. Ronnie loved to go down into that cool place and was in awe of the large supply of home-canned vegetables.

His great-grandmother told him how much work went into making maple sugar. He got a little sleepy-eyed as she related how they had to tap the best maple trees but always at the correct time of the year, capture the slow-moving sap, and then boil it down. They had to constantly stir the sap so that it wouldn't burn. He could hardly believe that it took 40 gallons of sap to yield one gallon of syrup. Making the syrup into sugar required more time and effort to evaporate it. Some-times they would harden the syrup by dropping it in the snow. They called that "sugar on snow". Even at his young age of seven or eight, he could appreciate how the hard-working farmers, like most Vermont farmers, managed to live exclu-sively off the land. He really didn't see himself growing up into a similar hard life, but this surely was a fun place to spend summer days with his brothers and cousins. It was always great fun when they made butter and ice cream.

In the summer of 1945, Ronnie was at his paperboy job delivering the Boston Herald to his 52 customers. In the winters he would deliver his papers by lugging them along on his sled, but now he was on his bike. He was as jubilant as could be when he saw the Wednesday, August 15th headlines proclaiming the end of the war, even though he had heard the good news on the radio. Nearly the entire population of his city gathered downtown to celebrate this momentous event, spontaneously and happily forming a huge, noisy parade.

One close-to-home true story of the war that affected eve-ryone in Ronnie's family very deeply was what they believed to be the loss in action of Lester "Russ" Russell, one of Ronnie's older cousins. Russ was with the Army Air Corps and had been on his 32nd mission over Germany as tail gunner in a B-17 "Flying Fortress" as part of a squadron on its way to bomb Nuremburg. It was November 30, 1944. As Ronnie's family would find out some time later, his plane lost one of its four engines while deep over German territory. Within minutes, it lost another. With both disabled engines starting to burn, it was clear to the pilot that there was no way they could keep up with the rest of the squadron. He told his crew to bail out. Nobody did. They all felt that it would be safer to go down with the aircraft and hope for the best. Fortunately for the crew, after the plane's crash landing they were all able to get out and head for the German woods where they hid until nightfall. Under cover of darkness, they headed west each night for three nights, subsisting on their Air Corps rations. On the third day, Russ and two of his crewmates came across an old barn that appeared to be deserted. The three of them watched it carefully from the cover of nearby woods and eventually figured that it would possibly make a reasonably safe shelter for a few days. Just as they were about to enter it, a German hunter, rifle at the ready, showed up. They immediately surrendered and were marched into the city.

They were brought into a house occupied by several men, women and children. Instead of being turned over to the Nazis, the compassionate villagers cared for Russ and the two other American airmen. However, harboring the enemy was cause for death in a concentration camp, so eventually a policeman was called for. As he took the flyers away in chains, one of the women of the house began to cry and rushed up to the prisoners giving them a sack full of bread, butter and meat. That extraordinarily generous gesture by the crying woman helped Russ and his buddies survive the coming ordeal. They were eventually sent to a prisoner of war camp on the Baltic coast. Russ spent several months in that camp until the Russians came in and liberated him.

He was soon in the capable hands of the US Army where he was fed real food and was sent home to Vermont a few weeks before Germany surrendered. Of course his family was thrilled to have him home, safe and sound, after believing that he was killed in action and not having known of his close call with the B-17 in Germany.

All during his confinement in the POW camp and for many years later, Russ would recall the crying woman and her courageous act of kindness. He often wondered why she was so moved to tears. After 63 years, he was contacted by a researcher for a German organization that dug into the stories behind the sacrifices made by American servicemen in World War II. Russ found out that the "crying woman" was still alive. The researcher contacted her to find that she was amazed to discover that Russ was still alive also, since she had been told all those years ago, that the Americans were about to be shot to death in a nearby cemetery. Russ, upon learning of those details, explained to those around him that what he experienced was "An atrocity that didn't happen". He and his buddies were not shot, he explained, due to the kindness of the crying woman and her family. He is convinced that they saved his life and are an example of the good that people can do, no matter the circumstances.

Once the boys' father returned from active duty with the Navy, he went right back to being Chief of the Montpelier fire department and things were back to normal at the Lawson household. Although Ronnie and his brothers did attend their Methodist church regularly, their father rarely, if ever, managed to get to any services. Their mother would attend on a regular basis. While they all believed in God, no one in the family could really be considered as having a particularly strong faith. Other than Ronnie's mom, none of Ronnie's immediate forebears were religious or were known to even attend church. As hard working country farmers, getting to a church service was often nearly impossible mainly due to the lack of a nearby house of worship. There was no expectation that any of the boys would ever have a call to serve the Lord. All three brothers attended Sunday School until the eighth grade. They were however very happy to be connected to the social aspects that came with belonging to their church. Ronnie, who had been with the local Methodist Church since the age of seven, was soon a member of the junior choir, then the teen choir and finally, the senior choir. He acquired a great love of music through those experiences and it became a key factor in his eventual spiritual life.

Ronnie's mother, a regular churchgoer, served a term as President of the WSCS (Women's Society of Christian Service), a Methodist organization for women and later held the position of Church Trustee. For several years, she spent a lot of time working on the annual Christmas bazaar. Her efforts always resulted in raising lots of money for the church. She was highly skilled as a knitter. Her hand-knit specialties were always a bit hit at her Women's Group bazaar and were among the first items to sell out every year. In her capacity as President she also supervised the Women's Group meetings known as Circle Meetings.

Ronnie felt that pretty much the whole state of Vermont was in one way or another connected to his family after he had been told of some of his family's background. His mother's great-great grandmother was Amanda Luce and was born in 1795 in Hartland, Vermont. Her father, Moses Luce, along with his brother, Oliver, founded Stowe Vermont back in April of 1794, being the first settlers there. They had come from Martha's Vineyard when the state was first formed and was opened to settling. This is the same Luce family that the very well known Clare Boothe Luce was part of after she married Henry Robinson Luce about a year after Ronnie was born. Her husband was the publisher of *Time, Fortune* and *Life*. She was famous in her own right for being a playwright, editor, journalist, ambassador to Italy and was one of the first women ever in the US Congress, as a Republican in the House representing the state of Connecticut.

Ronnie always loved the milk, cheese and other milk products made by the Cabot Creamery in Cabot, Vermont. The extra enjoyment he derived from their goods was principally due to the fact that he had several cousins from nearby farms whose cows regularly contributed to the creamery's operation over the years. He felt that if it weren't for the Lawsons and their extended family, Vermont just wouldn't be the same.

As he approached his high school years, his Mom and Dad filled him in on a bit of other interesting Lawson family background. He found that he is in the 11th generation of descent through his great-grandmother, Dora Tompkins Lawson, from Elder John Strong born in 1605 in Taunton, England who settled in Northampton, Massachusetts and died there in 1699. The ship that Elder Strong crossed the Atlantic in was none other than the *Hopewell* that only a few years earlier had been commanded by Henry Hudson in his search for a Northwest Passage. (In Ronnie's adult years he would discover that Elder John Strong was also an ancestor of Diana, Princess of Wales.)

Through the influence of a distant cousin, Ronnie became interested in family research. This cousin, Zepherine Towne Shaffer, descended from family in Calais, Vermont. She was an ardent genealogist and a prominent member of the Mayflower Society. She also was very involved with the Daughters of the American Revolution in Washington DC.

He found that he is descended from three of the Mayflower passengers, who arrived from England via Holland at Plymouth, Massachusetts in 1620. The list continues. He is a 10th generation descendant of Henry Samson, born in 1603 at Henlow, England and who died in 1699 in Northampton, Massachusetts; a 12th generation descendant of Elder William Brewster, born in 1566 at Scrooby, Nottinghamshire, England who died in 1644 in Plymouth, Massachusetts; 13th generation descendant of John Billington born circa 1580 in England and died by hanging in Plymouth. He had been tried for murder. The only available explanation for his crime is that the Billington clan was not as "genteel" as some (hopefully most) of the others.

With this long and (with the one exception of old John Billington) proud heritage to reflect upon, Ronnie just knew that he was destined for a great future. But there was high school and college ahead and then most likely a career in the US Navy, as an officer out of Annapolis.

CHAPTER 3

HIGH SCHOOL YEARS

Montpelier High School was fun for Ronnie. He never really had to study, but always maintained high grades and was on the honor roll every semester. In spite of being such a whiz kid he was also very sociable, going to all the dances, school events and ball games. For a while he dated a cute girl named Sue, but they were never serious. They were really very good friends.

One of his passions was the stage. He was in every play and operetta that the school put on and was in *Masque*, their theatrical group. In his freshman year he had a lead role in the George S. Kaufman and Moss Hart comedy, *The Man who Came to Dinner*, bringing down the house with his performance. His character in that play was a nerd and he felt that he didn't have to reach too deeply to empathize, although none of his friends really thought of him as a nerd since he was so sociable and out-going.

But operettas became his main love on the stage. He played the Mikado, the Japanese Emperor in *The Mikado*, a comic opera in two acts by Gilbert and Sullivan. This is probably the most popular opera ever written and he really enjoyed bringing the Emperor to life on the school's small stage. He also had a major singing role in *H.M.S. Pinafore*, another Gilbert and Sullivan collaboration.

He was so taken with the excitement of the floodlights and grease paint, that in his senior year, he enjoyed the homework of writing his own play. It was part of a drama class exercise and had a Christmas theme. The assignment was to compose a one-act play, and then have it performed with the student's choice of actors and actresses. Of the various plays developed and performed as part of this assignment, Ronnie's was well received and may even have been one of the best.

Ronnie was also blessed with the gift of a wonderful singing voice with near-perfect pitch. He was very involved in the Men's Chorus as well as the Mixed Chorus, both ensembles very popular with everyone. The teacher who directed these groups, Miss Newton, was a tough taskmaster, but brought out the best in her vocalists. Ronnie began as a second tenor, but as his voice changed he switched to baritone where he continued his singing over the years. Music, especially vocalizing, stayed very important to him throughout his life.

As if all his acting and singing weren't enough, he also was drum major of the high school band, where he enjoyed himself immensely. He particularly loved the yearly excitement of traveling to the Vermont State Music Festival in Burlington. Each year the band members, after performing proudly, would stay the weekend in a local hotel; chaperoned of course. They had lots of silly fun without doing anything really outrageous and never got into any trouble.

The school faculty appointed him the Treasurer of the Athletic Association. This involved his controlling all the monies that were paid at all the school's athletic events, mainly football and basketball games. He was completely responsible for taking the collected cash, counting it and properly banking it. Another task at which he excelled.

In spite of all this activity (practically a whirling dervish) he continued to keep his grades high, stayed on the honor roll and enjoyed all the social life his high school had to offer. In his senior yearbook for the Montpelier High School Class of '52, he was voted *Most Popular Boy* and *Best Actor*. No surprise there. Other significant yearbook entries were: "Won't we miss... Ronnie's horse laugh"; "What Our Star Dealers Would Have (meaning our wish list) ... Voice like Ronald Lawson"; The Class Will... "I, Ronald Lawson, do hereby bequeath my 'horse-laugh' to Roy Kelley so he may be accused of having 'Hysterics' in chorus also"; The Class prophecy notes: ... *Ronnie Lawson – learning about the French – firsthand.*

Older brother Milan, just one year ahead of Ronnie continued to be one of his good buddies along with several classmates. Until Milan graduated with the class of '51 and went on to study Civil Engineering at Northeastern University in Boston, the brothers often double-dated. They continued to be more than brothers, but best friends as well. Of course it also helped that Milan had a car.

Milan also did well in high school, maintaining high grades (getting the *Pro Merito* award) in spite of having a job every day after school and somehow managing to fit in time to get his homework done. In his junior year he was in 4H and competed at the Washington County Fair & Field Days, a major local event. He was proud to take first place, winning a blue ribbon in dairy judging and cattle showmanship. As if that wasn't enough, he also took second place in tractor driving. He loved photography and used that skill to capture some great photos for his class yearbook.

Kid brother Sid, Jr. followed in Ronnie's footsteps in his fascination with being on stage and with singing. He also took over on the drum major's duties and graduated from Montpelier High School with the class of 1958. He was to eventually receive his BFA in Drama at the Boston Conservatory in 1972, attending that college on the GI Bill. He went on to have a long and enjoyable career in the theatre.

In Ronnie's senior year it was time to get serious about selecting a good college to attend. His various language teachers as well as his Guidance Counselor strongly suggested nearby Middlebury College. It was very well known as a top institution for the study of languages. Since he had displayed a natural affinity for such a curriculum, as well as all the other courses he took, this seemed a perfect match. He was not completely convinced and so he applied to Harvard and to the University of Vermont as well as Middlebury. He was pleased to be accepted by all three colleges, but the kicker that really made the choice easy was that Middlebury offered him a full, four-year, all expenses paid scholarship. That made Mom and Dad not only proud, but relieved that the normally high cost of four years at a top college would be taken care of for them.

After a short period of reflection on what he might do in the future, he decided to major in Russian. When his high school buddies heard that, the reaction was pretty much along the lines of "What? Are you nuts? Russian is impossible!" He wasn't worried about that and felt that a working knowledge of that language would potentially be useful in a number of ways given the world political condition at the time. The continuing Cold War that deepened the rivalry between the U.S. and the Soviet Union and the attendant propaganda, espionage, and weapons development kept the world off balance. He was sure that being fluent in Russian would be of great use to his country.

Although he knew that Middlebury had Army Reserve Officer Training Corps (ROTC) on campus, he still felt that he could get an appointment to Annapolis somehow, so that his dream of a Navy career could be realized.

CHAPTER 4

MIDDLEBURY COLLEGE

On a glorious September day in 1952, with the leaves showing off their best colors and with the unmistakable scent of autumn in the air, Ron Lawson began his freshman year experience at Middlebury College in Vermont. This was to be his first time away from home, even if it wasn't very far and he was enthralled with the whole idea of college life. Getting to know his fellow classmates and finding his way around the large campus were his initial priorities. Learning the names and hometowns of the other freshmen was made easier by the requirement that all these newcomers were obliged to wear tags clearly showing those facts. The few extra days that were provided for freshman orientation did the trick in helping him feel comfortable with the thought that he would be able to find any particular building for his various classes. They were scattered all around the large campus and a lot of fast walking would be required to get to where he needed to be and to get there on time.

For the first semester, he had a very crowded room with three other guys in Starr Hall, one of the men's dorms, built over 50 years previously. One of these fellows, Chuck, who hailed from New York City, had been enrolled the previous year at Vermont College located in Ron's hometown. He was known to Ron back at Montpelier High School in his senior year, since Chuck had been dating one of Ron's classmates. She was the best girlfriend of Ron's steady date back then, so the kids frequently doubled dated. Ron enjoyed Chuck's company and when it developed that both of them would be at Middlebury, they planned to room together.

Both of the old girlfriends had gone off to other colleges and were no longer in the picture. Ron's other two roommates included a real introvert, who was hard to get to know and a semi-serious young man interested in sports, girls, beer and occasionally college classes and homework.

It wasn't very long before one of the things that really took a lot of Ron's attention was the fact that the fraternities and sororities had ramped up their search for new pledges. He found himself being invited to nearly all the fraternities on campus to be interviewed by the upper classmen members. Ron took an almost instant liking to the men at the Alpha Tau Omega (ATO) house and the feeling was mutual. But he went to all the fraternity open houses he was invited to, and that included practically all of them. When it came time to make a choice to "go Greek", several fraternities extended offers to him, but he chose ATO.

He went through all the hazing and mischief that the fraternity culture demanded and was still able to attend to his classes and get all his homework done almost always on time. Like all fraternities on just about any campus at that time, each of the pledges was obliged to perform some inane or wacky stunt as part of the hazing before initiation. His assignment, which he carried out very well, was to measure a particular distance along the main street in Middlebury in hot dog lengths. This portion of that piece of Middlebury topography had been measured over the years by any number of fraternity pledges using very unorthodox measuring equipment. This had included various items of women's underwear, frozen whole fish and athletic supporters. Ron had been given an actual hot dog to use as his measuring instrument. When he went from being a lowly pledge to being a fully initiated brother, he was happy with his choice and the fact that from now on, perhaps he would have a little more time for his studies. He reminded himself that his parents really expected him to perform well and even though that was his own plan too, he sometimes needed the thought of their faith in him to get himself to buckle down and give the social life a break for a while.

31

He was carrying a heavy course load and, not surprisingly, did very well with it. He studied German, French and Russian among other liberal arts courses. He also joined the ROTC, which it turned out was a bit ironic since he had, for as long as he could remember, planned to go Navy. He had applied for an Annapolis appointment, but none was available. He was told by the senator who was working the issue for him that he would surely get an appointment to West Point with no problem at all. He refused that, since he really had no strong interest in the Army. However, he did join Middlebury's ROTC since it seemed like a way to at least get some conditioning and military discipline that might come in handy if he were to eventually get into the Navy. The particular branch of ROTC at this college was Army. It would be emphasized in his junior and senior years and would require a commitment to serve as an officer in the US Army after graduation. One of the ROTC branches he could choose from at the end of his senior year was Army Intelligence. He had to admit that it did sound interesting. Perhaps even more so than being a naval officer.

Although the original choice of room and roommates in his freshman year was OK, the room was simply too crowded with four young men in it, so for the second semester Ron moved to another dorm, Gifford Hall. Here, he roomed with a senior who was a fraternity brother and who would graduate with the class of 1953. This five-floor residence facility was much newer, having been built just 12 years previously.

In his sophomore year, he lived in the ATO house and shared a room with a fellow from Long Island, New York who was also pretty bright and did very well in all his studies. They got along very nicely with each other and were able to not only study in deep thought at the same time in the same room, but also could have a great time at the several frat parties that came along nearly every weekend. Alan had taken piano lessons in his younger days and still enjoyed knocking around on the piano down in the game room. Usually after most parties, he could be heard playing the only tune he could still perform: an old blues piece. And it sounded pretty good. It was funny how the same tune played by the same guy the next afternoon just didn't sound quite the same.

The ATO brotherhood was pretty nearly constantly on the move, always up to some good-natured fun and occasional mischief when it wasn't time to cram for a major exam or simply to complete assigned homework. One of their favorite things to do in the wintertime was to flood the flat side lawn before too much snow piled up, and play ice hockey. Pucks were constantly getting buried and lost in the snow at the sides of their homemade rink. A solution to that problem was unwittingly provided by their cook, "Mrs. S", a wonderful and good-natured woman from nearby Cornwall. She always prepared delicious meals for the guys' suppers and saw to it that their favorite dishes were cooked just the way Mom used to. Every week she would make up a batch of doughnuts that made a hit with everybody. But in the winter, she was prevailed upon to cook up a few extras, which were purposely left aside in someone's room. After a few days - - voila! Hockey pucks.

Ron was elected Social Chairman at ATO in this, his sophomore year, a job usually held by upper classmen. He was responsible for organizing all the weekend parties and being sure that each one had a theme to help make them memorable as well as lively. Chaperones were required at each fraternity party, and all the frats had to abide by the rule that no women were allowed above the first floor. The campus-wide rule was that the women, who all resided on the Women's Campus across the street from the Middlebury main campus, had to sign in to their respective dormitories by midnight on weekends. On weeknights, they were required to be signed in to their dorms by 10 pm.

Also during Ron's sophomore year he attended Winter Carnival again, a major yearly event at the college. It was the oldest and largest student-run carnival in the country. One could expect to see fireworks, an ice show, ski competitions and a host of other exciting activities. For example, there were fraternity parties, a ball at which a carnival king and queen were crowned, ice sculpture competitions among the fraternities and many other memorable events for the enjoyment of all. Often, the college a cappella choir would entertain, conducted by the world-famous German-born pianist and composer, Jean Berger. Ron had been an active member of this choral group almost from day one as he continued his love of singing. Having such a notable and gifted music educator as Herr Berger on the faculty was one of the many reasons he was glad that he had chosen Middlebury for his college education.

Each year the winter program seemed to be better than the previous one, if such a thing were possible. (In his senior year he was among the men chosen to be in the Carnival Court as a competitor for the position of Winter Carnival King. Although he wasn't selected as King, he was pleased at being in the running.) But at this Winter Carnival, Ron ran into an old acquaintance, a lovely young lady who was then attending the University of Vermont (UVM). They had first met the previous summer when they both worked at a resort known as the Bonnie Dunes at Lake Dunmore, Vermont. She had been a chambermaid while Ron was a bus boy. At that time Ron was infatuated with her, but never expected to see her again. After running into each other at the Middlebury Winter Carnival and even more frequently since she was a sorority sister of Ron's best friend's girlfriend, they started going out together and had several dates. But it fizzled out for no obvious reason. Perhaps it was God's plan.

Ron really did enjoy his college days and was determined to get the most out of the social opportunities as well as the academic life. He rarely went home, except for holidays and special family occasions since he was having such a good time. To help remind him that he did have a home, his brother, Milan, would occasionally drive up for the weekend. He was studying Civil Engineering at Northeastern University in Boston and would look forward to spending at least part of a weekend from time to time with Ron, enjoying much of the social life on that wonderful campus. Milan was enrolled in the Cooperative Education Program (Co-Op) at Northeastern where, as part of that program he worked a portion of most semesters at companies that gave him some hands-on experience in his chosen field as well as a modest income to help pay his expenses. Although he graduated from Montpelier High a year ahead of Ron, Milan would be getting his engineering degree in 1957 since he had worked for a year before starting college in 1952, the year Ron entered Middlebury. The time spent in the Co-Op program added an extra year to his graduation date. It also turned out that he would be joining the Army about the same time as his kid brother. Milan was proud to be part of the Northeastern ROTC Corps of Engineers.

In his junior year Ron continued to live in his fraternity house and roomed with its president, who was one of his classmates. Ron was selected as Steward of the Dining Room, a paid position that required him to plan out all the meals, place the purchase orders for supplies, coordinating with the House Treasurer, and to supervise the brothers as they served the meals. He ensured that the proper decorum, or at least a minimum of horseplay, was evident during mealtimes. He had to watch the new pledges and even the newly initiated brothers carefully since they could easily get distracted and goof up a bit. As an example of everyone getting distracted, he watched one of the upper classmen waiters make a fancy presentation of a special covered plate to one of the brothers who was known by everyone in the house as a very finicky eater and who was never bashful about complaining loudly about the food. When the shiny cover was removed from the plate with a flourish, what had been delivered for this young gourmet's approval and comment was seen to be a dead rat. It took quite a while for the laughter and comments from the 50 or so diners to subside: nearly as long as it took for the color to drain back into the recipient's cheeks.

It was in this year that he was elected to the very prestigious position of President of the Inter-Fraternity Council (IFC). This was a very powerful assignment, since the IFC supervised the social activities on campus with the oversight of the Dean of Women, Elizabeth Kelly, a force to be reckoned with. "Ma" Kelly, as she was called, had been an Army nurse in the Philippines during most of WWII. Now she was married to the Middlebury football coach ("Red" Kelly) and was very much "with it". Ron spent many hours in her office along with other officers of the IFC as he kept her up to speed on the latest fraternity activities on campus as well as those areas of strict IFC rules that perhaps could be improved upon.

In the summer of 1955 right after completing his junior year, Ron attended ROTC summer camp. He drove with several classmates to Ft. Bragg in North Carolina. There, they spent six weeks at Fayetteville for the rigorous work of learning a bit of what Army life in the field could be like. The intense summer heat combined with fleas, gnats and ticks plus snakes crawling through the grass could easily have been dispensed with, but it seemed that was part of the fun of it. The exercise of going through the gas chamber was definitely no fun at all. It was filled with tear gas and this exercise was meant to drive home the importance of the gas mask and to gain confidence in its effectiveness. Ron paid careful attention to his Drill Sergeant's barked instructions, but still didn't manage to get it completely right the first time, along with most of his fellow officers-to-be. It was a powerful exercise and he eventually learned it well. Map reading training was much easier for him, but the night exercises in the woods with all manner of unseen but heard animal sounds was not a lot of fun. But crawling through mud and over obstacles while live fire was directed close over their heads was probably the most stressful part of the training.

The hard work of this summer camp resulted in not only getting some very important training, but also the bonding of the men as they developed good teamwork. There were quite a few of Ron's classmates from Middlebury at the training, good buddies he had known there, but he also met several others who would remain close friends for years.

The one bright spot in the entire six weeks of summer camp was the weekend of July 4th, the only time the young soldiers had off. Ron, along with a group of others, went to Myrtle Beach, South Carolina to spend the weekend on the beach. They were warned that it would be a punishable offense to return with a sunburn. They ignored the warning, soaking up the sun while enjoying the sandy white beaches and playing football in the salt water. Of course they all went back to Ft. Bragg with painful sunburns, but agreed to tough it out, pretending that there was no problem at all. Finally, they were civilians again and could enjoy what was left of the summer before starting their final year of college.

Big Man on Campus

After a swim, back at the Lawson homestead, 1955

In his senior year he and his fellow members of the IFC had a difficult issue to deal with and still remain friends with other classmates. It turned out that a Junior Prom weekend party at the Phi Kappa Tau (PKT) house was such a stupefying success that it seemed to the brothers that carrying all their living room furniture out to the side lawn and setting it all on fire was a great idea. Ron and others on the IFC had to penalize them. After some sobering discussions a workable penalty was levied. PKT was put on social probation for the rest of the school year, meaning that they could have no house parties during that time. Many of those brothers suddenly became best friends with classmates from many other fraternities and often managed to get invited to attend one of their parties.

Senior year was critical in other more serious ways, but none so much as the great difficulty he was having with his major, Russian. He was so busy with all sorts of extra-curricular activities that he just wasn't putting in the time and effort such a difficult language demanded. He was having a particularly tough time with reading *War and Peace*, a famous novel by Leo Tolstoy. Simply reading it in its native language was tough enough, but having to read it out loud in Russian and conduct a discussion in the language as part of his classroom activity was pure torture. During this final year he lived in the old dormitory known as Hepburn Hall, located right next to Mead Chapel. In this dorm he had the role of Resident Advisor, in charge of just about everything there. With 300 men in that building, there was always something to interrupt his attempts to study, as the highly spirited young guys found all sorts of ways to test his patience. What was so much fun about rolling a keg of beer up and down the corridor late at night? When he wasn't disciplining portions of the population, he often filled the role of big brother to many, helping with all sorts of issues. Little wonder that he had so much difficulty with his own studies. His comprehensive exam in Russian, which covered all four years of study in his major, was nearly his downfall. But he made it.

A very special event also took place for him in his senior year. As is typical of most colleges, Middlebury had a senior honor society, complete with a sense of secrecy and special importance. It was known as the Blue Key and was very selective about adding to its membership. He was surprised and honored to be chosen to be in this prestigious group. At a special ceremony held in Mead Chapel he, along with five other active, high performing leaders in his class, was inducted. With the chapel packed with students, present members of Blue Key solemnly moved among the audience. One by one as they got to a newly chosen member, elected previously in a secret meeting, they would stop behind the seated inductee and somberly place a blue ribbon that had a blue-painted key on it around his neck and then tap his shoulder. The ceremony continued until the last person was "tapped" and then the existing members as well as the new inductees would wordlessly walk out of the chapel with a solid round of applause ringing out until they were all out of sight.

Members of Blue Key had certain assignments given to them by the hierarchy of the organization. Ron's first one was to get the freshmen from the class of 1959 in his dorm to learn to sing the "Midd" songs so that they could loudly perform them at football games. Other members of Blue Key were directed to rouse the poor guys from their beds in the middle of the night and escort them over to the steps of nearby Mead Chapel while they were still in their bed-clothes. There, by the light of a full moon, Ron passed out song sheets and led them through the ones that were best for singing during football games. His own strong voice would not let up until he was satisfied with their performances. Eventually, the now energized freshmen were allowed to head back to their dorms to try to get a bit more sleep. Chances are that they caught up on it during their next lecture classes. At each football game, Ron gathered as many freshmen as he could find and led them and everyone else through the rousing songs. It wasn't tough to locate the freshmen, since they were obliged by the upperclassmen to all sit together. The players on the field seemed to do their jobs with reckless abandon spurred on by the singing. It didn't always result in a win, but no one could deny the strong sense of spirit felt by all.

Overall, his college experience was very positive and he relished the entire four years of it. In spite of being so intimately connected with an exuberant student body and being very active in his fraternity, he drank only in modera-tion. He never had a drink before his Middlebury days. As he matured into adulthood, that aspect of his personality changed slightly in that he would learn to enjoy occasional wine or cocktails at social gatherings.

He reflected back upon the many good friends he had made as well as the professors who had ignited his love for learning. He recalled especially his best friend for the four years, Jerry Ocorr, who hailed from Rochester, New York. Although they were not fraternity brothers, they found that they had a lot in common. Jerry was elected president of his fraternity, Delta Kappa Epsilon, and was Vice President of the IFC when Ron was President. So many other friends came to mind, such as Bob Vuillet who had represented Sigma Phi Epsilon in the IFC, as well as Bob's girlfriend, Sally Smith.

One particularly memorable professor whose class in Contemporary Civilization really enervated him was Prof. Waldo Heinrichs. The good professor, born in British India of Baptist missionary parents, had been a WWI ace in air battles over Germany. He had been shot down, severely wounded and taken prisoner by the Germans and subsequently released. He was a fascinating person and always held his students' attention.

Ron's love of music was enhanced even further as he spent each of his four years studying music and music appreciation under Professor Alan Carter. That gifted violinist had created the Vermont State Symphony Orchestra. Professor Carter also founded and presided over the Middlebury College Composers Conference and Chamber Music Center, Inc. In his spare time he guest-conducted many orchestras including the Hartford (Connecticut) Symphony and the Boston Pops. Ron felt really fortunate to be lucky enough to study under such an amazing and talented individual.

Of course he could never forget the great Robert Frost who came to the campus a couple of times a year to read his poetry to an overflowing hall with students in rapt attention. He was the best-known and most beloved American poet of his time and had won the Pulitzer Prize four times and received 44 honorary degrees. The students loved him. He served at Middlebury's Bread Loaf Writer's Conference for many years. This conference, designed for aspiring authors and poets, was a summer school experience located at nearby Bread Loaf Mountain in the Green Mountain chain. It has been described as the oldest and most prestigious writers' conference in the country.

When graduation weekend, in June of 1956 finally arrived, marking the end of an era for him, he was pleased to have his parents and kid brother, all of them glowing with pride, in attendance at the ceremonies. Ron had made arrangements for Sidney, Jr. to stay in one of the dormitories on campus, giving the teenager the feeling of being rather grown up. Unfortunately, Milan was unable to attend due to a conflict from which he simply could not escape. In addition to graduating with a Bachelor of Arts in Russian degree, Ron was also commissioned a 2nd lieutenant in the Army with his forthcoming specialization in Intelligence. This was to be a two-year commitment, but became much more than that.

For the summer of 1956 and until January 1957 Ron worked as an assistant director of Admissions for Middlebury while he lived in one of the dorms. This was a paid position during which Ron visited a number of high schools and prep schools in various parts of New England. His job was to get the seniors interested in attending Middlebury. He had enjoyed the school so much that he was an enthusiastic messenger. He loved meeting so many interesting people and felt that he had been a good emissary for his alma mater.

In early January he was off to Baltimore to begin his Army career, no longer feeling the least bit unfulfilled at not being in the Navy.

CHAPTER 5

US ARMY COUNTER INTELLIGENCE
1957 – 1959

With the cold and snowy January of 1957 making the area around Middlebury College a winter wonderland again, Ron looked forward to his assignment in the warmer climate at Fort Holabird in Baltimore, Maryland. He faced 12 weeks of training, which included learning about Army Intelligence, its history and function. Students at this facility learned debriefing and interrogation techniques, surveillance, and the handling of weapons. This U.S. Army post, founded as Camp Holabird in 1917 had changed not only its name but also its principal role several times over the years. Now the U.S. Army Intelligence School and Counter Intelligence Records Facility was its main purpose. It was not a large site and was not very appealing, situated among foul-smelling factories in the southeast area of Baltimore and abutting the small, yellowish Colgate Creek that poured into the Atlantic Ocean.

His living space was in a World War II type Bachelor Officers Quarters or BOQ located on one side of the parade ground. Facing the base one would see an American flag directly in front of Headquarters (HQ). The BOQ and other enlisted personnel quarters were on the left of the parade ground; HQ in the center front; the library and training areas on the right. The Officers Club and Enlisted Club were located at the rear center of the facility.

Ron effortlessly made friends with his fellow officers and they all commiserated about the training that lay ahead and what a dump this place was, even if the food was not so bad. They knew that after their initial four months at this location, they might be located close to the nation's capital in Washington, D.C. That was something to look forward to.

Ron, always a quick study, soon learned that a Counter Intelligence (CI) agent is responsible to supervise and conduct CI surveys and investigations of individuals, organizations and installations to detect, identify, assess, counter, exploit and neutralize threats to national security. He needed to learn the skills necessary to accomplish these responsibilities by quickly understanding and using photographic and recording equipment and to assist in non-technical surveillance. He had to know how to prepare and disseminate CI reports and to maintain files and databases. He also would have to learn how to conduct investigations into sabotage, espionage, treason and sedition activities and to liaison with foreign agencies. He had to be able to apply fundamentals of military and civil law and to detect, neutralize and exploit CI targets. He would be expected to conduct overt collection, surveillance and non-technical operations and more. Some would refer to this as "spy-catching", but there was no denying that, although it was fascinating, there surely was a significant element of potential danger involved. Of course, no job, not even in the military or perhaps especially in the military, is over until the paperwork is done. This clearly was to be no exception.

It was good that his ROTC training and experience had conditioned him to pretty much know what was going to be expected of him in this assignment and also had helped to keep him in good physical condition. He was young and eager.

A very important part of his training would include weapons handling, especially rifle and pistol shooting. He focused mainly on learning to be quick and accurate with a holstered .45 or sometimes a .38 caliber pistol. He could be found at the firing range nearly every day for what would be a 12-week cycle of training. He became an expert shot and understood very well what it takes to keep your piece in top condition by regular cleaning and oiling. He practiced how to quickly and smoothly draw his pistol from its holster under his jacket. He wanted the casual observer not to be able to detect that he was wearing a weapon, but to be quite surprised to find it out and ready for use in the blink of an eye should the need arise.

At the end of the summer he was assigned to Fort Lesley J. McNair in Washington, D.C. This heavily fortified series of buildings, 10 minutes from downtown Washington, is the headquarters for the Military District of Washington (MDW) and is part of the Fort Myer Military Community. Fort McNair is still famous for housing the "Old Guard": soldiers who patrol the Tomb of the Unknowns at Arlington Cemetery. It is also the location of The National War College whose mission is to prepare future leaders of the Armed Forces, State Department, and other civilian agencies for high-level policy, command, and staff responsibilities.

The fort is located on the point of land where the Potomac and Anacostia rivers join. It is guarded and patrolled around the clock by members of the Military Police Corps, often using police dogs. It was an imposing sight and was quite a contrast to the wide-open collegiate life Ron had come to love.

Ron's rank of 2nd lieutenant and his ROTC training had him assigned in the Counter Intelligence Corps (CIC) with the 116th Detachment located right next to Ft. McNair at Tempo (Temporary) Building C. Others in a corresponding area of service were in the 902nd and were at the other end of the complex in Tempo Building A. Ron and his fellow officers were allowed no contact with the 902nd due to the high level of professional secrecy involved in all their assignments and training.

Now at Ft. McNair, he also developed his skills in self-defense using various methods of hand-to-hand combat. All this was excellent physical conditioning and he could feel his bodily strength being honed as he endured his training. This added to his self-confidence in his abilities to do his job well should the need to defend himself arise. As his training progressed he felt that he was meant to be in such a role, but also relished the social life to be had in the Washington area. Always, a social butterfly, he continued to make friends easily and never tired of finding ways to enjoy life.

For the first couple of months in Georgetown, his accommodations were in a small pie-shaped 2-bedroom house at the corner of Q Street and Wisconsin Ave that he shared with another CIC lieutenant. At a party, Ron, still his outgoing and personable self, was introduced to a few diplomats who were being reassigned to Europe for a couple of years. After hearing from him about his cramped living space, they offered to allow him and four of his friends, all recent college graduates, to move into and to live at their furnished and spacious four-bedroom townhouse at 4837 Reservoir Road. The rent of $250 a month was just manageable with each of the guys chipping in $50 apiece monthly. Overlooking the Potomac, and being only a half-hour bus or tram ride from Fort McNair while also being in the heart of lots of activity made this place even more attractive.

The four young men he shared the place with had recently graduated from Princeton, three of them serving in Navy Intelligence. The other was in training to become a Foreign Service Officer in the State Department. None of them ever had any real money, other than just enough to get by. Nobody had a car so whenever they went anywhere in this fascinating place with so many wealthy and famous residents, it was always by public transportation. The young officers did their own cooking and did their best to pick up after themselves. None of these young men were aware of the fact that Ron often carried a loaded weapon or, for that matter, what type of duty he had. A good CI agent simply did not discuss such matters.

Ron learned more than simply how to be good at his job. He also learned how to cook some pretty appetizing meals. Since he and each of his housemates had to fend for themselves, each young officer had to cook supper once a week or so, in a learn-by-doing sort of way. The gentleman in training for the State Department was studying Chinese and arranged for someone from the Chinese embassy to come to their house once a week and cook a Chinese dinner for them. No one was ever late for those meals. (This housemate, J. Stapleton Roy, or "Stape" as they all called him, had graduated magna cum laude from Princeton in '56. He became a senior United States diplomat specializing in Asian affairs. He rose to become a three-time ambassador, serving as the top U.S. envoy in Singapore, the People's Republic of China, and Indonesia. He attained the highest rank in the United States Foreign Service when he was eventually promoted to the rank of Career Ambassador.)

They were all fascinated by the Washington social life as revealed in the Washington Post and they dreamed of attending those fabulous diplomatic dinners. There always seemed to be a party at one or another of the many embassies, several of which were along nearby Foxhall Road. And of course, parties were a constant at the homes of the rich-and-famous, such as the very well known Gwendolyn Cafritz, wife of Washington Real Estate Millionaire Morris Cafritz, who had a luxurious mansion on Foxhall Road and was nearly always in the society pages of newspapers and magazines.

Not to be outdone, the young officers decided to organize a summer afternoon garden party and to make it a memorable event. Using their best diplomatic talents they enlisted the help of high-ranking neighbors whom they had all gotten to know. It was good that these neighbors, one an admiral, the other a senator, thought very highly of these clean-cut and well-mannered young men. Sure enough, Ron and his friends invited all the Cherry Blossom princesses to come in formal dress to an afternoon garden party in the beautiful rose garden at the back of their home. All the princesses showed up along with all the other invited guests from the neighborhood. Everyone was dressed in formal wear or in white uniforms. Ron had recently purchased a white dress uniform, usually meant for use only in the tropics, but the heat and humidity in Washington, DC surely made it feel like a tropical location. Everyone in his band of brothers agreed that he looked pretty sharp. One of Ron's housemates worked at the Navy Receiving Station and had arranged for a band to be at the event. With a full bar and classy guests, it was an extraordinary success and actually made the society pages of the Washington Post. Take that Gwen Cafritz! The cost to each of the five housemates to pull this off was $50. They had to cut way back on their usual expenses for a while, but it was worth it.

The energetic and resourceful young officers found other ways to enjoy this time in their lives. For example, in the summer of 1958, they heard that a family from Pope's Head Road in Clifton, Virginia was soon to be off on a two-year assignment with the State Department and would need someone to look after their home while they were away. So the five of them, along with a few other friends persuaded the family that they would look after their place for them in lieu of rent if they could stay there, especially on weekends. They agreed that at least one of them would stay there full time. It turned out to be a charming Civil War era stone farmhouse, complete with two horses and a small flock of geese, and a large in-ground swimming pool. They made a point of properly maintaining the property, feeding the geese, and taking good care of the horses as well as keeping the pool swimmable.

For real relaxing and fun when time allowed, Ron and a group of 14 young officers, some Army and some Navy, managed to rent a triple-decker unfurnished house located right on the water at Rehoboth Beach in Delaware. About a two hour drive from Georgetown, Rehoboth was sometimes called the Nation's Summer Capital, since it was so often a summer vacation destination for Washington D.C. residents. The cost was shared by all 15 and amounted to $15 each for the whole summer. On many 1958 summer weekends, this place would be home to the initial group of 15 plus nearly as many more invited guests. These guys knew how to have fun when not hard at work at their training to be "spooks" or whatever their particular military field was.

It is of course impossible for a gang of enthusiastic young folk not to make quite a racket as they enjoyed this facility, especially when partying around a bonfire after dark. Even when talking in what they considered to be normal levels, they would frequently find that the local police had been summoned to get them to keep the noise down. It became Ron's job to interface with the cops and to assure them that the message was received "loud and clear", or "5 by 5" as one of the pals who had some Signal Corps experience stated it. Ron quickly discovered that the source of the complaint was the gentleman who lived in the house that abutted their place. Ron went to this neighbor and in his charming yet serious manner, made friends with the fellow, explaining that he and his guests would do their best to be quieter. Once the neighbor realized that Ron and his buddies were really good folk, the complaints to the police were a thing of the past. Ron breathed a sigh of relief when he realized that the problem was a non-issue now. He knew that his group had to be very circumspect since they were all working for one form of military intelligence or another. Police complaints finding their way back to their respective units would have gone over "like a lead balloon".

Ron's brother, Milan, who had entered the Army about the same time that Ron had, after his ROTC training at Northeastern was stationed at Ft. Belvoir, Virginia. He would drive up to spend some time with Ron and friends at both the Georgetown house and the beachfront property as often as he could, enjoying their times together.

Ron's professional life in the District of Columbia was different, to say the least. None of his housemates were permitted to talk about their work and training in Intelligence just as none of them were ever aware of the fact that he usually packed a loaded pistol under his jacket. He was often assigned (sometimes with other more experienced Army personnel) to bodyguard duties whether it was at Arlington Cemetery wreath-laying ceremonies or at one of the Officer's Clubs in the District where his job was to protect the foreign dignitaries. Once, he had bodyguard duty for General

Lyman Lemnitzer and General Maxwell D. Taylor, both four-star general officers at the time and both with nearly unbelievable records of accomplishment. At that time, General Lemnitzer had just been promoted to Chief of Staff of the Army, succeeding General Taylor in that post.

Ron also acted as a Personnel Security Investigator, checking on a variety of people's backgrounds. Once, although he was nervous about doing it, he had to interview the then head of the Secret Service, James Rowley. This was a routine investigation in which the subject under discussion was updating his security status as a matter of form. The interview with this imposing figure left Ron feeling relieved when the task was completed. Then in retrospect he realized that he could do his job well with anyone at all at any level. A nice confidence boost.

Four young Intelligence Officers at Arlington National Cemetery. Do they look professional, or what?

Ron "wired for sound" on DC Mall with a demonstration about to happen. He's ready!

Ron and his co-workers were often directed, in duty-teams of four to six men, to be at Arlington National Cemetery at the Tomb of the Unknowns anytime a dignitary arrived for a wreath-laying ceremony. These dignitaries included Queen Elizabeth II, President Eisenhower, Fidel Castro and others. 2nd Lieutenant Lawson was on duty in mid-summer of 1958 at the amphitheater at Arlington for the entombment of the Unknowns from World War II and the Korean Conflict. In his Army white uniform, Ron found himself struggling to not show his excitement as he carried out his responsibility of ushering Admiral Nimitz to his seat. That white uniform was very unusual for a Counter Intelligence Corps agent but was required for this solemn event.

Ron hadn't been home to Vermont for over a year and a half. Thanksgiving in 1958 was approaching and although he had sent and received several letters, he thought it would be really nice to be back with his family for the holiday. He wasn't at all sure how to make that happen, until he discussed the thought with one of his Georgetown neighbors, a Marine Corps colonel, who was a pilot based at Anacostia Naval Air Station. The colonel, who flew aircraft carrier-based fighters, needed more flying time and asked Ron if he would like to hitch a ride home on his unique dive bomber. What a great opportunity! The aircraft, an old Douglass AD-5 Skyraider, a propeller-driven plane with foldable wings and side-by-side seating, was just the ticket.

Ron's taxi ride home for Thanksgiving.

This truly was a marvelous piece of aeronautical engineering. It was the last heavy single-engine plane built for Navy and Marine use to be flown and landed on aircraft carriers. Its engine, an air-cooled radial 18-cylinder wonder, was the same one used two on each wing, on the B-29 Superfortress. It cranked out a nearly unbelievable 2700 horsepower for takeoff. This was the largest engine ever used on a single-engine airframe. Its two-man crew sat up high and had an unparalleled view out the front. Although AD-5s first saw combat in World War II, where they were often flown in the role of submarine hunter-killer, several of them saw heroic use in Korea and would effectively come to see action in Vietnam as well, in a variety of roles.

Ron registered as co-pilot at the Naval Air Station, with his pilot buddy vouching for his sanity, if not experience. He donned a flight suit and with no visible trepidation, climbed up on the aircraft's wing. He then stepped through the opening made when the canopy was slid fully aft and settled into his seat to the right of the pilot. With plenty of instruction on what not to touch, push, twist or turn, (especially the control stick that was right there between his knees) and how to properly strap in, he had the ride of his life in this marvelous and historic airplane. This was not a fast aircraft by 1958 standards so with a cruising speed a little over 200 mph and flying at around 14,000 feet he was eventually delivered right to the Burlington, Vermont airport. All along the way Ron picked out familiar landmarks and was thrilled to be in the air on such a clear day and flying in such a unique aircraft.

Once they landed, his pilot buddy taxied over near the terminal. Ron took off his flight helmet, crawled out the plane's sliding canopy and stepped down onto the wing. From there he jumped down onto the tarmac. He whipped off his flight suit, tossed it back up to the pilot with a salute and a grin and moved out of the way as the plane quickly taxied and, with a deafening roar, was soon airborne again. The amazed folks that had been watching this unexpected landing and delivery as they stood, transfixed by their front row seats in the terminal, must have thought that this was a celebrity of some sort, even if his "taxi" was a really unusual aircraft.

Ron had previously called his brother, Milan, who was home on leave from his post at Fort Belvoir, to ask if he could pick him up at the airport without telling anyone in the family that they would have him home for Thanksgiving. Sidney, Jr. was also home for the holiday from his studies at the University of Vermont. The Lawson household enjoyed a special Thanksgiving with everyone there catching up with each other's activities since they had last been together. Ron felt a little brotherly one-upmanship as he described his unique ride home. He had almost forgotten how much he missed his mom's cooking and, as his brothers did, he dug in for second helpings and eventually his favorite desserts. And of course Mom and Dad made a big fuss over their three sons while really wishing that they could stay a lot longer, but knowing that all three of the boys were deeply into their new lives.

When it came time to return to base, Milan drove his brother back to Washington in his new Chevy recently equipped with snow tires. When they reached the Baltimore-Washington Parkway, snow was falling heavily, with six to eight inches of the unplowed stuff on the road. There was very little other traffic during the snowstorm, but it didn't seem like such a big deal for the native Vermont driver. After dropping Ron off at his place in Georgetown, Milan continued on his way to his quarters in Virginia, thinking that he would love to get a ride in a Skyraider. Ronnie always did seem to fall into the good stuff.

By June 1959, Ron had completed his two-year commitment to the Army as part of his ROTC program. He looked forward to civilian life. After a short job search he found what appeared to be an appealing job. He had taken an offer extended by Lockheed Aircraft Co. in St. Louis, Missouri in their sales/marketing team. It sounded interesting and that part of the country had always appealed to him. But when he visited the Out-Processing office in the Pentagon to sign all the necessary forms to conclude his Army career, he was surprised at an offer that was then made to him. His record of service during his two years was exemplary and it was noted that he seemed to have a flair for languages and that he had majored in Russian in college. This made him one of a few ideal candidates for a special assignment if he would agree to it. With his discharge paperwork pushed to one side, he was asked if he would strongly consider extending his Army duty by agreeing to go to a special, one-year language course in Germany. If he accepted, he would then be required to continue in the Army, once his language course was complete, for an additional two years at an undisclosed location, most likely in Europe somewhere. After considering the excitement and further adventures such a life could provide and comparing that to being part of an industrial organization, he accepted the Army's offer the next day. He called Lockheed and informed them that he would not be joining them after all. There is no telling what his life might have been like if this last-minute decision hadn't been made.

So in late June 1959 2nd Lieutenant Ron Lawson found himself heading for Bavaria to be enrolled in the Dual Area Language Course (German and Polish) at the Army's Intelligence facility. This facility was in the hard to pronounce, but enchanted village of Oberammergau.

CHAPTER 6

OBERAMMERGAU
1959 - 1960

In mid July 1959 and at age 24, Ron found himself boarding a Pan American World Airways flight that would eventually get him to West Germany so that he could make it to his final destination of Oberammergau in Bavaria where his new language training was to take place. He really had no other commitments or major plans so he looked forward to his first trip to Europe and the adventures that were bound to be a big part of his life. The large, four-engine propeller-driven aircraft was crowded and noisy as it lifted off from Fort Dix, New Jersey. Even though Pan Am and other airlines had begun using jet engine-powered aircraft such as the Boeing 707 at this time, Ron was somehow comforted to know that the vehicle he was now in was tried and true, with many safe transatlantic journeys. Commercial history was made October 26, 1958, when Pan Am inaugurated trans-Atlantic 707 jet service between New York and Paris. In the next few months, jetliners rapidly entered service throughout the world.

His first stop on this flight was at St. John's International Airport in Labrador, Canada for a quick refueling and to pick up a few more passengers. At the time, this airport was an American/Canadian Air Force base. (It was closed long ago.) Then they were airborne again and on their way to the next scheduled stop in Prestwick, Scotland, where passengers were allowed to deplane for a few minutes if they chose in order to stretch their legs. Then they flew on to Frankfurt,

West Germany where he changed planes and flew on to Munich. This was enough traveling for a while, even if he was not yet at his final destination. Thoroughly exhausted, he registered at the Columbia Hotel in Munich; a Bavarian hotel for American troops and their families.

In the morning, after a good night's sleep and a hearty breakfast he, along with a couple of other young men who it turned out were also heading for the same course of studies, boarded a train to their final destination in the village so high in the Alps that he was told that it could take a week for him to adjust to the altitude. Even though its elevation is about half that of "Mile-High" Denver, Colorado he was cautioned to take it slow upon arrival. Sure enough, once he was at his quarters in the Intelligence Facility at Oberammergau he did feel a little breathless and was more fatigued than he would have thought would be the case. He figured that his dizziness and decreased appetite were just the result of his long trip, but his superiors were well aware of high-altitude sickness and helped him ease into his routine, while ensuring that he drank plenty of fluids and ate the right kind of food. He was good as new before the week was out. But he felt that the spectacular views in all directions were going to keep him feeling light-headed for quite a while.

The facility was sometimes referred to as a Kaserne, the German word for barracks. Several dozen Kasernes with NATO forces were at that time spread all across Germany. After the Cold War most were closed, some even demolished. At that time his particular post was called Hawkins Barracks by the Americans. It was named in 1954 in honor of Lt. Col. Jesse M. Hawkins who lost his life in a gallant battle in the Bavarian theatre in World War II. This facility was originally known as Hötzendorf Kaserne, the home station of the 54th Mountain Signal Battalion of the Nazi Wehrmacht's 1st Mountain Division. After the Signal Battalion's departure in 1944, the Kaserne was used by the Messerschmitt organization for conducting secret experimental work on one of Hitler's top priorities, jet aircraft engines. Most of their actual work was done in the 22 miles (35 km) of lighted, air-conditioned caves that they dug into Laber Mountain directly behind what would later be the Hawkins Barracks' pistol range. The equipment for the plant was removed by the Allies after the war and the tunnel entrances were sealed by blasting. US personnel were never permitted to enter the caverns.

Oberammergau is located in Bavaria, in the southernmost part of Germany. Bavaria shares international borders with Austria, The Czech Republic and Switzerland. The Bavarian Alps are along the border with Austria and lay claim to the highest peak in Germany, the Zugspitze, which is usually crowded with tourists.

Ron was more than a little impressed with everything about his new home. The compound was surrounded by a high stone wall with guards posted at the entry. It included a parade ground and a helicopter landing area. There were several two-story Bachelor Officer Quarters (BOQ) and a dozen three-story apartment buildings that were home to married officers. Some of the American intelligence and teaching staff lived in the taller buildings also. The three-level apartments all had front balconies affording a wonderful view down the mountainside looking at the Oberammergau village and the surrounding Alps. As one looked east and up the mountainside, the Laber Mountain could be seen with its cable car that carried people up the steep slope. This mountain is not in the highest peaks of the Bavarian Alps but it offers spectacular views nonetheless. From the top of this mountain, one can see the foothills of the Alps, with their many lakes. On a clear day, even Munich and further north can be seen from there. There was also a marvelous restaurant, called a Gasthaus in German, on the summit. He looked forward to an occasional good meal there with his fellow officers. He also anticipated the great skiing to be had as well as simply riding the cable car to the summit and just relaxing in the sun; enjoying the views on those days when he would surely have a little time off from his training.

This scenery was all new to the Vermont native who was of course very familiar with the Green Mountain range in his home state as well as the neighboring White Mountains in New Hampshire. But, he had to keep reminding himself, he was here for the next year not for the views but to learn the languages the Army needed him to master as well as further training in counter espionage.

There were several buildings located within the confines of the stone wall that defined his new home and he would explore nearly all of them. Included in this compound was the Language School (his main reason for being there) a school for training of Military Police, and a Special Weapons School for training in atomic weapons. A high level of security clearance was required in order to enter the buildings in the Special Weapons School, since they were classified Secret. Since he did not have a need-to-know, he never did get to explore that intriguing part of the barracks.

When he, along with two other fellow officers whom he met on the train from Munich, first arrived in O'gau, as they sometimes called the place, they stayed in the building identified as BOQ 604, which was next to his school building. After going through an easy couple of days of "in-processing" the new students were assigned to their permanent quarters. Ron's was in Mann Hall, which today is known as Haus Edelweiss. (In 1995, when the German military, under NATO took charge of the base, the buildings that had American Names were re-named in the Bavarian fashion. The edelweiss is well known as a unique European mountain flower, growing only in the rare atmosphere of the Alps above the tree line.) Initially, they had all their meals in the Officers' Club. Ron never had a problem with getting up for breakfast, but now he could hardly wait for it since the views of the snow-covered Alps out the large windows were breathtaking. Not only was the Officers' Club the location for nearly all their meals, it was also where much of the socializing took place. He continued to enjoy that aspect of his life as much as ever.

Ron made good use of the pistol range and was there once a week for the duration of his assignment. There, as part of his intelligence training, he would have pistol and rifle practice on a regular basis. He was proud to be able to demonstrate that he hadn't lost his marksmanship and familiarity with weapons.

He also regularly spent time in the chapel attending the services and singing in the Protestant chapel choir, led by Mrs. Edna Storey, wife of Goeff Storey, a British major from Belfast. The choir, backed up by a pipe organ, usually had 20 members singing their hearts out and doing a beautiful job of it. This truly unique ecumenical chapel was set up in such a way as to have one hour for Catholics, another hour for Protestants, and another on Fridays for those of the Jewish faith.

Every now and then, on Sundays the choir members and other officers in the chapel at the time, would see a dignified priest in the sacristy where the choir robes were kept, getting himself ready for Mass. It turned out that he was a military chaplain known as Fr. Pius Fischer, OSB (Order of Saint Benedict) and was assigned to the 14th century monastery at nearby Ettal Abbey.

Ettal Abbey

He was the military's choice for chaplain in Hawkins Barracks, since he was fluent in English. He regularly said Mass for the Catholic community here in the military compound. The group in the chapel was fascinated by him, since they learned that in World War II he had been in the German Afrika Korps commanded by the "Desert Fox", Field Marshal Erwin Rommel. Even though Fr. Pius was an ordained priest, he still had had to serve in that outfit as a regular rifle-toting soldier. Ron and his fellow officers invited him to the Officers' Club for coffee after a Sunday morning Mass that he had just celebrated in the same chapel where they had worshipped as a Protestant community. All who met him were enthralled by his true-life anecdotes, his charming and charismatic personality and were interested in getting to know him better. One Sunday, he invited Ron and a group of four others to come and visit his monastery. No one in that invited group had ever seen a monastery and it surely sounded like a great idea. Somehow, Ron felt a special bond with Fr. Pius and became interested in better understanding the Catholic Mass knowing that he would take him up on his offer to visit the monastery before too long.

This assignment in O'gau was in many ways very different from his training at Fort McNair, but one constant was how quickly he integrated into the Army life in his barracks and at his school classes. He met many interesting people all working in Intelligence in its various forms and studying a variety of languages including Russian, Czech, Hungarian, Slovak, and Serbo-Croatian as well as German and Polish as he was doing. Although nobody had to read *War and Peace* out loud in Russian, he wondered if he could still do that if asked.

With the warm weather at this time of year, he was required to wear the Army's new short uniform (since discontinued), which was styled after the British summer uniform. With khaki short pants down to the knees, short-sleeved khaki shirts, long black knee stockings, black shoes and a visored officer's hat it was hard to believe that they looked at all intimidating.

His focus on the study of his assigned languages was intense. He studied Polish for seven months and then, with only one weekend off, moved on to his five months studying German. While studying these languages, he was obliged to communicate solely in Polish or German. That can, and occasionally did, provide for some embarrassing and comical situations. For example, they were all required to tell a joke once a week in the language being studied. The more ribald the joke was, the better it was judged to be. In one Polish class, someone attempted to use the phrase, "My Greetings" in his joke, which in Polish correctly translates as "Moje uszanowanie", but slipped up and, with the whole class in rapt attention used the verb "szuszac" instead of "uszac", causing him great embarrassment, since szuszac refers to urination. It took quite a while for the poor guy to live that one down. But his joke was remembered long after many of the others were forgotten.

Many mornings when Ron would enter his language class, he would draw a funny cartoon on the chalkboard. It practically cried out for nutty phrases to be added. The other students would, one after the other, add Polish or German words or phrases to add to its silliness. This activity took off some of the pressure of studying such difficult languages and provided a bit of comic relief. His instructor had no problem with the light-hearted silliness, but very quickly got down to business upon entering the classroom.

While studying German, taught by Herr Bachmann, a former U-boat officer in the German Navy, the best part of the day was when the students could get the teacher into describing his underwater battle experiences during World War II. He was a native of northern Germany, near Hamburg, and was amazed that he had made it through the war unscathed while cooped up in a steel coffin, dodging Allied depth charges and trying to sink enemy ships. He had been young then and doing what his country demanded of him. He was thankful that the war had ended when it did. He was even more thankful that he was now permitted to do what he really loved: teaching eager young minds.

While studying Polish, the class group would leave the barracks and travel down into the local countryside visiting restaurants and even the famous Neuschwanstein Castle and other well-known tourist destinations. There, in civilian clothes, they would conduct all of their conversations in Polish. The idea was to learn everything that they might hear (or overhear) in interrogations of, or in conversations among refugees. The same approach was used during their immersion in the study of German. They needed to learn the local dialects, slang phrases, swear words and strange phrases that they would surely eventually encounter in their future assignments.

Polish came quickly, if not effortlessly to Ron since it was in many ways similar to the Russian he had studied in college. Now he wished that he had put more effort into his major back then. He found that his Polish teacher, Marian Lewicki, had been an officer in the Polish Army at the beginning of World War II and had been a prisoner of war in the town of Murnau, not far from Uffing. He was never able to return to Poland after surviving the war because of the Communist takeover of his country. Although his family remained in Poland by force of politics, he settled in Uffing with the widow of a German officer who had died in the war. Barbara Schober had smuggled food and other items to Marian while he was in the POW camp. Now they lived together as husband and common-law wife. Professor Lewicki was a most interesting man who became close to his students, often inviting them to his home in nearby Uffing/Staffelsee with beautiful views of Lake Staffelsee. He reinforced his students' knowledge and use of Polish by continually using that language in his conversations with them, only switching to English if anybody was simply missing his discussions and had a puzzled look on his face. In future years, whenever Ron would return to this part of the world, he would make it a point to visit with the good professor.

Ron not only did extremely well in his studies, he also (not surprisingly) made many classmate friends that would remain important to him in his life as time went on. Captain Tom Blakey, who was the Headquarters Commander of Hawkins Barracks, and his wife, Ginny, and several others were part of his social group. They all had great times together in Oberammergau and in Garmisch-Partenkirchen a market town near the Austrian border. What had been separate communities of Garmisch and Partenkirchen until Hitler forced the two to combine in 1935 to improve the location of the 1936 Winter Olympics, was casually known as Garmisch. The residents of Partenkirchen never appreciated the snub and were proud of their cobblestoned streets and the many fresco style treatments on the facades of houses and other structures, offering a glimpse into the past. Even though Garmisch was slightly more progressive, it was not unusual for all traffic to be stopped in early mornings and late afternoons as dairy cows were herded to and from the mountain meadows. The group would occasionally spend an evening there in a café that specialized in Russian music. Sometimes they would dine at the officers' club in the Hotel von Steuben in the Garmisch recreation area. In Oberammergau, their favorite nightspot was a restaurant (or as the place was locally referred to, a Weinstube) called the Bemsl that specialized in serving wine. At these comfortable and relaxing places, they would invariably converse between themselves in English without feeling even a little guilty that their Polish, German or other studied languages would suffer from a little break in otherwise constant use.

Fortunately a couple of Ron's friends had cars at their disposal and didn't mind in the least driving the short distances through the beautiful terrain to get to Garmisch and other such interesting locales. Normally whenever any of the group of officers wanted to get from O'Gau to visit Ettal or the next village in the other direction called Unterammergau, they would simply walk, occasionally practicing their languages with each other. Somehow Ron acquired a bicycle that came in handy when he wanted to go in a different direction from the rest of the gang. For serious local travel, such as to Munich or Kitzbühel they always relied on the good German train system.

Ron and his friends found the village of Oberammergau truly fascinating for many reasons, not the least of which was the fact that so many famous wood-carvers plied their art at places all over town. All sorts of carved and painted statues and figures of all description were available for purchase, usually at prices that kept them out of reach for his group. Of course one couldn't be very long in this unique village without learning about the world-famous Passion Play, the story of Christ's last supper and crucifixion that the residents put on every ten years. The Passion Play began in the seventeenth century when the villagers promised God that if they were spared from the devastating effects of the Bubonic Plague that was overwhelming the area, they would perform such a work. Ron knew that the next performance would be scheduled in 1960, since they are enacted in years ending with a zero. He made it a point to be sure to attend.

Ron became close friends, and remained in contact over the years, with the Schmid family who owned a hotel and restaurant in Oberammergau called the Hotel Restaurant Friedenshöhe. It is an extended small villa that has lots of charm with dining tables both inside as well as out on an open deck. The outdoor tables featured magnificent views of the Alps. The hotel is still in business. In its early days, before it was owned by the Schmid family, the famous and prolific author, Thomas Mann, had been frequent summer guest. Paul Thomas Mann (his full name), a German Novelist, essayist and 1929 Nobel Prize laureate, was one of several distinguished guests. The villa had served for a short time, immediately after the end of World War II as an American Officers' Club. At that time, a young American Army sergeant named Henry Kissinger of the Counter Intelligence Corps could often be found there enjoying the camaraderie of his cohorts. The Schmid family has maintained albums of photos, autographs and scribbled messages from their many houseguests since World War II. Sure enough, future US Secretary of State Kissinger's autograph is proudly displayed to all who leafed through the albums in later years.

The Schmid family's place was of special interest to one of the lieutenants in Ron's BOQ. The young man had a crush on a very pretty waitress there named Heidi. He constantly talked about her beauty and how much he wanted to see her again, but was simply too shy to go there without reinforcements. He convinced a group of fellow students, including Ron, to accompany him to the place and to be sure that they would wind up in her serving area. The lovesick young officer realized that she was out of his league and when Herr Schmid came to their table to be sure everything was to their liking, he introduced his daughter, Heidi, and made a point of explaining that she was engaged to be married. In future years whenever Ron would wind up in O'gau he would make it a point to stay at the Friedenshöhe. He would often bump into Heidi and her husband there. They would all get a chuckle over the memory of how they had first met. Heidi's brother, Erich, and his wife, Gretl, have remained good friends with Ron over the years.

With their youthful exuberance and excellent physical conditioning, Ron and his pals made full use of everything this wonderful assignment had to offer. Several winter days they could be found skiing the mountain slopes, trying their best not to let the scenery distract their focus from their technique. Included among the peaks they skied was the Zugspitze, the highest mountain in Germany, located at the Austrian border in the town of Grainau of the district of Garmisch-Partenkirchen. In warmer weather, they often went mountain hiking in the nearby Alps. A fascinating feature within a short walk was "The Matterhorn of Oberammergau", the Kofel mountain top. It is shaped like a high stalactite pointing upwards all by itself. Although a bit treacherous, it was a favorite place for tourists to climb, so of course the enthusiastic officers just had to climb it. Ron couldn't help thinking that this assignment surely beat the daylights out of a job with Lockheed, or anywhere else for that matter.

In the middle of August 1959, one of his fellow officers, a Catholic, had invited Ron to accompany him to a 6 AM Mass in the O'gau village church of St. Peter & St. Paul. It was the Feast of the Assumption; a Holy Day of Obligation for Catholics and this particular Mass was for the children. Even at this early hour, the church was packed. He was enthralled at being witness to a liturgy with a full orchestra and choir, singing a Mozart Mass. This whole experience spoke to him at a deep level and he had thoughts then that perhaps there was something more fulfilling in a faith-filled world.

Before he knew it, the Christmas season of 1959 had arrived. Ron and his fellow officer students had a few days to themselves. A small group of about six other officers, at Ron's suggestion, headed by train for the village of Kitzbühel, Austria, for what they hoped would be some great skiing. Ron had done some research into truly special skiing locations and, although it would be hard to miss a good one if you walked blindfolded in any direction, Kitzbühel for some reason called out to him. At the suggestion of friends who had been there before, the group arranged to stay the week at the beautiful Park Hotel Sonnenhof in the heart of Kitzbühel. This turned out to be more than just a relaxing and fun-filled ski trip, but was the occasion of a turning point in Ron's life when, on Christmas eve, after a great day on the slopes, he found himself on his knees in a cold memorial chapel, blazing with the light from hundreds of burning candles. He had uttered the words, "Let me be a light," not understanding the deep meaning behind that phrase until quite some time later.

The group of happy, but tired young officers returned from their skiing adventure to their home at Hawkins Barracks in Oberammergau. On Christmas morning, they ran into Fr. Pius Fisher who was at the barracks Chapel once again to celebrate Christmas Mass for the Catholics. The priest reminded them of his earlier invitation to go to his monastery in Ettal for a visit. This seemed a unique way to celebrate Christmas so the group followed him to Ettal and were given a complete tour of the monastery. It was a fascinating place. Fr. Pius suggested that a very educational experience for one person could be had with a couple of night's stay-over in an interesting, though little known room in the monastery. Ron, always looking for a new and different learning opportunity, stepped forward and agreed to participate in whatever this might be.

He then spent a few nights in one of the monastery's very small bedrooms. It was of the type found in most convents, monasteries and the like for housing religious clergy and nuns. There was a main dining room, called a refectory in all religious houses and seminaries, where meals were available at appointed times. Bathrooms were located along the corridors with stalls and private showers. Cold Alpine water was available at the sink in his room. A large blanket called an eiderdown (a comforter filled with goose down) was placed on his narrow bed. It helped him to keep warm since there was no heat at night.

It turned out that this was the very room that had been occupied by one Fr. Rupert Mayer during World War II. He had been a Jesuit priest who was pastor of a parish in Munich. Because Fr. Mayer spoke out against the treatment of the Jews by the Nazis, the Gestapo put him under house arrest in that monastery all during the war. He had been sent to a concentration camp but it was discovered that he was a holder of the Iron Cross, the same medal that Hitler himself had been awarded. In World War I, Fr. Mayer had been an Army Chaplain who won that medal for extraordinary heroism. He lost his left leg in a grenade attack in Rumania. He had been fitted with a wooden stump that he managed to get around on. So instead of being in a concentration camp, he spent the war years confined to this little room in the monastery at Ettal, not allowed any visitors or even to speak in public.

The only time Ron actually spent in Mayer's "cell" was to sleep at night. During the days there, he was given a complete tour of the monastery. He learned the background story of Our Lady of Ettal, was shown the print shop, the brewery, the distillery and the farm buildings with their animals. He enjoyed cross-country skiing with Fr. Pius in the meadows surrounding the Abbey. He was solemnly introduced to several of the monks. They followed the monastic routine of "chanting the office" in the small interior chapel beginning at 4 AM. That was followed by Mass in the main church at 6 AM and then breakfast in the refectory. That delicious meal consisted of fresh boiled eggs, fruit, homemade bread with jam and coffee all prepared by the monks.

Ron was fascinated by the monks' chanting and was introduced to the centuries-old Gregorian chant that appealed to his musical sense in a whole new way. The only person he talked with during the daytime was Fr. Pius, since in the monastery there is Grand Silence all during the day; one doesn't speak to a monk unless there is a reason. It is all "ora et labora", prayer and work. But his easy discussions with Fr. Pius were very meaningful to him as he discovered more about Catholicism, not only directly from the priest, but also from the several books on the subject, written in English, that he was given to peruse. In this unusual setting and with no prior knowledge that he would become a student, he discovered the central point of the Catholic faith – that Jesus exists, Body, Blood, Soul and Divinity in the Eucharist. This whole experience, including spending his nights (from about 9 PM) in the very room that Fr. Rupert Mayer had been in during the war, left an indelible impression on the young Lieutenant.

As Ron's friendship with Fr. Pius strengthened, he became even more interested in the Catholic faith. What really spoke to his heart was the warmth of the people, their dedication to their faith, and the sincerity with which even young Catholics approached their faith. He was drawn to share in that and began to study the teaching of this faith with Fr. Pius who was very pleased to have an eager, interested (and interesting) young man as his protégé. Ron reflected back on his youth when he would occasionally accompany some of his Catholic friends to their church, mostly to be social. All he ever heard about from his friends in those days was Confession. His pals used to say that it was really cool to be able to confess whatever needing confessing, say a few Our Fathers and Hail Marys and then you'd be good as new. Then, if by some chance you happened to repeat a sin or two, all you had to do was go to Confession again and the slate was wiped clean once more. He thought that surely the intention of the sacrament was much deeper than that view. When he later learned that Catholics believe in the Body, Blood, Soul and Divinity of Jesus Christ in the Eucharist, it was another major step toward becoming Catholic. He had never in his youth, heard the words "Blessed Sacrament" or "Eucharist"; knew nothing about them. When he learned what Catholics really believe, he felt "I have come home." At the age of 25, he recognized his true faith calling.

This all culminated at Easter time in 1960 when Fr. Pius first received him into the Catholic Church by conditionally baptizing him at the high altar in Ettal Monastery beneath the miraculous image of Our Lady of Ettal. Even today, with so much breathtaking beauty in this historic church, the focal point is this white marble statue. Ron's baptism in the sanctuary at the high altar steps, where a pitcher of Holy Water was reverently poured over his head, took place on April 9, 1960, the day before Palm Sunday. He had been baptized into the Methodist church at age seven, along with his brothers by having water sprinkled on him in that ceremony. Since he did not have a copy of his baptismal paper with him to validate the Methodist baptism, and really didn't want to inform his folks of his intentions at this time by writing to them for a copy, this would be a "conditional" baptism. Conditional Baptism gives this sacrament on the condition that it can be received (using such words as: "if you are not baptized, I baptize you...").

A number of Ron's military friends were present at the straightforward baptism ceremony. Included among his sponsors were Virginia (Ginny) Blakey, whose husband, Tom, was HQ Company Commander and Frank Hanigan and his wife, Peg, also stationed at Hawkins Barracks.

During this ceremony, an old monk, who looked to be in his nineties, held the bowl or pitcher of water for Fr. Pius. At the end of the baptism, Ron asked the old monk what he did there at the monastery. The response was, with a big smile, "I'm the brew master." Ron knew from his previous visit and stay-over that this indeed was a very large monastery with over 200 monks. They ran a private high school for boys and girls and had a large farm, complete with farm animals. They plowed the fields, operated a brewery, with a distillery where they made schnapps. They also had a large printing press at which they turned out many books and beautiful postcards depicting many different saints. But now, he met the brew master and actually spoke to this monk who was able to reply back to him, something that was not normally allowed in the monastery.

Upon his return to his barracks, he found that some of his Protestant friends at O'Gau, Jerry and Barbara Schumacher, arranged to receive the whole group that had gone to the monastery baptism for a reception in Ron's honor. This small gesture really pleased him greatly and it helped him to feel even closer to his friends.

The very next day, on Palm Sunday, he received his First Holy Communion from Fr. Pius in the chapel at his barracks. It was ironic that he had this sacrament in the same chapel in Hawkins Barracks where he had just recently worshiped as a member of the Protestant community.

On the following Sunday, Ron and the same group of friends that had skied with him in Kitzbühel Christmas Eve, travelled for several hours to Vienna, Austria to attend Easter Mass in the imposing Saint Stephen's Cathedral. They were continuing to explore the part of the world they had come to love and it seemed to them that Vienna would be very interesting. They had read about St. Stephen's and looked forward to being there. Saying this Mass in the world-famous cathedral was Franz Cardinal König, Archbishop of Vienna. Ron was awestruck by the solemnity and special grace he felt when he received Holy Communion for only the second time in his life, receiving it now from the Cardinal.

When it came time for Ron to be confirmed, in May 1960, he was sent to the Bürgersaalkirche, "The Citizen's

Hall" church in Munich since the confirming Bishop there was a friend of Fr. Pius. There were about 100 people gathered there, with twenty of them, all adults, to be confirmed. Ron's sponsor was a US Army captain, Alfred Ferris, who hailed from New York and had been in Ron's Polish class. The confirmation was conducted by an auxiliary Bishop of Munich, Bishop Johannes Neuhäusler.

Father Pius Fisher

Bishop Neuhauesler

Ron took "Benedict" as his confirmation name, since Ettal Abbey was Benedictine. The bishop addressed Ron in Latin as "Ronaldus Benedictus". It is interesting to note that this also means "Blessed Ronald". In the Roman Catholic Church a definition of "blessed" is "beatified", the third of the four steps in the canonization process.

After the ceremony, Ron told the bishop that he was an American, as he was instructed to do by Fr. Pius. Bishop Neuhäusler had spent most of the World War II years at Dachau concentration camp just outside Munich. It was the Americans who freed him from captivity there. He was very pleased to provide Confirmation to a person who was not only well loved by Fr. Pius, but an American as well.

There was something else about this particular Munich church that spoke to Ron. It was the final resting place of Fr. Rupert Mayer, in whose little room Ron had spent a few cramped nights when he had visited the monastery at Ettal.

When Fr. Mayer, the parish priest, had been arrested at the beginning of the war, he was initially held at the notorious Sachsenhausen Concentration Camp for a short time until it was discovered that he was a holder of the Iron Cross medal. Then he was sent off to Ettal for the duration of the war. At the war's end in 1945, Fr. Mayer was returned to his Munich parish by an American officer with the townspeople giving him a hero's welcome. Sadly, within the year he was dead. He was in the middle of saying Mass when he had a massive stroke and collapsed. His last words were "The Lord, The Lord, The Lord." He was buried in the crypt of the Bürger-saalkirche, where many people frequently visit. Prayers are nearly constantly said through him to the Lord, and many candles burn continually in his memory at that crypt. At least two confirmed miracles occurred that were attributed to him, allowing him to be beatified by Pope John Paul II in 1987.

It was now nearing the time that the Passion Play would be opening. Ron and his cohorts wanted very much to get to see the performance. The entire cast of this production is made up of villagers, all amateurs, who make Oberammergau their home. All the marvelous costumes are made by villagers, working for weeks in advance. Performers must allow their hair and beards to grow naturally for several months prior to the performance since wigs are never used. Performances normally begin in the middle of May and continue six days of the week until early October. Each year nearly a half million people attend and are moved by this unique living tribute to Jesus Christ.

As it turned out, all the American and other nation's military (mainly instructor staff in the special weapons school) stationed in Hawkins Barracks were given free tickets to see the dress rehearsal performance just before opening day in mid-May 1960. This clearly was another highlight of Ron's time in Oberammergau. Getting to see this exciting and very moving production was not something that anyone could have anticipated when contemplating staying with the military as opposed to taking a job in the private sector.

The play that Ron and the others in his group saw opened with a German monologue in the Bavarian dialect while an orchestra made up entirely of local townspeople played an overture. The opening scene on the very wide stage had most of the children of the village (some 300) fully costumed, waving palm branches as an actor portraying Jesus rode across the stage on a real donkey. The performance was in the style of an operetta, with most of the lines either sung or accompanied by music. Ron was no stranger to operettas since he had performed in a few himself in his younger days. For the next four hours, the play depicted the beginning events of Holy Week. There was then a one-hour break for lunch, with all in Ron's group leaving the theatre and heading back to the Officers' club in the Kaserne. Most of the others in the audience headed back to their respective hotels for a quick lunch. All were back and seated within the hour. The entire fascinating and very reverent production lasted eight hours and captivated everyone with unbelievable portrayals of The Last supper, the Agony in the Garden of Gethsemane, the arrest, the ensuing scourging and the crucifixion. It ended with a spectacular Resurrection scene. This whole production touched Ron deeply and he could tell that several others around him had the same experience. He felt that this was about the most worthwhile eight hours he had ever spent. The images stayed with him for a long time.

In the spring of 1960 Ron had accumulated the required time and experience and so was awarded his promotion to 1st Lieutenant. In addition to exchanging his one brass bar for one silver bar, he received the pay increase that accompanies the promotion. He was also expected to perform at a higher level with increasing responsibility. He felt no problem with that at all and looked forward to his future assignments wherever they may take him.

Ron had just learned that he would be assigned to duty in West Berlin, at the end of June 1960 when his language course was complete. He felt very confident in his abilities in both Polish and German and knew that he had gotten the best training anyone could hope to get. He arranged to take the month of July off and to spend the leave time he had coming to him, sailing with two British friends who had been students with him in Hawkins Barracks. Stephen Finch and Robin Plummer were both British Army captains who had been stationed in the enchanting northern German town of Celle with its hundreds of beautiful half-timbered old houses. The Brits were attending the Special Weapons School in the Kaserne. Ron, Stephen and Robin met socially in the Officers' Club shortly after arriving at the post, and (no surprise here) formed a quick, close friendship. It turned out that they would remain good friends and keep in touch over the years to come.

Captains Finch and Plummer had both grown up knowing the joys and intricacies of sailing a boat and were highly skilled in the art. The two of them had talked sailing so much that Ron developed a strong interest in that gentleman's sport and was eager to be on the water. This was to be his chance.

CHAPTER 7

THREE MEN AND A (SMALL) BOAT

As their train rumbled into the port of Kiel in northern Germany, a little over 55 miles (89 km) north of Hamburg, the two experienced sailors and their wannabe sailor buddy could hardly wait to get started. On the short trip it was all they could talk about. As they eagerly got off the train, Ron found a locker to store those items he would need later in West Berlin and took along the few things he would need on the boat: principally his bathing suit, sneakers and a few casual clothes. And a case of Beefeater Gin and a bottle of dry vermouth. He figured that there would probably still be plenty of vermouth left when their sailing escapade was over.

The biggest sailing event in the world, the annual Kiel Week helped this area on the southwestern shore of the Baltic Sea, to become one of the main maritime centers in Germany. It was on July 3rd 1960 that the young officers went directly to the British Yacht Club in Kiel and rented a small 30 square meter sailing vessel with the charming name of *The Alemane*. They declared their intention of going sailing all around Denmark's eastern-most island of Zealand for most of the month of July. The small sailboat, or sloop, had been part of a fleet that had once belonged to the Nazis, and was taken over by the British at the end of the war, given its new name and lovingly restored. The princely sum of the equivalent of thirty American dollars from each of them would be all that was required for the use of the boat for the month. It was moored at the marina in Stickenhorn a short distance from Kiel proper. By way of explanation, the term "30 square meter" refers to the sail area, and was used in a very complicated formula, the Square Meter Rule, in the design of competitive sailboats. Its use dates back to at least the 1920 Olympics. Sailboats of this type are sleek and fast vessels with practically no two boats having the same overall length, beam and other dimensions, so long as the sail area remains within the defined "square meters". The Alemane, built to race, was just barely able to accommodate a crew of three in her small cabin. She was outfitted with a single tall mast with two sails, a mainsail and a jib. Actually two jib sails were provided so that the yachtsmen had a choice of which to use based upon weather conditions. Much of the time only the mainsail was in use and the jibs seemed to be constantly in need of repair. It was good that both Robin Plummer and Stephen Finch were highly skilled in the art of sailing since there was no motor on board. The Alemane surely looked to Ron like she would provide the guys with some exciting sailing.

The trip was memorable for many reasons, not the least of which was that, flying the British flag, they visited a different Danish port each night, usually spending the night on board tied up to the local wharf. They found the local people very friendly but not the least bit interested in conversing in German. These folks' memories of the German occupation of Denmark were still fresh in their minds and conversing in German was avoided. Their native tongue was Danish, but everyone there could carry on a conversation in English quite well, but without the British accent of course. At one of the wharfs where Ron and company tied up, a handsome young Danish lad of about seven years old asked in perfect English if he could have a cigarette. As he walked away without his prize, Ron was reminded of his own youthful snitching of cigarettes and hoped that this youngster would refrain from ever getting hooked on cigarettes.

It was late in the day of July 3 before they had made all their arrangements and had their gear stowed on board, so they spent their first night in a local inn. The next day, the 4th of July, the wind was at Wind Force 6 to 7, much too strong for easily sailing away without an engine, so the intrepid crew remained another night, and was only able to talk about sailing and hope for calmer weather. Measurement of wind levels as used in nautical discussion is done by reference to the Beaufort scale, or Wind Force (WF). This parameter is usually measured with an onboard anemometer, but both Robin and Stephen were able to accurately evaluate the Wind Force by examining the sea state, or size and shape of the waves, as well as the feel of the wind on their faces. Here is a brief overview of some Wind Force numbers that appear in the boat's log, and the conditions that accompany them.

0 = calm. Less than 1 knot = unable to make any headway
1 = light air. 1 to 3 knots = enough to barely make gentle forward motion
2 = light breeze = 4-6 knots = enough to sail at even speed
3 = gentle breeze = 7-10 knots = small boats sail at hull speed
4 = moderate breeze = 11-16 knots = crew fully extended; a learner's gale
5 = fresh breeze = 17–21 knots = ideal for experienced sailors; capsizing common
6 = strong breeze = 22-27 knots = only experienced crews race; seek shelter
7 = near gale = 28-33 knots = remain on shore or risk gear failure
8 = gale = 34-40 knots = tie down small boats to prevent them blowing way

(Note that 1 knot = 1.15 mph)

Finally, at 04:00 the next morning, with a light westerly wind of approximately WF 1 to 2, the excited officers cast off with the long narrow island of Langeland, north and slightly east as the destination for their first stop.

Stephen and Robin initially did all of the skillful and yet pleasurable work involved in properly and expertly getting underway and maneuvering their eager craft away from her mooring and out to open water. With no engine on board, the skill of the crew was fully tested each and every time they left or returned to a dock as well as when they navigated the busy waterways and coped with other marine traffic, constantly changing wind force levels and wind direction. Ron at first felt like a passenger and was laid back, enjoying every minute of this new adventure for him. In no time at all, he was eager to be a helping hand, and then to learn more and more of how to sail and navigate such a classy vessel. He enjoyed the uniquely calming hissing sound of the boat quietly slipping through the waves and then the quick work to be done to manage the sails and the rudder properly to control their direction. As he sat back in the open seat in the stern next to whoever was manning the tiller and controlling the rudder at the time, he found himself very close to the water: almost close enough to dip his hand into the sea to feel the cold thrill of it.

Robin and Ron aboard the Alemane

With a boat of this size he had to be part of the crew and not just a spoiled passenger. He learned his role, secondary as it was, very quickly. Always a strong swimmer he was not worried about being accidently jostled overboard by quick action on the part of one of the experienced sailors, and was sure that would not be an issue. He quickly settled into the fantastic adventure that he hoped was ahead of them and looked forward to the many interesting ports they would sail into as they made their way out from Kiel and into and around the waters surrounding Zealand. Stephen and Robin had previously charted the course that they would follow and they believed that their plan would give them ample opportunity to visit many beautiful and historic places.

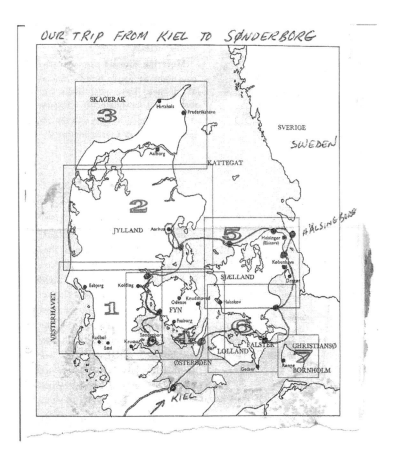

OUR TRIP FROM KIEL TO SØNDERBORG

The on-board accommodations were minimal, at best. There were four small, narrow beds, two on each side, one behind the other in the tiny cabin and a little space with appropriate venting for a gasoline fueled cook stove. They also had two insulated containers, one for ice and another for water. Of course no true English gentleman (and Robin and Stephen fit that description perfectly) would consider not having "high tea" daily, or as often as could be arranged. It was for the purpose of brewing their tea that the little cook stove was fired up. It was a rare day that the crew failed to have their tea at around four in the afternoon, provided that they were not preoccupied with the sails and with navigation. For a special treat, they occasionally had martinis, courtesy of Ron and his delivery of gin and vermouth. (Nobody teased him about not bringing along any olives.)

Without a toilet, known as a "head" in nautical terms, or a real galley (kitchen) on board, things were a bit primitive, which simply added to the fun of it all. They would spend nearly every evening on board while tied up to a dock. When they were sailing they would wait to answer the call of nature until they were berthed somewhere and ready for a good meal after working up a considerable appetite. Still, there was no denying the fact that one of the first skills Ron had to develop was the casual ability, when they were clear of other vessels and far enough from land, to urinate overboard. Of course, one had to be sure which way the wind was blowing before relieving oneself in this manner, or the familiar little ditty about the sailor who forgot about this and sang *Oh, it all comes back to me now!* , would suddenly be recalled.

The wind had dropped to between WF 1 and 2 (sometimes less) so it wasn't until just after noontime on July 5th that they actually sighted their destination island. The wind freshened to WF 2 – 3 and by nearly 6:45 PM (18:45 in military or sailing time) they tied up at the dock at Spodsbjerg, about half the way along the east shore of Langeland, ready for a good meal and a way to freshen up. Spodsbjerg offered the only east-facing harbor on Langeland and had an ample number of berths. The many beautiful beaches on this island offer great places to photograph stunning sunsets. There were more tourists here than one might expect, but that was clearly due to the fact that, although it is indeed an island, it can be accessed by a series of bridges and causeways, as well as regular ferry services. After exploring the area, the trio stopped at a local pub for some nourishment and to buy some sandwich-making items for the next day. They spent the night aboard their sturdy vessel and slept amazingly soundly. After a hearty breakfast the next morning in another local eating place, and a little more sightseeing, the sailors were ready for more open sea. They picked up more ice for the forthcoming leg of their journey, ensuring that their sandwiches would be fresh and that their martinis could be made properly, should the crew decide to enjoy such a libation later in the day. They cast off just after noon and sailed east across the Great Belt, a strait between the main Danish islands of Zealand to the east and the central island of Fyn. Their destination for this leg of the journey was Stubbekøbing.

Shortly after leaving the Langeland dock, the wind picked up to level 5, so Robin and Stephen set their course with a storm jib and a reefed mainsail. This adjustment would help keep the boat balanced and allow them to make reasonable safe headway. Ron thought, 'These guys really do know their stuff!' The sailing was great the whole day. By 8 PM (2000 hrs.) they were 1 mile west of the Masnedø road and rail bridge when the wind dropped to force 1 to 2 and the sailing was relatively calmer. They continued on a course for Stubbekøbing as the daylight faded, but had no worries about sailing in the dark. At around 11 PM, Ron detected a massive shape closing in quickly off the aft starboard portion of their little boat. He immediately alerted the guys to the impending danger. A large merchant ship was on a collision course. His crew quickly shined their flashlights upward on their sails to increase their visibility to the intruder, while doing their best to alter course away from the expected path of the big guy. Fortunately, the crew of the huge ship saw the sailboat and smoothly altered their course narrowly avoiding contact. Nobody yelled out any obscenities, but were relieved to still be upright and in one piece. It all happened so smoothly that one might have thought that the maneuver had been rehearsed, but the log has the ominous notation "23:20: Narrowly avoided by merchant ship." It was nearly midnight when they detected the harbor leading lights, and they smoothly and safely made their way to a berth in their destination's dock where they tied up for the night.

Stubbekøbing is an ancient little town and is beautifully situated on the Gron Sound. Here, Ron and crew explored the oldest church on the island of Zealand. The church features a Renaissance altar and a beautiful hand-carved pulpit. They felt that they just had to climb the church tower and were re-warded with a great panoramic view. They visited the old

Town Hall and made special note of an original inscription over one of the doors that read *Lad dem styre som forstaae det* (Let those who understand, govern). Not a bad thought.

The next day (July 7th) at noon, they were ready for more and different sights and cast off with a moderate breeze and were soon on their way to their next planned stop at the harbor in Rødvig on the east coast of Zealand on the way towards Copenhagen. Within about three hours the little boat was hit by a squall with winds gusting to WF 5 – 6. The experienced crew did all the right things while Ron looked on in awe of their skill. In under an hour, the squall died away and they smoothly continued, arriving at the port of Rødvig at 22:00 hours. Once again, after some nourishment at a local pub and provisioning for the next day, the 3-man crew settled in for the night aboard the Alemane.

At shortly after 08:00 next morning, they cast off from Rødvig and sailed north along the east shore of Zealand on their way to Rungsted, north of Copenhagen. At around 14:00 when they got into the narrow passage between Denmark and Sweden, near where the Royal Danish Yacht Club was located, the level of adventure changed significantly. Since their sailboat relied entirely on wind to go anyplace, and since they had no back-up means of propulsion, when the wind simply stopped blowing, they just sat on the water. That is exactly what happened in this busy waterway. For hours that seemed like forever, they were stranded there not terribly far away from a docking point, but stranded nonetheless. Ron remembered the phrase *up the creek without a paddle* and thought surely there must be, or certainly should be, a paddle or two on board. No such luck. It was extremely hot as they sat, becalmed for what would be over four hours with limp sails and the Alemane just drifting along. About the only entertainment for them was that they had a great view of the nearly life-size statue known as "The Little Mermaid" from the Hans Christian Andersen fairy tale about a young mermaid who fell in love with a prince who lived on land. In the story, she often came up to the edge of the water to look for her love. He was not aboard the Alemane. They ran out of water as Ron recalled the old nautical theme, *Water, water everywhere, and not a drop to drink*. But they could see civilization a mere few hundred feet away and knew that they'd be fine – in time. Eventually the wind picked up just enough to fill their sails a little and they slowly made some progress. By nearly 19:00 an east wind of WF 2 came up and they sailed right past the main entrance to Copenhagen Harbor, as was their plan. At nearly 21:00 they tied up at the Rungsted Yacht Club docking area. Famished after the hard work of trying to make the wind come back, they chowed down in the Club's pleasant restaurant, and realized that it was too late to continue exploring so they made their plans for the next day. This whole area had much to offer well-rested young gentlemen.

They again spent the night aboard their floating home and almost got a good night's rest. But by next morning, July 9, they were awakened at nearly 05:00 hours by the heavy rocking motion of the boat. Once they stuck their heads out of the cramped cabin, they found very strong winds and a heavy swell in the entrance of the harbor where they had tied up. Stephen and Robin hoisted the storm jib and sailed in to a more sheltered part of the harbor where they would be better off. At this point the boat's log has the brief notation "One of the crew made a rather undignified entry into water." Stephen, always a proper English gentleman, was standing on the aft portion of the adjacent boat and was working to help Robin tie up at the new location. As he stepped across the short span of open water between the two boats, the one he had been standing on moved away, making the gap suddenly too large. Still dressed in his pajamas but wearing his ever-present monocle, he flailed his arms around, uttered an oath and then disappeared, feet first into the cold water. He was up in a flash, his monocle intact, and swam to the side of his boat. Once Ron and Robin had stopped laughing at the comical scene they had just witnessed, they both reached over the rail and hauled Stephen aboard. Now fully awake, he dashed into the cabin to get out of his wet PJs and into more appropriate clothing to go to breakfast with his mates.

Later that day the crew met with an old friend, Major Søren Wissum and his wife who were now living in a small cottage in this charming part of the world known as Rungsted Kyst. The city's name literally means "the coast of Rungsted". It is one of the north coast suburban areas of Copenhagen with much of it populated by the well to do. Major Wissum had been a student at Hawkins Barracks in Oberammergau and was in the Special Weapons (atomic) course with Robin and Stephen. Ron had known him casually then, since it could be said without fear of contradiction, that he knew everybody there and was very good friends with most of the population. They were royally entertained by the Wissums at the Officers' Club of the King's Artillery Regiment and were treated to cocktails and dinner.

The next day, Sunday July 10, was also spent tied up in the harbor at Rungsted, not so much because of heavy seas, but because Major Wissum insisted upon more touring around the area with the three visitors in his car. Before the touring about would begin, however, the major, who was Catholic, brought Ron to an early morning Mass in a beautiful cathedral in downtown Copenhagen. Robin and Stephen, both of the Anglican faith and both very religious were happy to come along as guests. Ron was more than pleased to realize how much it meant to him to be able to go to Mass. Since it was still said in Latin and he knew the rite so well, he was able to devoutly follow along. There was no language problem here. Both Robin and Stephen were aware of their buddy's recent conversion to Catholicism and they frequently would discuss the topic while the sailing was smooth and relaxing. They were keenly interested in his comments to them that hinted at the fact that he was beginning to feel a stronger calling to a religious life. They made it a point to be sure to find a Catholic church each of the following Sundays while Ron was with them. This was not always as easy as it may sound, since the percentage of the Danish population that professed the Catholic faith was as low as 1 percent.

After Mass, the sightseeing trio was off to explore, with the major doing all the driving while describing everything in sight. An absolutely fascinating place was Elsinore castle where they spent most of the day. Also known as Kronborg Castle in Helsingør, it is famous since it was the setting for Shakespeare's *Hamlet* and is the best-known castle in Denmark, having been a fortress hundreds of years ago.

Their evening was spent partly onboard the boat docked next to them, the Kuckuck, and partly at the world famous Tivoli gardens amusement park in Copenhagen. The outgoing trio from the Alemane had easily made friends with the fun-loving British sailors of the Kuckuck and exchanged sailing stories and misadventures along with cocktails. Soon the boys from O'gau were on their way to the home of the Wissums to go to the Copenhagen Park. To call the Tivoli Gardens an amusement park is missing the point. The three sailors, escorted by Major and Mrs. Wissum, enjoyed a few carnival rides, walked around the flowered grounds while eating pølser sausages, and drinking a bit of øl (Free Beer) in the beer garden. Despite its name, they still had to pay for the beer. The bright red boiled sausages were practically a national dish in Denmark and they just had to sample these unique treats, finding them really delicious. They watched a free pantomime theatre, took in a symphony concert and wound up the evening in an elegant restaurant. All in all, they had a wonderful time. As they bid their old friends and new hosts goodbye, they assured each other that they would keep in touch.

The next day, July 11th, the sailors set their course to sail past Elsinore castle so they could take a few more snapshots of the marvelous place they had visited the previous day. This time their photos would have an interesting view from the water. As Ron faced east, he realized that Sweden looked to be about three miles (5km) away. In the afternoon the adventurers sailed east across the strait and tied up in Helsingborg, Sweden after experiencing difficulty on entering the harbor due to heavy cross current. The members and staff of the Helsingborg Yacht Club treated the new arrivals as long-lost comrades and made them extremely welcome. They had another very enjoyable evening, this time at the Club's new restaurant. They were reminded that in about 1940 the good

Danish King Christian had seen to it that many Danish Jews had been ferried to this port in the dead of night in order to escape the Nazi's plan to ship them all to Auschwitz.

After spending another night in the Alemane's cabin, the trio cast off at a little after 10:00. The experienced sailors really had to pay close attention to detail as they found themselves competing with the several ferryboats, but soon they were out of the harbor. However, they couldn't relax just yet, since the wind came out of the west at WF 5 and proceeded to strengthen until after they had tied up at their destination of Gilleleje shortly after 1 PM. This charming fishing town is at the northernmost point of Zealand in Denmark. Ron, Robin and Stephen spent a pleasant evening with the crew of the *Lily Maid* berthed nearby. This crew's home base was at the Isle of Wight Yacht Club located on the south coast of England. Robin and Stephen enjoyed conversing in their "native tongue" for the evening while Ron found their accents considerably more difficult to follow, but was pleased to see the enjoyment in it for all.

After spending the night onboard their little home away from home once again, the crew of the Alemane was up early, had a nourishing breakfast in a little restaurant right there on the wharf and cast off just before 10:00 after having purchased some great-looking sandwiches for later on. With gentle to moderate breezes, they headed to the next planned stop at Odden Havn, one of Denmark's finest marinas on a skinny, westward pointing peninsula at the northwest portion of Zealand. They sailed all day, eventually docking at nearly midnight after searching for the harbor lights as they carefully navigated the darkness. It was helpful that the wind had dropped to a light breeze after sundown.

The next morning the guys set out with Tunø, a tiny little island to the west, as their destination, with a gentle to moderate breeze helping them out of the marina. The sky was grey and somewhat ominous. Shortly after noon, they were hit by a squall with heavy rain soaking the three of them and strong winds whipping up the sea. Ron's buddies adjusted the sails quickly to best manage the situation. Once again, they performed with great precision and flawless technique. Everyone was dripping wet as a result of the heavy rain and spray from the sea, but remained cheerful and in high spirits. All three of them were great jokesters and there was always much merriment on board, especially in time of stress. *What? Me Worry?* might have been the name of their craft had they been the ones to christen her. Luckily, the squall died away in a little over an hour and the wind dropped to a very comfortable level for sailing. However, they were surrounded by a heavy mist and therefore slowed their forward progress accordingly. In a little over an hour, the sun broke through the clouds and seemed to announce that it was planning to stay out to help the sailors to dry off a little. By 16:30 they were tying up at the dock on their destination island of Tunø, and noting that their mainsail had gotten slightly torn during the storm. The damage presented no problem since they had the equipment and knowledge to repair it later.

The next morning, after once again enjoying the cramped comfort of the Hotel Alemane, they relaxed by swimming in the clear waters in a cove near the island. The darned red jellyfish were a nuisance, but didn't cause any real trouble for the swimmers. Then with seemingly little effort, Stephen and Robin, with Ron's help, mended the torn mainsail. It was then better than new and they began searching around the island for new things to explore. They sighted an interesting building not too far from the dock. As they approached it, they realized that it was a combination church and lighthouse. What an ingenious way to make extra good use of the steeple in the church that was built on one of the island's highest points. They had never seen a lighthouse in a church steeple before finding this unique building. The hungry trio enjoyed a meal in the Det Gamle Mejeri Inn (The Old Dairy), with live music all around them. They saw no cars at all on this island and soon discovered that cars were simply not allowed. They did find a footpath that led all around the island and were about to set out for a stroll. But after Stephen discovered from someone who made Tunø his home, that the walk would take about three hours, they realized that they did not have the time for the whole circuit. Instead, they made their preparations for the next leg of their trip. By mid-afternoon they set sail northwesterly for Åarhus and tied up there by about 9 PM. This new destination was in the second largest city and principal port of Denmark on the main peninsula known as Jutland. However, the weather was so appalling all day that they quickly gave up on the idea of sightseeing and, of all things, took in a movie where they spent a pleasant afternoon seeing the film, *South Pacific*, which was of course presented totally in Danish.

Over the next several days, more sailing and visiting charming ports of call continued with each of the crew members maintaining a high level of fascination with their good fortune in making this cruise. They continued to encounter a variety of weather: more heavy winds as well as plenty of perfect conditions. Every day was a freewheeling adventure with detailed advance plans rapidly adjusted to suit the weather and their own interests.

The time on the sailboat flew by much too fast, with several other ports of call and more fabulous sights, but the month was soon up. Ron felt that he had been treated to a special gift by being such good friends with fellows who knew the ins and outs of sailing so well and who had the same adventurous spirit that he possessed. He knew that he'd never forget either of them. They made a pact to reunite in the future, no matter what the future held in store for them. It turned out that they truly did have a reunion more than 40 years later in London. But that is another story. With great reluctance and hearty good-byes and wishes for continued good luck, near the end of the month he left his sailing buddies at Sønderborg, a town in the southern part of Denmark. From there he took the ferry to cross to the German town of Flensburg near the Danish-German border. Here in Germany's northernmost town he proceeded by train to Frankfurt/Main. Then, on August 1st 1960, with a minimum of baggage, but a head and heart full of great memories, 2nd Lieutenant Ronald Lawson boarded a military train for an overnight trip through East Germany into West Berlin, at nearly the peak of the Cold War, where his counter-espionage assignment awaited him.

CHAPTER 8

WEST BERLIN
1960 – 1961

Aboard the overnight military train that was delivering him from Flensburg into West Berlin, Ron's catnaps were full of quick little dreams of sailing and swimming. He knew that his adventures of the past month were truly special, but now he needed to alter his focus. He needed to be recalling his training in counter-intelligence and all that went with it. He would soon be waist deep in some never-before experienced activities, although he felt well prepared. Still, training was one thing. Actual hands-on CI work was something else. He was also recalling the recent strong feelings that led to his being called to become a member of the Catholic faith. There were so many events that had occurred within the last year or so that had shaped his religious beliefs that he was beginning to wonder what else lay in store for him in a faith-based future.

He had been on several different trains in the past, but this particular one seemed a little old-fashioned. This thought was reinforced when his train switched rails and made an unplanned stop in the city of Magdeburg situated at the edge of the Elbe River, apparently to allow another train to go roaring past, on its way to the East. The Duty Train NCO made a strong point of telling all the passengers to refrain from looking out the windows while they were stopped. This was a security issue since the Army did not want any "accidental" photos being taken of the military personnel on board. At the beginning of this trip, he had noted that all the shades were drawn down in a closed position in his "bedroom" which consisted of two double-bunks and four male passengers. On impulse, he slowly raised the shade in his window enough to see out. Standing on the platform next to him and looking right back at him was a Russian lieutenant. Magdeburg was in the middle of East Germany and had several Russian military installations there, so the quick sight of the Russian officer should not have been completely unanticipated. It was hard to tell which of the two lieutenants was more surprised by the quick, unexpected sight of one another. Ron quickly closed the shade for his window and was thankful that the Russian did not have a camera. Soon, his train slowly resumed forward motion, was back on track and headed once again to his destination, with nothing ever coming of the eye-ball-to-eye-ball contact of the two officers.

Since the end of the war, Berlin had been divided into four sectors of occupation, each controlled by a different nationality. The French Sector was in the northern portion, the British in the middle while the American Sector enveloped the southernmost portion of the city. By far the largest in area was the Russian Sector that contained nearly half of the pre-war boundaries of Berlin. This area was known as East Berlin while the other three sectors collectively made up West Berlin.

After an uncomfortable few hours in his compartment, Ron was finally in West Berlin. All his traveling companions were American military, some with their spouses, and all headed for various assignments inside West Berlin. As far as he knew, Ron was the only intelligence officer on board. He did his best to freshen up a little, gathered his luggage and made his way to the Command Post where he was directed to temporary quarters in a BOQ (Bachelor Officers' Quarters) at Andrews Barracks. Within a couple of days he was assigned to his permanent BOQ apartment quarters at No. 1 Flanaganstrasse. His apartment was not at all spacious, having a small bedroom just big enough for his single bed, a bathroom, and a small kitchen. However, the living room/dining room could comfortably accommodate six people. Perhaps once he got settled and had a chance to make some new friends, he could invite a few over for socializing after hours. He shared a housekeeper with the other apartment dwellers. She was a short plump war widow named Frau Gräbert, who was always very pleasant and helpful. Years later, on reflecting back on this time in his life, Ron's principal specific memory of Frau Gräbert was her insistence, almost lecturing him, on not keeping beer in the refrigerator. Germans, at least the ones known to Frau Gräbert, did not chill their beer; it was to be kept at room temperature. He was finally able to persuade her that a few bottles should be kept on ice for the American personnel although he would respect her demands for warm beer for the locals.

He learned that the street where his new home was situated was named after Father Flanagan of Boy's Town fame, who had died while he was in Berlin in the middle of a European fund raising trip in 1948. This street was parallel to and not far from the US Headquarters compound on the Clayallee where Ron's main reason for being in West Berlin was located. That street or "allee" was named in honor of the dynamic and highly respected postwar military governor, General Lucius D. Clay who had seen to the rebuilding of Berlin and also served during the crisis of the Berlin Blockade. He is considered the father of the Airlift that helped keep Berliners alive and which took place in 1948 and 1949.

This compound, a 19-acre facility, included ten major buildings housing the offices of the Commandant, US Army, Berlin; the Commander Berlin Brigade; the US Minister, Department of State; and their administrative staffs. In Ron's time there, it was simply referred to as the US Headquarters. It was later named in honor of General Clay, after his death in 1978 since military protocol dictated that such facilities not be named after active duty service persons. In 1979, on the 30th anniversary of the lifting of the Soviet blockade of Berlin, the compound officially became General Lucius D. Clay Headquarters.

Ron's unit was the 513th Army Intelligence Corps Group, Berlin Station. After a minimum of searching, he found that it was located in the building on the right just as he entered the main gate. Guards were posted inside the doors of each of the buildings in the compound. Other than the honor guard sentry posted at the entrance to the US Headquarters on Clayallee, none were ever seen outside any of the buildings. He was welcomed by the Personnel Officer and given a quick tour of the facility. He found that it consisted of three floors of offices. The first floor housed the main administrative offices as well as the Security Office. That group saw to it that all personnel had the proper clearances and they checked ID cards of everyone coming and going. The second floor was divided into various sections according to function: overt collection of intelligence, counter-intelligence, counter-espionage, etc. The top floor housed the section that dealt with fun and games. Here they specialized in equipment such as lie detectors that would be used in interrogations and spying. High-tech stuff for its time. He couldn't help but think that James Bond might have been envious of some of this special gear: concealed or disguised listening devices, miniature photographic equipment made to look like mundane things, and some real Rube Goldberg type gimmicks.

Ron was assigned to counter-espionage. With his uncanny ability for instantly making friends, he soon got to know many of the good people that were assigned in the offices with and around him. However, none of them was ever allowed to discuss the slightest details of their business with anyone. Everything was on a need-to-know basis. In the office area that was his home for this assignment, there were about 20 people working at desks. They were all deeply into projects that could never be shared or discussed at all with anyone else, even those who may be sitting at the adjacent desks. The only exception to that rule was that discrete conversations pertaining to one's specific task were allowed with one's supervisor and the few selected team members who might be working on the same case.

The few telephones scattered around the offices were strictly for routine, non-intelligence use. All personnel were forbidden the use of phones for anything even remotely connected to active cases being worked. Details were always discussed face-to-face, occasionally in a team group setting. There were severe penalties, including court martial and potential jail if security was broken. Ron never did know what the other folks did, what cases they were working on, or even what sort of operations were being conducted. More than once he had the thought that it was entirely possible that more than one person could be working the same issue and it would be great to be able to share some hard-earned knowledge. But he was never to find out.

The various Intelligence Departments were identified by color. Ron was in the Gold, Counter-Espionage team. The officers assigned to the overt collection of intelligence were on the Orange team while the ones whose primary tasks included Polish interests were assigned the color Yellow. Red (not surprisingly) was the code color for those whose principal tasks included targeting Russian interests. The select few who got to work in the "fun and games" high-tech stuff were identified with the color white. This color-coding scheme was never used on any uniforms or other clothing, but aided internal security within the office settings. For example, one never had to call out for a meeting with "the Counter-Espionage team", but would simply request that the "Gold Team" gather for a meeting.

Within a few weeks, Ron was assigned to a private office. There, each morning as he reported for duty, he would find a large stack of papers on his desk, delivered before sunup by the local CIA station, for his attention. He had to go through the mountain of paper, sheet by sheet and comb out leads. These piles of papers consisted mainly of telephone intercepts and copies of all postal mail going into and out of the Military Missions assigned to West Berlin. The types of "leads" he dealt with were such things as the name of a person-of-interest gleaned from either (or both) a postal or telephone intercept. It would usually give specific information such as a city where an East German intelligence unit was located for example. Usually this could resolve down to the actual name and specific location of a person that they determined, with a reasonable degree of certainty, would be able to be "vetted" or talked into working with US Intelligence.

The many Military Missions in the city were all diplomatic missions that had been set up at the end of World War II by the Allies and the Russians. Military Missions were a technicality of the status of Berlin being an occupied city, with a military Commandant as mayor. They functioned as diplomatic listening posts. Allied Intelligence saw them as fronts for intelligence activity.

Part of 1st Lieutenant Ron Lawson's work involved surveillance along the streets of West Berlin. He was instructed to look for foreign and even Allied personnel who were suspected of espionage activity against West Germany or the Allies. This always-exciting task was undertaken as a real team effort and was only started after he had been given a very thorough briefing by the Command. Critical names, places and addresses were provided to him ahead of time. When he identified a suspect (from photos or other previously supplied data) the arrest was always made with the help of a German police officer who shadowed him as he surreptitiously made his way along the streets and alleys. While he performed this type of work, he used an assumed name, and carried an official US passport and driver's license both with the false name. Of course in such assignments he did not wear a military uniform, but could (and did) pass for a well-dressed ordinary citizen, who it just happened was armed with a .45 caliber pistol holstered unobtrusively under his jacket. When using the undercover identity, he was never allowed to carry any of his real identification papers. They had to be left locked up in the safe in his office. If he were to be in any way compromised or overpowered by any of the people he was out to corral, his true identity could be kept secret. However, because of the team concept of operation and the exceptional training, he felt that he was never really put in a dangerous position. But there was always an element of intrigue as well as the unvoiced thought that the unexpected could occur at any time. This all added to the thrill of the job for the adventurous young lieutenant.

Well dressed man about town.
West Berlin

Occasionally, he was involved in manning a listening post as part of a team eaves-dropping on conversations in an adjoining apartment or building. His language skills benefitted him greatly as he, with intense concentration, tuned into conversations of persons who were actively working against US interests inside West Berlin. He also debriefed selected double agents. These were citizens of East Germany or other Eastern European Communist countries, who were working for their own country's intelligence service, but who had been doubled somewhere along the way and also reliably worked for the US intelligence services. There was, of course an element of doubt. How far could he trust these people? However, he knew that his superiors knew what they were doing and much good eventually came from these missions.

Many people who would become double agents, had been picked up in the refugee stream. In the late 1950s, West Berlin became the focal point of disaffected persons in the

East who managed to escape to the West via West Berlin. It was part of an open city at the time. It would remain open until the famous wall was erected in August of 1961. The refugees who had come into the Western Sectors would end up at refugee camps, which were organized and run by the Western Allied intelligence services. The main American camp was located in the West Berlin suburb of Marienfelde. This refugee-processing center was the first stop for over a million refugees fleeing communism in East Germany. People arriving at the center received medical treatment, food, identification papers and housing until they could be permanently re-settled in the West.

At Marienfelde, US teams would identify people knowledgeable of East German and other intelligence activities and refer them to the various safe houses to be debriefed and interrogated, etc. Some of these people were successfully doubled in the process and would then be smuggled back into East Germany with a specific mission to work for American interests in the East. Unfortunately, many such persons became compromised or were discovered for what they had become. Several either turned up missing or ended up in an East German prison. In one memorable debriefing, Ron's team discovered that the person had escaped from a certain East German prison. Ron spent all day with the fellow and had him describe in detail every room and passageway as well as locations of doors and windows. He stayed with this individual and encouraged him to make the best possible sketches of the prison showing the fenced-in outdoor areas and to carefully explain just how he had defeated the security and was able to free himself. The thought was that perhaps it would be possible to arrange an escape for others by helicopter in the near future. Ron was never aware of whether or not such a daring rescue was ever implemented during his time in West Berlin.

Another episode at Marienfelde that would stick in Ron's memory for many years was his interview of a refugee from Leipzig, Germany who had been brought in by agents at this center. That large city, heavily damaged by allied bombing during World War II, was captured by American forces near the end of the war. In accordance with the occupation zone boundaries, the US turned the city over to the Red Army in East Germany. Again, the principal reason for interest in this young man was that he was knowledgeable of Eastern/Russian intelligence operations. Ron met with him one-on-one in an interview room and could tell from the beginning of their conversation that he had a nearly venomous hatred for Russians. Surely, there had to have been something in his past to cause such deep-seated loathing. Eventually, well into the interview after much valuable information had been obtained, the Leipzig native confided to Ron that as a young boy, he had been made to watch as a group of Russian soldiers raped his mother as she cried out for help. Ron could almost feel the young man's pain and hoped that the unburdening of that unspeakable horror would somehow help him to carry on. The refugee volunteered to be a double agent, and was eventually smuggled back into East Germany. Ron did not hear from him after that, but prayed for his safety.

Other than the morning routine of combing through the stacks of mail and telephonic intercepts left for him from the CIA, every day was different for Ron. Some days, under his false name, he and his team were out on the streets for what appeared to be a casual stroll. Of course there was nothing casual about it as they continued to search for trouble. At one point, relatively early in his arrival at Command, he was given the assignment to be the agent-in-charge of a safe house in the West Berlin suburb of Dahlem, about 10 miles (16 km) from Marienfelde. The three-floor house had been a family residence years ago. It now was occupied by a team of people including a sergeant who lived at the place and supervised the team's activities. The interior of the house was unique. The first floor looked pretty much like it must have been when the family lived there. It had a fully applianced kitchen, a dining room and a couple of bathrooms. What must have once been the living room was now occupied by a small group of secretaries at typewriters. They were usually busy typing up the results of interrogations held there. In addition to the American sergeant, who was the only permanent resident of the house, and the handful of secretaries, there was a German housekeeper and four German interrogators, three men and one woman. Ron (or whatever his undercover name was) had to sign for the contents of the house. In the military, all property is under the supervision of a responsible individual. In this case the house and all its contents needed to be 100% accounted for, with monetary values assigned to everything. Every penny had to be accounted for. "Signing for" was a task that nobody really wanted to do, but Ron took that extra assignment in stride and kept careful records.

The second floor of this house contained several interrogation rooms, each of which was fully soundproofed. Also on this floor was a comfortable room for the live-in sergeant, who now reported to Ron. Up one more flight of stairs to the top floor of the building was the location of two more interrogation rooms fitted with two-way mirrors and hidden recording devices including movie cameras. The debriefings and/or interrogations here would be recorded for future evaluation as may be required. Every non-American who was in any way connected with this house knew Ron only by his cover name and had no real idea of his background.

The basement of this unique building contained more than just a boiler room and furnace. As one proceeded down the poorly lit stairs into the dank cellar, one would find three barred holding cells that looked as though they may have once been in use in a prison somewhere. They actually were normal cellar storage rooms that the group made over into holding cells with barred doors and windows. The occupants locked in these cells all were considered of serious interest because of their knowledge of intelligence activity in the East or wherever they came from and were watched carefully. At one time while Ron was in this assignment, one of these prisoners was a notorious Ukrainian refugee who had killed a Western agent in London in what had become a famous case just a couple of years previously. Shortly after

Ron's arrival he found that the CIA came into the building and removed the prisoner, bringing him by air to one of their holding facilities in West Germany.

The many people he interfaced with daily at the headquarters on the Clay Allee became very close friends and stuck with each other socially, even if they didn't really know their true identities. He was not allowed to socialize with any of the people he saw so often in the safe house since they were all German nationals and the live-in sergeant saw to it that there was no fraternizing. The other folks would often attend parties and functions together in each other's homes, enjoying a break from the stress as well as the sometimes routine work they were doing. Sort of reminiscent of Middlebury's fraternities, but without the hazing and goofiness that usually went on back then. As it would later develop, there actually was a fair amount of good-natured goofiness in this part of the world too. One example of this was the time a young, fun-loving and highly spirited British lieutenant was caught driving a British tank down the Herrstrasse in the middle of a Saturday night at the end of a great party. Brigadier Hamilton's daughter, Carolyn, who also had been at the party, was happily sitting on top of the tank and enjoying the whacky ride. The event was a sort of cause célèbre among the young party-going crowd. Unfortunately, the stoic British humor of the senior officials saw nothing at all funny or in any way humorous in the act and in no time at all, the rogue tank driver was reprimanded and shipped out to West Germany. No one in Ron's social circle ever heard from him again.

As a new Catholic, Ron got in the habit of attending daily Mass at 7 AM in the ecumenical American Community Chapel on the Huettenweg in Berlin-Dahlem, a short walk from his quarters. As the weeks went by, he found great solace there praying in front of the tabernacle in the small Blessed Sacrament chapel off to one side that was reserved for Roman Catholic use. He was especially taken with the beautiful Oberammergau crucifix that hung above the tabernacle. He became very attached to that crucifix and felt deeply that Jesus on the cross was watching over him and summoning him to do His work. He was somewhat conflicted about these notions since he had been trained well and was performing at a high level in what he had previously thought of as his profession. But now he felt very deeply in ways that he could not really verbalize, that a higher calling was in store for him.

Attending Mass with him was another lieutenant named Bob Deshler who became a close friend. The ability to easily and quickly develop close friendships was a constant in Ron's life. He hadn't changed in that regard since his school days. Now, in this foreign place, that ability was even more important. Ron and Bob, if they were not assigned to duty, would spend many weekend evenings at the British compound at Montgomery Barracks. There they would bowl in the former German bowling alley and have a casual beer as they simply "hung out" together and decompressed. This compound was located in Berlin-Gatow on the western side of Spandau, where the Nazis convicted at Nuremberg of war crimes in World War II were incarcerated. The first of several Brits that Ron and Bob became friendly with was a group from the First East Anglian Regiment, (a former infantry regiment of the British Army) and later, they got to know a few folks from the Durham Light Infantry. When they visited the Montgomery Barracks on Sundays, they always looked forward to the noontime dinners. They would be served truly delicious curried chicken, Indian-style. Years later, just the memory of that great meal could set Ron's taste buds longing for it again.

Ron made a number of life-long friends at the British Barracks, all young officers of about the same age, and kept in touch with most of them over the years. One of these friends, Tony Berry, would, in future years, rise through the ranks to become a British Brigadier, a one star general. He would also become a holder of the high honor, the MBE (Member of the British Empire) given to him by the Queen of England. Another close friend, Bill Hill, was an officer with the Durham Light Infantry. Eleven battalions of that top-notch British group fought gallantly in World War II in theatres such as Dunkirk, North Africa, Malta, Sicily and Burma. They also were a significant force during the invasions on D-Day and continued the fight right up to the final defeat of Nazi Germany in 1945. Bill was proud to have that heritage to look back upon as he fulfilled his duties in West Berlin. In future years, whenever Ron visited the UK, Bill and his wife, Diana, were wonderful hosts to him as Bill and Ron recalled their Berlin assignment.

During Ron's social activities with the British in West Berlin, he never mentioned his intelligence duties or in any way described his assignments other than to simply say that he was assigned to Berlin Command Headquarters. Of the many young officers with whom he became friendly, one of them struck him as having particularly strong leadership qualities. This was Norman Schwartzkopf who was at that time, aide-de-camp (personal assistant) to the American Brigadier General in command of US forces in West Berlin. Norm was one of the dozen or so members of Ron's social crowd and always had lots of good fun with the group. He later became famous as Stormin' Norman, the senior American general in the 1991 Gulf War, known as Desert Storm. Others in the group included the delightful daughters of the British Brigadier Goff Hamilton (British Forces Commander in West Berlin) and his Indian-born English wife, M. M. Kaye. She always used her maiden name and became famous in her own right as the author of the worldwide best seller, *The Far Pavilions* and many other popular works.

One of Ron's closest colleagues while in West Berlin was Bill Tyler, the handsome aide-de-camp of Major General Polk who was US Commander of Berlin. Bill lived in an apartment on the floor below Ron in the BOQ at #1 Flanaganstrasse. Bill's dashing good looks and his smooth approach ensured that he was the one who invariably would escort the most beautiful and charming young ladies in Berlin. The time Ron spent with his new friend occasionally included double dating, with Bill always selecting their companions. One memorable evening on the town in just such an arrangement, Ron's date for the evening was a young (almost 20) and pretty German movie actress, named Elke. She was very bubbly and enjoyed describing her life story to Ron, with little or no prompting on his part. He quickly learned that she had been born in Berlin to a Lutheran Minister and his wife, and as a child moved with them to a small town in the south of Germany where she went to high school, or as it was known to her, Gymnasium. She continued, with Ron simply listening and not really getting a word in edgewise, with the information that when her father died when she was only 14, she moved to England to be an au pair and to help perfect her English and to earn a living. While she was on a brief vacation in Italy, she caught the eye of the noted film director and actor, Vittorio De Sica. She had started playing small parts in movies in the late 50s. She proudly pointed out to Ron and Bill and his date that she was now getting starring roles that emphasized her seductive blonde good looks as well as her acting talent. It turned out that her full name was Elke Sommer and she would soon move to Hollywood, become one of the most popular pin-up girls of the time, be featured in Playboy Magazine at least twice and go on to have a movie and TV career in which she made nearly 100 appearances before essentially retiring from that career in the 1990s. On the way back to their quarters at the end of the evening, Ron and Bill agreed that Miss Sommer would eventually most likely do very well in the film business.

Ron typically had brief dates with different young ladies on several weekends, mostly due to his being good friends with Bill Tyler. One of these dates was a CIA secretary named Jeanne Rowley. He knew that her last name sounded familiar, but was surprised to learn that she was a cousin of the head of the US Secret Service in Washington, James Rowley, whom he had interviewed in a security investigation while on assignment in Georgetown. Small world. Ron and Jeanne would be seen together at a variety of parties and social events over the course of the next few months.

In the late summer of 1960, the general that Bill Tyler worked for had received two tickets to attend the annual Nobility Ball in West Berlin. Such regal affairs were traditional in Germany and dated back to the days of the monarchy. The nobility would show up at these fancy affairs with all their jewels and decorations prominently on display. Even after the First World War put an end to the monarchy, the celebration of the Nobility Ball continued when it could. It was a way for people who could recall those glorious times to re-live the grandeur once a year. Bill asked Ron to attend with him, since the General was not interested in going. Dressed in formal uniforms, and looking pretty sharp, they attended what was probably the most intriguing event ever for them. This dance, somewhere in the British Sector, consisted mainly of waltzes, a favorite of the elder generation of Europeans and seemed to be right out of the 19th century. The people in attendance were of the German nobility and had been suppressed ever since the end of World War I. The proud and dignified attendees wore decorations crossed over the front of their clothing with spectacular medals lovingly affixed.

At this gala event, Ron and Bill were seated at one of several large round tables with ten other people. There were at least 200 persons in attendance that evening all enjoying the live orchestra and each other's company. As soon as the young officers were seated, introductions were made all around the table. One of the young ladies at their table was introduced as Cecilie, the Crown Princess of Prussia, the granddaughter of the late Kaiser Wilhelm II. In later years, she would go on to become the Duchess of Oldenburg in northern Germany. Another person at the table was a young Freiherr, or member of the lesser nobility, such as a baron or equivalent. His name was Lutz-Henning von Lehman and, really was a regular guy. He and Ron not only had a great time chatting over the background noise at the gathering, but the two of them would become life-long friends and remained in touch over the following years. Most of the people at this table, with the exception of the Crown Princess, joined Ron and Bill at Ron's quarters at 1 Flanaganstrasse in Dahlem after the dance for coffee and cordials.

The military chain-of-command above Ron included a captain and a lieutenant colonel. However, the officer with whom he interfaced almost daily and whom he thought of as his boss was Colonel Tom McCord. The colonel was a Russian linguist and he and the 1st lieutenant had a lot in common. Ron had been doing his assigned jobs as an agent in Intelligence work so well and at the same time was such a people person that it was not unusual for Colonel McCord to occasionally invite him out to dinner with him. On one of these evenings he was out with the Colonel, his wife, and her parents who were visiting from Texas. Colonel McCord was driving around the area after their dinner to give his in-laws and his wife an interesting tour. As he drove and described the landmarks all around, Ron suddenly noticed that he actually had driven them into East Berlin and around the Potsdamer Platz (Potsdam Square). Ron spoke up quickly and said, "Oh, oh, boss. We better get out of here!" Masking his embarrassment at his momentary lapse of good judgment, the colonel smoothly swung the car around and rapidly drove back into West Berlin. At this time, Berlin was still, outwardly at least, an open city for the most part. Allied personnel stayed in West Berlin. Intelligence agents most definitely were forbidden from entering East Berlin, except on assignment. This little goof could have ended up with great embarrassment to the Command and by association, to the colonel especially. Fortunately, nothing ever came of the error.

Ron had an opportunity to become a charter member of the American Yacht Club Berlin. Remembering his recent escapades on the Baltic Sea, he couldn't let that excitement pass him by. The AYCB was located on the Wannsee, a beautiful lake, two lakes really, in West Berlin on the edge of the East German city of Potsdam. Many American and other troops went to these lakes for R&R (Rest and Recuperation). It was one of the best recreation areas in West Berlin. However, Ron's sailing instructor probably needed some R&R himself after watching his new student perform what appeared to be dare-devil stunts while single handedly sailing in the busy waters. Ron was doing his best to imitate the slick moves performed by his buddies, Robin and Stephen just a short time ago. No sailboats or innocent bystanders were harmed in the development of this sailor.

In the fall of 1960, Ron felt fortunate to get to know an unforgettable School Sister of Notre Dame known as Sister Maria Alfonsa Uciecha. She was a native of Breslau in German Silesia, which later became known as the Polish city of Wroclaw. He found that near the end of World War II, Sr. Maria and a group of other sisters from her convent somewhere in the inner city of Breslau had walked the nearly 400 miles (640 km) all the way to the city of Berlin. They kept ahead of and away from advancing Russian troops. Once in Berlin, the small group of nuns settled in an abandoned Nazi villa located on the outskirts of the Berlin suburb of Marienfelde, an area well known to Ron and his fellow agents.

Sister Maria Alfonsa in 1962.
At a parade featuring JFK.

When Ron first met Sister Maria Alfonsa, she was still wearing the same, second-hand shoes that she had worn in 1945 during her trek to Berlin. Since the habit she always wore covered most of her head, but left her compassionate, usually smiling attractive face on view, it was difficult to discern her age. Ron thought that she was most likely in her mid-forties, but could have been off on that assessment in either direction. Sr. Maria worked tirelessly as a teacher of religious education for American and British forces and was very good at her vocation especially since she had an excellent command of the English language. She had been a sister for over 20 years, with the first five of those years in Breslau. She had been in Berlin for about 15 years and had worked as a teaching sister in a school owned by the School Sisters of Notre Dame. She explained her fascinating background to Ron, impressing him with her total commitment to the Lord's work and her personal humility.

Without really meaning to, she inspired Ron to consider following her lead in his life's work. He felt a close connection to her and he helped out the sisters whenever he was able to, both with food, material goods and money. Others in the American community in the area followed Ron's work and joined in his effort to assist. They took to calling her "Sister Mary" instead of Maria. She loved it. As the years went by, Ron and others kept in touch with Sister Mary by letter, fondly recalling their brief time together. In less than four years, poor health wrapped itself around her saintly body, and she died of heart failure.

Between busy days and nights working his CI role under his assumed name and managing to enjoy himself whenever the occasion presented itself, the second half of 1960 had slipped by and it was now Christmas time again. This would be Ron's first Christmas as a Catholic and he was eager to celebrate it in a more meaningful way than in previous years and have fun as well. He also was looking forward to some accrued time off, away from base command. He talked his good friend and frequent date, Jeanne Rowley, into taking a train all the way to Kitzbühel, Austria with him to enjoy the fabulous skiing that he knew from experience could be had on those spectacular slopes. It was only last year that he had been there with Oberammergau friends and not only had a great time skiing, but also stumbled into a strange and somewhat mysterious episode in a candle-lit memorial chapel. That overpowering encounter still occasionally would enter his dreams leaving him wondering once again about the meaning of what had occurred. Perhaps he wondered what effect being in that area again might have on him. Ron had been in touch by letter with Tony Gillespie and his wife, Vivian, both of whom he had known very well back in his time in Washington, DC. Tony, now out of the Army, having worked in Intelligence himself, was now working as a Foreign Service officer for the State Department. The Gillespies now lived in Western Europe and loved to travel. Both Tony and Vivian, as well as a few of Tony's friends were all planning on joining their old pal for Christmas and looked forward to the time being spent on the slopes at Kitzbühel.

Shortly after he celebrated his 26th birthday on December 21st, Ron and Jeanne set out for Austria. Jeanne had a hard time not giggling at the way Ron was dressed. In a throw-back to college days of the Roarin' Twenties, he was (in his mind at least) pretty smartly attired in what had been his great-uncle Ivan's full-length raccoon coat. He also knew that since several of his friends had practically begged him to let them borrow it once in a while, it must really be a pretty special coat. He knew he'd be warm with that nearly 50 year-old fur piece wrapped around him. Their long trip to the ski slopes would be via a series of trains starting with an over-night military train ride through East Germany to Helmstedt and on to Frankfurt. Once there, they boarded a regular train to Munich, and chugged through the German countryside for a few hours.

The next part of the trip involved boarding a train bound for Traunstein. Easy enough to do. All that is required is to show up on time. As luck would have it, the train they had been on had mysteriously slowed to a crawl as it made its final approach into Munich, arriving several minutes late. They had to rush. In fact, they had to grab their bags and their skis and run for it, since their train was already slowly pulling away. People watching from a distance must have worried about what may have looked to them like a young woman being pursued by a strange-looking, bear-like animal that was gaining on her. Ron and Jeanne, young and nimble as they were, each made a running leap onto the platform of the last car along with their baggage and all-important skis. The Traunstein-bound train was home to them for a few hours. One more change of trains put them on a southerly route and they were eventually at their destination of Kitzbühel.

It had been a tiring ride, but enjoyable nonetheless. They soon caught up with Tony and Vivian and their friends. Everyone was totally enchanted by their surroundings. They all spent the better part of a week in Kitzbühel skiing, sightseeing, shopping (mainly an exciting thing to do for the ladies in the group) and enjoying each other's company. Many of Ron's friends went on to have distinguished careers. Tony Gillespie was no exception. He later held a series of significant government positions. These included Deputy Assistant Secretary for Inter-American Affairs in the US State Department; US Ambassador to Grenada for one year, followed by US Ambassador to Columbia for four years, and then US Ambassador to Chile for four years. He then served on the US National Security Council as Senior Director for Latin America and the Caribbean.

It was Christmas Eve when Ron, Jeanne and some of the rest of his group attended the Midnight Mass in the village church. This church was near the memorial chapel Ron had stumbled upon the previous Christmas Eve and had been overwhelmed by all the burning candles within. After this Mass the rest of his group left the church along with everyone else, but he told them he wanted to stay behind for a few more minutes and would catch up with them soon. He was thinking about the words he had inexplicably uttered last year, 'Let me be a light', and searching for meaning in them when he was drawn to an unoccupied darkened corner of the sanctuary in this church. As he approached, he saw that hanging on the wall in the dim light was a portrait of a pope. (He later discovered that the portrait was of Saint Pius X, who would be important in his future life.) He got as close to

107

it as he could while he wondered why such a beautiful and important painting should be hung in such a poorly lit area in this little-known church. He dropped to his knees in front of the image while he prayed through the saintly pope for guidance in his life. It seemed almost as though the image turned to him and spoke to his heart, suggesting that he give his life to the Lord Jesus as a Catholic priest. It was a powerful and most significant event and was the real beginning of a major change in his life. He now understood why he had been so intent upon traveling the distance he had from West Berlin all the way to this particular location.

Pope St. Pius X

He went outside the church into the cold night air and soon found his friends waiting for him. All agreed that the Midnight Mass had been beautifully done and would remain a special memory of this particular trip. Ron heartily agreed. They all concurred on a plan for the next day as they made their way to their individual quarters. Ron confided his revelation to Jeanne as they walked back to their rooms. She was not surprised, but rather very moved by the knowledge that her good friend might be called to the priesthood.

After a week of great weather, loads of skiing fun and enjoying meals in a variety of local eating-places, the group disbanded with Ron and Jeanne heading back to West Berlin.

Shortly after their return to base, Ron sought out the council of the military chaplains, thinking that if they supported his current thoughts about how his religious life should grow, that one day being an Army chaplain was a very appealing thought. They all knew that he still had loads of CI work to accomplish and he wanted to be sure to meet those obligations. However, the way Ron presented himself to these chaplains convinced them that he should eventually put in his application to be released from the military in order to enter the seminary. But there was still work to do.

The stressful work of spy-catching, always under an assumed name, continued as 1961 rolled by. Ron continued to find good social outlets for any internal stress that would build up as part of his assignments and was as outgoing and sociable as ever. In July, one of the secretaries who worked with him went on leave to the US for the summer. Trusting his judgment and character completely, she left her two-door blue Chevy coupe in Ron's care. He called it the "blue tank". It was often seen at the British compound at Montgomery Barracks in Gatow. Ron would use the vehicle on a regular basis to visit his friend there, Captain Bill Hill. He was with the Durham Light Infantry and that outfit had a great stress-relaxer in the basement of their Officers' Mess. They would spend hours at the bowling alley down there. Knowing that this facility had originally been built for the Nazi troops several years ago, did not diminish their enjoyment of trying to outscore each other.

Some of Ron's other British officer close friends were assigned at the British HQ at the Berlin Olympic stadium, in the British Sector. Water-loving Ron made frequent good use of the Olympic swimming pool as often as he could manage to get there.

Ron's discussions with various military chaplains continued in earnest as his spiritual faith became stronger and stronger. The Army chaplains in West Berlin put him in touch by mail with Bishop William Arnold, who was the Military Vicar for US Catholic military throughout the world. Bishop Arnold was stationed in New York City, functioning as an Auxiliary Bishop of New York. He suggested that Ron write to Bishop Joyce, of the Burlington Diocese that embraced all of Vermont, Ron's home state. Bishop Joyce had been an Army chaplain during World War II and was happy to be of help to this serious potential new candidate for priesthood. Once he had reviewed Ron's credentials, he quickly accepted him as a candidate for the priesthood for the Diocese of Burlington. Bishop Joyce was so impressed with Ron that he suggested that he go to Rome to study in the English College of Saint Bede. This unique place, referred to as "The Beda", had been organized many years previously by the Bishops of Great Britain especially for more mature (older) candidates for the priesthood. At first, this sounded like a great idea to Ron, but as he considered it a little more closely, perhaps it would not be the best place for him. He explained to Bishop Joyce that at age 26, he had never really been inside a Catholic Church in the States, not counting the few times he accompanied his friends just to be social. Perhaps it would be better if he were to return to the US to study there. The bishop fully agreed and arranged for him to attend St. John's Seminary in Brighton, Massachusetts. But before that could happen, he had to be released from the Army. The request went all the way to the Secretary of the Army because of the serious cold war situation in West Berlin. The senior officers involved in granting such a release were not at all happy to be losing one of their best Intelligence Agents and somehow hoped that this young man who had been doing such a great job and certainly seemed to be a real people-person would soon come to his senses and stay put. His most ardent supporter in gaining the required permission to leave the Army and enter the seminary was his "boss" Colonel Tom McCord, who truly understood the young 1st Lieutenant's mindset. When the others interviewed him privately, they knew that his request had to be granted. They all hoped that they would see him again sometime in the future as an Army chaplain. Permission to muster out was eventually granted with departure arranged for late August 1961.

Near the end of July, Ron and his very good friend, Jeanne Rowley, went together to what was then the Berlin Hilton Hotel (now the Intercontinental) for a late dinner. At nearly midnight, they took the elevator to the lounge in the roof garden, a lovely enclosed setting surrounded with glass, to view the city lights and to have drinks before heading back to their respective quarters in Dahlem. They had a good view of the famous Kurfürstendamm, the main drag that runs through the center of the city, into East Berlin at the Brandenburg Gate, and is the most popular shopping street in Berlin. They were sitting alone, enjoying the views of the city in all directions, when Ron looked over Jeanne's shoulder and whispered to her, "That guy who just came into the lounge looks an awful lot like Willy Brandt." She turned and confirmed that indeed it was the Mayor of West Berlin. She added, "And look who he has with him! It's Vice-President Lyndon Johnson!" In no time at all the area was swarming with security personnel and Ron realized that a few guys he had previously noted who looked suspiciously like Secret Service people, really were just that.

A tall well-dressed gentleman casually approached Ron and Jeanne's table. In the dim light, Ron didn't recognize the man until he was right next to them. It was a person he had known in Washington, DC as a member of the Secret Service. The fellow recognized Jeanne, but she could not recall ever meeting him. She thought that maybe he was someone who knew her cousin, James Rowley, head of the Secret Service. His job for this evening was to accompany the US Vice-President and see to his safety. He had been escorting LBJ who was on an official visit with specific instructions from President Kennedy, to shore up American interests in this part of the world in the face of threats from the Russians over the refugee problem. With a minimum of small talk, the tall agent asked them if they would like to be introduced to Mr. Johnson. Of course they simultaneously answered in the affirmative and soon found themselves being ushered over to him and being formally introduced. The agent explained to the VP that he had known Ron from back in his days in Counter Intelligence training in DC and that he was a top-notch talent. He also assured the Vice President that Jeanne was a highly qualified secretary with the CIA. After a short visit with Mr. Johnson, Ron and Jeanne shook hands with him, returned to their table and soon left the hotel. During their brief chat, the second highest-ranking civilian in the United States had asked his visitors what it was that they did here in Berlin. Ron described his job in detail. This was the first and only time he ever told anyone the true details of his assignment. Ron knew that the VP was about the only person he would be allowed to discuss the details with. Jeanne kept her secretarial duties simple and was out of earshot while Ron spilled his story for the Vice-President. Ron couldn't help notice that through most of his frank and complete discussion, LBJ's eyes seemed to be mostly trained away from him and more toward Jeanne.

As Ron and Jeanne made their way back to their separate quarters, they were laughing at the chance meeting. What were the odds? They agreed that evening was one to remember. But the excitement could have continued. The next morning, Major General Watkins phoned Ron at his unit and asked him to come to his office immediately to explain something. During the short walk to get to the general's office, Ron kept asking himself what this could be about. Once inside the office, the general asked if it was true that Ron had met Lyndon Johnson last night. Ron confirmed the meeting. The general laughed as he explained that now it made sense to him. It turned out that the VP had his people phoning many of the US Headquarters offices around 1 AM trying to get in touch with 1st Lieutenant Ron Lawson and his friend. Evidently he had been so taken with their cool-headed manner and obvious knowledge of their jobs that he wanted to invite them to a late night dinner with him so he could get to know them better. The general was smiling from ear to ear as he and Ron both enjoyed the sudden, but brief brush with fame. Ron was only slightly deflated when the general laughingly made the observation that it may very well have been Ron's date that Mr. Johnson was really interested in getting to know better.

On the night of August 13th Ron was guest of honor at a party for him since he would soon be shipping out to leave for the US to enter a seminary to study for the priesthood. This celebration was touched by a note of sadness for those who would surely miss the very sociable and friendly new priest-to-be. The gathering took place at the quarters of a married officer, Jerry Schumacher and his wife, Barbara. Ron had met Jerry and Barbara at Oberammergau. They had invited lots of Ron's friends, American and British. Soon the place was packed with folks all trying to be sure to let Ron know how much friendship with him had meant to them.

The party quickly was silenced at about midnight when the telephone rang. It was their HQ in Dahlem. In no uncertain terms, they were all ordered to report to their respective offices or units immediately. That night, Ron got no sleep at all. It turned out that the East Germans had begun to close all the highways and railroad lines coming into West Berlin. Barbed wire barriers were being strung across the entrances to the city. All East Germans were forbidden to enter West Berlin. The East German regime did more than string barbed wire barriers. What was reported to amount to 40,000 heavily armed soldiers and police, with the support of armored cars, tanks, trucks rigged with water cannons as well as other military vehicles providing back-up, had lined the sector border between East and West Berlin. They went so far as to chop down trees, causing them to fall across streets, cut and bent streetcar tracks to block access to passage, dug trenches across plazas and parks, and installed concrete posts. By mid-morning of the next day, the East German government had a blockage in place along the entire border. Where there had been 80 crossing points between East and West, now there were only 13 left open and these were controlled by heavily armed East German guards. The construction of an actual wall would come soon.

Ron was assigned to the task of going to the Military Police station at the famous Brandenburg Gate in the city center and thoroughly interviewing the last East German refugee to come west on the S-Bahn, an elevated railway. The MPs at the Brandenburg Gate had called Ron to tell him that the last person had just made it through. It would be valuable to "pick his brain" to get a better understanding of any details he could recall about what the East Germans were doing to the fencing and crossing points that he saw as he rode the S-Bahn. Ron's subject turned out to be an 18 year-old boy, who looked younger than what he gave as his age. He had come to West Berlin from Leipzig to join his older brother as a refugee and head to West Germany. He was lugging a zipped up canvas bag that was nearly as long as he was tall. It contained a collapsible sailboat; something that Ron had never even known existed, but was impressed to see. The youth was hefting the unusual sailboat as a ruse that he was coming to Berlin to sail on the Müggelsee in East Berlin. When he had arrived in West Berlin, as the last person on the S-Bahn he was scared to death. After debriefing him, Ron drove him to where the kid's brother was living in Zehlendorf. He never saw either of them again.

It was a very tense time for everyone in the area. There previously had been talk that a wall would be built to seal off the Russian-controlled border at East Berlin. In fact it was Ron's "boss", Colonel Tom McCord, who had information several days earlier from one of his agents that West Berlin would be sealed off by August 13th, but until now it was only talk. Concern was expressed by many that soon, if someone happened to be in the wrong part of Berlin, they might just find themselves being hauled off to Siberia. Just two days earlier nearly 4,000 refugees streamed through the Marienfelde camp.

Ron spent a few days checking on the construction of new fencing along the borders of the British sector abutting East German territory in Spandau and Gatow. His job was to learn as much as possible about the material being used, how impenetrable it looked and other potentially useful data. He was surprised at first to realize that the fences were being located a full meter back into East German territory. He wondered why they would be giving up all that area, but soon understood that the space would shortly be needed as they built the concrete and mortar block wall. He had a driver assigned to him to take him wherever he needed to be. This young fellow was from Norfolk in Great Britain and was happy to be referred to as a "Geordie" as were most of the folks who hailed from the vicinity of Newcastle upon Tyne. His unique dialect was like nothing the well-trained linguist had ever heard. It was so unusual, practically a language of its own, that Ron couldn't understand most of what was said. Extra effort was required so that he could convey information to the driver about the places he needed to be and to stop so that he could inspect the fencing. Ron was trying to get the driver up closer to a particular critical spot when the driver said, "Gan canny or we'll dunsh summick. Ye knaa what ah mean leik?" Ron translated this as "Be careful or we'll crash into something. Do you know what I mean?" Eventually the task was completed to Ron's satisfaction with the driver mumbling either approval or total lack of comprehension.

For the next two weeks Ron, along with everyone else, was preoccupied with what was happening along the borders. Practically every day he was in plain clothes, snooping and gathering as much useful data as possible as he inspected the rapidly increasing lengths of new wire fencing along the British sector. Using his best local dialect German, he tried to engage the workers in conversation, hoping to obtain more data. No luck. None of them would say a word to him.

The barbed wire fencing was quickly being replaced with the construction of a thick concrete block and mortar wall nearly 12 feet high. Near the end of his time in West Berlin, Ron learned that one of the other teams in the Command was able, under cover of darkness, to help nearly 20 East Germans escape under a portion of the wall that had just been erected. The team made good use of an abandoned subway tunnel that led them into an old sewer system. They ignored cat-size rats as they waded through a couple of feet of fetid water, leading their charges to freedom through a manhole in West Berlin. When Ron was told of the details he thought that he had watched that scene in a movie once somewhere, but this was real and gave a whole new meaning to the phrase, "The light at the end of the tunnel".

Since he was to be leaving the Army soon, much of his remaining time was spent getting his household goods ready for shipment home and signing what seemed to be an endless collection of paperwork. He had to turn in those items he had been using on a regular basis that belonged to the government; things like weapons, special equipment used in his surveillance work and undercover ID stuff. He also had to debrief and turn over responsibility to one of his agents, and in turn, be debriefed by the Command on all the secret material and information he had been dealing with. Of course, all during this time, everyone he had been working with was very heavily involved in the unprecedented closing of the border, at first with the wire fencing, then the wall that would eventually run for over one hundred miles (160 km) in length. A city was being cut in two. But there was still time for a number of informal luncheons in his honor, sponsored by his many friends. There even was one midnight bash at the British HQ Olympic pool. He knew that he would really miss these folks.

On August 28th Ron left West Berlin on the overnight military train from the Wannsee Bahnhof (railroad station). A large group of his close pals and co-workers were there to see him off with hugs, handshakes and wishes for success in what would be the next chapter in his life. As Ron waved back to the crowd from the boarding steps of the train, he realized that he would in all likelihood, never see these good people again. He simply could not fall asleep or rest easily as the train took him through East Germany to Frankfurt/Main. All the recent events including the potentially dangerous Counter Intelligence work he had done, combined with all the fun social times he had enjoyed, played like a movie in his head. When such images managed to slide back from the forefront of his memory, thoughts of his new calling and what that would be like took their place.

In Frankfurt/Main he boarded a large commercial jet bound for New York. On the long flight, Ron's mind was nearly completely occupied with thoughts of spirituality and how it was that he had made the decision, mostly unexpected by many of his closest friends, and even himself, to become a Catholic priest. His parents and brothers also were surprised and a little unsure of his mindset. It was difficult to properly convey to them, as he tried to do in his frequent letters, the momentous and life-altering convictions he now held. He knew that as always, they would be supportive of whatever path he may choose, but without actually talking to him and feeling the strength of his calling, it was probably a bit concerning to them.

If someone were to sit next to him on this plane and ask him outright just how it was that he had come to embrace Catholicism, and eventually to feel the call to the priesthood, he was sure that he would find it difficult to put all that into meaningful words that made sense. He pretended that the person next to him had just asked about this. His response, in his mind, dealt with both a feeling initially and then an intellectual exercise. By "feeling" he realized that he felt attracted to the many Catholics that he had met in the Army, particularly in Oberammergau and then by the local people wherever he found himself who exhibited a unique faith; very devoted, very deep, very expressive and very pious. He had never seen anything quite like that devotion in his Protestant experiences. The "episode of light" in the Austrian chapel at Christmas of 1959 was, no doubt, an opening of a door by the Holy Spirit for him to explore and search for meaning in his life. Then he began his dialogue with Fr. Pius Fischer at Ettal Abbey who tutored him in many aspects of the Catholic faith. Fr. Pius opened another door, so to speak, and sparked in Ron a keen interest in searching for truth. Here was the intellectual aspect of his answer to the as yet unasked question. Once Fr. Pius explained to Ron the origins and belief in the True Presence in the Eucharist, it was then that he had the strong revelation that was almost a voice in his head saying 'This is what I believe!' He felt that there probably always was a longing in his involvement in Protestant liturgies over the years to put meaning into Holy Communion that not only made sense to him in a deeper way, but also gave him a personal message. As he thought back on his younger days he recalled that he had always felt that there was something special about what was above the altar, perhaps a kind of tabernacle. He could not identify the source of that thought, since no one had ever suggested it to him. But when Fr. Pius explained the tabernacle on every Catholic Church altar and what it traditionally contains, he felt a strong kinship and knew in his heart that he had already embraced that belief. That it was unambiguously defined as containing the Body, Blood, Soul and Divinity of Jesus Christ made it completely an article of his faith. Ron's fascination with the miraculous image of Our Lady of Ettal, resting above the high altar at that abbey, became the door through which he learned to embrace the role and position of Mary, the Mother of God. Of course, the powerful message he had taken from his prayer in front of the special painting in the chapel in Austria last Christmas Eve, seemed to encapsulate all of these beliefs and was the major turning point for him.

Our Lady of Ettal statue.

118

He also knew that he had been given many gifts by his creator, such as a keen intellectual ability to understand anything he put his mind to, a loving and outgoing fun-filled personality which helped him to relate with and befriend nearly everyone he would encounter, and a healthy and strong body. He felt very confident that he would indeed make a good priest.

He slept comfortably for most of the rest of the long ride to New York. Once the aircraft had landed and he gathered his luggage, he made his way to Fort Hamilton in Brooklyn. There, with a fair amount of paperwork, he was processed out of the Army and now was a civilian again. From there, he traveled directly to his parent's home in Montpelier, Vermont.

In an amazing side note, a theft of the very special marble statue of Our Lady of Ettal took place much later. It is worth recalling here. In March of 1991 an unbelievable, sacrilegious event occurred in the beautiful and venerable monastery church, or Kloster, at Ettal Abbey. The extremely precious and world-famous marble statue of Our Lady of Ettal was stolen from its perch high above the altar. It had been alarmed for years against any possible theft, so its sudden disappearance came as a real shock. This statue, that measured only about 12 inches (30 cm) tall but weighed nearly 26 pounds (12 kilos), had been a gift in the year 1330 from King Ludwig der Bayer at the founding of Ettal Abbey. It had been venerated for all those years and was a key attraction for visitors for over 600 years.

A British soldier, who had been on an assignment in Saudi Arabia, had been part of a tour group that visited the Abbey and surrounding villages. He saw the small, but famous statue and inquired about its history, asking many questions that centered on its value. He pretended to be fascinated by its craftsmanship and was allowed to get very close to it and the alarm system, which he studied carefully. After leaving the monastery, he devised a means to by-pass the security system. He was clever enough to have a plaster copy of the statue made even though he knew that it would fool absolutely no one on close inspection. He was counting on the thought that so long as something reasonably close to the original was up there in its usual position, nobody would notice an imposter; at least for as long as it would take him to stash the real item away where only he would know its location.

Somehow, he was able to gain entry into the monastery church with the fake in a plastic bag. He climbed up to where his prize was, disabled the alarm, removed the original and put the plaster imitation in its place. He was surprised at the weight of the ancient statue but quickly wrapped it in a military sweater and stuffed it into a plastic bag as he left the premises. No one saw or heard him as he did his dastardly deed. He was soon on the grounds of the Schilcherhof Hotel in Oberammergau, about two miles (three km) from the Abbey, as was part of his plan. Under cover of darkness he dug a shallow grave for it in an out-of-the-way part of the garden area on the grounds of the hotel, stuffed his prize into the hole and quickly filled it in. He was satisfied that its hiding place would not be easily discovered, but he would be able to identify its location when his plan to ransom the statue was put into play.

He returned to England and made phone calls to the hierarchy within Ettal Abbey and began to negotiate a substantial ransom of around $750,000 for information that would identify its location. He was very clever about concealing his identity, but was frustrated by the fact that no one connected with the Abbey would consider such an outrageous scheme. The Abbot and Ettal community immediately got the German police and Interpol into high gear on the theft. It took nearly five months before the statue was found in August of 1991.

The proprietors of the hotel on whose grounds it was hidden, the family Schilcher-Thilo, placed a memorial plaque at the foot of the tree in their garden where the priceless statue, considered a miraculous image, had been hidden. That area is now a pilgrimage site, with many people making it a point to stop there to pray.

The culprit was sentenced to three years in prison.

CHAPTER 9

BACK IN MONTPELIER

When Ron, now a civilian, walked through the door of his parents' home, he was received like royalty by his family. He had so many tales of his adventures to relate that he knew it would take days to convey his experiences. Of course, one of the principal topics for discussion with his parents was how this young Protestant man had made the decision to enter studies for the Catholic priesthood. At first, it seemed an unlikely development, sort of sudden and a little foreign to their minds. His amazing choice was not entirely understood by them. After all, Ron was half way around the world while this metamorphosis was taking place so no one in his family had had the option of sitting down, face-to-face with him. There had been no opportunity to witness the development in his thinking. He played over in his mind the imagined discussion on the flight across the ocean where he silently did his best to explain his change in direction to a non-existent seatmate. He hoped that his folks would understand. And he prayed that he would be as eloquent in fact as he had been in his mind. He knew that his family had great faith in him and that they knew that their son and brother was a very capable man. He also knew that they saw him as a person of high standards who knew his mind and heart. He hoped that they would come to believe that he would not only be successful in his new career, but would be very good at it.

He couldn't help but notice that a large plywood box nearly four feet wide, four feet tall and about 15 feet long was sitting to the side of the driveway. It was covered with shipping information and had been sent by the Army from Germany to his parents' home. Although he had been the principal driving force behind the gathering of his personal stuff while he got ready to leave West Berlin, he was surprised to realize how big a box was required to hold all his "junk". But it was hardly junk. This box contained his clothes and the household goods he had accumulated. It also contained souvenirs and priceless items that would always remind him of the time in his life when being in Counter Intelligence was how he had defined himself.

Fortunately, the weather was good, with no rain in the forecast so Ron and his dad were able to peel back the shipping straps, crowbar back the lid and get all of this material put under cover. As they handled each item, Ron did his best to relate the story behind it to his folks. But there was one surprise. A sealed envelope was tucked between packages of clothing and on it were the words "Go for the Gold". It turned out to be a photo of his Gold team, everyone smiling and waving to the camera. Priceless.

Now in the late summer of 1961 as Ron unpacked his suitcase in the spare bedroom, he thought about how long it had been since he had been with his parents. The house they now owned was not the one he and his brothers had grown up in. It was purchased as a way to downsize once the three boys had moved on with their lives. It was just what his folks needed and fit their requirements perfectly. He did not feel like a stranger there, and knew that he never would feel that way about his parents' home no matter where it may be. Except for the Thanksgiving ride home in the Navy dive bomber a few years back, it really had been quite a while since he had last seen them. He had been involved in an amazing assortment of experiences. Even he was hard-pressed to believe all that he had done and seen in the nearly five years since leaving Vermont soon after college in 1957. There was a lot of catching up to do.

He was pleased to see that his folks were in good health and were enjoying this phase of their lives. His dad was still the Fire Chief and his mom continued to be very active with the Methodist Church Women's Group. She sold greeting cards from her home and saw to it that all the proceeds went directly to the church. His brothers simply weren't around that much at this time. Milan had gotten married to Corinne Kelley who hailed from nearby Calais, Vermont. The wedding took place two years ago, in September of 1959 while Ron was doing his thing in Oberammergau, so of course there had been, unfortunately, no way for him to have attended the gala event. Although Ron and Milan had frequently double-dated in their high school, college and even subsequent years, Ron had never met Corinne. Milan had "robbed the cradle" and chosen for his wife a lovely woman, seven years younger than himself. He always was pretty good at making smart choices.

Bride and groom, Corinne and Milan Lawson. Sept. 1959

The newlyweds made their home nearby in Montpelier, so it was not too difficult for them to visit with Ron a couple of times before he was to head for the seminary. Milan, who had graduated from Northeastern with a Bachelor's Degree in Civil Engineering, was employed in that capacity by the Vermont Highway Department. He enjoyed being close enough to his parents to pop over and help out with whatever may be needed and to have occasional social visits.

Sidney, Jr. had, since 1959, been a scholarship actor for the Champlain Shakespeare Festival located at the University of Vermont. He was a student at UVM at that time and was majoring in speech, but was developing a growing interest in the performing arts. He was happy to be back at his parents' home for the summer, and therefore could spend a little time with his brother, Ron, who it seemed was going through some sort of metamorphosis.

Ron's parents and brothers had received several letters and postcards from him mailed from his various ports of call as he moved through his intelligence training and assignments. Some of these missives were the equivalent of "wish you were here" types of quick notes with pictures and words describing the beauty or historical aspects of his then current location. But several of the more recent communications had contained his thoughts and strong feelings of his call to Catholicism and his latest bombshell . . his desire to become a Catholic priest. It was difficult for the folks at home to really understand what he had been experiencing. No written words could truly convey the essence of what had transpired in his life for him to be so strongly called.

Ron's dad was pretty much OK with the idea of having his son become a priest since his connection with the Methodist Church was tenuous at best. He was a man who could see the good in nearly all religions. He recalled that of his three boys, it was only Ronnie that had shown a real interest in religion, even in high school. He knew that his second son was a very intelligent man who had an easy way about him, a trait that had always attracted people to him. But more than that, he had confidence that Ron had thought his decision through very carefully. If he thought that having his son out of the Army and therefore out of harm's way was also not such a bad deal, he didn't voice it.

Ron's mother also had a world of respect for how her boy had turned out. She always eagerly looked forward to any kind of communication from him no matter where in the world he might be. However, she was initially not so comfortable with what appeared to her as a sudden change in his religious life. She worried that he may regret not ever being allowed to marry and have a family. She knew that he would make a great dad. But more than that, she had been concerned about what may have been a failing on her part to instill in him a full appreciation for the Methodist religion. One of her first actions upon getting long-distance notice that she was evidently going to be the mother of a Catholic priest, was to discuss this whole business with her minister. That good man knew Ron from the time he was called Ronnie and he very truthfully advised Mrs. Lawson that this career path was going to be just fine for her son. He assured her that in no way should she or her husband take this turn of events as a rejection of their values and beliefs, but as a spiritual call for Ron to serve the Lord in a deep and meaningful way.

Neither Milan nor Sidney, Jr. really had very much to say about their brother's new plans. They tended to assume that Ron, who always knew what he was doing, was still his own man and would do just fine at whatever he chose to do next. Privately, they may have felt that if he made it through the intensive training of the seminary, it might be rather nice to have a Catholic priest for a brother. But they never actually voiced those thoughts to him on the rare times they actually caught up with him.

In a couple of short weeks that seemed to everyone to really fly by much too quickly, it was time for Ron to head for Brighton, Massachusetts and St. John's Seminary. Ron's dad was happy that he had the time available to drive his son to his new home. Sidney, Jr. was glad that he also had free time so that he too could be part of the transportation team. He also knew that it would be a lot better that his dad had company on the long ride home. They all consulted maps to determine the best route to take. Unfortunately, the Interstate Highway System had yet to have extended very deeply into the geography that the Lawson men would be covering. Ron's mom prepared a nice picnic lunch for her guys to carry along with them in the car. There still were plenty of places along the planned route for them to stop by the side of the road and refresh themselves with tasty treats from home.

And there would be enough left over for the Sidneys to munch on as they traveled home after they had completed their "special delivery". Ron said farewell to his mom once again and gave her a peck on the cheek. She let him know that she was sure that he was going to have a wonderful experience and that she looked forward to phone calls and letters keeping her up to speed on his progress. She also let him know that she was going to be really proud to have a Catholic priest as a son. Neither of Ron's parents let their emotions show and didn't make a scene at farewells, but everyone knew that down deep, this was another momentous occasion. And they fully expected that there would be more to come.

During the nearly five hours it took to wind their way through parts of Vermont, New Hampshire and Massachusetts, the banter between father and sons was light-hearted and easy, with very little mention of the new direction Ron's life was about to take. When they got close to the winding, unpredictable maze that defined Boston and surrounding towns, they really had to pay close attention to their maps. But shortly after noontime they made it to their destination of St. John's Seminary in the busy but attractive area of Brighton. They found that it was located not far from the Boston College main campus on Commonwealth Ave. They noticed that although the seminary was located in the heart of the city, it was surrounded by green space that helped to give it a relaxing, meditative aura. It was an inspiring sight.

After Ron had found his way to his new residence in St. Clement's Hall and the car was unpacked, it was time for the pilot and co-pilot to return to Montpelier. The men shook hands and then all spoke at once as they wished each other well. He thanked his dad and brother for not only being so good as to drive him here, but for being such great traveling companions. Ron noticed that his father's eyes seemed a little moist, although that might have been a trick of the sunlight. He was surprised to find himself temporarily at a loss for words. For some reason, he couldn't quite manage to articulate the thought that he was thankful to have such a terrific man for a father and that he would always do his best to make him proud. As Ron watched his dad's car recede into the distance, his thoughts quickly became 100 percent focused on this new chapter in his life soon to begin in this beautiful setting. He couldn't wait to get started.

CHAPTER 10

SEMINARY YEARS: 1961-1962

Ron was used to being in beautiful surroundings, such as the many Bavarian locales he had lived in and visited. Although the grounds and buildings that made up St. John's Seminary did not rival the breathtaking aura of Oberammergau, he was impressed with the architecture and landscaping of this little part of Boston. He knew that by comparison to some European monasteries and cathedrals that date back several centuries, this place was relatively new. It had opened its doors for the first time in May of 1884 with provisions for 100 seminarians. But it had all the charm and impressive solemnity of anything else he had experienced. This indeed was going to be a very pleasant home for as long as it would take him to achieve his strongly desired goal of becoming a Catholic priest. He also recognized that his most recent training and experiences in Army Intelligence did not matter very much in this new chapter in his life. But, he thought, once he got to know some of his fellow seminarians, he would have some fascinating tales to tell. Of course the various escapades would need to be watered down a bit for security reasons, but he was thinking that very few of the other young men living and studying here could match his stories.

It was cool and tranquil in the shade of the many large trees on the campus this warm, late September afternoon. He found that it was pleasantly cool inside the first building he was directed to, St. Clement's Hall. This would be his residence, along with about 200 other students. They all would be studying Philosophy for the next two years. He was quickly introduced to several dozen young men. He rapidly zeroed in on those in that group who were in the same course of study as he was, *First Philosophy*. Although most of his classmates were probably about nine years his junior, (he was 26, going on 27) he in many ways still felt like a kid, at least from a physical point of view. He knew that he would have no trouble keeping up with any of them at any sports that might be available. As was the pattern ever since college, very soon he had come to know several people who it was clear would become great friends.

The basic path, or rite of passage, through which a young man would grow and learn and eventually become a Catholic priest, involved eight explicit steps. At the time Ron entered St. John's Seminary these eights steps were: tonsure, four minor orders; Porter, Lector, Exorcist and Acolyte followed by the three major orders; Sub Deacon, Deacon and Priest. Tonsure (from the Latin tondere: "to shear") at that time involved the clipping of about two inches of hair from the back of the crown of the head. This ancient practice preceded the investiture of the cassock. (It was amazing how quickly that sheared hair grew back. Was it due to a few extra prayers for its return?) The entire seminary experience was expected to be a six-year journey during which time the seminarian could clearly focus his heart and mind on his journey and his eventual goal.

In his not so distant past Ron had been fitted for a variety of uniforms, including what he thought of as strange looking attire similar to a British officer's summer uniform with shorts, knee-length socks and a visored officer's helmet that he had worn in Oberammergau. But soon he found himself being fitted for a uniform of a different style. This outfit consisted of a cassock, which was a long black cloak with a wide belt, known as a cincture. This black belt was about five inches wide, and after fitting it around the waist it was allowed to loop down about two feet to hang along the side of the cassock. A black cape was to be worn over the cassock. The attire was not complete without its special black hat, known as a biretta. This is a square cap with three ridges or peaks. Ron knew that the biretta is worn by all ranks of the clergy, with the black ones with a red pom-pom worn by monsignors, the red ones worn by bishops, and the scarlet ones of silk worn by cardinals. The birettas worn by seminarians, deacons and priests are always black. He was also fitted with a surplice, a white-sleeved shirt-like vestment to cover the top part of the cassock and was to be worn for use in the chapel. At this point in time, these garments were only provided for fitting purposes, not to be actually worn until Ron was formally invested. This important and memorable ceremony would take place in early October in St. Clement's impressive chapel.

At St. John's Seminary, 1961

To call the chapel impressive is understating its beauty and its unique, ornate design. It has been described as one of Boston's landmark religious edifices. It was constructed with the Eucharist in mind, having only one altar, unlike many local churches that typically contain one or more side altars. This design detail was incorporated in order to help remind the seminarian, even from his first day on the job that his future life as a priest would be centered on the Eucharist. Ron spent a lot of time in this chapel from the very first day he entered it, absorbing its beauty and spiritual messages that spoke deeply to his heart and soul.

He was told that with the wearing of the cassock, he was legally considered a cleric under the law and therefore could not be called up to serve in the Armed Forces. However, that issue was irrelevant to the young man who had until a few weeks ago been very involved with the Army and who had thoroughly enjoyed the experience.

Ron soon met the Seminary Rector, the person who presided over all the activities and day-to-day business there. He was the formidable, but honorable and very supportive, Monsignor Matthew P. Stapleton, an Irish son of South Boston. At their very first meeting the Monsignor was impressed with Ron's military background. But Ron soon found that there was a certain similarity of mindset between those in positions of power in the military rank and file, and the seminary hierarchy. Monsignor Stapleton seemed to Ron more like a Sergeant Major who doggedly insisted that all residents strictly adhere to the many seminary rules. And many rules there were. Ron soon discovered that all the seminarians were to live in what was practically a monk's way of life. This was acceptable to him, but the rules, strictly enforced, included: no visiting in each other's rooms, maintaining silence above the ground floors, lights out at 10 PM and the maintenance of what was referred to as Grand Silence from 10 PM until 6 AM. Radios and TVs were not allowed in the rooms, nor were telephones, newspapers or magazines permitted. They were also not allowed to leave the seminary grounds without permission. Using a telephone to call anyone, parents, relatives or other friends, required special permission, and when granted, the admonition to "be brief" was always part of the deal. Ron and the others with him were good about maintaining the strict rules for the two years he spent in Philosophy House and in subsequent years.

He found that he was really enjoying himself, settling in fairly quickly and finding that being back in an academic setting, even one with so many strict rules, was not bad at all. It had been about five years since he had been in a college level program, and for the most part, he liked it. He had already had four years of Latin in high school, so another year of it was nothing to him. They studied, among other things, canon law, Scripture, Liturgy and moral theology. He found the study of philosophy to be absolutely deadening due not only to the professor's presentation of the subject matter but, at least in the first semester, the fact that this difficult subject was taught in Latin. Whoever said that Latin is a dead language never had to experience this unexpected use of it.

One of the most unusual things about the course in philosophy was the textbook. It had been printed totally in Latin in Italy and had pages that required the reader to slit them with a knife or scissors. For example, pages 1, 2, 3 and 4 were printed on one large sheet and then folded over together. The same approach was used for all the other pages as well. These folded over sheets were bound into the book folded in that manner, and a fair amount of slitting or cutting was required by the first student to have the book before it could be considered anything more than a strange paperweight. After several weeks into the semester, the professor asked to borrow Ron's book, since he had forgotten to bring his own to the class. Ron somewhat reluctantly handed his book to the teacher. Standing in front of the class, the good professor soon had a strange look on his face and made the observation, "You haven't even slit the pages!" All Ron's classmates burst into laughter since it was now obvious that he had not even read the Latin text. Ron had been able to keep up with the professor, just barely, since the instructor used English from time to time in his teaching. He also reviewed his classmate's notes and had discussions with them to help him stay reasonably current. The whole idea of teaching a subject in Latin in the first place was an attempt to follow what had been perceived as a decree from Rome that such a thing should be done. Pope John XXIII had made the casual suggestion to someone in Rome that it might be interesting to teach seminary courses in Latin. It was never a command, simply a thought from the Holy Father. In an attempt to please the hierarchy, the ill-fated Latin-based philosophy curriculum was put into place. By about mid-semester, after it was seen as much too difficult with no redeeming qualities, someone in a position of authority at the seminary appealed to Rome to change the rule. The request was immediately granted and that was the end of that.

No matter how difficult some of his classes were, he enjoyed the camaraderie with his classmates, even if they had to behave in a reserved manner most of the time. They were always able to see the humor in things that somehow seemed to escape their professors.

Ron enjoyed the food in the dining hall, known as the refectory, and always seemed to have a good appetite. He thought it was pretty nice that St. Clement's Hall had both its own refectory and chapel. Almost a community of its own. When this community's residents were out in the local area, they had to be in groups of four and dressed in black suits with white shirts and black neckties. Each seminarian wore a felt homburg with its upward curled brim completing the sartorial splendor. Umbrellas were carried if there was even a threat of rain. On Thursdays each week, the group was allowed to be out of the seminary and on their own between the hours of 1 and 5 PM. They had to be back in time for chapel Vespers, which were their evening prayers. Vespers always started at 5:30 PM after which, supper was served. Once when Ron's group walked past Monsignor Stapleton on their way out onto Lake Street they were all laughing at a remark Ron had just made. "Guys. We look like a bunch of nuns!" The Monsignor was glad that his men were enjoying themselves, but wondered what was so funny. He thought about having that evening's Vespers run a little longer than usual, just in case this young bunch was having too good a time somehow.

Most of the time, Ron and his group enjoyed their walks around "Beantown", especially when they approached an intersection on Boylston Street at Boston Common. Invariably, the traffic cop there would see them approaching and would stop all the traffic in both directions to allow them to safely cross the street. They felt like dignitaries. However, occasionally something would happen that was not quite so pleasant. For example, once at that very intersection, a disheveled and obviously upset drunk rushed over to the group and spat on him, all the while uttering incomprehensible curses. As the inebriated fellow stumbled away, Ron did his best to control himself by thinking that he needed to pray for that person's soul, even if that might not have been his first reaction.

It wasn't very long before a slightly older seminarian, named Steve, who was impressed with Ron's natural fit with his surroundings, asked him to help him out with a difficult project he had been doing alone. He needed help teaching CCD (religious education) to some inner city elementary school children. Ron agreed to assist even before he knew the details, since he always loved kids and felt strongly that aiding in their spiritual growth and understanding was a powerful idea. The location they had to travel to was a very tough neighborhood: Columbia Point in Dorchester. It was a run-down, drug and crime-infested housing area that sat on the former city dump. It was such a bad scene that it was well known that the fire department and police were reluctant to answer calls there. Getting to their destination of St. Christopher Church was a serious challenge. Once they had ridden the "T" (subway and street cars) to get close to where the church was, they had to make their way over a sea of broken bottles and all sorts of refuse. Of course they were wearing their typical Thursday afternoon attire; black suit, tie, etc. Talk about standing out in a crowd. The church, a fairly new facility, shined like a jewel in the midst of less than ideal surroundings. It was built to address the spiritual needs of the thousands of Catholics who lived in the area. Once inside, the familiar arrangement of religious items was soothing, especially the beautiful altar and statues.

The CCD classes, held every Thursday through the school year from October through May, were held in the downstairs hall. Ron was pleased to see several enthusiastic groups of children, arranged by age. His assignment was to teach fourth grade boys and girls. They were a little suspicious of him at first, but it wasn't long before he had them under his spell. By and large, they were really nice kids who appreciated the attention being given to them. With just a couple of exceptions they were reasonably respectful and most likely came from families that prized religious education. Ron was determined to relate to each and every one of these kids, especially the ones who, by their actions and attitudes let it be known that they really didn't want to be there. By the time his assignment was over for the year, he felt that he had indeed made a difference in these children's lives. He connected especially well, for no apparent reason, with a well-behaved redheaded boy named Kevin who took his lessons seriously. Ron kept in touch with him by mail until the youth finished high school, with Kevin keeping him posted on happenings in his life. It would develop that Kevin attended the ordination of Father Ron some nine years later in Vermont. Ron's seminarian friend, Steve, who would be Fr. Steve by then, got Kevin to the special event.

Summer had slipped by and it was now the end of November. Thanksgiving was spent in the seminary with all hands enjoying a traditional sumptuous turkey dinner with all the extras. As a special treat, everyone was allowed to watch football games on television. Almost like home. Lots of folks were homesick and all looked forward to the Christmas break. They were released on Christmas morning and sternly reminded that they had to be back on campus not later than the end of the first week of January 1962.

Ron was pleased to be back in Montpelier again with his folks. They were all eager to know how everything was going so far on this strange path he had chosen. He assured them that it was all excellent and that he was very happy with his decision. But it was while he was in Vermont that he did something unusual that was to have extraordinary ramifications in his life for years to come. Just before being released for the holiday season, he had been in the seminary bookstore where he picked up a copy of *The Story of the Trapp Family Singers*. One of the things that caught his eye right away as he skimmed the book was the fact that this family, headed by Maria von Trapp, was now living in a lodge that she ran in Stowe, Vermont. This was the area of Vermont near where his relatives in the Luce family had resided. That whole region is still referred to as Luce Hill. He was greatly impressed with the story of this refugee Austrian family who had escaped the Nazis and ended up settling in "his" part of Vermont in an old farmhouse on Luce Hill near where his ancestors had once lived. What an amazing coincidence. The unusual thing that he did was to send off a quick letter to Mrs. von Trapp giving a few details of his current enrollment in the seminary and describing how his ancestors had lived very close to where she and her brood were now settled. He indicated that the next time that he had some time off and was in Vermont, he would very much enjoy visiting her. He thought they would have lots to talk about, since he had found the book of her life so fascinating. He had never seen the Broadway play, *The Sound of Music* that had opened in 1959 starring Mary Martin as Maria, but was sure that it was highly stylized anyway. He mailed the letter and really didn't expect much of a reply, if any.

He was astonished to get a letter back from Mrs. von Trapp by return mail in which she indicated that she would like to have him come to the lodge right away - - now.

Original Trapp Family Lodge   Maria von Trapp

He really only had a few days available to him before he needed to be back at St. John's, but he quickly packed a few things and managed to travel the short distance to her lodge. When he met her, she instructed him to simply call her "Mother", short for Mother von Trapp, and she put him right to work. She knew that he had only a few days now, but she felt sure that she would see a lot more of him as time went on. Technically, he was not permitted to work for money as a seminarian, but she insisted that she needed someone to help out at the front desk, greeting guests and getting them settled in. She was the most charismatic person he had ever met and he was fascinated not only with her life story, but with her great spiritual strength. She would gather all the young people who worked in the lodge, along with whichever of her children were in residence at the time and kept all of them occupied, discussing spiritual issues, singing, celebrating a variety of things or events and sharing everyone's thoughts and concerns. Everyone there attended daily Mass in the house chapel whenever a priest was in residence. It was amazing how often a priest would actually be on the property, either just making a quick visit on the way to some other destination, or to be spending some relaxing time at the Lodge. Mother had many fascinating things to say, based upon her own background, and she shared wondrous ideas for those who may be heading into a life in religion, as was he. She quickly became Ron's spiritual mentor and would remain important to him in that capacity throughout his journey to the priesthood. In a very few days, Ron had to travel back to his beginning point in that journey, but they both knew that he'd be back.

In short order, Ron discovered much more of Mother Trapp's fascinating life story. She had been born Maria Augusta Kutschera in Vienna, Austria in 1905. As a very young child she was orphaned, was raised by an abusive relative and was taught to be an atheist and socialist. As she grew up she attended the State Teachers' College of Progressive Education in Vienna. One day she attended what she thought was to be a concert of Bach music, but in actuality was a Palm Sunday Mass in a Catholic church. She listened carefully to the words the priest said and it was as though the flame of the Holy Spirit suddenly touched her. She knew in her heart that all the nonsense her uncle had spewed all her life about bible stories being inventions and folk lore was in reality just that - - nonsense. She was so moved by the words of the priest and the message that seemed to be meant just for her and had spawned her religious awakening, that as soon as she graduated college, she entered the Benedictine Abbey of Nonnberg in Salzburg as a novice. She had a difficult time there with the rules and discipline but flourished spiritually. She had been accustomed to plenty of exercise and fresh air, neither of which was plentiful in the Abbey. The result of that was that her health suffered.

Out of the blue one day, the Reverend Mother of the Abbey selected her for a special assignment. A retired local Austrian Navy hero of World War I by the name of Georg von Trapp, 15 years Maria's senior, and sometimes called "Baron", had lost his devoted wife (Agathe Whitehead) to scarlet fever. She had borne him seven beautiful children who were now motherless. His whole family was totally devastated by the passing of that caring woman and mother. He could not bear to continue to live at their old homestead where they all had been so happy, so he sold that property and bought an estate in Salzburg. One of his daughters (also named Maria) had become quite ill, so he approached the Reverend Mother looking for a teacher for this daughter as well as someone to look after her health. With Maria's training and level of skill as a teacher, she was chosen for the task. The plan was that she would stay with the von Trapps for 10 months. After that, she would enter the convent formally.

At the von Trapp homestead, Maria tutored her young charge and fell in love with all seven children. She enjoyed singing with them and getting them into outdoor activities where they all had wonderful times together. As Georg observed the interaction with his children and the "borrowed" teacher, he fell in love with her. He asked her to forget about going back to join the convent but rather to marry him and become a second mother to his children. Since Maria by this point was so emotionally connected to the seven von Trapps, she agreed. They were married in 1927 and eventually had three children of their own. All of the original seven children were musically gifted, primarily as talented singers whose voices blended beautifully. In time the three newest members of the family continued with that gift. In fact, as the local economy became depressed, Maria turned the family hobby of singing together into a profession as they sang in public. The family took first place in the Salzburg Music Festival in 1936 and were well-known singers of Renaissance and Baroque music, performing madrigals and folk songs.

In 1938, the Nazi regime annexed Austria. Georg and Maria, after careful consideration of the bad political situation they saw happening all around them, made the decision to move away from their estate and all their possessions. It was a heart-rending choice, leaving behind a way of life that they knew and loved, as well as relatives and friends and of course the beautiful property. After many moves within Europe, they eventually sailed to New York and continued to search for a place that would really call to them as "home". For a time, they lived in Pennsylvania and while there, their third child, Johannes, was born in Philadelphia in 1939. It was in the early 1940s that the family found just the place they had been seeking in Stowe, Vermont. They continued on tour as a musical family, but ran a music camp on the Vermont farm most of the time. The family flourished in this great setting, as nearly all of them became American citizens. Georg never filed to become a citizen, stating that he would soon get to it. Unfortunately, he passed away in 1947 and was buried in what would become a family cemetery especially created at that time for him on their property.

As Ron learned more about this amazing family and especially about Mother Trapp, he knew that he would be spending time gaining perspective and understanding of his own calling even more fully with her as his mentor.

Back at St. John's Seminary, things quickly got back into gear shortly after the start of the new year. Ron continued to excel at his studies and felt an even stronger bond to the path he had chosen. In the spring, the special ceremony of tonsure was held for his class. Origins of tonsure date back many centuries when the unique shaved portion of a cleric's head would set him apart from the layman. This ceremony was held in the chapel where Ron and all his classmates lined up while Bishop Luke Riley, an Auxiliary Bishop of Boston cut a good clip of hair off the top of each young man's head. This was the beginning point for the Minor Orders, which would be conferred, in the coming years.

As he progressed along the path he had chosen, he found that his parents were becoming accustomed to his development. They realized that he was still the same Ronnie they had always known and loved. At the next vacation time, a few of his seminarian friends and religious novices would make it a point to visit his Montpelier home. His parents got to meet and know quite a few of them. They both liked the young men, appreciating their sincerity, their helpfulness around the house and their good sense of humor. They realized that Ron's friends were a good bunch of guys and were grateful that their son was part of this special group.

Spiritually, Ron developed well, learning to meditate and pray effectively. He also learned to select good spiritual reading material in the library. One of the first books he borrowed was *Faith of Our Fathers* by Cardinal Gibbons. This is and always has been an incredibly popular and successful book explaining the basic tenets of the Catholic faith and (more importantly) why Catholics hold them. As he took the book off its shelf to inspect it, something fluttered out from between some pages and fell into his lap. It turned out to be a holy card of St. Pius X, the same saint whose image had so moved him on Christmas Eve in Kitzbühel, Austria in 1960. He had no idea about the identity of the person captured in that painting back then, but recently had spotted a picture of Pius X in a library book dealing with the Popes and made the connection. The unexpected dropping into his lap of the holy card of Pope Saint Pius X was but one of several manifestations the saint made toward Ron mystically, spiritually. As other strange events, all having to do with some aspect of St. Pius X occurred over the years, Ron became convinced that the good Pope was simply trying to catch his attention.

It was during the middle of 1962 when Ron first noticed an unexplainable phenomenon. As he would be alone, praying or meditating, sparks of light would show up. These brief sparks might be right next to him or across the room, but although not a constant or continuous event, they did happen, sometimes even when he was in the presence of others. This manifestation has continued. He came to accept the strange lights as the presence of angels. The more he developed spiritually, the more he came to feel that the presence of angels would be a normal thing for someone trying to tune in deeply into God's world. How else to explain unsummoned sparks of light? Especially after various eye examinations revealed no physical anomalies.

He learned to appreciate the daily Latin Mass and to assist the clergy at private Masses in the crypt chapel. The crypt was the basement area consisting of rows of small altars where the seminary clergy would celebrate private Masses. At that time the concept of concelebration did not exist, and wouldn't until after Vatican II when it became a liturgical norm. So when Ron was in the seminary a priest would celebrate a Mass by himself with an acolyte in attendance.

Always one to enjoy sports, Ron soon took up tennis and loved playing almost daily. A seminarian friend named Jack was his instructor and taught him the fine points of the game. At the beginning, it was not unusual for Ron to have to retrieve a ball he had eagerly smashed right over the court fencing. In very short order, Jack had a worthy opponent in his new student. Ron eagerly found other seminarians with whom to enjoy the game and was soon playing both singles and doubles, developing a reputation as a natural on the court, with a powerful serve and great volleying skills.

In early May, Ron was informed by Steve, his Dorchester CCD training compatriot, that he had been selected to attend a special workshop at a Massachusetts lake where he would be trained as a Water Safety instructor. After completing his training by the end of May, he was ready to teach swimming, diving and lifesaving. This training came very easy for the strong swimmer who had previously taught local kids in his childhood home's nearby lakes when he was not much bigger than they were.

His instructions for the six weeks of summer were to join all the seminarians that hailed from Vermont in teaching and supervising at a boys' camp. It turned out that there were seven of them from St. Augustine's, the Montpelier parish. However, they were studying at seven different seminaries and religious communities all along the Eastern seacoast. As instructed, he arrived at Camp Holy Cross for Boys at Mallet's Bay, Lake Champlain located north of the city of Burlington, Vermont. He found a well-laid out series of cabins, a chapel and a large building similar to a parish hall that would be used for activities, especially in rainy weather. There was ample waterfront to accommodate all the boys, who no doubt would keep their supervisors busy. However, as it turned out, he did not work there that summer. That would come later. His superiors in the Burlington Diocese, responding to an urgent call from a nearby orphanage whose staff had requested an experienced and compassionate seminarian, sent him directly to St. Joseph's Child Center in Burlington. This pleasant complex was located at the partially sheltered waters of Burlington Bay on Lake Champlain. It housed nearly 200 orphaned boys and girls all of whom needed someone to look after their physical, emotional and spiritual well-being.

He settled in there for the last two weeks of June and the month of July with another seminarian named Bill, both of them wearing their cassocks while in the building. Their job was mainly to accompany the young orphans, approximately 20 at a time, to the waterfront to teach and supervise the active kids in all their swimming activities. Out at the waterfront, the seminarians wore swimming trunks while doing their jobs and casual summer clothes for other times. They got to know each child by name and soon heard their individual stories. For many of them, he and Bill were like uncles and usually were treated with respect and sometimes even awe, as the men would tell stories around an evening campfire near the water's edge. Both men were pleased to be able to attend daily morning Masses in the center's chapel and encouraged all the kids to follow their lead in that regard.

A couple of times they took a group of boys on overnight hikes up to the top of Mount Mansfield in Stowe. This is a premier skiing destination for winter sports lovers with scores of excellent trails, nearly a quarter of them designed for expert skiers. It is the highest peak in the Green Mountain chain. Although all during ski season there were several lifts in constant use, it was not an unusually difficult hike in the summer, depending on which particular trail one picked. The path that these explorers followed led from an already elevated location in Smugglers Notch to the summit of Mt. Mansfield. The kids (and the supervisors) loved the adventure, the cool mountain air and the views from the summit at nearly 4,400 feet. They spent the night in the rustic lodge before hiking back down the next day. The boys were usually quiet and a little laid back for a day or two after one of these adventures. Once they were back to their usual selves they talked for hours about their great hike and loved telling anyone who would listen about the natural air conditioning in the lodge up there. It was only an open-air square-shaped structure with a real roof but no walls; only having support columns at each corner. They unrolled their sleeping bags on the cement floor, trying to get as close as practical to the warmth from the fireplace which was kept going all night by some miracle. The ones who didn't sleep as well as others knew that the miracle was that Ron and Bill managed to take turns keeping the fire going through the night. It was surprising just how cool the night air could be during the heat of summer, providing a science lesson as well as a great get-away for the kids.

Once during a spell of very humid days, the seminarians took the boys on a ferryboat ride on the Burlington – Port Kent ferry across Lake Champlain to the New York shore and back, taking all afternoon to do so. All the kids loved it and talked about the ferry and the views of New York for days. Nobody could tell when they had left Vermont and were actually in New York when they were in the middle of the lake. No "Welcome to New York" signs were floating and the kids got a kick out of running to the front of the vessel to be the first ones in New York. Some of the sisters from St. Joseph's Child Center came along to help keep the children in line. All of the sisters were very nice, caring women who enjoyed the partially controlled antics of the kids.

Sister Henri Alfonse Lippens, the superior of the Child Center was particularly nice to the seminarians and spent time with them discussing the life of a religious, as well as current events, including major league baseball happenings. One day, Ron and Bill drove her and another sister to Montreal to inspect their order's newly constructed Mother House. It was located in the Pierrefonds section of Montreal and was a huge, attractive 10-story building. They were amazed to discover that the designer of this edifice was none other than Sister Henri Alfonse, who was pleased with the way it had turned out. Within a year, Sr. Henri was summoned back to Montreal to the Generalate of the order. This is the central house of the congregation where the General Administration is located. Sr. Henri was asked to take over the prestigious position of chief administrative officer over finances, engineering & building construction. She was thrilled with the appointment.

The 20 sisters at the Child Center were French Canadian, each of them having a wonderful sense of humor as well as being fully committed to her calling. An event that had Ron and his pal laughing for days was an unplanned visit to their quarters early one evening by Sister Emilie, who among her other duties at the Orphanage, worked in the kitchen as a chef. She came to their door, put a finger to her lips to signal "silence" and unceremoniously pulled a six-pack of beer from out of the folds of her plentiful habit, then left as quickly as she had arrived.

Ron spent the month of August at the Trapp Family Lodge, having looked forward to this ever since his first visit there on his Christmas vacation. The seminary was good about allowing their students the freedom to pursue pretty much whatever they wanted during the month of August and most of September as well. His superiors were very pleased with his choice of summer activity.

During this time he got to know each of the Trapp Family members who were in residence there at the time. They all became great friends as well as becoming confidants. Each had a special, unique personality, traits no doubt instilled in them by Mother Trapp. Not only did Ron get well acquainted with the von Trapps who were on the property while he was there, he also learned tantalizing facts about all seven of the original descendents of Georg von Trapp and his first wife, Agathe Whitehead, and also of the three who had been born to Maria (Mother) as well. He was told that all but the youngest of the ten children had been born in Austria, most in Zell am See.

The oldest of the von Trapp children was Rupert, born in 1911 in Pola, Austria which would later become Pola, Croatia. He was followed two years later by Agathe, named for her mother. Then came Maria in 1914, who now went by her nickname of Mitzi, which eliminated any confusion with "Mother". Werner, born in 1915, now lived a few miles from the Lodge on a farm in Waitsfield, Vermont with his wife Erika and their six children. Hedwig was the third girl, born in Austria in 1917, followed two years later by Johanna and finally, in 1921, along came the last of the original seven, Martina who was born in Klosterneuburg, Austria. Sadly, she had died in childbirth in 1952.

The children born to Baron Georg von Trapp and Maria were: Rosemarie born in 1929 in Salzburg and two years later, Eleonore, also a native of Austria. The only one of this bunch born in the United States was the last one, Johannes, born in 1939 in Philadelphia.

Ron and Johannes, who were only five years apart in age, became very close friends and found much in common. Johannes, who was a student at Dartmouth, two of his half-sisters, Mitzi and Hedwig, as well as his sister, Rosemarie, were the only von Trapps who actually lived at the Lodge while Ron was there at that time. The seminarian soon found that this portion of the family was really a fun-filled group, including Mother, and when chores were done, at least for a while, they often would roam through the woods together. Sometimes they would bring a picnic lunch and hike along until they came to a stream where they would swim and then enjoy their picnic together, laughing over some silliness or other.

Ron learned that Hedwig had spent a number of years working as a schoolteacher when she lived in Austria, but now was happy working the family gardens there in Stowe. With her wonderful sense of humor, it was always a treat to get to listen to one of her many true-life stories. He found that Mitzi, a very charming and charismatic woman, had spent years in Papua, New Guinea working with Austrian missionaries. She was much happier in Stowe, Vermont, but was proud of the work she had done in New Guinea.

Johannes' sister, Rosemarie, who went by the nickname of Illi was also lots of fun to be with, but spent most of her time helping out in the kitchen which she thoroughly enjoyed. She continued the use of "Illi", a name she gave herself as a toddler who, try her best, simply couldn't pronounce Rosemarie. Ron was in awe of her magnificent apple strudel, an Alpine favorite, and couldn't wait for the times when she would produce this delicate apple-filled pastry.

Other members of the extended family would visit the lodge periodically, especially those who lived nearby such as Werner. When he came to visit from Waitsfield, he usually brought his wife, Erika, and whichever of their six offspring were not off at their own activities. Also living in Waitsfield was Eleonore, known as Lorli, with her husband Hugh and their eight daughters. This group or at least parts of it would also stop in to visit and help out whenever possible.

Ron learned that the oldest of the clan, Rupert, now 52, was a doctor and was married with six children. In his younger days he had played accordion and piano and sang bass with his family. He and his wife now lived a little too far away in southern New England to simply drop in for a visit, nor could he leave his practice unattended very often, but would do his best to visit whenever possible.

When it was time for Ron to return to the seminary, he knew that he would surely be back at the Trapp Family Lodge at the very first opportunity.

In the photo above, Erika and Werner von Trapp celebrate their 50th wedding anniversary in Waitsfield, Vermont in 1998.

CHAPTER 11

SEMINARY YEARS
1962 – 1963

In September 1962, Ron was back at St. John's Seminary and in his second year of Philosophy. He had also returned to his familiar living space in St. Clement's Hall. There were a few new faces and some that he looked for had not returned. He was still very motivated and determined to master all that the seminary had to offer. Although he continued to do very well in all his courses of instruction, he felt the need for more physical exercise. Although he had never played soccer before, he soon found himself actively involved with the sport. He knew that he would never play at the highest skill level, but he enjoyed the action and fresh air (even if it was sometimes darned cold) as well as the spirit of competition. Another benefit of being so active with this sport was that by the end of the soccer season he had lost 25 pounds. He looked and felt better than ever.

The staff at the seminary encouraged the students to share their own individual talents and skills with others. Ron happily got right into the teaching of both Polish and German and had five classmates in each program. He knew that one of the best ways to master any particular subject is to teach it to someone else. He hadn't had a chance to use either of these languages in a while now and he was happy to realize that he had not lost much, if any of his proficiency. One of his students was particularly interested in mastering German and was a quick study. Ron was sure that it was his effective teaching technique that helped this young man do so well. It would develop a few years later that this person became a student in theology at Regensburg University in Germany. His instructor there was Professor Josef Ratzinger, who went on to become Pope Benedict XVI. Ron wondered if his ex-pupil had mentioned to professor Ratzinger that he had previously been trained by none other than Ronaldus Benedictus, the name Ron was given at his confirmation in 1960.

Most of the seminarians continued to have assignments off-campus teaching CCD, since skilled, committed teachers of Christian Doctrine were in short supply. Also, this was another way to reinforce in their own minds many of the basic concepts that the men had long ago accepted as articles of faith. Ron's assignment was at St. Clement's Church in Somerville where he taught marginally interested 9th grade pupils. At his first meeting with the group of about 20 or so students, he got the distinct impression that each of them had someplace else they would rather be. He quickly got their attention when he gave some of the highlights of his times in Germany when The Wall was being constructed and the terrible repercussions of all that the barrier would entail. He followed the syllabus that he was given, but amplified it with real life experiences that helped keep his charges connected to the main messages he was there to impart.

When Christmas break rolled around, Ron brought several of his classmates to the Trapp Family Lodge to work for Mother Trapp in whatever areas she needed. A side bonus for the seminarians while they were in Stowe was that they had the chance to get in some great skiing when their tasks were out of the way.

In the spring of 1963, Ron and his classmates received the first of the Minor Orders, and it was a very minor order indeed, that of Porter. In the very early days of the Church, one of a Porter's principal tasks was to open and close the church doors, guarding that no unbaptized persons could enter during the Eucharistic celebration. In more modern times, the Porter would perform these tasks at the doors of the Sacristy and elsewhere in the church. Additionally, since the seminarians had to serve at Masses at various times for monsignors or bishops in the different seminary crypt chapels, they had to learn how to be a bugia-bearer. This refers to the one who used to hold a candle ceremoniously all during the Mass. In times past, this was necessary for the one saying Mass to be able to read more easily in the otherwise dim light. Learning to be a bugia-bearer was not all that challenging.

However, the curriculum all the seminarians studied was difficult and required lots of effort and outside reading. The study of Philosophy II dealt with the history and development of philosophy by such luminaries as Aristotle, St. Thomas Aquinas, Descartes as well as more modern philosophers. Learning to paraphrase these learned giants of the subject was about as difficult as anything Ron had faced in any of his previous studies. They all studied Scripture in each of the seminary years, emphasizing a different section of the bible each year. Canon Law was studied every year and since it is such a complex legal system, going back to the rules (canons) that were adopted in the 1st century and is kept current, it too required careful study. A great deal of detail effort was put into studying Liturgy, the meaning behind the celebrations and actions during a Mass. Learning how to present meaningful and interesting homilies during a Mass was given a high priority. This subject was identified as "homiletics" and was taught every semester. Ron took to this subject in a very natural way and impressed his teachers with his native ability to deliver homilies that seemed to keep his audience not only awake, but interested in his message. In the theology years, one of the areas emphasized was known as catechetics, or the teaching of the Faith. This subject formed the root of the well-known "catechism". A considerable amount of memorization was needed to do well in this area. Another important part of the curriculum was the study of the sacraments and their celebration, although this was not covered until the last two years in the seminary. Both sacramental theology and moral theology were very important parts of this high-power learning experience. These complex topics were presented once the students had a good understanding of ecclesiology, the theology of the church. One of Ron's most enjoyable experiences in the seminary was learning how to sing Gregorian chants in community. His fellow priests-to-be practiced this beautiful singing style at least weekly and sang it every day in chapel. The natural acoustics were perfect for helping the combined voices sound all that much the better. In the past, he had often been moved by the rich harmonies and unusual melodies whenever he heard the chants and was now delighted to be part of a group producing such awe-inspiring sounds.

In July of '63 he was assigned to the special camp for boys that he first saw the previous year when he joined his fellow Vermont seminarians, but instead of working there in 1962, he had been redirected to the orphanage in Burlington. This time he actually did supervise at Camp Holy Cross for Boys. He was a swimming and diving instructor and by the time the summer was over, he realized that he had taught about 200 boys. Some of them had been afraid of the water and felt that they would never learn to swim. Others had overconfidence and told him that they could probably swim all the way to New York if they really wanted to. He worked closely with all of the boys and was pleased to find that they all were swimmers by the time he completed his assignment. Some of the original non-swimmers perhaps could not make it very far, but they had learned the sidestroke and knew how to save themselves in an emergency. Others of that bunch turned out to be like fish and came out of the water with prune-like fingers. Ron worked hard with the hot shots and got them to focus on diving and lifesaving. When this assignment was over he wasn't sure who had had the most fun, the kids or himself.

The month of August was really special for Ron since he was fortunate enough to spend it working at the Trapp Family Lodge once again. He was able to earn a little money working the front desk but the main attraction for him was getting to know even better than the previous year, those of the von Trapp family who were living there at the time. He was in awe of their musical talents and came to truly appreciate their close friendship. There was a private chapel on the second floor of the main lodge building where they attended daily Mass whenever a priest was on site. Mother Trapp was always on the lookout for priests who would come to Stowe to spend some time either on private retreat or simply for rest and relaxation. Just about every day, after chores were finished Ron enjoyed swimming in the Lodge pool. After supper, hours would be spent, usually in groups, discussing the religious life with Mother. Many evenings were spent discussing Pope John XXIII's ministry, his life and his books. This was when Ron first began reading of the Pope's spiritual journeys. Here was a pope who began writing spiritual notes daily from his early days in the seminary in 1895 and continued throughout his lifetime. Much of this fervor was captured in his *Encyclical on Christianity and Social Progress* published in May 1961. Ron became very familiar with this long and carefully worded document. He also was captivated by the Pope's autobiography, *The Journal of a Soul: Exercises and Spiritual Notes, 1895 – 1962*, published shortly after the Pope's death in June of 1963.

One of the things that all who visited at the Trapp Lodge really enjoyed was the way Mother would entertain the groups as they sat around a campfire in the evening. She would relate stories of saintly happenings in her native Austria. Some of the stories were about the lives of saints and good portions of them were really folklore. She told all her stories with a fervor and heightening sense of anticipation that kept all quietly transfixed. One of the stories that Ron heard more than once was intended to highlight the lengths to which clergy and lay people would go to protect the Blessed Sacrament from desecration. In this story, an altar boy felt the need to protect the consecrated host from evil non-believers who were out to do it harm. He took it while it was in a monstrance. (A beautiful vessel used to display it during Eucharistic adoration or Benediction.) In order to keep it safe, he snuck it into a secret room behind a confessional in his church. No one knew he had done that. Centuries later, he was found locked in that room, adoring the Blessed Sacrament in a state of suspended animation. When air came rushing into the room, the boy turned to ash. Mother had many such stories.

CHAPTER 12

SEMINARY YEARS
1963 - 1964

In the fall of 1963, Ron began his year of First Theology back at St. John's Seminary. He had new quarters for this year in St. William's Hall. It sat on a hill separate from the other buildings and was adjacent to the diocesan chancery buildings, where all written documents that concern the diocese were handled and stored. Meals were served in the large refectory in St. John's Hall, a short distance down the hill from his quarters. Ron joined the seminary choir and wondered to himself why it had taken him so long to do that since singing in a choir always brought him such great pleasure. He found that the talent possessed by these choir members exceeded any he had witnessed in previous locations. This choir sang at most liturgies in the chapel in St. John's Hall.

Everyone who was an adult in November 1963 remembers clearly exactly where he or she was and what he or she was doing in the mid-afternoon on the 22nd of that month. Ron had just finished a class in Scripture at St. William's Hall. That was the day that John Fitzgerald Kennedy, the 35th (and only Catholic) president of the United States was assassinated in Dallas, Texas. This tragic event moved Ron and everyone around him deeply. They were all glued to the black and white television set in the common room, with full permission granted of course, to watch the endless replays of what happened in the open car the President had been waving from, and to listen to the news reporters trying their best to deal with the developing story. This was unbelievable.

Later, the choir from St. John's Seminary had the great honor to participate in the Month's Mind Mass at Holy Cross Cathedral, celebrated by Cardinal Cushing in the presence of the entire Kennedy family. The Mass was Mozart's Requiem and was played by the Boston Symphony Orchestra. The seminary choir's role was to sing the psalm refrain between readings. Of all the times in the past that Ron had performed in a choir, this was the first time that he felt choked with emotion, but his voice stayed strong as did everyone else's in the choir.

After the Christmas holiday everyone in Ron's class moved out of St. William's Hall to the third floor of St. John's Hall overlooking the inner courtyard. There had only been room for about 20 people in St. William's Hall so it was put to use as a place to house visiting clergy, occasional conferences, and perhaps even for retreats. It also became quarters for a few faculty members.

Ron, as usual, had made several good friends. Two of these friends included a young man named Ron and another who went by his nickname of Camillus. That was actually his middle name, so one may have thought that he was possessed of a really strange or weird first name. However, his first name was Ed, and it turned out that he simply preferred a less common name. Ron and Ron and Camillus were not a threesome and didn't hang out together all the time, but rather joked around and shared thoughts, concerns and homework issues. Camillus was a very talented artist and cartoonist with a great sense of humor. He drew at least one cartoon of the ex-lieutenant Ron that was a real keeper. For whatever reason, neither the other Ron nor Camillus ever managed to get up to Vermont to visit at the Trapp Lodge.

Ron's CCD assignment in the academic year 1963 – 1964 was at St. Camillus in Arlington. It would have been a most unusual class if his pal Camillus were chosen to teach there. The students would have had a great time with the play on words. As it was, Ron really enjoyed the interaction with the high school boys who made up his class. They were all bright kids, most of them high school seniors and were fun-loving and interested in learning what Ron had to teach. He was totally unprepared for the trauma of hearing that one of his star pupils had been rushed to the hospital for an emergency appendectomy and had died on the operating table. He met with the youth's family and grieved with them, doing his best to help them cope with their sudden inexplicable loss. Several of his CCD lessons were taken up with the discussion of the tragic event as he tried his best to help the boy's classmates deal with it and to find meaning in their developing faith.

In the summer of '64 he once again was on the shores of Lake Champlain at Camp Holy Cross where he was in charge of the activities at the waterfront. He thoroughly enjoyed this summer where in addition to paying close attention to the excited kids as they learned to swim, he also supervised a cabin full of teenage junior counselors. They were a wonderful group of young men who were very keen on learning all that he had to offer and doing their best to make the precious days as meaningful as possible. They all helped him in one way or another on the waterfront. With a minimum of input from him, these junior counselors could often be found repairing or painting equipment.

It is often said that one never really knows the impact one has on other people's lives and that it is a rare opportunity to somehow be graced with that knowledge. While this book was being written, the following message was received from Bruce T. who was part of the group of youngsters at Camp Holy Cross in '64 and was 15 years old at the time.

.... *"What I do remember vividly is that Ron was very different from everyone else (seminarians and other counselors alike) and he was quite comfortable with it. While others were constantly and consistently boasting or proving themselves, Ron did not. It was unusual for me to see someone who did not seem to want others to be impressed with him. He is/was always my concept of a gentleman. I don't know that I can even define that term*

*adequately but in my mind he was/is the only man I
have met that fit the role.*

*I know that he struggled with his faith as he spoke freely
of that. It made it ok for me to question my faith at 15 yrs
old. Not long after I turned 19 I left the Catholic Church
and later in life became a deacon in a Christian and
Missionary Alliance church. I was able to teach/speak in
a Catholic church during that time in one of the towns
here ("once a Catholic always a Catholic") in Vermont. I
believe having known Ron helped me not to "write off"
the church and made it possible to work positively, in-
terdenominationally towards God's purpose.*

*Interestingly though Ron had a relationship with the
Trapp family (who are a very big name here in VT.) he
spoke little of it and certainly did not flaunt it. The only
thing he would do that was unusual for some of us was
to attire himself in suede shorts with suede suspenders,
knee high socks, and a loose fitting shirt. A very Austrian look. He cut quite a figure in that outfit. Very handsome.*

*(Years later...) He spoke briefly with me about being in
Berlin and standing under manholes while rescuing, I
believe it was children, out of East Berlin. He did not
mention he was with army intelligence. The way he
spoke of it took any thought of war being something glorious from me. Though I was a Marine in Vietnam I realized early on that my "enemy" was a lot like me and all
that entails. I don't know how Ron felt about his enemy
but something tells me hate is not a word in his vocabulary. I can see him caring as much from his heart
for the enemy as a friend.
I can't say at camp Holy Cross he ever treated me as an
equal but he never made me feel he was better than
me, though I always thought he was.*

I am honored to have known him..."

At some point during 1964 both Ron and his fellow seminarian, Camillus, had been discussing the fascinating activities
at the Second Vatican Council, and in particular the many
faces from around the world that surfaced there. The two

students undertook a letter writing campaign to a few famous bishops, mostly just to see if they would respond. The likelihood of a real reply seemed fairly remote considering all that these very busy giants had to deal with. Ron wrote carefully and thoughtfully in each of the bishops' native language, expressing his deep faith and his strong calling to the priesthood as well as his honest reaction to some of the changes that he understood would be forthcoming from their historic meeting. Ron and Camillus were happily surprised to get responses from each of the bishops they had written to. Ron wrote periodically to Cardinal Wyszynski of Warsaw, Cardinal Beran of Prague, Cardinal Slipyi of the Ukraine, the Ecumenical Patriarch Athenagoras of Istanbul, and Cardinal König of Vienna. He treasured this collection of letters and kept them with him wherever he would be stationed. The only remaining ones are those from Cardinal König; the rest tragically were lost in a rectory fire in 1997.

The month of August was again spent at the Trapp Family Lodge where he worked mainly with guests at the front desk. He enjoyed meeting the visitors, showing them to their accommodations and in the process, learning a lot about their life stories as well. Of course swimming in the large in-ground pool was a side benefit that was hard to beat. He wondered if Mother Trapp had run out of stories to tell around the campfires. She most definitely had not.

Maria von Trapp in the Lodge,
ready for hungry guests.

CHAPTER 13

SEMINARY YEARS
1964 - 1965

In Ron's second year of Theology, he lived in a rather special area of St. John's Hall. This was a place that had the unusual nickname of "Popcorn alley". It was called this simply due to its architecture since it was the hallway of rooms on the third floor level that ran directly above the center of the refectory where they all enjoyed their meals. There were no faculty rooms up there, which to the spirited young seminarians translated to the fact that there was no one around to "snoopervise". For the most part, rules were a bit relaxed up there, although the deep spiritual strengths and belief in the seriousness of their calling kept all the young men in line pretty much of their own volition. They had what they called their own "beach front" in this unique setting. One could go out on the roof from up there and not be seen from any direction. (Except from Heaven!) They had an occasional chicken fry up there on the roof. Innocent and at the same time, great fun.

Ron spent a lot of time with the seminary choir, continuing to hone his technique and enjoying every minute of it. This choir attended the funeral of every local priest, at which event they sang the liturgy. When Cardinal Cushing consecrated St. Mary's Church in Lynn, the choir was there to sing the lengthy and complicated parts of the liturgy for that ceremony. They were also in fine voice for the consecration of several other beautiful churches, including St. Leonard Church in the North End.

The familiar and enjoyable routines that by now had become almost second nature to Ron continued. For example, Christmas Holiday '64 was spent working at the Trapp Family Lodge and also getting in some good skiing in Stowe. He again taught CCD to school kids, spent six weeks on the waterfront at Camp Holy Cross, and once again in August '65 he worked at the Trapp Family Lodge.

At the end of August he was given a marvelous opportunity to visit Europe again. This wonderful trip was not only the inspiration of Mother Trapp, but she financed it entirely as a gift to him. So that it wouldn't seem to be what it really was, a way for him to get a break from his day-to-day life, she told him that she needed him to pick up some dress material from an old friend of hers in Bavaria. She would use the material to make the Austrian style clothing she enjoyed wearing as well as for extra outfits to sell at her lodge.

Although the trip was a quick one, Ron did manage to pack in some very special visits. He began with a brief trip to West Berlin where he was given a warm welcome by some of the members of his former intelligence unit. Several persons were new to the command since he had left four years previously, but the many that knew him from back in the day, were fascinated with his progress in his new direction in life and were pleased not only to see him again, but also to realize that he was very happy with his calling. He was given a special tour of the Berlin Wall, which by that time was fully built up and formed an ugly reminder of how bad the political situation really was. In the four years since he had been in West Berlin, many people had been killed attempting to scale the wall or to tunnel under it to get to freedom or to join family. There was no joy in that part of the world.

He made a quick visit to the village of Oberammergau and found it as beautiful as ever. He didn't have the time to obtain the clearance required to get into Hawkins Barracks, but he did manage to meet briefly with some friends at the Officers' Club. Then, using the specific directions on how to locate Mother's friend, he drove to visit Fr. Franz Niegel in the village of Unterwössen in order to pick up the special package for her, remembering that that was the main reason for this trip. The package was, as he had been told in advance, rare material that was used in the making of the unique dresses that women wear in the Alps. It was from a friend of Mother's, Annette Thoma who was the widow of the famous Bavarian poet, Ludwig Thoma. Although Ron had no way of knowing it at the time, Fr. Niegel and Unterwössen would become very important in his life within a few short years. (But Mother Trapp knew it in her heart.)

Although Ron thought of this trip as a short one, he really was on the move and covered a lot of ground in a relatively short time. At that time, getting around in Europe by commercial aircraft was reasonably affordable. He got to Denmark where he had a brief but wonderful visit with the Wissums at Rungsted Kyst near Copenhagen. He reminded them of how much he appreciated their wonderful hospitality when he was sailing in the area in 1960.

He managed to get north to Oslo, Norway to visit a young fellow who had been a classmate of Johannes von Trapp when they were both at Dartmouth College. Ron had met Jens, who was about the same age as his own brother, Sidney, Jr., and Johannes during one of his summers at the Trapp Lodge. They had become good friends. When Jens learned from Mother Trapp that Ron would be coming to Europe, he got word to him, complete with directions, to be sure to come see him at his home in Norway. While Ron visited there he learned that during World War II, living in that neighborhood, was none other than Vidkun Quisling, the Nazi dictator of Norway all during the German occupation of that country. Sometimes referred to as "the Hitler of Norway", he was tried for high treason and executed by firing squad in 1945. The term "quisling" has become a synonym for traitor. The Norwegians managed, by keeping a low profile during the war years, to escape any harm from their unwanted neighbor. After a short visit with Jens and his family, Ron was off again to continue his whirlwind trip.

He then arrived in England where he was fortunate enough to actually catch up with both Robin Plummer and Stephen Finch, the principal facilitators of his sail boating all around Denmark. They both wanted him to stay and really visit, since they said that they indeed still had a little left over vermouth to waft near some gin, but that would have to wait for another time. They had a great, but very brief reunion and pledged to meet again in the not too distant future. As it would turn out, another get-together did eventually take place, but much later than their eager promise.

On his way back to America, he got a chance to locate his British military friends, Bill and Diana Hill in London. They had a wonderful time recalling their earlier work and fun together. They too, voiced the thought that a longer visit in the near future would be a high priority. An enjoyable reunion with these two friends from the UK would indeed take place in about five years.

Ron was back at the seminary in what seemed to him to be a very brief time, after stopping at the Trapp Lodge to deliver his amazingly large special package to Mother Trapp. She was pleased, not only with the material he brought to her, but the look of contentment he had about him. She felt certain that her special assignment for him on the trip to Bavaria had accomplished what she had hoped it would, especially when he voiced the thought that he was eager to resume his studies.

The rest of Ron's academic year of '64 – '65 went by smoothly and he continued to truly enjoy everything about it. He looked forward to his next term and felt that he was making great progress towards his goal of becoming a priest.

Those unexplainable sparks of light that first manifested themselves around him in 1962 still showed themselves from time to time and had become a fairly regular occurrence. This usually happened only when he was alone praying. He no longer thought of them as odd or strange, but somehow comforting. The message he took from this unusual pheno-menon was that God's angels continued to look over him.

CHAPTER 14

SEMINARY YEARS
1965 – 1966
THE "DEMONSTRATION"

During the '65 – '66 academic year of Third Theology, Ron's Sub-Deacon year, he resided in Bishop Peterson Hall, third floor center. He had a great view of the ball field from his window. That was where all the seminary athletes and would-be athletes gathered for their afternoon games. Depending on the season or the whims of the students they would get into games of touch football, soccer or softball and all would have a great time. Occasionally he would go to his room to study, take a quick look out his window and realize that he really needed to be out in the fresh air and "helping" his pals enjoy whatever game was going on at the moment.

He was enrolled in a seminar for Third Theologians on the subject of Moral Theology, taught by Father James O'Donoghue. This was a very difficult subject with homework for this course demanding the reading of one relevant book a week. St. Thomas Aquinas' 5- volume work, *Summa Theologica*, part of the required reading, is still considered the premier treatise on the topic. One of the many books on the subject that made an impression on Ron was a book by Martin Luther King, Jr. that dealt with the question of the *Just War Theory*. This complex theory combines a moral abhorrence of war with the belief that war may sometimes be necessary. Deep stuff.

A lot of things were happening all over the world that seemed to be pushing everyone toward big life-style changes, making "The Sixties" a catch phrase for freedom and at the same time for turmoil and unrest. Demonstrators were assembling in Selma, Alabama in support of civil rights for our nation's black people. The assassinations of John F. Kennedy and his brother, Robert, caused much unrest and suspicion throughout our nation. The unpopular Vietnam War appeared to be in a quagmire. At many universities and colleges all around the country, the theme seemed to be one of unrest.

At St. John's Seminary, things, at least from the perspective of some of the young seminarians, seemed to be downright out of touch with the modern world into which they would be thrust once they had completed their studies and were ordained. There were, and had been for weeks, several discussions in relatively small groups of students about what changes really ought to be made in what they perceived as a monastic life-style; a way of being treated that they felt was simply not appropriate. They began to realize that many of them shared the same views; that there needed to be some changes in their personal and academic freedoms. For example, wouldn't it be great to remove the restrictions on visiting each other in their rooms, at least for a couple of hours a day? And how about removing the insistence on the Grand Silence at night? And becoming involved in community action projects concerning the poor, the aged and the disadvantaged was something that these young "rebels" felt was absolutely the right thing for them to be doing. The seminary hierarchy did not wish for the same things.

These thoughts and feelings came to a head on May 26, 1966. It was discovered that Richard Cardinal Cushing, Archbishop of Boston, was to be at St. John's Seminary Library on that day to address the pastors of the Boston Archdiocese on the subject of how to implement the important changes that were now directives from the recently completed second Vatican Council in Rome. These dealt with revisions in liturgical practice in the churches, such as saying the Mass in the vernacular, whereas it had been said in Latin for centuries, turning the church altars around so that the celebrant would no longer have his back to the congregation, but would be facing the people, and other important modifications.

What a great opportunity for the group of young men who felt that they were in synch with the times, to make their thoughts known to the highest levels in their church structure. Most of the seminarians who agreed with the relatively small vocal group who had been concocting the plan to get the Cardinal's attention and thereby make their feelings and wishes known, suddenly called what they were about to do, a "demonstration". Others labeled it a "revolt". Someone made up a sign that read "Freedom Now!" Pretty heady stuff for this place. At any rate, the purpose of the planned demonstration was to create a dialogue with Cardinal Cushing relating to their issues. They felt sure that if they could get him to understand their plight, he would be supportive.

Ron and a few of his fellow students in the Moral Seminar were asked to join the rebellious group and assemble in front of the library where there would be the best chance of actually getting close to the Cardinal. So when the bell rang at noontime, Ron and a few others left their classroom in St. John's Hall and walked outside the building, just past the kitchen area. There they saw a large group of seminarians milling around, expecting something. Word had gotten around. Ron, used to being in a lead role, without being prompted (and without really knowing the issues) and expecting to be followed by a crowd, walked briskly up the hill to the seminary library. That was where the Cardinal should be. When Ron got to the library there was no sign of the Cardinal, but more importantly, when he turned around there was hardly any sign of any other seminarians. What had happened? He suddenly realized that only seven others had followed his lead, while the organizers and self-proclaimed rebels had stayed back where it was safe.

Suddenly, Ron realized that cameras were clicking. Reporters from out of state newspapers had gathered to cover the cardinal's visit. The Boston newspapers were on strike at the time, but there were always others. He spotted a TV

164

reporter with his cameraman and could hardly believe it when the aggressive guy stuck a microphone in his face and asked him about the *Freedom Now* sign and what the group of eight seminarians was up to. Before he even had a chance to respond, one of the seminary professors stepped between Ron and the TV camera and sternly told him that he was not to represent the seminary in these, or any matters. It was just as well that he was prevented from responding since for essentially the first time in his life, he felt tongue-tied. All during this short-lived demonstration that never really happened, Cardinal Cushing was nowhere to be seen. Almost as suddenly as it began, the event vaporized leaving Ron feeling as though he and the seven others had somehow been set up. As the groups of would-be protestors headed back to their respective destinations, most seemed to be carefully inspecting the ground under their feet.

For the next week, Ron's discussions with his fellow students resolved nothing, with many people taking evasive action and constantly changing the subject. Eventually, he was summoned to the office of the Seminary Rector, Monsignor Lawrence Riley. With very little in the way of preamble, he was asked if he had participated in "that demonstration". Ron looked the monsignor in the eye and replied in the affirmative. The response was totally unexpected. He was to be immediately expelled from the seminary. He was to leave that day. Ron felt that this was some sort of twisted joke on him and that the monsignor would soon break out in a huge smile and tell him, that of course, the faculty at St. John's held him in high regard and in no way were they about to lose such a promising candidate for priesthood. But the smile and the kind words never came. He could feel his face flush with a combination of anger and disbelief as he left the office.

In the days immediately after the event (or really, non-event) and the notice of expulsion, TV shots of the demonstration had been obtained and reviewed by the Auxiliary bishops and Cardinal Cushing. A total of eight seminarians including Ron were identified as the culprits, and the decision was to expel all eight promising candidates for priesthood. An example had to be made. No nonsense would be tolerated. Soon, the headlines in the Manchester NH Union-Leader exclaimed **Boston Eight Expelled**. That type of headline always sold newspapers. The editors loved using numbers like that, such as *The Chicago Seven* and others. The Boston newspapers were still on strike or surely they would have gladly jumped on the bandwagon.

The eight "bad guys" arranged to meet on Tuesday after the expulsion notice was public, at the south Boston home of one of them for the afternoon to plan their next moves. They contacted a sympathetic leader in the seminary and were told that they could have an appeal with the Cardinal the following Saturday. Ron immediately went to his home in Vermont. His folks were surprised to see him and once he explained the reason for his sudden, unannounced visit, his mother said, "Haven't you had enough of this Catholic stuff?" Ron smiled and said, "Probably not. We'll see."

The next day Ron paid a visit to Bishop Joyce. He had been ordained to the priesthood in 1923 and appointed bishop of Burlington, Vermont in 1956. Ron had corresponded with Bishop Joyce on a regular basis during his years in the seminary to that point. He felt comfortable writing and keeping him up to speed on his progress since the Bishop had been so instrumental in getting him into St. John's Seminary in the first place. He knew that the Bishop, who had been an Army chaplain, liked him and was impressed with his military background. He had called his office and told him the unbelievable news. The good Bishop asked Ron to be sure to come back after his upcoming meeting with Cardinal Cushing and to fill him in on exactly what transpired. He was very interested and determined not to lose a promising candidate for the priesthood.

The following Saturday, as directed, Ron was the first of the banditos to visit the Cardinal. He showed up at the Cardinal's residence in Brighton early that morning. At 9:00 AM, he was ushered into the large reception area on the ground floor. The Cardinal was cordial and greeted him warmly and eventually spent nearly two hours with him. However, very little discussion centered on Ron's plight. Most of the time the Cardinal talked about the Kennedy family finances, the Cuban Missile Crisis and the need for him to raise money, something he was good at, to help rescue the Bay of Pigs militia who had been captured by the Cubans. The discussion, which was really more like a monologue by Cardinal Cushing, was interesting and Ron felt that perhaps all would be forgiven for his role in the "demonstration" during which he never even saw the Cardinal. After over an hour or so of progressively more fascinating topics being explained, Ron felt that it was time to bring up the subject of the reason that he had this audience with His Eminence. When he did manage to get this topic out for discussion, it was summarily dismissed by the Cardinal. He rather abruptly indicated that the pastors of the Archdiocese would have his head if he allowed the eight perpetrators back into the seminary. All during this meeting, Ron took extensive notes of everything that the Cardinal said. At the end of the two-hours, Ron, in awe of the heavy issues of real importance that this impressive man was dealing with and not at all sure of his own future, left for Vermont after shaking the Cardinal's hand and thanking him for his time.

He went directly to Bishop Joyce and handed him the notes he had taken during his visit in Brighton. The Bishop carefully read Ron's neat transcription and said not a word about it. Nor did he make any reference to the Cardinal. He did indicate that he would do his best to "straighten out" Ron's situation. Before leaving Bishop Joyce's office, Ron voiced the thought that perhaps he could spend the remaining month of his third year of Theology at the Edmundite Seminary in Burlington, Vermont. There was a small seminary located there for the Edmundite Fathers, who ran St. Michael's College in Winooski, Vermont. It was obvious that Ron still felt strongly about his calling and was not about to be deterred from the path he had been on until being so abruptly knocked off his feet. Bishop Joyce knew a good man when he saw one and within a few days had made the arrangements for Ron to be enrolled there.

Ron quickly adjusted to his new surroundings and spent the balance of the academic year there surrounded by some very nice and thoughtful Edmundite seminarians as he took a course on the writings of Teilhard de Chardin, a prominent French philosopher and Jesuit priest who had also trained as a paleontologist and a geologist. This fascinating priest had also taken part in the discovery of Peking Man. Ron found his writings to be truly fascinating. He had no trouble with the final exam for this course, which was an oral one; an exam style that was somewhat new to him, but at the same time, right up his alley. He aced the course. It was no surprise that he managed to make some very good friends at this seminary in the short time he was there, and he enjoyed the experience.

In June, almost as if nothing unusual had happened, he reported once again to Camp Holy Cross at Mallet's Bay for another six weeks of working on the waterfront. He was back to teaching swimming, diving and life-saving and enjoying the fresh air and sense of freedom that went along with the task. This was a much-needed calming down period for him, allowing his thoughts to coalesce and to realize that he was as committed as ever to becoming a priest. One of the seminarians there, who was also providing swimming instruction to the kids, was from Montreal and was upset to learn of the trouble that Ron had gotten into. He was of the opinion that Ron had been treated unjustly and was determined that he be allowed to continue along his path. He suggested that Ron visit the city of Montreal and meet the very impressive Archbishop, Cardinal Paul-Emile Leger, who had been elevated to that position by Pope Pius XII in 1950. He had recently returned from the Second Vatican Council that took place from 1962-1965 where he had been a leading liberal force.

Ron and his new friend from Montreal went to that city together by bus. Once there, arrangements were soon made for Ron to meet with the Archbishop who quickly suggested that he spend his deacon year in the Grand Seminary of Montreal. Ron was impressed with Cardinal Leger and after thanking him for his time and consideration, returned to discuss the plan with Bishop Joyce who was excited with the idea. He revealed to Ron that he himself had completed his seminary studies in Montreal and knew that Ron would find it to be very pleasant. He was glad that Ron had taken the opportunity to be interviewed by Cardinal Leger, whom he thought the world of. None of them could know at the time, how close Ron came to not being able to meet with the Cardinal who would, in April of 1968, resign as Montreal's Archbishop to move to Africa where he would do missionary work with lepers and handicapped children.

Once again, Ron spent time at the Trapp Lodge where he did his best to explain to Mother Trapp how he had come to the situation that would have him completing his seminary years in Canada. She made him repeat the story several times since she had a hard time seeing the logic behind his expulsion. However, she was as proud as ever of him for sticking with it and just knew that he would do very well in Montreal.

After spending a couple of weeks at the Lodge, he was on his way to Montreal's Grand Seminary for the year 1966 – 1967. If all went per plan, this would be his final year as a seminarian. At the end of this year, he would be ordained a priest. Little did he know that his trial was not that close to being over.

Once settled into his new home, and he was so used to being in different places that he settled in very quickly, he was surprised to discover that the horarium (schedule) was somewhat relaxed. He was even more amazed when he found that attendance at scheduled events was not absolutely mandatory. Quite a change. The entire seminarian community was very friendly towards him. But then that had been his experience no matter where he was. They were all accepting of his status and quickly came to see that he had been railroaded, but all were glad that he was now one of them. He was actually given a key to the front door. Unbelievable! He thought he'd gone to heaven.

It was very fortunate for him that he knew French well, since just about everything was in that language. A couple of the courses were conducted in English for the benefit of those seminarians who really had no background with the French language. There was one bi-lingual student, fluent in both languages who was thoughtful enough to make copious notes of other courses for the benefit of the English-only crowd. Ron's background in French included two years of it in high school, and then 2 years at Middlebury College. He was a straight "A" student of that language in both institutions. But he automatically became more proficient in that language since he had used it quite a bit growing up in Vermont. Many Vermonters used French as their normal language in their homes. Also, he spent some of his summers between college years working on a survey crew for the Vermont Highway Department, a job that his brother, Milan, had helped him line up. Some of that work involved conducting interviews of people who were traveling the Vermont highways. He would always be the one to whom the crew chief would delegate the task of interviewing the folks who had driven down from Quebec and were not bi-lingual. Occasionally, he would wave goodbye to some of them who were pleasantly surprised to find that someone in a highway survey crew knew their language, even if it wasn't perfect quite yet. He had always been a proponent of the learn-by-doing approach to just about anything.

Ron really enjoyed the food that was served in the Grand Seminary. It was prepared by French nuns whose cooking skills were excellent. They always came up with a varied and healthful menu and were pleased to get positive feedback from the diners who never left the tables hungry. He particularly looked forward to the chicken pot pie that was usually served on Wednesdays. On one of these evenings while all eight at his table were enjoying the nuns' specialty, he made the casual comment that one of the bones that was left in his dish after he had enjoyed the meal didn't look like a chicken bone. His dinner companions all smiled broadly at his comment. The person sitting to one side of him told him in

French that he was right. The bone indeed was not from a chicken, but was from "lapin" or rabbit, and wasn't it delicious? He assured Ron that it was not lapin de garenne, which Ron knew meant wild rabbit. All at his table had a good laugh when Ron pointed out that he now realized that the nuns had succeeded in fooling him, just the way his mom had done when he was a kid. They ate a lot of pot pie at home in Vermont, with Ron and his brothers all believing that it was made with chicken. But it was always made with rabbit that his dad had caught. He and his siblings never knew that until they were adults when his mom 'fessed up. He said that he was raised on lapin de garenne and looked forward to next Wednesday's supper.

A large portion of the academic work in this year was devoted to the study of the theology of marriage. Of course it was conducted in French, a fact that slowed him down very little, but from time to time caused him to seek out his French-English dictionary. He felt that the extra effort required by that slight detour helped him to more fully understand the subject.

As a means of fulfilling the requirement of "Field Education", Ron also visited the many Montreal churches that belonged to the Eastern Rites and found them all fascinating. Some Sundays he went to Mass attending the liturgy in a different Eastern Church, such as the Ukrainian Greek Catholic churches of the Byzantine Rite and others such as Syrian, Armenian, Coptic and Chaldean Rites. At each of these churches, the Mass was conducted completely in the corresponding language and yet still felt so close to his heart. During the week, the English language seminarians, including Ron, attended Mass in the seminary chapel, where it was celebrated in English.

He enjoyed the fact that every weekday contained a recreation period. This was much better than recess during elementary school, and he enjoyed the free time even more. A group of hardy young guys, Ron included, played football on the wet field calling it the "Mud Bowl". He loved playing handball in the court provided for just that. In the winter they often played broomball, a version of hockey using sawed off brooms. When the hockey rink was flooded, Ron learned to play hockey under the expert guidance of his hockey coach who was a seminarian in the year behind him. This coach was a really nice guy named Marc Ouellet from Amos, Quebec. He was ordained into the priesthood in 1968 and went on to become the Cardinal Archbishop of Quebec and primate of Canada. (The term primate in this use was taken from the Latin *Primus*, "first".) This wonderful, outgoing person continued to keep in touch with Ron over the years and still remembers their hockey games. Ron kept a pair of skates, his coach's old ones, at his Vermont home so that he could make use of them during Vermont winters in the future.

Marc Cardinal Ouellet, fluent in six languages, English, French, Spanish, Portuguese, Italian and German, is known for his missionary work in South America. He was in Rome in 2005 at the papal conclave as a cardinal elector and remains eligible to vote in any future papal conclaves until his 80th birthday in 2024. He is well known as someone who could easily become Pope since he was among twenty papal possibilities according to a report in *The National Catholic Reporter*, an independent Catholic newspaper. Talk about having friends in high places!

One of the major wintertime attractions for all the seminarians was attending the Montreal Canadiens hockey games in the Forum, located just a block away from the Grand Seminary. That they were all able to get in free after the games had started somehow added to the fun of being there. Ron did a lot of swimming at the nearby "Y" pool to keep himself in shape and for the sheer joy of it. The Seminary was located on the edge of Montreal's downtown area and the students were able to get around in the city freely and on their own, taking in a lot of sights and enjoying the ambiance. McGill University was just a few blocks away to the north and they would occasionally run into some of the University students and strike up interesting conversations. The relative freedom to get around and be off the seminary grounds on their own was positive motivation for each of the seminarians to do their best in all their courses. It allowed them to keep in touch with the general population, and to keep current with the concerns of the community.

In the spring of 1967 Ron was approached by Montreal's new English Auxiliary Bishop, Norman Gallagher. He had been the Military Ordinary for Canada and had recently retired from that position. (The term "Ordinary" here refers to a prelate who exercises jurisdiction over a specified territory or group.) The Bishop was impressed with Ron's military background and invited him to become his secretary, or aide, and to move in with him at the Basilica of St. Patrick's which was located not far from the Grand Seminary. Ron would be able to continue his seminary training and learn more about church business this way. Ron took him up on his offer.

A happy seminarian in Montreal.
1967

CHAPTER 15

UNTERWÖSSEN

The springtime weather in Montreal in 1967 was chilly and overcast a lot of the time. But Ron thought that he had a pretty neat set-up so his spirits were high no matter the weather. He was on his last leg of his seminary journey but now had started living at St. Patrick Basilica in downtown Montreal, not far from the Grand Seminary where he had a great bunch of friends and excellent teachers. He was just beginning his task of serving as secretary to Norman Gallagher, Auxiliary Bishop of Montreal. He soon discovered, however, that his job was one that required more brawn than brain. For the first few weeks he told himself that he was lucky to be selected to live in the Basilica and be able to serve the Bishop. But it wasn't very long before he seriously questioned what in the world he had gotten himself into and he felt chilled even when the weather was beautiful.

The month of June had been extraordinarily busy, mostly because Montreal's Expo '67 was in full swing. It was hailed as the most successful world's Fair of the 20th Century. By the time it closed at the end of October, it had been host to over 50 million visitors from all over the world. Many bishops, who had gotten to know Bishop Gallagher while they were together in Rome for the Second Vatican council, came to Montreal to visit with him and take in the sights of Expo '67. Most of the bishops came from Scotland. Ron's main job for several days was to pick them up at the airport and chauffeur them around, showing them whatever places and attractions they really wanted to see. Ron acted as valet and chauffeur for the Bishop and all of his guests; a job that kept him totally preoccupied for nearly every waking minute of several days. He also served cocktails at the appropriate hour on a regular basis. He was extraordinarily busy and had absolutely no time for himself. He was even busy writing sermons for the Bishop who was preoccupied with all his guests. Of course, he was missing many of his seminary classes and would have a hard time catching up with the program in which he had, until just recently, been doing so well. After many days of this type of crazy busy work, he looked at his reflection in a mirror and asked himself what he was doing. This was clearly not what he had been called to the priesthood to do. He began to feel depressed and concerned about his future. He thought, "This is not what I signed up to do!" He could feel himself sliding into a spiritual slump, feeling unsure of what was going on and just where he was headed. He also may have been experiencing at that time, a delayed reaction to his expulsion from St. John's the year before. Whatever the cause, he was definitely feeling that his spiritual life was falling apart. And he didn't like that feeling at all.

He bravely approached Bishop Gallagher and asked for time off. His request was readily granted, probably because the Bishop could see for himself what was happening to this serious young seminarian. Like a duckling returning to its mother, he went directly to the Trapp Family Lodge in Vermont. He poured out his woes and troubles to Mother Trapp who gave him her full attention. Surprisingly, she brightened, smiled at him and with her unique manner somehow let him know that if he followed her lead now, he'd be OK. She wasted no time in telling him very authoritatively that he must return to Bavaria. She knew that if he took the time to do that, he would recapture the sense of faith that he had initially received over there not that long ago. She asked him if he remembered meeting Father Franz Niegel when she sent him on his whirlwind trip around Europe a couple of years ago. He was the one who had the special dressmaking material she needed. Ron clearly did recall the kindly priest and remembered that he was in the Bavarian village of Unterwössen. Mother Trapp picked up her phone and in what seemed to Ron to be no time at all, was talking to Fr. Niegel in Bavaria. In her straightforward style, she got right to the point and asked if he would be willing to take the good young man on as a house guest for about a year or so in order that he might become re-acquainted with his spiritual roots. Fr. Niegel responded in the Bavarian dialect, "He is already here!" Three days later, fully at Mother Trapp's expense, Ron Lawson arrived in Unterwössen.

He had flown to Germany via Icelandic Airlines and landed in Luxemburg. He gathered his luggage and boarded a train to Frankfurt, where he transferred to another train that was bound for Salzburg with a few stops along the way. One of the scheduled stops was in Prien, a few miles west of Salzburg, where he disembarked according to Mother Trapp's instructions. He knew that it was most often referred to as Prien am Chiemsee and was a lovely municipality on the western shore of Chiemsee Lake. It was often known as "the Bavarian Seaside." As he searched across the faces in the crowd, he wondered if he would recognize Father Niegel when he saw him, or if the priest would easily pick him out. He thought to himself that it would surely help if his host was wearing his priestly garb. He knew that he should not expect to see him wearing a Roman collar, since German clergy do not wear that familiar and distinctive article. When not dressed in their vestments for Mass, those priests traditionally wore a thin black sweater over a white shirt with an open collar. As it turned out, they both knew each other immediately, with Ron easily recalling his visit a couple of years earlier.

Fr. Niegel, who was young, jovial and fun loving, greeted Ron warmly and talked a mile a minute with Ron having a little trouble with the priest's Bavarian accent in otherwise good German. He told Ron that before they could go to St. Martin's Church rectory, where he was based and where Ron would be living, they first had to attend a wedding reception. So with Ron hardly even fully aware of his surroundings, he was whisked off to a party. The wedding reception was held in one of the nicest hotels in Unterwössen, known as the Post Hotel. When they arrived, the reception was in full swing with the many guests enjoying the open bar and the bride and groom shyly receiving their guests. They knew Fr. Niegel, of course but had no idea about the young man who accompanied him. As Ron was introduced to the newlyweds, he did what anyone back home would have done. He kissed the bride. There was an audible gasp from the large crowd, followed by sudden silence. Ron had unknowingly broken a local taboo. It had been the custom forever in this part of the world that on her wedding day, only the groom kisses the bride. Once that was quietly explained to Ron by Fr. Niegel, his face reddened and he wondered how to correct his faux pas. The ebullient priest quickly explained that Ron was his guest from America and had simply done what everyone does at a wedding there. And by the way, wasn't that a nice custom and perhaps it was time to update the antiquated rules they followed. Once everyone understood that Ron was a foreigner, all was forgiven and he was actually asked to dance with the bride. He became a big hit with most of the guests and was soon engaged in spirited discussions with many of them as he explained that he was nearly completed with his studies for the priesthood and hoped to be ordained in the not-too-distant future. In subsequent weeks, the bride and groom started attending Mass where they sat in the front row. Sitting at the front of the church was something that young people in that part of the world rarely did.

After a respectable amount of time at the wedding reception, Fr. Niegel drove Ron to St. Martin's Rectory, called a Pfarrhof locally, where he was shown to a nicely appointed guest room. The priest made it abundantly clear to Ron that he wished to be called Franzi, a familiar form of his first name and didn't expect it to be preceded by the designation "Father". He also told him that he must learn the Bavarian dialect, because speaking in "High German" simply did not suit him. This was just one more small challenge for the linguist who was sure that he could master the dialect in short order. It was harder than he expected, finding it to be quite different from High German, but he finally got the hang of it, (or at least, most of it) hoping that it would not ruin his normal German in which he had become passably fluent.

Ron was introduced to the live-in housekeeper, a deeply religious young woman named Anny. In addition to keeping the Pfarrhof neat and clean, she was also the cook, and as he would soon discover, a very good one at that. She had a beautiful little dog, a well-behaved and well-trained long-haired daschund that she called Waschi. After a short period of getting to know Ron, little Waschi took a real liking to him and they both enjoyed frequent walks around town. With his long, floppy ears and soulful eyes, the pup made a hit everywhere they would go.

Ron was to call his room in the rectory home for the next eight months as he got to know Franzi and to understand what was expected of him. Franzi turned out to be a wonder-ful, kind and gentle priest who was only about ten years older than Ron, who was 32 at the time. Franzi was pastor of this small village parish church located in the Achental region of the Chiemgau, bordering the Austrian Tyrol, high up in the Alps. The small town had a population of about 2,000 at the time and it seemed to Ron that each and every one of them was very cordial and kindhearted. He enjoyed seeing them in their traditional Alpine clothing, such as lederhosen as well as the hats with the hair of a mountain goat arrayed upright on the back. That particular hat detail was called a goat's beard, or locally "Gamsbard". The townspeople were all hard-working, serious-minded folks. Most of them worked as farmers, forest workers or civil servants, such as border police. Others were teachers, storekeepers and much-needed business people.

Ron was a bit surprised when Franzi told him that he could do whatever he wanted in his parish, even going so far as to say that he didn't have to go to church if he didn't feel up to it, or felt that he needed a break from it. For a few minutes Ron thought that was some sort of a test that the priest cooked up to take a measure of his mettle. Then he realized that Franzi was quite serious and he gave it though-tful consideration. It didn't take him long to get into the routine of attending daily Mass, participating in most parish activities and serving as a Eucharistic minister at Mass.

In short order Ron became acquainted with the teenagers of the village, who were impressed with the newcomer's background and fun-filled personality. Several of these kids took him mountain hiking in the lower Alps once he had told them about his escapades on the mountains near Oberammergau. They were impressed that an old man over 30 could keep up with them so easily. He suggested that Anny, the Pfarrhof's housekeeper, come along on several of these hikes, an activity that she thoroughly enjoyed. The easy talk between the youngsters and the "old man" covered every topic imaginable including ideas about religious faith and the purpose of life. To bring the conversation down to earth a bit, Ron was educated about the kind of clothing the locals wore and some of the customs of the town, especially singing. The teenagers would regularly gather in the parish center, called the Pfarrheim, adjacent to the Pfarrhof, where they spent a lot of time "rapping"; singing, planning activities and parties. Nearly every day, these kids would have get-togethers in a local pub, as young people (teenagers and older) will do almost everywhere in Europe. After Sunday Mass, they would gather in a village pub for an hour or so to have a beer, in a tradition known by the local name of Frühschoppen which simply means "morning pint". It turned out that all the men of the village enjoyed the Sunday Frühschoppen as well, perhaps as their way of staying youthful. All the women were at their homes preparing Sunday dinner so that when their "youthful" spouses and others of their family returned, they could sit right down to their favorite meal. Other local customs he participated in included going to Friday and Saturday evening village dances where just about everyone, young and old alike, was singing and dancing the night away. He never saw anyone there not having a good time and was impressed by the whole community's light-hearted spirit.

Partly in order to not stand out from the group and partly because he thought they looked good, he began to wear their kind of clothing, especially enjoying the Bundhosen (knee-britches with long stockings) and mountain boots. Those boots were worn in all seasons, a very practical idea. In the summer, he wore Lederhosen, the leather shorts that were held up with shoulder straps. And to follow the lead of the kids, he wore a plain shirt, usually white, but sometimes red or blue plaid and woolen knee stockings. His outfit was not complete until he put on his special Alpine hat with the goat's hair feather. The local girls wore blouses and full skirts, with matching aprons and woolen knee stockings, usually white, and simple shoes that often had a tread pattern on the soles. The girls' hair was often long, usually blond and frequently braided from just behind their neck into a halo that went around their head. They all looked pretty and, in spite of being full of energy and enthusiasm, maintained an air of innocence about them.

Ron with hunter's hat at
welcoming party.

Not very long after his arrival in this village, he was invited to a party at the home of the folks who lived just across the street from St. Martin's rectory. He was the guest of honor since these good people were happy to have him in their town and did their best to help to make him feel even more welcome than he already felt. He was given a many-feathered hat to wear, of the type that young men from the town who were drafted into the military wore at parties held in their honor. He was posed for a quick photo seated in front of the wall that displayed the hunter homeowners' rifles. He thought it best to not divulge his familiarity with weapons, acquired during his counter-intelligence days.

He and his teenage pals wandered around together for the better part of a month, and they really got to know one another very well, finding that they had a lot in common; love of the outdoors, sports, (especially swimming in the summer and skiing in the winter), reading and discussing current events. Every afternoon when the weather was nice, they gathered at the local lake (the Wössnersee) to go swimming. In the evenings they would head for a local café for beer, coffee or soft drinks. The owners of the cafés always enjoyed this carefree group since inevitably someone would have a guitar and the kids would spontaneously break out in song. Most of these were songs that Ron had not heard before, but he quickly picked up the melody and the upbeat words and was soon blending his voice in harmony.

A major treat for him was a visit by a Montreal classmate, Guy-Marie, who having just been ordained was on his way to Africa to serve with the Foreign Mission Society from Quebec. He and Ron had kept in touch, mostly by postcard and when he read that Ron was in Unterwössen he made it a point to track him down and spend nearly a week visiting there. He immediately became part of the regular gang along with Ron and since he was a very accomplished singer, who also was very good on the guitar, he fit right in. There most likely would not be very many chances to play guitar and sing in Africa, but Guy-Marie decided that he would do his best to bring those enjoyable forms of self-expression to whomever he could, wherever he might be.

At the end of July 1967, Ron sent the following letter to his parents.

Dear Mom and Dad

I have my feet back on the ground and have decided to continue with the idea of the priesthood. The priest here, Franzi Niegel, is a wonder and a great friend. The church here and everything surrounding its activities is so different from Montreal and Montpelier as to constitute a lovely breath of fresh air. The Mass, for instance, is entirely in German and the people all sing with gusto. It's a moving experience. And the boys of the town have adopted me as one of their own, so I am like the Pied Piper, going mountain climbing, or swimming or bicycle riding. Franzi and I have made tentative arrangements for me to do some apostolic work. So, when the work permit comes through, I will begin work sometime between 1 – 15 August as an orderly in the large hospital in the city of Traunstein, about 30 miles northwest of here. I'll travel back and forth everyday from Unterwössen. The cardinal in Munich is granting me permission to distribute Holy Communion in the church here on Sundays; that way I can be of great help to Franzi.

Near the first of August, Franzi (Ron was still having a hard time calling him that, as opposed to Pfarrer [Father] Franzi, but that's the way the priest wanted it) talked to Ron about finding a job that would earn him some pin money to make him feel somewhat independent. Franzi made several phone calls to friends of his with possible short-term job openings. He took Ron with him on a couple of interviews. It didn't take long for them to agree that a great opportunity was to have him work as an orderly at the district hospital in Prien, about a half-hour bus ride from Unterwössen. For the next seven months Ron left the rectory before 6 AM for Prien and worked at the well-equipped hospital there. Although he never had any real medical training, he knew that an orderly's job normally did not require much more than having a strong back for lifting and helping patients and doing a lot of grunt work. He knew that this could possibly include helping to physically restrain combative patients, but he was sure that he could handle that should the need arise. He also understood that he may be asked to assist with the application of casts, or to transport patients around the facility as may be required.

He was supervised by the Mahlersdorfer Sisters who ran the hospital and also made up the nursing staff. The Mother Superior, Frau Oberin, who, not surprisingly, turned out to be a strict disciplinarian, was his immediate supervisor. He was very well treated by the Sisters and he enjoyed the company of the staff, who appreciated him for being a good worker. He was young and energetic and could lift beds and patients with ease, and was always in good spirits. It developed that he was perceived to be a medical student, since in Germany one cannot just be an orderly. In the Sisters' experience, an orderly was always one of the jobs performed by a medical student; therefore he was addressed as "Herr Doktor". He liked the ring of that and got used to being called that very quickly.

This Herr Doktor attended a variety of operations, observing the skill of the trained professionals and finding real medical practice to be fascinating. He wondered for a few short moments if he perhaps should have gone to a medical school after Middlebury. He soon rejected the thought and knew that he was eventually going to be just where he belonged; doing God's healing work as a priest.

One day, as he began his morning duties, he saw that a Caesarean section was the operation that was about to begin. He put on his usual scrubs assuming that he would be observing as he had so many other operations. As he headed for the operating room, the nun who was in charge of the O.R. cut him off. She made it abundantly clear that because he was perceived as a candidate for priesthood, he would under no circumstances, be allowed to witness such a procedure. He did his best to convince her that he would have no problem with being in the room for the very interesting operation, but his logic failed to win her over. He never did attend such an operation.

One unforgettable day that Ron had been thinking was just beautiful with the warmth and peacefulness of late summer, suddenly turned into one of his worst experiences when he heard the wail of another ambulance cutting through what had been tranquil surroundings. Although it clearly was not unusual for ambulances to be rushing to the Emergency Room door, he had a sense that this time was different somehow.

A young child was rapidly delivered from the back of the emergency vehicle, his distraught parents jumping out of their car as it pulled in next to the ambulance. The emergency medical technicians who were attending to the young boy were obviously shaken by the extent of his injuries. They had been summoned to the child's home, a farmhouse in the picturesque village of Bernau am Chiemsee, on the south shore of the "Bavarian Sea", a short distance from Prien and the hospital. The seven year-old boy, whose name was Lorenz Baumgartner, was unconscious and horribly pale. He had been innocently playing on the hillside above his family's home and got too close to some moving farm machinery. Somehow, without his even being aware of any danger, his heavy wool sweater got caught up in the spinning gear shaft mechanism on the nearby manure-spreading contraption, and he was whipped violently around by the uncaring machine. He had blacked out, not realizing that both of his arms had been ripped off above the elbows. He was immediately tended to by his father, but the unbelievable violence to which he had been subjected made it look hopeless for him. The hospital was called as quickly as possible, but even that seemed to everyone around the distraught father to take too much time. After what seemed like slow motion, but actually happened quickly, Lenzi, as he was fondly called, was being loaded into the back of an ambulance with trained personnel keeping the stumps of his arms bandaged and under pressure.

Once he was in the Emergency Room, the highly skilled doctors and nurses worked feverishly to save the life of this blond, blue-eyed, pudgy-cheeked young child who had suffered so much blood loss. His nearly hysterical parents, certain that he would not live, prayed fervently as they waited for a miracle. Lenzi did indeed survive his trauma with the extra special care he received from the dedicated doctors and nurses. In a few days he was actually out of his hospital bed and, with amazing youthful energy was running up and down the corridors even if he was bandaged around his upper body almost like a mummy. He had no recall of the accident that had caused him to be in this strange place. When it came time for the bandages to be removed, he suddenly realized that his arms were gone. The doctor who had tended to him and who now removed the bandages was a specialist in such medical conditions and had been brought from his usual hospital in Munich to do his best for the young patient. Lenzi looked tearfully into the doctor's compassionate eyes and asked where his arms were. The gentle doctor asked him if he liked to ski and to play football (soccer). Lenzi quietly responded that he did, but wondered out loud how he could ever do those things with no arms. The doctor stated with confidence that he would continue to be able to ski and play football and do all sorts of things, but it would take practice and determination. He would need to learn how to keep his balance without having arms stretched outward to help. The youth proudly stated that he would learn to do whatever he had to do. Although he had tears in his eyes when he made that solemn pledge, Ron was sure that the little guy would be up to it.

During the four weeks that Lenzi spent in this hospital, he really became quite attached to Ron who, with his gentle and calm demeanor, became like an uncle to him. As they both got to know each other better, one of Ron's tasks was to ensure that the active little armless dynamo didn't hurt himself or any of several pieces of hospital equipment as he ran up and down the corridors like a kitten on the loose. Most of the time however, the pair could be found walking

185

together and exploring the place as much as possible. Since Ron was fluent in German and also remembered some favorite children's stories, Lenzi looked forward to spending time with "Onkel Roni" every day. (In Prien everyone called him "Roni" which, oddly enough, is a nickname for Jerome, but was closest to his own nickname, Ronnie.)

When the staff felt that he was ready, Lenzi was sent to a special school in Munich called the Royal Bavarian School and Home for Crippled Children, for continuing therapy and to eventually be fitted with artificial limbs. With courage and determination, he learned to write by grasping a pencil or pen in his toes; he learned to use an electric typewriter with his toes, and he was able to play cards with his friends by using those nimble digits. All who came in contact with him were in awe of his amazing accomplishments. In the winter he learned to balance properly and was able to ski. And he was a member of a regular football team where not having arms was really not an issue as he controlled the ball so well with his feet, upper torso and head. He always managed to be happy and adjusted to his situation unbelievably well. Ron hoped that he would somehow be able to keep in touch with this courageous youngster as time went on.

During Ron's assignment at the hospital, he got to know just about everybody there, but became very good friends with Dr. Klaus Remberger, one of the talented surgeons on the staff. The doctor invited Ron to his home for dinner a few times where he had a delicious meal prepared by Monica, the doctor's wife. All three of them enjoyed lively discussions all during dinner and with after-dinner cordials. The Rembergers were especially interested in Ron's background in the Army as well as his calling to the priesthood. They were of one mind when it came to believing that Mother Trapp surely was a very special woman and that her plan to have Ron search for and regain his initial spirituality was bound to work.

Another person that Ron became very good friends with was Dr. Andreas Glasser, a young intern assigned to work at the hospital. They spent some time together during off-duty hours and he also came to visit Ron in the Pfarrhof at St. Martin's. Dr. Glasser lived in a neat house in a small village just outside of Prien on the shores of Lake Chiemsee where Ron visited with him a few times. They enjoyed conversations on a wide variety of topics, but Ron found that the intern was fascinated by his exploits in West Berlin as well as his tales of sailing around Denmark.

During the weekends, or other free times, Ron would enjoy a variety of activities. In the early fall, the local head of the Provincial Border Police, Josef Schlagbauer, an accomplished mountain climber, learned of Ron's love for mountain hiking and that he had had some climbing experience. Herr Schlagbauer thought that Ron would enjoy some of the places he and his 16 year-old daughter Gitti (short for Margaret) had experienced. Sepp, which is "Joe" in the Bavarian dialect, drove Ron and Gitti to the Austrian Tyrol village of Elmau well before sunup on what promised to be a beautiful day. They arrived at their destination before dawn. At 5 AM, with the sky just beginning to brighten enough so that they could see where they were stepping, they began slowly climbing the Wilder Kaiser, the Wild Emperor. In a very authoritative voice, Sepp told his followers to never look down from where they were climbing and to follow his instructions exactly. Although Ron had been tempted a few times to grab a quick peek downwards just to see the view, he thought better of it and followed Sepp's admonition to the letter. The day had, as promised, turned out to be a great one for mountain climbing, although it was beginning to get a little warm, even at their elevated altitude. Ron thought that perhaps it was the energy he was expending in this near-vertical climb that was making him perspire and not the weather. Several hours after they had started, they arrived at the summit at The Elmauer Tor (The Elmau Gate). With a happy smile on his broad face, Sepp then told his charges to look back at where they had climbed. Ron was astounded and could hardly believe his eyes. It looked to him as though they had climbed up a sheer precipice. In reality, they had climbed, single file, up a very narrow trail that indeed was extremely steep and would have probably seemed so even to a mountain goat. Once he could stop marveling over the route they had followed, Ron began to appreciate the view. He commented on it all to Gitti who told him that she had made that very climb many times before and had never enjoyed it more. All during their ascent, Ron had entertained the other two by singing, using up his repertoire of German songs then switching to French, and eventually to some fraternity songs in English. Occasionally Sepp and Gitti would join in on the songs they knew. He felt that he could definitely get used to this type of exercise.

Gitti and Ron take a break
at top of Wilder Kaiser.

After enjoying a light lunch, which they had carried up in a backpack, Ron and Gitti climbed down the other side of the mountain. Gratefully, the descent turned out to be very much easier than he imagined. Sepp had backtracked down the way they had come up in order to more easily get to his car so he could pick up the others where he knew they would be. At just about the bottom of the down trail, Ron and Gitti found a bubbling Alpine stream and immediately removed their boots and soaked their tired feet in the ice-cold mountain water. Fabulous.

In October of '67, Franzi took Ron and some of his young friends with him to the nearby village of Oberwössen, a place where Fr. Franz had once served as a priest. It turned out that the young men riding along with them were semi-professional musicians who specialized in typical Bavarian and Alpine music. They taught Ron a lot of music that day. They all climbed up the Watzmann peak in Berchtesgaden, the second highest peak in Bavaria. This dramatic appearing Alp cluster looks from a distance like a jagged tooth. The folklore in the vicinity is that the various peaks in the cluster are a "family", a father, a mother and three children. Variants on that story have the cruel King Watzmann turned to stone and forever looking down on Berchtesgaden with his wife and seven children, the Kleiner Watzmann and Watzmann Kinder peaks, by his side. The old-timers must have had lots of imagination to have come up with such romantic notions since it is actually hard to identify these families, but it is not at all hard to appreciate the beauty of the area with its extensive forests, steep rock faces and sparkling glacial lakes. Ron and the whole group climbed to the summit of the peak they referred to as the "mother", finding it cold and beautiful. Surrounded by Alpine snow and ice, Franzi suggested that it was as good a place as any for Ron to learn how to sing an Alpine yodel. Ron had heard yodeling in cowboy movies when he was a kid growing up in Vermont, but soon found out that there was absolutely no resemblance between what he had previously heard and the beautifully melodic sounds his fellow climbers produced for his educa-tion. First they sang their yodels in short phrases so that he could easily recall them. Then, they put them all together and, facing out towards the mountains, his instructors sang out their yodels. They signaled for silence and cupped their hands to their ears. Ron likewise cupped his ears. What he heard was nearly unbelievable. Someone out there, maybe the old King Watzmann, sang the songs right back at them - - repeatedly. Ron thought that he heard about seven repeats of the original song. This was fabulous. Could he do it? His friends had him face away from the mountains and rehearsed him a few times as he faced the glacial ice until he got it right; everyone was amazed at how quickly he picked it up.

When they were satisfied that he had the yodel just right, they had him turn and face into the mountains and belt it out into the wind, with his head held high. He didn't have to cup his ears to hear his voice echo back to him from at least seven different mountain peaks. It was a fantastic experience that he repeated several times, with his teachers all glowing with pride at how well their student had done. In his later years Ron often used this experience as an example of what happens when a person performs a good deed for somebody. It comes back to the person in so many ways. Eventually, they had to climb back down from this magical place and found a small café at the mountain base where the group enjoyed well-deserved beer or soft drinks.

One afternoon when Ron had no responsibilities at the hospital, Franzi took him and another young man from the village to visit a special person in the Austrian village of Zell am See, not far from Unterwössen. The widow they visited was locally known as Mimi. In fact, she was the Baroness Falkenhausen, whose husband, Baron General Alexander von Falkenhausen, at one time the military commander of Belgium and Northern France, had been deeply involved in the "Plot of 1944" to assassinate Hitler inside his "Wolf's Lair" field headquarters. The plot was the culmination of the efforts of the German Resistance to overthrow the Nazi regime. Its failure led to the arrest by the Gestapo of at least 7,000 persons and the execution of nearly 5,000 of them. The Baron von Falkenhausen was arrested and jailed in Niederdorf. He was freed by American troops in May of 1945 before the Gestapo could carry out their planned execution of him. He died in Germany in 1966.

Mimi, an Austrian Imperial Countess, had met Fr. Niegel several years earlier when he was serving as a priest in the village of Reit im Winkl located on the Austrian border. She had been away from the church for many years, but through conversations (mainly with Fr. Niegel) and confession, she returned to the practice of the Faith. Before the war, she and her husband had lived in Silesia in the German village of Giesmansdorf. They also lived there during the war, but after the Baron was jailed by the Gestapo in 1944, she relocated to her family's property in Austria. Ron found her to be very interesting, entertaining and enthusiastic about life and just about any subject one would wish to discuss. As he was leaving the next day, Mimi asked him to visit her cousin in Vermont the next time he was back that way. Her cousin, born the Princess Hilde de Auersperg, was a member of the Austrian nobility. Ron was amazed to think that a person of such prominence would be living in his home state. She was the second wife of Baron Louis de Rothschild, whose Austrian palace was famous for its exquisite art collection and hundreds of antiques. After Austria was annexed by Nazi Germany in 1938, the Baron was arrested by the National Socialists solely because he was of the Jewish faith. After his family had been terrorized by the Nazis and forced to give up all of their possessions, they fled Austria for America, winding up in Barnard, Vermont. They never returned to their roots. The Baron died in 1955 after suffering a heart attack while swimming in Montego Bay, Jamaica. Baroness Hilde continued to live in Barnard, a little over 40 miles (67 km) due south of Montpelier. Small world.

Ron did make a point of visiting Mimi's cousin Hilde some years later and they became great friends. He found her to be a most interesting conversationalist and was fascinated by her many experiences as she described not only her life as a baroness, but her more recent activities. She had become secretary to Dorothy Thompson, the famous journalist and author who was the second wife of Sinclair Lewis. *Time Magazine* in 1939 declared Ms. Thompson to be one of the two most influential women in America: the other being Eleanor Roosevelt. Ron visited with the Baroness Hilde from time to time before she passed away in the 1980s.

In the wintertime of 1967 and 1968, Ron became acquainted with the Schweinöster family who ran a hotel and Gasthaus (guest house) up on a mountainside. It was known as the Auschuster Stüberl Gasthaus and was a typical Bavarian inn with a bar and restaurant as well as the hotel rooms for rent. They had five boys and one daughter with their ages ranging from 20 down to 5. The oldest, named Tony, was what we would call a lumberjack, but in Bavaria was known as a Holzknecht which defined a person who worked in the forest, chopping down trees and looking after the woods and the animals there. Tony and Ron became fast friends and often, with a group of other friends, with nicknames such as "Grischei" and "Jokei" would go skiing in the mountains. On one of their excursions the group went to the Hotel Gasthaus at Streichen, which was right on the Austrian border and on top of an Alp. They went there to help the owner, one of Tony's friends, remove the huge amount of snow from a recent avalanche that covered over the road leading to the hotel. It was a lot of work, but they made it look easy and had a ball while doing it. The owner's 18 year-old daughter thought it would be fun to throw snowballs at the hard-working shovelers. Ron picked her up and laughingly tossed her into the huge pile of snow that they had just made. Everyone had loads of fun there and then finished the day off by skiing in the nearby mountain village of Achberg, adjacent to Streichen. Ron soon got to know everyone in that little mountain village and spent a lot of his free time together with them. Some of these young people very rarely saw the inside of a church, leading Fr. Niegel to comment that while he looked after the church-goers, Ron was a missionary to the "unchurched".

Over the months that Ron was at St. Martin's Pfarrhof, a number of the houseguests that came by were rather famous people, or would become famous. For example, a seminary classmate of Fr. Niegel, who had also served with him in the German army at the end of World War II, had come to visit. Together they had been POWs in Traunstein, a place not far from Unterwössen, under the American Army with both soldiers being released from their prisoner status at the end of the war, and allowed to go home. This friend was Professor Josef Ratzinger and he had come by not only to see Franzi, but to enjoy some mountain hiking as well, during which time they brought each other up to date on what had transpired in their lives since the end of the war. Professor

Ratzinger, who went on to become Pope Benedict XVI, was from the same Alpine region of Bavaria as Franzi and they had been close friends for years. He enjoyed his brief conversations with the American seminarian and wished Ron good luck in what he felt sure would be a successful career in the priesthood.

Prof. Josef Ratzinger eager to
go mountain hiking.

Another frequent visitor was the very beautiful actress Hildegarde Kneff, whom Fr. Niegel had brought into Catholicism. She was his most famous convert and he was very pleased that he had helped her regain her faith. She was a German actress, just nine years older than Ron, who had a long career in the film business, not only in her home country, but in the United States as well. One of her best-known performances was her starring role as Trilby in *Svengali*, one of several film adaptations of a classic novel about hypnotism written by George de Maurer. She also starred in the 1955 Broadway hit musical *Silk Stockings*.

Annette Thoma, the widow of the Bavarian poet Ludwig Thoma visited often, since she was not only a friend of Franzi's but was very interested in Bavarian music and culture. She knew that Franzi would gather musicians from all over Bavaria, who would come to Unterwössen to present concerts, especially at the beginning of the Advent season. Ron thought the musicians were truly spectacular as they performed on local favorite instruments such as the zither, the hackbrett and the Jew's Harp, locally called a Maultrommel, as well as the long Alphorn. Some of the musicians played more conventional instruments such as the guitar and the accordion as well as a full complement of brass instruments. Ron had seen and heard the zither's beautiful sounds as well as those from the Jew's Harp before his trip to Bavaria, but the hackbrett and the long Alphorn were new to him. The hackbrett, he discovered, is very much like a Swiss hammered dulcimer since both have a large flat trapezoidal sounding board with metal strings that are struck with hand-held mallets by the musician. It can easily be a solo instrument, but integrates beautifully into an ensemble. The melodies, usually fast and upbeat, that can be produced on the hackbrett, depending on the skill of the instrumentalist, are very pleasing and often have appreciative audiences clapping in time with the music.

The long Alphorn was definitely something that belonged in the Alps and was truly unique. Very early Alphorns were used to signal warnings and to announce daily activities. It is a very long (ranging from over 10 feet [3 meters] to over 13 feet [4 meters] in length) hollow conical tube with an upturned end that is bell-shaped. The often beautifully painted or carved bell rests on the floor with small feet under it to stabilize it, while the musician holds the instrument so that the mouthpiece is conveniently accessible. The sound it produces is mellow and reverberant and can often be heard for long distances. It typically has a four-octave range, but is limited in the notes that it can produce since it has no valves, keys or slides and can only produce tones in its overtone series. It was probably the most unusual orchestral instrument Ron, or many others for that matter, had ever seen or heard. And yet, its unique voice blended perfectly when the skillful musicians performed.

Another frequent visitor was a spiritual director from the Freising seminary, Praelat (Prelate or Monsignor) Dr. Michael Hoeck, who had been interred in the Dachau Concentration Camp for a long period during the war. He became a close friend of Ron's and the two of them often shared stories of their call to the Faith. It was rejuvenating for Ron.

The stream of visitors seemed endless. One day, Franzi brought a 16 year-old British boy to meet with Ron. The youth, named Tad, had been hitchhiking along the Autobahn to Salzburg. Ron had never heard of anyone trying to get a speeding car on that notoriously fast highway to stop to pick them up, but Tad had been reasonably successful at it and hadn't gotten killed yet. He explained that his parents had been refugees from Poland and had settled in the UK. He was a typical high school student and confessed that he was not sure of how to sort out the various religious beliefs to which he had been exposed. He had not spoken English for several weeks during his hitchhiking journey through the Alps, and Ron hadn't spoken English in several months, so the two of them had a "language feast", occasionally struggling to find the right English word. Tad spent about a week at the rectory and seemed to enjoy every minute of it. (Ron and Tad kept in touch over the years and sometime during the 1970s Father Ron conducted the boy's wedding to his sweetheart in the Anglican Cathedral of Ripon, England, which had been a pre-Reformation Catholic cathedral. The Dean of the Cathedral told Father Ron that he was surely the first Roman priest to conduct a sacrament in that church since the Reformation.)

The most surprising visitors however, were none other than Mother Trapp with her stepdaughter, Mitzi, who both showed up in December 1967 to see how things were going. They spent about a week there enjoying the Bavarian community and rehashing some fond memories with Fr. Niegel, whom they also called "Franzi". Mother Trapp, then at the ripe old age of 62, continued to amaze Ron with her vitality and no-nonsense approach to just about everything interesting; with very few things that weren't of interest to her. She had known Annette Thoma from years before and enjoyed visiting with her and having Annette join with Franzi and his groups for the Bavarian music concerts he so often organized. Ron and Franzi traveled around the area with the Trapps as they made it a point to visit Maria's beloved Salzburg and then on to enjoy the many sights and activities in nearby Berchtesgaden. They spent enjoyable times visiting with Mother's old friends in various mountain farmhouses in the area, where she was consistently greeted with great hugs and tears of joy. She continued to brighten the area immediately surrounding her with her outgoing (some might say strong) personality. She was constantly on the go, not resting for a minute and often very amusing, as had always been her style. The folks around the Pfarrhof missed her the minute she had left to return to the US.

With Franzi and all those around him, Ron was having such a good time that he could hardly contain himself. The best part was, just as Mother Trapp had predicted, his spiritual life had come alive again. As he contemplated the meaning in all of this, he thought for a while that maybe this was a sign that he should stay in Bavaria and become a priest there. To test this out, he arranged for an interview with the Archbishop of Munich, Cardinal Julius Doepfner, who was kind enough to take time from his busy schedule to talk with him. The Cardinal told Ron that he could finish out his studies at the seminary in Freising if he really wanted to, but he should beware. He would always be known behind his back as "Der Ami", "The Yank". That was a slur at that time. Even more important to the Cardinal was that if Ron really wanted to remain in Bavaria, he should get some experience with another parish situation before going forward with that plan. His logic was that Fr. Franz Niegel was an outstanding priest and human being and really was the exception rather than the rule.

After Ron's discussion with the Cardinal, he talked it all over with Franzi, who seemed slightly embarrassed by the high praise from Cardinal Doepfner. At any rate, for quite a while they talked over the pros and cons of having Ron get some first-hand experience in a local parish in order to be comfortable about staying in this part of the world. Eventually, it seemed very clear to them both, that Ron's real place now was back in the US. With feelings of deep gratitude for the opportunities that Franzi had provided for him to regain his calling, Ron made plans to return home sometime in late February 1968. He had to finish up at the hospital before leaving, being sure to turn in any material that he may have taken out and saying his goodbyes to the very supportive staff. He was glad that he had the experience there in that caring hospital and wanted to be sure that he would always have a way of staying in touch with Lenzi Baumgartner. Ron's last work with Franzi was to help him for a few days with religious education classes in the local elementary school.

It had been eight months that Ron was so closely allied with the good priest, Fr. Franz Niegel. He had learned so much from this impressive man that he was sure that he could not adequately express his gratefulness, but knew in his heart that Franzi understood. His benefactor, the good friend of Mother Trapp, saw him off at the train station in Prien. They both knew that he would become a fine priest and had had just the right set of experiences in Bavaria. Ron promised that he would return to visit and that he would, for certain, make his return as an ordained Roman Catholic priest.

During the congested train ride to Frankfurt and then another to Luxemburg, his mind, still working in the Bavarian dialect, was full of the nearly unbelievable events of the past eight months. He knew that it would be very unlikely that he would ever meet up with another priest like Fr. Niegel. What a treasure! And how perceptive of Mother Trapp to have facilitated that adventure. Eventually, he arrived at the Icelandic Airlines terminal in Luxemburg and was headed for Vermont.

After spending a few days at his parents' home reliving as many of his experiences as possible and answering their thought-provoking questions (along the lines of "Are you really sure?") he headed once again for Stowe and the Trapp Family Lodge to rehash it all with Mother Trapp who beamed her approval at how things went for him, even if he still may have had some lingering doubts. She could tell that he had regained his strong faith and was ready to resume the path that had been interrupted.

He had the incredible opportunity to teach high school in Northfield, Vermont. A dear friend of his mother was the Director of the Vermont Department of Education. When she heard Ron's mom proudly describing her son's background and current situation, she knew that he would be a perfect fit for an opening that existed in Northfield. This was an extraordinary experience that brought a lot into focus for him and allowed him to clear his head. He continued to attend daily Mass in Montpelier early in the mornings, taking great comfort in receiving the Eucharist, as always, and finding a few homilies that seemed to be sent straight to him. Amazing.

After morning Mass, he would drive the short distance to Northfield High and his students, where he taught English and Latin. The students in his classes had higher test scores and showed a better overall understanding of his subjects than did most previous students there. He was honored a year later by being the graduation speaker for the NHS class of 1970.

At the end of the school year in May of 1969, he made the decision to return to the authority of Bishop Joyce in Burlington. The Bishop was very pleased to have Ron back with him and had a sense that his eight months in Bavaria had been very good for his spiritual health and overall well-being. Bishop Joyce arranged for him to return again to Camp Holy Cross for Boys for six weeks in the summer. Once there he quickly found that the new crop of needy boys was thrilled to have his attention as well as his calm water-safety instruction. Most of them were swimming within a few days. He still enjoyed his assignment there and tried to calculate just how many young guys he had taught to swim over the years he had been there. It had to be over a hundred - - perhaps many more. A good feeling.

Most of the month of August was spent at the Trapp Family Lodge where he continued to enjoy the company of the family members who were in attendance while he relaxed as he looked forward to finishing his seminary training. However, he was not to finish this in Montreal as he had assumed. The upper echelons of the church hierarchy had been carefully following his moves. They really wanted to be sure not to lose such a promising candidate for priesthood, and yet wanted to ensure that the final phase of his preparation was done in an environment that they believed to be best for him. At the end of summer, he was informed by Monsignor Gelineau, the Chancellor of the Burlington Diocese, that it had been decided that he needed a year of "rehab" so to speak, by returning to a strong seminary environment, since he had been away from such surroundings for nearly two years. The Monsignor told him that Bishop Joyce thought it best if he were to go to Our Lady of Angels Seminary. This was located in Bethlehem, New York, just south of Albany. His first reaction was that he felt somewhat disappointed, since he was looking forward to the familiar campus and seeing some of his former classmate friends in the Grand Seminary in Montreal. He very soon came to the thought that rolling with this unexpected twist in his path just might be a very good move. He was happy with the choice.

In late September he entered the Seminary of Our Lady of Angels in New York. He very quickly adjusted to his new surroundings and was back into the academics in no time at all. He was pleased to find his new home to be very accepting and open, with very few restrictions. He mentioned this happy news in a letter that he wrote to his parents, adding that it was even more open than the Grand Seminary in Montreal. Of course, as had been his usual operating procedure throughout his entire adult life, he quickly made several great friends. Many of his new friends were solidly committed to their calling and were soon to become priests.

During the first semester, Ron helped out at the social service center in downtown Albany's St. John's Church. The pastor of that church, Fr. Peter Quinn, often visited the seminary. He had asked the rector for some help. He specifically asked if he could borrow some 4th year seminarians for some part-time work. His church was in the middle of downtown Albany where there were very few Catholics. Although he did have Sunday Masses, usually not heavily attended, the principal use of St. John's Church was as a center for distributing food and clothing to the poor and needy. Ron and a seminarian who had hailed from Washington, DC, were selected to assist Fr. Quinn. They spent a couple of mornings each week for about four months doing this extra-curricular work. Also, Ron often served as a sort of secretary to the pastor, answering his huge pile of daily mail. Frequently, Ron would take dictation in his own unique shorthand, which no one else could decipher, as Fr. Quinn dictated letters. He would then type them on church stationery using the church's clunky old Royal typewriter for his "boss's" signature. The time spent helping out there was very educational and Ron found it to be interesting and rewarding. He felt that he was doing some good in a community that sorely needed it.

A few weeks after he had arrived at his new seminary, Our Lady of Angels, he was out for a run by himself in the wooded area that was in a distant portion of the property. It was a crisp, gorgeous fall day with the trees getting ready to put on their yearly show of brilliant color. Some of the trees were already changing color as if in a race with the stragglers. As he ran easily along, he contemplated the nearly unbelievable chain of events that had occurred in his life and reaffirmed that he was ready and eager to become a priest. He suddenly heard what sounded like a strong wind, but noticed that the leaves on the trees and on the ground near him were not moving. Then he felt someone behind him lift him about 20 feet into the air and hug him from in back and then set him down gently. The sensation, like nothing he had ever experienced, was over before he knew it. Of course this did not actually happen physically, but rather was a spiritual event. It was the most moving and mysterious feeling in his life. He sat down, with his back against an oak tree to regain his senses. Shortly, he was convinced that he had been hugged by the Holy Spirit and lifted gently from his earthly domain. He spoke of this to no one, but relived it in his dreams for many nights. Beginning shortly after that strange experience, he felt the closeness of the Holy Spirit again. At Masses, he would often assist in distributing Holy Communion, by opening the chapel tabernacle to take out the consecrated hosts in their ciborium. Every time he did this, he felt the spiritual presence of the Holy Spirit reaching out from within the tabernacle to embrace him. It was an over-powering feeling that often stopped him in his tracks for a few seconds. This mysterious force continued regularly for a period of nearly three months. Then it disappeared, just as suddenly, as if to indicate "O.K. Now that I have your attention, let's really work together." Ron felt certain that these manifestations were gifts from the Lord for fidelity to his calling in spite of all the obstacles he had faced. He continued to recall the special feeling, wishing that it would return, but knowing that the memory of it was really what was important.

The unexplainable sparks of light that had first danced around him nearly eight years previously, continued to show themselves on a fairly regular basis, adding to his feelings of closeness to the Holy Spirit. He would never have predicted that anything like all these phenomena would become part of his life.

In mid-January 1970 Ron was ordained a sub-deacon in the private chapel of Bishop Joyce in Burlington. One week later, in the same chapel, ordination as a deacon took place. Now with that rank, he was assigned to work at St. Mary's Parish in Glens Falls, New York. This was a good experience for him as he visited the sick, took Holy Communion to the elderly and other shut-ins and preached at Masses. He loved delivering his homilies and watching the reaction of the congregation, especially when they stopped reading or gazing around and actually paid attention to what he had to say.

After another three months of study, he had completed all the requirements to be ordained a Catholic priest. What an amazing journey. Although he could not possibly know what the future would bring him, he was solidly committed to his calling and eagerly looked forward to serving on the front lines in his priesthood as he would bring the word of God to many.

CHAPTER 16

MAY 5, 1970
ORDINATION

St. Augustine Church, Montpelier, VT

Ronald Curtis Lawson's ordination into the Catholic priesthood took place on May 5, 1970. Except for the late afternoon rain, it was a glorious day. It took place in St. Augustine's Church in his hometown of Montpelier, VT; the first ordination ever held there. The size of the crowd in attendance was mind-boggling. Including then Governor Deane Chandler Davis, there were over 900 guests. A special pleasure for Fr. Ron was to see Maria von Trapp there along with family members Mitzi, Rosemarie (Illi), Hedwig and Johannes, all decked out in Austrian Tyrolean costume. His brother, Sidney, noted that Mother Trapp, at a youthful 65 years, made a grand stage-type entrance, and did so at the last minute. Her group paraded all the way up to the first pew and was clearly noticed and appreciated by all.

Even the church was especially nicely dressed up for his special day. It had been newly renovated in what Fr. Charlie D'Avignon, the parochial vicar at St. Augustine's, labeled "neo-Puritan" style, with royal blue wall-to-wall carpeting and freshly painted solid white walls. The raiments of the dozen vested priests and the mitered Bishop Robert Joyce, followed by two magenta-robed monsignors; the pastor, Monsignor Harold Field, and Monsignor Louis Gelineau, who was the Vicar General of the Diocese, added a striking contrast. Bishop Joyce, who had been such a solid supporter of the young seminarian through his various trials and confused times, was glowing with pride and happiness that the Church would finally be receiving this sincere and devoted young man into the priesthood.

Happily, practically all of Fr. Ron's Protestant family was in attendance. They had long ago gotten over his transition from Methodist to Catholic and were very proud of the dedicated young man who obviously had a natural affinity for his faith. Also proudly in attendance were students from Northfield High School where Fr. Ron had taught English and Latin during the 1968-69 school year. The chorus from that school was there to sing *Climb Every Mountain* from *The Sound of Music*. Fortunately he had advised Mother Trapp in advance about the song they would be singing, giving her ample time to let that sink in to prevent her from feeling embarrassed about being spot-lighted once again. Of course she and her family were pleased at the selection.

The ceremony included Mass and the Rite of Ordination and took place at 7:30 PM. The Rite of Ordination to the Priesthood within a Mass dates back many centuries. Although beautiful and very moving for all in attendance, the event went by for Father Ron in a sort of a blur. He went through the entire ceremony in what he would describe later as a daze, and he couldn't help but think that perhaps many brides and grooms went through a similar state at their weddings.

He remembers many solemn portions, including the Chanting of the Litany of the Saints, while prostrate in front of the altar and the Laying on of Hands, and being vested with his priestly stole and chasuble (the outermost vestment). A moving part of the ceremony was the anointing of his hands, from the ancient Jewish custom of anointing priests, prophets and kings. He was also presented with the Book of Gospels, commending him to preach the Word, and eliciting his promise, as the bishop held Fr. Ron's hands in his own, to be obedient to him and his successors. He has good recall of his first priestly blessing when, as part of the Rite, Bishop Joyce received this new priest's blessing. What a marvelous experience, even if the whole ceremony pretty much flew by for him.

Chanting of the Litany of the Saints

After the ordination was complete, the new Father Ron Lawson, guests and dignitaries were escorted to the church hall for a wonderful reception put on by the women of Trinity United Methodist Church. This welcoming of the newly ordained priest was truly an ecumenical occasion, with several Protestant ministers in attendance. Two of them had been pastors of his family's Methodist Church. Also present was the local Congregational minister, Wally Short, who had been in the class ahead of him at Middlebury College.

Fr. Ron actually missed most of the reception himself, since he spent the better part of two hours in the church proper, bestowing first blessings. It was just as well that he did this since it allowed him to personally and warmly greet nearly everyone who had come; something that pleased him very much. He was surprised and very moved to find among the guests, none other than the red-headed youth, Kevin, who had been a CCD pupil of his at Columbia Point, Dorchester. Kevin, who now was a student at Boston College, had been driven to the ordination of his former teacher by Fr. Steve who had been a seminarian with Ron and had also taught CCD with him at Columbia Point in 1962 and 1963. That priest also was the one who got Ron into attending the Water Safety program in May of 1962. The main reason for Fr. Steve to be here now was to have the distinct privilege of being a concelebrant at this special ordination Mass.

Mother Trapp beaming as Fr. Ron admires her gift statue

The newly ordained priest received many gifts, for which he was very thankful and expressed his appreciation enthusiastically. But perhaps the most precious gift he received was a colorful baroque statue of the Blessed Virgin Mary given to him by the Trapp family. It was a little over two feet tall and was a beautifully painted wooden carving made in the Austrian Tyrol. Mother Trapp presented it to him on the condition that he keep it always in his bedroom. He has been faithful to that requirement ever since.

Fr. Ron had decided a few weeks prior to the date of his ordination, that he would dedicate his ordination Mass to both John F. Kennedy and Robert F. Kennedy, whose assassinations were still a troubling ache in our country's memory. He knew that their mother, Rose, who was at that time residing in Florida, would surely not be able to actually attend his special day, but he sent her an invitation anyway and included mention of the special dedications he hoped would please her. A few days before the main event he received a hand-written letter on stationery embossed with the Rose Fitzgerald Kennedy monogram. It read,

Dear Father Lawson,

I hope that Almighty God may shower upon you His choicest blessings on May fifth, and that you may continue in His service during many fruitful years.

Please remember all the members of the Kennedy family in your prayers.

Your respectful child,
(signed) Rose Kennedy

Palm Beach –
April 8, 1970

Fr. Ron was very touched by the letter and had it nicely framed. He has kept it with him always.

After the last guests had departed around midnight, Fr. Ron went to his home, where the party continued, with nearly 50 people there including priest friends from Boston, Albany and Montreal, military friends from Philadelphia and Washington, DC and a number of local people as well. This party went on until 5 AM. He couldn't help but think, "Did all Catholic ordinations wind up this way?" His surely was memorable in many ways.

Newly ordained Father Ron.

CHAPTER 17

OFF TO EUROPE

According to plan, the next morning (actually later that same morning) at 8 AM, Father Ron and his younger brother, Sidney, Jr., who was 30 years of age, began the long trek that would take them on an exciting excursion to Europe. Sidney was a 2nd year student on the GI Bill at the Boston Conservatory and was residing in the Fenway in Boston, while he was studying for a Bachelor of Fine Arts in Drama. He took the time off even though he was preparing for the year's final exams. A visit that was planned for the end of this trip was to the National Gallery in London and it would be about the best possible homework for an upcoming exam in his elective in Fine Arts. He would be able to study some wonderful artwork up close and personal in a way that couldn't be matched by textbook study.

The main driving force behind the trip to Europe for Fr. Ron was the unshakeable thought (dream might be a better term) of saying a series of "first" Masses back where so much of his spiritual strength was rooted. They awoke to a snowstorm in spite of the fact that it was May in Vermont, and rushed to get ready to drive first to Burlington, about 40 miles (64 km) to the northwest on the shores of Lake Champlain, and then to Montreal in Quebec. They had airline tickets to Europe from Montreal's Dorval International Airport, renamed in 2004 the Pierre Elliott Trudeau International Airport.

Also, as planned, when they arrived in Burlington, they stopped at St. Joseph Child Center. It was operated by the Montreal-based Sisters of Providence for about 200 boys and girls who were either orphaned or came from home situations that caused them to be placed in protective custody with the sisters. Fr. Ron had worked at the Child Center teaching swimming during the summer after the completion of his first year in St. John's Seminary in Brighton, MA. All of the children he interfaced with really touched his heart back then and he looked forward to saying one of his first Masses there for them. The mass was really for the sisters, since most of the children Fr. Ron once knew were no longer in the Child Center, having become too old or having returned to their homes. After the Mass with the children and sisters, the brothers had lunch and continued on their journey.

After arriving in Montreal, they stopped at the beautiful and very familiar St. Patrick's Basilica, the mother church to Montreal's English-speaking faithful. With its Neo-Gothic architecture, it was an imposing sight on Dorchester Boulevard, now known as Boulevard-Rene-Levesque. In St. Patrick's Rectory, they had dinner with Bishop Norman Gallagher who was an Auxiliary Bishop of Montreal, as well as Archbishop Wilhelm of Windsor, Ontario who was visiting. Fr. Ron had developed a close friendship with Bishop Gallagher while a seminarian in Montreal's Grand Seminary, when he worked as the bishop's secretary. After a satisfying dinner that included robust conversation including how the world (and the Church after Vatican II) had changed since Fr. Ron's time as a seminarian some three years previously, the two church leaders drove the brothers the short distance to the airport at Dorval, Quebec. Fr. Ron was permitted to leave his car in St. Patrick's parking lot to save on a parking fee at the airport. As Fr. Ron and Sidney were being dropped off at the gate, Archbishop Wilhelm pointed out, with a sly grin, that as a newly ordained priest, this door-to-door treatment was not to be expected all the time.

After checking their baggage and carrying newly purchased snacks, the brothers were seated in their crowded Lufthansa jumbo jet for their flight to Frankfurt, Germany. Fr. Ron had previously been to Europe several times so he was rather blasé about it, but it was Sidney's first journey abroad and he couldn't hide his excitement and even a little anxiety: especially since he really should be studying for his final exams. Even though the events of the previous couple of days had left them a bit overtired, they were still youthfully energized and they didn't get much sleep on the flight. Early in the morning, just as they were starting to doze off, they were awakened by the commotion of preparations for their descent to their destination.

After a brief stopover in Frankfurt/Main, Germany, they were airborne again and were shortly at their destination of Munich. As they deplaned, Fr. Ron explained to his kid brother that Munich, the capital city of Bavaria was the 3rd largest German city. One fascinating fact that did not seem to be quite real until Sidney got sight of the city's coat of arms, was the origin of its name. It had been derived from an old German word that translated to *monks*. They both knew that in a couple of years this city would host the 1972 Summer Olympics. Neither could have imagined the tragedy that would eventually befall the Israeli athletes at the hands of Palestinian terrorists.

They were met at the airport by friends from Ron's time as an orderly in Prien, Dr. Klaus Remberger and his wife Monika. Fr. Ron and Sid, in their rented VW, followed the Rembergers to their home on the Dachauer Strasse a short distance away, where the good friends caught up on the latest happenings in their lives. The brothers were so exhausted from all the recent activity, that it was a pleasure for them to catch a couple of hours of sleep in the Remberger's guest beds. Then a marvelous dinner prepared by Monika was enjoyed by all, with more catching-up conversation.

Shortly after dinner, Fr. Ron left Sidney with the Rembergers and drove off in his Beetle for the 25-minute drive to the site of the former Concentration Camp at Dachau where he had previously arranged to celebrate Mass at the Carmelite Cloister. As he drove the narrow streets he couldn't help but feel a little bit bad for his kid brother, being left alone with a couple who spoke very little English. Sid's German vocabulary was limited to such phrases as "Kaffee! Danke." and not much more. For some brotherly reason, the thought of his struggles really only did so much as to bring a quiet smile to his face as he drove on.

People are not normally admitted into the Cloister that is set up within the confines of the former Concentration Camp. The Carmel, or Carmel of the Precious Blood as it is known (Karmel Heiliges Blut), was built as an addition to one of the guard towers and presents an eerie sight with its rooflines resembling those of the former barracks. Entrance is gained through the large door in one of the old guard towers. A church is included within the convent complex.

Fr. Ron was introduced to the 12 young nuns by their superior, Mother Prioress, Maria Gemma. Ron had visited Dachau several times dating from his Army assignments in Oberammergau and Berlin, and corresponded with the Prioress regularly. She had invited Ron to celebrate one of his first Masses at Dachau. Mother Maria Gemma later was reassigned to Berlin, where she founded the Berlin Carmel known as Carmel Queen of Martyrs (Karmel Regina Martyrum). After celebrating Mass in German, Fr. Ron talked to the nuns (auf Deutsch) about the beauty of their particular self-dedication and how it really touched him. As he was preparing to leave the complex, the nuns presented him with a beautiful candle they had made. On it was the inscription *Wandelt in Licht* that translates to *He walks in the Light*. Another unexpected reference to being a "light-bearer". It was among the first of many such allusions.

After returning to the Remberger home, Fr. Ron treated Sidney to a visit to the Hofbräuhaus, the most famous pub in the world that, in addition to serving the best beer in the world, captures one's spirit with traditional Bavarian folk music. A local word that describes the feeling one gets while there is *Gemütlichkeit*. This word can best be translated as bringing to mind the pleasures of belonging, social acceptance, cheerfulness, the total lack of anything hectic and the opportunity to spend quality time with friends, new and old. Sidney and Fr. Ron enjoyed it fully. While there was still a bit of time left in this busy evening and with the brothers still somewhat energized from their enjoyment of the Hofbräuhaus, Fr. Ron drove on to the bohemian district of Schwabing. This unique area had been a gathering spot in Munich for actors, writers and artists for nearly 50 years. Its ambiance could remind one of New York's Greenwich Village with its eclectic shopping, cafés and stalls along the Leopoldstrasse, the main drag through Schwabing. This was about all the excitement they could handle for this day, so they headed back to their friends' home for the night.

Up early the next morning, Fr. Ron described his plans for the next few days to his hosts, but especially to his brother who was enthralled with everything so far and looked forward to new adventures and sights. After saying their heartfelt goodbyes to their friends and hosts, the brothers were off in their little VW to head for the Royal Bavarian School and Home for Crippled Children in Munich to visit Lenzi Baumgartner, the young armless child Fr. Ron first met when he was an orderly in the Emergency Room at the hospital in Prien in 1967. In the intervening three years between Lenzi's accident and now, Fr. Ron had visited his family and him at their farm in Bernau am Chiemsee whenever he had an opportunity to do so. He was always very pleased at the youngster's strong spirit and lively enthusiasm. When Fr. Ron and Sidney showed up at the special school where Lenzi now was enrolled, the ten year-old was overjoyed to see his great friend again as they reminisced about their initial meeting at the hospital. It was good to see that he had continued to maintain his upbeat attitude and appeared to be doing very well. Fr. Ron told him about an upcoming "first Mass" that he would say in a few days in nearby Unterwössen and invited the boy and his family to be there. They all looked forward to that Mass and promised to attend.

After saying *auf Wiedersehen* to their little friend, they were off to the south through the foothills of the Alps to get to Oberammergau, the village with so much special meaning for Fr. Ron. Arriving after an hour and a half drive, they did some shopping, took a bunch of pictures and then as a special highlight, checked in at the guest quarters in the beautiful Kloster Ettal, the baroque monastery. This was a pre-planned accommodation since Fr. Ron planned to say his "first" Mass in that stunningly beautiful church. The monastery ran a large Internat, a high school for boys and girls, and maintained a sprawling farm where they harvested home-grown vegetables. The monastery also ran a printing press, a brewery, a distillery and a bookstore. It was there, at the monastery's high altar that he had been baptized 10 years previously. He felt that he had returned to his religious spawning ground.

After freshening up a bit, they drove off to the nearby village of Uffing am Staffelsee, for an afternoon and evening of reminiscing with Fr. Ron's former Polish teacher in the Army's language school at Oberammergau. Marian Lewicki, along with his partner, Barbara Schober, were thrilled to see him again after only getting glimpses of some of his adventures over the past ten years in the occasional post cards that Ron would mail to them. They were grinning from ear-to-ear as Fr. Ron gave them an animated account of his sailing adventures around Denmark, and then briefly did his best to recount the highlights of his time in West Berlin and his convoluted path through the seminaries. He blessed his friends' grotto that contained a statue of the Blessed Virgin Mary. It was amazing to note that still clasped in the hands of this statue, was the Jerusalem Cross that Fr. Ron had left there ten years ago at the time of his conversion to the Catholic faith in 1960.

The lively dinner conversation was a fascinating blend of German, Polish and English. Sidney, who was thoroughly charmed by Marian and Barbara, was able to enjoy a reasonable amount of the discussion, but resolved to work harder on his knowledge of German. Since Fr. Ron had a full schedule planned for the next day, they just had to break away from their pleasant evening and he drove back to their accommodations at Ettal Monastery.

They were out of bed by 5:00 AM the next day and in that amazing abbey church, which was still very cold inside since it was not heated, Fr. Ron celebrated a solemn Mass in Latin and German at 6:00 AM. The regular early morning worshipers (approximately 40 parishioners) were in their usual pews. A dozen local priests concelebrated the Mass with Fr. Ron, while several monks performed the duties of altar servers. The Mass was in memory of Major Tom Blakey, who had been HQ Commander at the military installation in Oberammergau when Ron was stationed there. Tom and his family had become close to Ron, since Tom's Catholic wife, Ginny, had been one of Ron's sponsors at his baptism. Tom had not been a Catholic, but converted in 1962. He had died of cancer in his early 40's in January 1970. Ron, at that time a newly ordained transitional deacon, conducted the funeral and burial of Tom in Arlington Cemetery, Washington DC. The Army chaplain at Arlington was the celebrant of the funeral Mass, while Deacon Ron proclaimed the gospel, gave a short, heartfelt homily and conducted the burial. This sadly impressive ceremony was carried out with full military honors including a horse-drawn caisson, a burial flag and three rifle volleys by seven riflemen. Taps was played by a military bugler. Formal folding and presenting of the flag concluded the service. The gravesite was just across the road from the Amphitheater within the cemetery.

The chalice that Fr. Ron used during this memorial Mass in Ettal's Abbey Church was a commemorative one, given in Tom Blakey's memory by the Knights of Columbus in Scottsdale, AZ where the Blakey family had settled after leaving Oberammergau sometime in the late 1960's. The chalice had been given to Ettal Monastery at the suggestion of Tom's widow, because of their close connection to Fr. Pius Fischer, the same priest who had baptized Ron in 1960. It turned out that Fr. Ron was the first to use that chalice. Coincidence?

After this special and very moving Mass, the brothers Lawson along with Marian and Barbara were treated to a delicious breakfast with the monastery's Abbot in a dining room on the Abbey's second floor. The room was full of magnificent baroque antiques, including the table and chairs they were using. Fr. Ron and Sidney couldn't help but try to imagine what dignitaries sat in those very chairs as they enjoyed meals long ago. It was a unique and pleasurable occasion for everyone.

As a parting gift, the Abbot gave the newly ordained priest, who had really impressed him very much with his presentation and demeanor, a hand-stitched pall depicting The Last Supper; beautiful and unique. The pall, which is a square stiff cover, lays on top of the chalice during Mass. This gift would be kept with Fr. Ron always.

Before much longer, the adventurous duo was on the road again, for the short ride to Füssen, where they visited the Wies Church (meaning church in the meadow). It is known as the Pilgrimage Church of the Blessed Virgin Mary and is one of the oldest, if not the oldest of such churches in Bavaria. Then they continued on to the striking Neuschwanstein Schloss (Castle). It had been built by the "Mad" King Ludwig II over 100 years previously and has been a major tourist draw for years. It was such a fanciful sight that it became the model for The Sleeping Beauty castle in Disneyland.

Then, to rekindle a very significant and meaningful friendship, they drove south to Schliersee, a small town about 34 miles (55 km) from Munich, for a visit with Fr. Pius Fischer, OSB, the marvelous priest who had baptized Ron in 1960. He had been the strongest influence on Ron's growing interest in Catholicism back then. He was now temporarily at the Schliersee church, helping out the parish in the absence of the regular pastor. As soon as he saw Father Ron, he was overjoyed with the sight of his protégé. They had supper in the rectory at the Schliersee church, during which they enjoyed animated conversation that no one wanted to end, but finally they gave up and then were off to bed in the spacious rectory for some much needed sleep. Fortunately, there were plenty of rooms available, dating back to when several priests would have been living there. Fr. Ron and Sidney got a good night's sleep and awoke rejuvenated and ready to press on with their adventure.

After the restful overnight in Schliersee, and a "see you later, not goodbye" type of farewell to Fr. Pius, the brothers were back in their VW. They drove to Innsbruck and then over the Brenner Pass through the Alps into the Italian village of Cortina d'Ampezzo about 27 miles (44 km) south of the Austrian border. It is one of the most charming ski resorts in Italy and locally is known as *Regina delle Dolomiti* or Queen of the Dolomites. Unfortunately the heavy rain at the time spoiled their ability to fully appreciate the beauty all around them. They stayed overnight in a local hotel and then drove north the next morning to Salzburg, the fourth largest city in Austria. It is world-famous for its baroque architecture, and, among other things, being the birthplace of Wolfgang Amadeus Mozart. But for the Lawsons, Salzburg was especially fascinating since so much of Mother Trapp's history was rooted there. Of course, it was also well known as the setting in 1965 for the musical film, *The Sound of Music*. That hugely popular film starred Julie Andrews as Maria von Trapp, and although very entertaining, was also very highly stylized with several significant differences between the real story and the movie. Fr. Ron was very aware of the differences, since he had been so close to "Mother Trapp" and several of her children, but he had enjoyed the sound track immensely.

On the way to Salzburg, they took a side trip to visit the village church in Kitzbühel, Austria, where during the Midnight Mass in 1960, Ron felt the strong calling to become a Catholic priest. He recalled clearly that at that time he had been gazing at a portrait of St. Pius X. Now in this side trip, they visited the little church once again. Once inside, Fr. Ron asked where he could locate the beautiful, large portrait of St. Pius X. He was eager to see it once again. He was informed by a very reliable source that there never had been such a portrait; in fact no portrait of any kind had ever been hung there. That thought stayed with him for many days as he attempted to attach a special meaning to his detailed memory of the portrait that didn't exist.

They spent two days in the exciting city of Salzburg and

toured everywhere the typical tourist would. Then they made another side trip, this time to Berchtesgaden, a picturesque mountain municipality about 17 miles (30 km) south. Since the end of the war this location had been one of the American recreation centers for the military stationed in Europe. There they visited Obersalzberg, a mountainside retreat famous for having been the location of Adolf Hitler's private home, the *Berghof*, as well as the home of Hermann Göring and other highly placed personages in the former Nazi government. This whole area was heavily damaged by Allied bombing attacks in World War II and there are no longer any signs of those homes, having been completely obliterated by the Bavarian government. Currently, the sole facility remaining on the Obersalzberg from the Nazi era is the so-called Eagle's Nest, built as a birthday gift for Hitler back in the 1930's. From there one has spectacular views of the Alps. They continued on to the Koenigsee, a lake near the German-Austrian border, the deepest and allegedly cleanest lake in Germany.

At Salzburg-Aigen; the Villa Trapp

On their last day in the Salzburg area, they went to Aigen to visit the former von Trapp family estate. The famous Trapp family, which by this time (except for the Baron and elder children who had passed away) had become almost a second family to Fr. Ron, had lived in this villa until their emigration in 1939. The SS-Reichsführer, Heinrich Himmler lived on that property from 1939 to 1945. In 1953 that beautiful real estate was given by the Trapp family to Missionaries of the Most Precious Blood to be used as a residence and seminary. More recently it has become a Bed & Breakfast.

After their visit to Aigen, they were off to Prien am Chiemsee, on the western shore of the Chiemsee lake in the district of Rosenheim, Bavaria. Here they purchased some Bavarian clothing for themselves, thinking that the outfits would be wearable souvenirs. After a brief visit to the District Hospital where Ron had been "Herr Doktor" in 1967-68, they visited the nearby village of Bernau am Chiemsee. They made it a point to stop in at the farmhouse where the Baumgartner family resided. Lenzi had come home from his special school in Munich to join the family during the Lawsons' visit. It was a happy occasion for all, with them looking forward to the Mass Fr. Ron would celebrate the next day. Fr. Ron and Sidney couldn't help but notice that Lenzi had a happy expression on his face that hinted that he had some sort of surprise in mind for his favorite Onkel Roni.

The Lawsons next visited some of Fr. Ron's pals in Achberg, which is located in the district of Schleching right on the border of Tyrol. It is a small and quite beautiful village in the high Alps with about 20 family homes and their farms. Once there, they were entertained in a genuine old Bavarian farmhouse kitchen. This something ordinary tourists would never experience, and most likely were not really eager to do so at any rate. The reason for the fact that this place was not on the list of "must visit" eating establishments was the odor of cow manure from the nearby adjacent stalls that added a bit of "spice" to the meal being served.

The next stop on this frenetic escapade was at Unterwössen, the major skiing locale south of Lake Chiemsee
and Bernau and was, of course, the area that Fr. Ron had
called home for almost a year not that long ago. They went
directly to the St. Martin's Church rectory where they were
met by none other than Father Niegel. There was no friend
that Fr. Ron was more eager to see again than Fr. Niegel, or
"Franzi," who had played such a significant role in helping
seminarian Ron to regain his footing and realize the depth of
his calling. The good Bavarian priest could not have been
happier to greet his former houseguest. He had never
doubted for a minute that they would meet again as brother
priests. The housekeeper, Anny and her daschund, Waschi,
were also pleased to see Fr. Ron. The four-legged pal was
ready for another walk around town any time.

Then more great friends greeted them as they drove up to
the Auschuster Stüberl Guesthouse. This was a place that
Ron had visited often during his eight months in Unterwössen. These folks, especially Tony and most of the rest
of his family, the Schweinösters, who owned the property,
were thrilled to see him again, with all of them welcoming
Sidney as though he were a long lost pal. Fr. Ron enjoyed
filling them all in on what had transpired in his life since he
last saw them. Tony, the eldest son, was still enjoying his job
as a *Holzknecht*, a woodsman or forester in the mountains.
The Lawsons were then escorted by Tony and others to the
8th century Benedictine chapel of Streichen on the mountain-
top of the nearby Austrian border town of Schleching. Fr.
Ron celebrated Mass in that chapel, where a number of his
lumberjack friends were in attendance. These were more
young men of the mountains who had befriended Ron during
his last stay here; taking him mountain hiking and skiing and
teaching him to yodel back then in the high Alps. Fr. Ron did
his best to yodel for them again and even though he didn't
face into the mountains and belt out his best serenade, they
were all impressed that he hadn't lost much technique.

When they returned to Unterwössen, they were enthusiastically greeted by the local town band, a typical Alpine

ensemble that played "oom-pa-pa" music, loudly emanating from their shiny brass instruments. There were about a dozen red-faced musicians creating wonderful sounds. They were all dressed in local costume, with their Alpine hats featuring a shank of mountain goat's hair, called in the Bavarian dialect, a *Gamsbart* or goat's beard. Even though the new priest was really not used to so much of that type of attention, he was very touched to be the object of their sincere and heart-felt welcome. Actually, the visit of a new priest was considered an honor for the village, which made the fun-filled celebrations all the more important.

The next day, after touring Reit-im-Winkl, a small village famous as a tourist resort especially for winter sports, Fr. Ron celebrated the truly special evening Mass that he had been anticipating so eagerly. This was to be the "first Mass" that he had invited Lenzi and his folks to attend. It was held in the Unterwössen parish church of St. Martin. His dear friend, the church's pastor, Father Franz Niegel (Franzi), had organized the whole Mass, making all the arrangements for the choir and talented musicians to be there. Franzi had always known that a day such as this would be in young Ron's future and was pleased that he had been blessed to have played a role in helping it to materialize.

The local populace turned out in colorful costume for this Mass. World War II veterans were in attendance with their veterans' flags; a common sight during local events. The choir sang the German Farmers' Mass (*die deutsche Bauernmesse*), written in 1933 by the very well known composer, Annette Thoma. At age 84, she had been a longtime friend of Fr. Niegel, the Baroness von Trapp and Fr. Ron as well. Her composition was sung in the traditional dialect of Bavaria. Especially poignant was that Fr. Ron's little friend, Lenzi, was there with his family, as they promised that they would be. Also there were the nuns and nurses from Prien who had attended to Lenzi and who had gotten to know Ron as he fulfilled his duties as an orderly They proudly presented the new priest with a small oil painting depicting a beautiful view of Our Lady's Island (die Fraue-

ninsel) located in the middle of Lake Chiemsee. At the end
of the Mass, Lenzi shyly but proudly gave a very special gift
to Fr. Ron as an ordination present. It was a beautiful wood-
en plate, actually a shallow bowl about 10 inches (25 cm)
across that was inscribed in Bavarian German with the words
from the Lord's Prayer, *Unser täglich brot gib uns heute*, *(Give
us this day our daily bread.)* What really touched Fr. Ron
deeply was that Lenzi had signed the back of the plate with
his full name by holding a pen with his toes. That plate
would always have a place of honor wherever Fr. Ron might
reside.

Fr. Ron with Lenzi, nuns and nurses from Prien.
Franzi holds gift for Fr. Ron from the nuns and nurses.

Later that day, they had a glorious celebration at the Auschuster Stüberl Guesthouse once again, with just about
everyone, farmer and lumberjack friends included, having a
wonderful time until about three in the morning. Fr. Ron had
known that a characteristic of these small Bavarian mountain
communities is that they knew how to party all night, all in
good spirit.

By the time they got back to Munich, Fr. Ron and Sidney had accumulated so many gifts and other items that four new pieces of luggage had to be purchased so that it could all be brought on the plane. Included in these newly acquired treasures was a beautiful baroque crucifix from Oberammergau, several beautiful beer mugs, antique diamond earrings from Cortina, Italy for their mother, some new clothes and assorted odds and ends.

They flew from the Munich airport, the second busiest airport in Germany, to Brussels where they were enthusiastically greeted by American friends, Judi Rosenthal and her husband David, who was a great friend from back in the days of Army Intelligence in 1957 and 1958. He and Ron had lived next door to each other in Washington, DC back then. It seemed a lifetime ago. Now, David was Merrill-Lynch's representative for Benelux. This precursor of the European Union was the economic union of three monarchies: Belgium, the Netherlands and Luxembourg. David entertained his good buddy with fascinating stories of his recent activities in his assignment and how much he loved Brussels. Then he and Judi escorted the Lawsons to a diplomatic reception held at a local restaurant and attended by several NATO officials from Western European countries. This formal and staid party could not have been more of a contrast to the one just the night before, with Fr. Ron's lumberjack and farmer friends in Unterwössen.

They had a hectic two days in the Brussels area, touring and visiting as many famous places as possible. Of special significance was a luncheon visit with American friends, Tony and Vivian Gillespie. They both had been assigned to the American Embassy in Brussels as Foreign Service officers and had been stationed with Ron in the Army in Washington DC in the late 1950's. The two of them had also been with him on Christmas Eve 1960, skiing in Kitzbühel, Austria. They reminded him that they knew back then that he would soon be headed to the priesthood. Meeting with him now as "Father" Ron was a logical and fulfilling conclusion to their expectations for him.

Then, it was off to London. This would not be much of a chance to catch up on sleep, since the flying time was less than a half-hour. And with London being one hour behind Brussels, according to their watches this short-haul international trip would get them there before they left.

Upon their arrival in London, Fr. Ron had a surprise in mind for his kid brother. They immediately traveled by train to Stratford-upon-Avon, about 100 miles (160 km) to the northwest and were soon at the Royal Shakespeare Company. Almost before he knew what was happening, Sidney was enjoying the famous Shakespearian play. *Richard III,* and hearing the opening monologue, *Now is the winter of our discontent*...What a phenomenal gift! Of all the memories of his trip with his brother, this side trip was a highlight that would be remembered and appreciated perhaps more than any other. Fr. Ron was more than a little pleased to see how much his actor brother enjoyed this unique and unexpected highlight.

After the performance, they were met right outside the theatre, as was Fr. Ron's plan, by Peter Johnston, a friend of his from their time together in West Berlin. After the two former military buddies had quickly brought each other up to speed on the happenings in their lives, and Peter and Sidney had a chance to get acquainted, they were driven back into London in Peter's auto. Peter had been with the First East Anglian Regiment when the two good friends served their respective countries in Berlin. They kept up a light-hearted banter on the nighttime drive to London, as they reminisced about their fun times when 1st Lieutenant Lawson would visit at the British Barracks. Their destination that evening was the London home of other great friends from those same barracks, none other than Bill Hill and his wife Diana, who were eagerly awaiting this reunion.

It wasn't very long before they arrived at the Hill's comfortable place and were soon enjoying cocktails and renewing old times. Peter, after getting in a few good-natured digs about the relative merits of his Regiment's valor versus

Bill's Durham Light Infantry's capabilities, was off to his own place, promising to keep in touch with everyone.

The next day, the Lawsons were escorted around London by Bill and Diana as they all enjoyed the historic city and everything it had to offer. Fr. Ron knew that they must stop in at the well-known, but often overlooked Eltham Palace since two more of his British military pals, Geoff and Edna Storey were stationed there as part of the Royal Army Education Corps. Fr. Ron had known them years earlier in Oberammergau where Geoff had been assigned to the Special Weapons School in Hawkins Barracks. Pressed for time, they had a short, but enjoyable visit with these good folks in this building with its Art Deco interior and beautiful gardens.

Of special interest, especially to Sidney, who was eager to get there, was their planned visit to the National Gallery at Trafalgar Square. This marvelous place, with no entry fee, houses one of the greatest collections of Western European paintings in the world. There, he could closely observe its unique collections, as he took all sorts of notes on about as many of the works of art as he could.

Before they knew it, the exhausted duo was boarding a BOAC jet bound for Montreal. On the long and uneventful return journey to Canada, Fr. Ron reflected upon how wonderful this whole trip had been and how much he knew that his brother had enjoyed it as well. As he reviewed all their hectic activities of the past two weeks he breathed a sigh of relief and offered a silent prayer of thanks that there had been no glitches along the way.

Bishop Gallagher met the brothers at the airport and they all talked at once on the short ride back to where Fr. Ron's car was parked at St. Patrick's. After the brothers had the car loaded with their luggage, he remarked to the bishop about his amazement that no glitches had occurred. He soon discovered however, that his car would not start and that the battery was dead. The energetic bishop did his best to get the car going by bodily pushing it. Not surprisingly that didn't work, so a new battery had to be purchased and installed, delaying the departure. It wasn't much longer before the exhausted men were home in Montpelier being deluged with all sorts of questions about the trip.

Sidney had to take a bus to Boston that very night and go through a grueling set of exams the next day. The jet lag from the exciting trip abroad didn't seem to impact him much since he got an "A" in his final exam in Fine Arts. This high grade was a direct result of his having had a chance to closely study many of the paintings in the huge collection at London's National Gallery. The one that really made it for him was the Dutch painter Jan van Eyck's *Portrait of Giovanni*. He had been able to describe it and the impression it made on him so well that his professor just had to give him an "A". Sidney also had a lifetime of fabulous memories of the fascinating places and people he had been fortunate enough to experience with his brother.

Sidney, Jr. 1970

Father Ron eagerly looked forward to beginning his assignment at St. Mary's church in Middlebury.

226

CHAPTER 18

FIRST PRIESTLY ASSIGNMENT: 1970 – 1972

Father Ron had no more than one week to catch his breath upon returning to his parents' home in Montpelier. It was hard to catch his breath since so much of it was used up telling his folks about the phenomenal trip he and Sidney, Jr. had experienced. He wrote down most of the highlights of that trip so that he would be able to recall details of it many years later. He knew that memory can sometimes play tricks on a person and he wanted to be sure to be able to describe it with accuracy in the future. He was especially pleased at how much his mother loved the diamond stud earrings her boys had purchased for her in Cortina, Italy.

Within a few days of his return, he got a phone call from the Chancellor (the principal record-keeper) of the Burlington Diocese, Rev. Msgr. Louis Gelineau (who subsequently retired as the Bishop of Providence, Rhode Island) informing him that it was now time to get to work. He was being assigned to the Parish of the Assumption of the Blessed Virgin Mary in Middlebury, and that he needed to be there right away. The parish church, locally known as St. Mary's, and its rectory were located right at the edge of the Middlebury College campus. In his four years on that campus enjoying himself as a student, fraternity brother and all-around social butterfly, not once had he had the slightest inkling that he would be a priest in that church, or for that matter, that he would even set foot into the place. What an interesting turn of events.

Early in the morning of the day after he had gotten word to be there, he drove the hour and a half from his parents' home to the parish church in his '69 Volkswagen Beetle, purchased new just the year before. In addition to a couple of suitcases packed with the few things he would need he also carried the beautiful carved wood statue of the Virgin Mary presented to him at his ordination by Mother Trapp. He had carefully wrapped and padded it against any possible damage in transit. He also carried along with him some of the meaningful mementos he had acquired and wanted to always keep close to him, such as Lenzi's specially autographed wooden plate, Rose Kennedy's letter in its frame and other priceless items.

As he entered the rectory, he introduced himself around to the folks he met and was pleased at their welcoming smiles. It was obvious that they were expecting him, the newly ordained priest. He appeared a little older than the usual greenhorns, but radiated warmth and an interesting personality. He met Father John Shorthill, the pastor, who showed him around the property and brought him to his small but clean room. Fr. John, a very pleasant, older priest, originally from Maine, described precisely what Fr. Ron's duties would be. A young priest had just left this parish having completed his three-year assignment and it was understandable that Fr. Shorthill was eager to get his replacement up to speed. His principle tasks were to say a number of the weekday and the Sunday Masses, giving the homilies at them, to hear confessions every Saturday and to help organize all the marriages as well as to be the priest who conducted the weddings. Fr. John would celebrate most of the funerals, say some of the Masses and conduct all the baptisms, most often with help from Fr. Ron. This arrangement worked out pretty well and Fr. John was obviously very pleased to get the extra help. He couldn't help but notice, however, that it wasn't very long before the faithful were showing up in larger numbers for the Masses that were to be said by the newcomer as announced in the weekly bulletin. In spite of the considerable age difference between Fr. John and Fr. Ron, their different views of Catholicism and life experiences, they really got along quite well together and formed a good team.

The live-in housekeeper, a dynamo of a lady in her late 70s, Doris Shambo, had entered the Sisters of Mercy in the Burlington diocese. Very soon after becoming a novice, she learned that she wasn't cut out to be a Sister, and subsequently left her order. She had worked for a number of years as a waitress in a small restaurant in Burlington. At some point, a priest from St. Mary's was occasionally one of her customers and eventually learned of her background with the Sisters of Mercy. His church was in dire need of a good housekeeper and she agreed that she just might like to give that job a try. In spite of her hard-as-nails demeanor, a cigarette nearly constantly hanging out of the side of her mouth, and a vocabulary that often included profanity, she became an important part of the day-to-day operations of the rectory and took her job to heart. She only resorted to swearing, putting together a creative combination of colorful words, when she was angry about something. She was angry a lot.

She turned out to be a real friend to Fr. Ron with the two of them sharing many thoughts on a variety of subjects. They both often saw the humor in situations that others simply missed. When the pastor was away for an extended time, she got a real kick out of surreptitiously helping the new priest put on dinner parties for a few select friends from the parish and college communities. These clandestine gatherings always were a real hit with the small groups.

Many of the young women who attended Middlebury College wore mini-skirts, the fashion at the time. Doris could be counted on to make a ribald comment or two on the appearance of the young ladies as they passed the rectory on their way to or from the campus. Fr. Ron couldn't help but wonder what she might say were she to spot them in their revealing bathing suits.

Since the parish church was in the middle of renovation when Fr. Ron first showed up, he often found the interior in a state of disarray with much of it torn up and with scaffolding everywhere. He kept a careful watch on what appeared to be a haphazard collection of planks, beams, tools and a variety of unidentifiable objects to be sure that no parishioners would be in danger of being harmed by tripping over any of this stuff or having any of it come crashing down on them. When the remodeling was completed in about a year, it turned out to be quite beautiful. The pastor, with the concurrence of Bishop Joyce, gave Fr. Ron the responsibility of consecrating the new altar. The newly ordained priest located an old ceremonial book in the rectory safe that described the ritual and the procedure of performing this important, rare and very special ceremony. This was a topic that had not been discussed in any seminary setting in which Fr. Ron had been enrolled. After carefully studying the procedure described in the old ceremonial book, last used some 100 years previously on the original altar, Fr. Ron performed the consecration. He was surprised that it took nearly three hours to complete, mostly because of the lengthy prayers and the need to anoint the entire marble surface with Holy Chrism (a mixture of oil of olives and balsam that had been blessed by a bishop) and holy water using a balsam branch, a technique he found very quaint and at the same time very interesting. The relics, bones from the 1st century martyrs, Saint Januarius and his colleagues, had been removed from the old altar and were cemented into place in the new one by a carefully supervised local craftsman as a critical part of the consecration ceremony. Father Shorthill was very pleased with the excellent job his new priest did with the difficult, although interesting, assignment he had been given.

The Vietnam War was in full swing at that time with no end in sight and occasionally Fr. Ron's preaching tended to reflect his strong feelings against his country's involvement. Many people shared that view, with the Vietnam War being one of the singularly most unpopular conflicts. Once or twice when he evidently got a little too political and spoke out strongly against that war, he was surprised to find a few parishioners get up and walk out of the church. The first time this happened, at least they didn't say anything or make any gestures, but it was obvious that he had struck a nerve with somebody. The next Sunday, when he again gave voice to his strong anti-Vietnam War sentiments it was evidently a little more than some in the church could deal with by simply walking out. A couple of men stood up and loudly voiced their reactions as they stormed out of the church. One of them stepped right up in front of the pulpit on his way out and with his voice tinged with rage angrily proclaimed "You have no right to stand in that pulpit and say such things!" Fr. Ron, feeling the man's pain, did not react or try to reason with him. After Mass the young priest and former US Army Intelligence Officer reflected on his preaching and made the decision that in the future he would express his beliefs about America's presence in Vietnam only to small groups outside of a Mass setting. He understood that there indeed was a group of Americans, who were in favor of an American-led all-out crash effort with the hope of winning the war quickly, even at the risk of Russia and/or China entering the war. He also felt strongly that he needed to be sure that these unhappy events in his church did not drive the dissenters from Catholicism. He worked diligently at that goal, meeting privately with the men who had been so angered with him. He had no intention of getting into a rehash of the controversial subject, but rather focused his chats with them more along the lines of his own lack of experience as a preacher and that he realized that there were far more appropriate topics for his homilies. He could never be sure if he had succeeded in that important task, although he did see them back in church from time to time.

From then on, his preaching was not about the war. He would talk directly to his audience (using the voice that his old high school classmates had loved) looking the parishioners right in the eye, one by one, while he delved into life's problems. He passionately discussed lack of faith, sin, as well as love of neighbor and dealing with the problems caused by the inability of some young people and their parents to live together in peace and harmony. He did his best to keep his homilies reasonably brief and could tell by the people's reaction better than his watch, when it was time to wrap up. He felt that this part of his ministry was quite a challenge and he worked hard ahead of time to prepare well, often finding a humorous story to open with. But it was still a challenge and he would often rehash in his own mind what he had said and what he thought the reaction of the congregation had been. He learned very early in his priesthood how not to be bothered at all by crying babies and noisy little kids in the pews, knowing that their parents were doing their best to keep the kids under control while they fulfilled their obligation to attend Sunday Mass.

At various times during the week, usually after a morning Mass, he got to meet many of the parishioners and found them to be really fine, upstanding and caring individuals. Many of these good people were farmers. One of his Sunday Mass homilies dealt with the topic of the need to give of self, not necessarily money, but of whatever a person may have that may exceed his own requirements. For example, perhaps one might give extra produce to help the poor. In a matter of days, the church hall was inundated with farm vegetables and all sorts of produce. Fr. Ron thought the response was outstanding. Fr. John was not amused. However, he soon was pleased to be known as the pastor of one of the most caring churches in the Burlington diocese.

Fr. Ron was most impressed with one particular couple, Lena and Albert Cyr, who each evidently had more than a green thumb since they consistently brought to the rectory, amazing quantities of all kinds of food that they had raised themselves.

With Lena and Albert Cyr

The bounty from their fertile fields was happily brought to church on a regular basis to help to feed the poor. Fr. Ron gave each of them a special blessing each time they came in with a truckload of their resources to give to the Lord. He silently wished that somehow, all of his preaching at Masses would be so well received. As for Lena and Albert, who unfortunately would never have any children of their own, this was the beginning of what would become a long-term connection to the young priest's developing career as they followed his changes in assignments with great interest; occasionally actually traveling to wherever in the world he may be stationed.

Fr. Ron, still his usual people-loving self, quickly made many great friends, several of whom have stayed in contact with him throughout his career. Although the social group he enjoyed spending free time with was quite large, he remained in close touch with Raymond and Teresa, Julie and Don, Howard and Ivis, Buster and Jeanette and Earl and Madeline. Some of these folks were not Catholic, which mattered to him not a whit. They all had camps at Lake Dunmore, a short drive south, so in the summer the enthusiastic swimming priest could often be found in those waters with any combination of those people, all having a grand time. Some of these folks confided to him that not only had they never had such a good time swimming with a priest, but never in their wildest dreams had they ever expected to do such a thing. They most probably also would not have predicted that they would go snowmobiling with a priest, but when the swimming season was long over and the area was covered with fresh snow, that is precisely what the group enjoyed doing. They all had a blast.

Earl, one of the gentlemen in his group of friends, had been the Chairman of the Board of Selectmen and he invited Fr. Ron to serve on a commission to study the provisions of the Middlebury Town Charter. This commission spent the better part of a year re-writing the original charter that was then forwarded to the Vermont State Legislature for approval. That was Fr. Ron's brief service in politics, an event that didn't seem to him to conflict with the idea of separation of church and state. The changes that were proposed to be made to the charter were not at all controversial since most of them were made necessary in light of the growth of the community in the 200 or so years of its existence. With uncharacteristic speed, the Vermont Legislature voted to endorse the submitted rewrite. Fr. Ron was soon asked to become a Selectman for Middlebury, a job he would have found interesting and challenging. The Bishop vetoed the idea ending any further political ambitions.

One of Fr. Ron's tasks in his "free time" was to serve as Newman (Catholic) Chaplain to the students at Middlebury College. He was happily surprised to find that the college chaplain, Charles Scott, who was the college chaplain when Fr. Ron was an undergraduate there years ago, was still there and proudly serving. The Episcopalian Chaplain Scott, lovingly referred to as "Charlie" by many on the campus, went on to have over a 50-year association with "Midd" and touched the lives of nearly the entire college community including persons of all faiths. He was a great help to the new priest in getting his bearings and helping him to conduct such a chaplaincy. In relatively short order, Fr. Ron had his duties there well under control. Among other things, he conducted a lot of weddings of college students, most right on campus in Mead Chapel. A couple who have remained great friends over the years, George Kuckel and his then fiancée, Pinny Bristol, were engaged when Fr. Ron, as Newman Chaplain, met them. He later conducted their wedding in Fire Island's community of Point O'Woods just off the southern coast of New York's Long Island in 1975.

At some time during 1971, Fr. Ron was approached by the head of the Russian Department at Middlebury's Russian Summer School. His first reaction was that there was no way he was going to read *War and Peace* out loud to anyone. He soon discovered that what they wanted was to find out if he would be willing to celebrate liturgies in Russian. After all, he had been a Russian major during his undergraduate years there and now that he was a priest, it seemed like a logical fit.

He told them he would have to investigate the issue and get back to them. He contacted the Ukrainian cardinal in Rome, Cardinal Josef Slipyi, to inquire about receiving an indult (permission) from the Vatican to celebrate Mass in the Russian Byzantine Rite. He felt comfortable writing to Cardinal Slipyi since he was one of the bishops that both Fr. Ron and his friend, Camillus, had written to while they were in the seminary in 1964. The fact that Cardinal Slipyi and the others had actually responded to their letter writing campaign back then and subsequently continued to exchange correspondence, gave him hope that his letter would be read. In about three months, his request was granted in a letter back from the cardinal, or at least the cardinal's office, with the provision that he would go for special training at Montreal's only Russian Byzantine Church, the subsequently closed Church of the Visitation of the Blessed Virgin Mary. The pastor of this beautiful old church, Father Leoni, was a famous Italian priest who had been a POW under the Russians in World War II. He graciously taught Fr. Ron exactly how to celebrate the Russian Byzantine liturgy, with the help of a Russian Orthodox friend from the Middlebury Russian Summer School. Both of them were amazed at how quickly and seemingly effortlessly (although Fr. Ron didn't feel that way) their star pupil learned the complex liturgy and how strong and melodious his voice was as he sang it. He had always truly enjoyed singing in choral groups and other opportunities such as in Gregorian Chants, so the fact that the liturgy in this rite was always sung was a real plus for him.

Fr. Ron, a little unsure at first, but rapidly gaining confidence, celebrated Mass in the Russian Byzantine Rite for the Middlebury Russian Summer School students and the faculty several times during the 1971 summer session. He thoroughly enjoyed this unexpected use of his college major.

He was truly touched by the special effort made by Doris, the housekeeper at his rectory, to make appropriate vestments for him out of gold brocade material. She had heard that there were some significant renovations going on in the parish convent for the Sisters of Mercy. She had been told that there was a nice collection of odds and ends available to anyone who could put any of it to good use. She and Fr. Ron had located a special book that clearly showed what Byzantine-style vestments looked like. Doris went to the convent, and found beautiful gold brocade drapes that had been the backdrop behind the altar and were no longer wanted. She happily brought that material back to the rectory. Following the images in the old book and in what seemed to be no time at all, she had fashioned perfect reproductions of just what Fr. Ron needed for celebrating Mass in authentic Russian Byzantine vestments.

Fr. Ron was given the task of supervising the religious education for the children of the parish, an assignment he thought of as both interesting and challenging. It was challenging partly because in his ecumenical approach to "getting through" to not only the Catholic children who were indeed part of his parish, he felt called to reach out to all the kids, regardless of their family's religious beliefs or which physical church they may attend. He interpreted his task as working with several nearby communities, including the villages of Cornwall, Weybridge and East Middlebury to organize after-school and/or weekend religious education opportunities. He became great friends with the minister of the Congregational parishes of the nearby Cornwall and Weybridge neighborhoods. With the eager help of the minister of the Methodist church in East Middlebury, he and his associates in his grand scheme put together an imaginative religious education program that was truly ecumenical. The Catholic sacraments were taught separately, while much of the balance of the educational material could be taught universally. The group of dedicated "persons of the cloth" used the Protestant churches as the locale for the classes to be taught. In Cornwall and Weybridge, the children were granted a bit of release time from their schools one day a week to go to the local church for religious education. In time, the schools permitted the classes to be held within their school buildings. In East Middlebury, Fr. Ron gave First Holy Communion to the Catholic children at a Mass that he conducted in that town's small Methodist Church. He felt that the experience was a very successful solution to a significant challenge. Several volunteers from each of the parishes helped to provide the religious education using material supplied by Fr. Ron and by his colleague, Rev. Murdale Leysath, minister of the Congregational Churches in both Weybridge and Cornwall. She was a great friend of his then and continues to remain a great friend.

In late spring, 1972, Bishop Joyce, who had been such a consistent supporter of Fr. Ron's development and was the one who had ordained him, retired. He was succeeded by Bishop John Aloysius Marshall who had come to the Burlington Diocese from Massachusetts. This new bishop had a different mind-set and viewed a Catholic priest's role in a parish in a much more conservative and contained way. He had heard many enthusiastic reports from all over his new domain about the gregarious and fun-loving wonderful Fr. Ron.

One day, while Fr. Ron was visiting the Chancery, where the diocesan business was transacted and recorded, he met the new bishop in a hallway and was invited to come into his office for an introductory chat. Or so Fr. Ron thought. It was soon obvious that Bishop Marshall had heard a lot of praise from many areas about this young, energetic new priest, however, he was not appreciative of his unorthodox approach to the various challenges he had been given. As soon as they were both seated and right after the very brief introductions to each other were dispensed with, the bishop began questioning him about his ministry in Middlebury. There were lots of questions asked before Fr. Ron was able to answer any of them. With his head held high, he decided to tell the bishop all about everything he had been doing and why and how he had been doing it. Fr. Ron realized that much of what he was about to convey was indeed very good by any standard. However, some of it would not necessarily measure up to strict parish discipline. Perhaps he dwelt too much on the latter aspects, but he had a feeling that the bishop had previously heard about a lot of it and most likely had already formed an opinion. He thought that hearing it all directly from his perspective could only be helpful - - maybe. Fr. Ron told Bishop Marshall that he would occasionally conduct a special baptism up on Bread Loaf Mountain, in the forest that had been dedicated to the memory of the great Robert Frost who used to read his poetry at the Writer's Conferences held there. That part of the story only caused the Bishop's eyes to widen slightly, but when Fr. Ron told him the reason for having a baptism out in the woods as opposed to the "correct" location of a baptismal font within the physical confines of a consecrated church, the reaction was a lot stronger. The reason was simply that in a few cases, the new parents and Godparents just did not like the pastor. So Fr. Ron made them all happy and brought in a new Catholic soul in the bargain.

The new priest related a few other episodes, none of which he thought of as serious infractions of the rules or of what Fr. Shorthill had expected of him. He included his occasional swimming parties with groups of young folks, some of whom were parishioners, others who held different faiths or no faith at all. That seemed to be especially shocking.

That very same day, Bishop Marshall decided that it was a good idea that Fr. Ron be transferred from Middlebury to some other parish. When this news reached the parishioners of St. Mary's as well as lots of other good people of Middlebury, it caused a significant outcry and many phone calls and letters pleading that Fr. Ron be allowed to remain. Fr. Ron was not pleased with the abruptness of it all and went to Montreal to discuss the matter with Bishop Leonard Crowley, an Auxiliary Bishop in that city. The bishop quickly suggested that Fr. Ron stay in Montreal and that he would put him to work in more favorable conditions, although he just might have to tone down his desire to be liked and pay a little more attention to "The Rules". Fr. Ron returned to Middlebury to find that Bishop Marshall still wanted him to be reassigned, although he still had Masses to say and parishioners to attend to.

In the summer of 1972, Fr. Ron drove the 135 miles (217 km) to Montreal letting Bishop Crowley and Cardinal

Leger's office negotiate with Bishop Marshall back in Burlington. In no time at all it seemed, it was settled that he could remain in Montreal indefinitely. He went to live for the summer at St. Augustine of Canterbury Parish in the section of Montreal known as Notre-Dame-de-Grâce, a residential district located to the west of downtown. There, he helped out doing parish census work. While Fr. Ron was there, he met an astounding and very interesting Jewish convert to Catholicism. This was the famous neurologist and psychiatrist, Dr. Karl Stern, who was in his mid sixties at the time. Dr. Stern had published the story of his conversion as well as reminiscences of growing up in Germany and his decision to emigrate to Canada before the Nazis destroyed his family, in the book *The Pillar of Fire*. During their long conversations, Dr. Stern captivated Fr. Ron with the terrible facts of what had happened to him and to his family. They both prayed that the world would never again see such horror inflicted upon human beings by other "humans".

Bishop Crowley came to visit with Fr. Ron one afternoon soon after the young priest's arrival back in Montreal. He had a warm smile on his face as he suggested that Fr. Ron could choose any one of six assignments that had been put forward for his consideration. He chose the first, to become Chaplain at St. Thomas High School in Pointe-Claire with his residence to be in the neighboring town of Dorval in the parish of St. Veronica. The other five choices offered to him at that time really did not interest him much at all; in fact except for choice number two, none of the others remain in his memory. His second offered choice was to set up an office in the Ville Marie office tower in central Montreal. There, he would have been available for spiritual counseling in French and English to the 17,000 or so working people. There was no contest. The energetic young priest preferred to work with teenagers.

His assignment as Chaplain at St. Thomas High became a pleasant and fulfilling experience that continued for the next 12 years.

CHAPTER 19

HIGH SCHOOL CHAPLAIN
1972 – 1984

Father Ron had always really loved the island of Montreal. Not too many people thought of it as an island, but since it is surrounded by the waters of the St. Lawrence River, even though driving to and from that dynamic portion of Quebec is facilitated by countless bridges and a few tunnels, it qualifies as being just that. An island; the second largest city in Canada and the largest in the province of Quebec. Its population approaches 4 million, and it is the second-largest French-speaking city in the world after Paris. In ways, it was somewhat like an island of religious freedom of expression for the newly developing priest. His time in the Grand Seminary there as well as his excellent relationships with various bishops and priests helped him to feel comfortable being there for the next phase of his own development. There continued to be a strong hierarchy of Catholic Church leadership in Montreal, as well as devotion to the Eucharist and all the liturgical teachings that made that faith so important and personal to Fr. Ron. He was sure that his new assignment there as chaplain at St. Thomas High School in Pointe Claire was going to present him with an exciting and fulfilling way to bring the Word of God to young people and to help to shape their lives in a positive way. He fully expected that he would be relatively free to express his deep faith in ways that this audience would find captivating and that would also increase their devotion to the Catholic Church.

He eagerly moved into the rectory at St. Veronica's Church located in the neighboring town of Dorval, within easy driving distance of the high school. He soon met the pastor there, Fr. David Fitzpatrick and knew instantly that there would be a good relationship between the two of them. That feeling was based upon more than intuition, since he had known Fr. David well in 1967 when Fr. Ron was a seminarian in residence at St. Patrick's Basilica. Also living at this rectory now was Fr. John Walsh, the high school chaplain at the neighboring John XXIII High School in Dorval. The three of them got along quite well, living together for the next three years until Fr. Ron's next challenge saw him moving into an exciting new and different type of set-up with the High School. He knew that he would be helping out at St. Veronica's, especially on weekends when he would be hearing confessions on Saturdays and saying Masses and preaching on Sundays. As soon as he had settled in, he dashed over to St. Thomas High.

He arrived at the English-speaking Catholic high school, whose enrollment approached 2500 students in grades 7 - 11, just a few days before the start of classes. He found that there was a French high school of the same name, St. Thomas High, located right next door with an equal number of students, however all the teachers and students were French. They also had a French priest chaplain as well. Fr. Jean-Guy Vincent, CSC (the French abbreviation for the "Congréga-tion de Sainte-Croix") who was a member of The Brothers of Holy Cross. This Order administers the Basilica of St. Joseph on the northern slope of Mount Royal. There was no doubt in Fr. Ron's mind that the two chaplains would be working very closely to maximize the effectiveness of their goals. In fact, Fr. Ron and Fr. Jean-Guy became very good, close friends over the years there together. They even sponsored a joint English-French student trip to Stockholm in 1975 and conducted a bilingual Mass in a Swedish Lutheran church. There was no Catholic church where they were visiting on that student exchange in the district of Nacka. Rather than go without saying Mass, the two people-oriented priests simply approached the minister of the Lutheran church and made their request to celebrate a Catholic Mass in his church. He not only rapidly agreed, but attended the Mass and spoke warmly to them after the service feeling the ecumenical power of prayer and faith.

His first order of business was to meet with his principal, a charismatic fellow named Luc Henrico, with whom he immediately formed a close bond of friendship. That friendship was to continue for the entire duration of Fr. Ron's 12-year association with St. Thomas High and beyond. Luc took Fr. Ron on a retreat that was being conducted for 7th graders in the nearby Laurentians, one of the world's oldest mountain ranges located in southern Quebec. They spent a pleasant day there talking with many of the teachers and several students. It was a great way to be introduced. Fr. Ron could almost feel the many pairs of eyes on him as his new associates tried to size him up. He was sure that he had passed muster when by the end of the day, all the teachers and many of the students continued to hover around him asking lots of great questions and finding the honest answers sometimes amusing but always fascinating. He couldn't have asked for a better introduction.

Back at the school, he was given a temporary office inside the library. He made do with this cramped space for a couple of months. He had noticed a large room that was tucked into the corner of the spacious cafeteria. The room had windows that afforded a great view: not of any of the local scenery, but of the cafeteria itself. This place was being used as a storage room, with a seemingly haphazard collection of audio-visual apparatus, outdated books, parts of chairs and desks, boxes of unidentified treasures, some sports equipment and more. The room seemed wasted on this collection. With his best persuasive techniques in full-gear, Fr. Ron soon convinced Luc that it would really be a great place for his office. The new chaplain eagerly helped carry the many treasures out to other storages areas and soon had a pleasant space with his own desk and telephone. It became the center of activities for him for the next 12 years.

There was another requirement that Fr. Ron had been quietly trying to resolve from day one in this assignment. He needed a chapel. He was eventually told that just off the front entrance of the building there was a room where the school board would meet for their infrequent on-premises meetings, and that he could make use of that space if he wished. He wished indeed and took command of the space. Fr. Ron outlined his ideas for transforming the room into a chapel to several faculty members as well as many of the parents he had come to know. A few of these parents were highly skilled craftsmen who were eager to put their talents to use on such a noble cause. He described his ideas for a tabernacle to these men and in relatively short order, they had created a truly unique and beautiful one made of handsomely grained select hardwoods. What really set it apart from any other tabernacle was that its front cover was finished with a Byzantine icon of Christ the Teacher. The former owner of that beautiful icon was gratified to see it put to such prestigious and holy use. All who saw it were touched by the symbolism it conveyed, with Jesus looking directly at the viewer, His left hand holding the Sacred Word of God, His right hand raised in blessing. His dark blue cloak and crimson red tunic signifying the mystery of His divine life and His human blood respectively.

The same talented craftsmen also fashioned the base for an altar, upon which was installed an altar stone, complete with relics. It had recently seen use in a nearby church that had installed a new stone and perfectly fit the bill for this new chapel. Chalices and similar liturgical implements were purchased out of the small operating budget, as was a beautiful standing crucifix that saw double duty on the altar and occasionally for processions. Some of the chapel items were gifts from neighboring churches, many of which had excess liturgical items. For example, there were 10 English or bi-lingual parish churches in Montreal's West Island. Word of the new chaplain's efforts to create a unique chapel in his High School rapidly spread to them and they were happy to donate their excess items.

Various people were so moved by the transformation of the old, empty room that they felt compelled to donate a beautiful collection of religious artwork for the freshly painted walls. The end result was a very attractive chapel in which up to 40 people could be seated on the folding chairs provided. Fr. Ron, using his own vestments, said Mass in the new chapel daily at noon for a number of students, faculty and occasional parents who might just be there at the time. Many of these parents made it a point to be there for these uniquely moving celebrations of the Holy Eucharist.

Fr. Ron was surprised to discover that as a school chaplain he was considered a Quebec government employee and so was paid not by the church, as he would have expected, but rather by the government. He actually belonged to a labor union for school employees, working for the Baldwin-Cartier School Commission. This Commission at that time embraced three English high schools, three French high schools and seven bilingual (French/English) elementary schools. The schools were separated by language, but had the same name as their neighboring parish church and were often located right next-door to their church buildings. All these schools were located in Montreal's West Island communities of Pointe Claire, Dorval, Pierrefonds, Beaconsfield, Baie d'Urfe, Ste. Anne de Bellevue, Kirkland and Senneville.

The Quebec system does not start high school with the title of grade 7, but rather what is referred to as Secondary I. Instead of having a separate junior high school of grades 7 and 8, the Quebec system embraces them into a Secondary system that ends with "grade 11". The grades progress through Secondary II, III, IV and V. Graduation follows at the end of Secondary V. Students then go to what is called a CEGEP. This is a post-secondary institution that is only found in the province of Quebec. (Ontario has a similar program under an English name.) Grade 12 and an additional grade 13 are part of the CEGEP system, a kind of junior college that is free. CEGEP is a French acronym for Collège d'enseignement général et professionnel, which means "College of General and Vocational Education". This gives the students two years of a junior college experience – all free. After that, going on to university is an option if they should choose to avail themselves of the opportunity.

As a special way to make the opening of the school year memorable, Fr. Ron celebrated a Mass outdoors in the playground area shortly after the school year had begun in earnest. This was a very well attended event with a reporter from one of the local newspapers picking up on it. The photo of the unusual activity made the front page over the caption *Mass Mass*. Such extra publicity was good for the school and for Fr. Ron and his overall objectives. Outdoor Masses became something to really look forward to with the students, encouraged by their new chaplain, developing original musical accompaniment for these liturgies. As the school year progressed, the outdoor Masses were held most of the time in the auditorium, and became seasonal events. Once a year, Fr. Ron invited 50 year-old Bishop Leonard Crowley, the English auxiliary bishop, the one person most responsible for Fr. Ron being the school chaplain, to be the celebrant. The bishop thoroughly enjoyed interacting with the teenagers, seeming to glow with his own newfound youthful feelings. The students made a point of telling their chaplain just how much they liked the bishop and looked forward to his return.

Fr. Ron very quickly made friends with the faculty. Making friends easily and in record time had been his hallmark no matter where in the world he might be at any given moment. Several of the faculty that were closest to him were teachers in the physical education department, especially Gabriel Takacs and Barbara Trenholm who were obviously sweethearts. Fr. Ron conducted their wedding the next year at Christmas time, 1973. Gabriel and Barbara quickly became stalwart supporters of Fr. Ron's weekend retreat movement in the mountains of Quebec. Eventually, these popular retreats were to settle at a rustic outdoor education facility aptly named The Round Hearth, about an hour from Montreal and within 10 minutes of Mont Orford. One of the features at that place was a round meeting room on the main floor around a central open fireplace with a fluted chimney above it. There was sleeping space for over 50 people in bunks on the lower, ground floor. Eventually, two dormitories for students and staff, an outdoor swimming pool and a tennis court were added to this facility. Hiking on the nearby mountains, especially Mont Orford, was one of the most popular activities, but came in second to the special feelings resulting from the midnight Masses celebrated on the mountain top on clear nights with millions of stars winking down. In the 12 years that Fr. Ron was devotedly connected to St. Thomas High School, at least 50 such weekends were conducted.

From the very beginning when this new chaplain began organizing and implementing his retreat movement, a number of outstanding students, leaders among their peers, supported the great fun to be had at these getaways. For reasons that never became obvious, this stalwart group called themselves *Ron's Raiders* as they talked up the exciting events. As a way to help ensure a good attendance at his retreats, even before his "Raiders" materialized, Fr. Ron started out by talking the very popular athletes on the football team into coming along with him. He knew that nearly all the rest of the student body would follow. He was right.

His lunchtime discussions with the athletic faculty soon lead to the fact that there was a real need for staff to help coach the ski and football teams. With no prodding at all, he quickly volunteered to be involved with both sports, but stipulated that rather than coach the gridiron guys, he would be available as a chaperone for away games. He emphatically stated that he would be more than willing to help coach alpine skiing. Whether it was his unique coaching skills or simply that the talent and dedication to their sport the skiers possessed, they ended up with several years of championship ski racing. Most of the skiing was done in the nearby Laurentians and the Eastern Townships of Quebec. However, over the next few years he and other faculty members wound up taking the ski team to Europe on three or four occasions. They were all amazed and awe-struck by these adventures since they included Davos, Switzerland twice and in subsequent years they travelled to Stockholm, Sweden and Chamonix, France. The school kids raised their own funds through a variety of imaginative raffles, dances and appeals to the public via the local newspapers.

The first overseas ski trip, to Switzerland, found 52 students making the trip along with a dedicated group of faculty, including Fr. Ron of course. Upon their return, he made the observation that it was nearly unbelievable that with 52 pairs of skis, 52 pairs of boots and countless other articles and pieces of equipment, nothing was misplaced or lost. A logistical miracle.

In his role as chaplain to 2500 teenagers, Fr. Ron was much more than a priest to the students who had quickly come to admire and respect him. His door was always open to anyone (student or faculty) who needed to unload a problem situation, just needed a bit of advice or had issues that simply must be resolved. More often than not, such counseling or confession opportunities took place right in his office.

As background material for this biography was being collected, the following unsolicited message arrived from Don H., one of the young men who had been one of Fr. Ron's former students at St. Thomas High School, Pointe Claire, QC.

.... As kids we took a lot for granted and didn't always appreciate the work and support of the people around us, particularly at school. So, 31 years later - thank you. And as an observation - those friends who participated actively in pastoral activities and who were Ron's Raiders ..... have all become quite incredible, accomplished adults. I'm not saying it's all your doing, but...

Over the years as high school chaplain, he conducted at least a couple of dozen weddings, some for former students and others for faculty. Sadly, he also had occasion to conduct several funerals for deceased faculty.

In the spring of 1974 he organized and ran a walk-a-thon, which netted $21,000 for the poor of Senegal, Haiti as well as Montreal. The French in Quebec have long had an affinity for what goes on in Haiti and have a number of activities to collect money for this impoverished nation. St. Thomas High School students happily turned over the proceeds of their walking efforts to be divided beneficially between their own neighbors who were living in poverty and the many Haitians who were without some of the most basic needs.

His living quarters during his 12 years as high school chaplain were normally in the rectory of one of the parish churches where he would assist at weekend Masses and also preach there as well. He wound up housed in the rectories of St. Veronica in Dorval, St. John Fisher in Pointe Claire, St. Thomas à Becket in Pierrefonds, Transfiguration of Our Lord in Cartierville and at Corpus Christi in Senneville where he also served as Administrator.

As he moved from one rectory to another during his 12 years, he was happy to bring along his very special gift statue of the Virgin Mary given to him by Mother Trapp at his ordination as well as other personal and significant objects that he would always keep nearby.

By the time the Christmas season neared in 1973, Fr. Ron was approached by priests from Pointe St. Charles. Locally known as "The Point", it was about 25 miles (40 km) from Dorval and was part of downtown Montreal. This was one of the most ethnically diverse places in Canada and had a significant percentage of its population who lived at or below the poverty level. The visiting priests, who had heard of the good work being done by the new high school chaplain, asked if he might have any ideas for raising funds to help the poor children of St. Gabriel's Elementary School in their community. Fr. Ron, never at a loss for creative ideas when it came to helping people, eagerly met with the Head of the Religion Department, Neil Patton, and they jointly came up with a plan for a Christmas party for the St. Gabriel's kids. He involved a significant portion of the St. Thomas High population in planning the details and organizing the whole event. The elementary kids were matched up with his students who committed themselves to acquiring special gifts for the little ones. The head of the Religion Department played Santa Claus, while the St. Thomas students went dressed as elves, angels and other Christmas characters including Santa's reindeer. The elementary children put on a traditional Christmas play with the usual cast of characters and Baby Jesus. The gang from St. Thomas High brought all the food, ice cream, cake and sweet treats plus the special presents for each child. This event was a great hit and was repeated for the 12 years that Fr. Ron was there. It is most likely still being done.

In the first few summers of his enjoyable role in Montreal, he attended Boston College where he was enrolled for six weeks in courses leading to a master's degree in education. Having such a degree was a requirement for the position he already held so he was eager to get the course work behind him and take his degree. He found the six summer weeks quite stimulating and knew that the extra education would be very useful. The course he was taking also provided his classmates, a large group of priests, sisters, brothers and interested lay persons, the format to share ideas about related types of work in which they were involved. Just chatting with his fellow students gave him additional good ideas about how to approach some difficult topics. And surely his kids could present some difficult topics indeed.

In August of 1974 he travelled to Bavaria again especially to visit what he thought of as practically his second home in the village of Unterwössen. He explained to his students and fellow faculty before he left for this trip, that that village was where he had so many positive and faith-filled weeks and months during a confusing period in his life, and was where he had lived with Fr. Franz Niegel. Once he was back there again, he and Franzi enjoyed each other's company during his short visit. While in Bavaria he also visited some dear friends in Oberammergau, at Kloster Ettal as well as the Bavarian Forest where some of his lumberjack pals still worked and yodeled. When he returned to Montreal he felt that the trip had been refreshing to him both physically and spiritually. He was sure that he would make that trip again.

In the early winter of 1974, all the students at St. Thomas High again worked very hard to make their Christmas project a roaring success. They put on a variety show at St. Gabriel's School in Pointe St. Charles that brought down the house, making him think that some of these kids just might have a stage career in their future. Not only did the students distribute 350 wrapped gifts to the eager elementary children, they also were able to provide the school administration nearly $1,000 that they had raised through a combination of bake sales, class auctions and other imaginative fund-raising activities. As if all this wasn't enough, they also brought 3,000 cans of food and half a room full of warm clothing that they had rounded up, and gave it all to the poor families at St. Gabriel's.

Another one of the activities that these High School students did at least once a month while Fr. Ron was chaplain there, was to go to the neighborhood known as la Petite Bourgogne (Little Burgundy). Although it was not a distant trip for them, their reason for going there regularly truly made him proud of them. They would go into the Benedict Labre House to prepare and serve meals to the street people who wandered in with hopes of getting fed. The destitute men and women who found their way into the warmth and comfort of the place, if only for a short time as they enjoyed the food that was presented to them, would soon be back out and into their dilapidated area with other impoverished people. The kids expected nothing in return.

All of the non-stop activity; interfacing with the many students, their families and the school faculty as well as the various citizens of the local area, saying Masses, hearing confessions and planning new projects and field trips, kept Fr. Ron in a constant state of renewal. He was always finding and dealing with new challenges and situations and through it all, constantly growing in his faith and dedication to his calling, feeling very much that he was right where he belonged.

Fr. Ron was a natural traveler and truly enjoyed jetting off to distant locales. In February 1975 he accompanied a group of 130 students and teachers to Stockholm, Sweden on a unique exchange program. The entire group enjoyed the two weeks they spent there and were very pleased at the warm, enthusiastic reception they were given. It seemed as though everyone made new friends and many promised that they would keep in touch "forever". It was during this trip that Fr. Ron and Fr. Jean-Guy Vincent, from the French St. Thomas High, celebrated a bilingual mass in the local Lutheran church. The second part of the exchange was planned for the following February at which time a group of an equal number of students would travel from Sweden to spend two weeks in Montreal.

When the Easter holidays rolled around, Fr. Ron took a group of 45 students, members of the ski team, and several teachers to Davos, Switzerland: their second trip there for training and fun. In spite of the season, late spring, they were surprised to find that it seemed like deep winter there and were almost snowed in. Their mission: to train and have fun, was highly successful.

Again during the summer recess, Fr. Ron continued his course of study at B.C. working toward his master's degree in education. He continued to enjoy the mental stimulation this provided but looked forward to completing the course the following summer and getting his advanced degree. As soon as his six weeks at B. C. were over, he was on his way to a retreat in the Benedictine monastery at Ettal, Germany where he had been baptized into the Catholic Church in 1960. So many beautiful, and at the same time powerful memories of his time there 15 years ago came flooding back to him as he felt the deep significance of it all. It took his breath away. To help him return to earth, he spent a week mountain climbing in the nearby Berchtesgaden Alps, loving every minute of it. He especially enjoyed climbing Bavaria's second highest peak, the Watzman, and clearly recalled climbing it when he was younger, in 1967 while he was Franzi's guest in Unterwössen. He returned to St. Thomas

251

High School refreshed and ready to take on whatever challenges lay ahead.

During the latter portion of 1975 a group of seasoned Montreal priests had been studying the possibilities of creating "community" among the diocesan clergy. Their efforts towards their goal of oneness seemed elusive. But then, Fr. Ron and another high school chaplain, Fr. Joe Sullivan from Pierrefonds Comprehensive High School, with Bishop Crowley's permission, got the ball rolling by moving out of their respective rectories and into a furnished home they had rented. It was located near the parish church of St. Thomas à Becket in Pierrefonds, one of Montreal's suburbs not far from Pointe Claire. There, they started a *House of Prayer and Hope*, and often referred to it as Becket House, with plans to provide the kind of family atmosphere that they felt was needed at that time in order to be mutually supportive. They started off with just two young teen-aged boys who both really needed a place to live. Their eventual goal was to grow into a community that would include lay people, both married and single, religious sisters and four or five local priests as well as Protestant clergy. A bold new idea, and an exciting one at that.

Shortly after moving into their new home, they invited the two teenage boys to move in with them. One of these young men, Tony Shaw, had been enrolled in the CEGEP (post-secondary school) and doing very well, when his parents found that for job-related reasons, they needed to relocate to British Columbia. Tony could have stayed with family members, but they were not in close enough proximity to Montreal and his school. He was a top-notch athlete with the St. Thomas High School track team, being its captain and coaching the runners in his final year there. Living at Becket House was the obvious solution to his problem and he was a real contributor while there.

The other young man, Pierre, came from a troubled home, was known to Fr. Joe and was in desperate need of a stable and caring place to live. He brightened up from the very beginning even if he may have thought that this place was too good to be true. He buckled down to his studies and presented no problems to the two priests who took advantage of any opportunity to show by example how to live a God-centered life.

While both youths were good kids, Tony really was a role model for Pierre. Both priests were in awe of Tony's actions late one night. Fr. Ron and Fr. Joe were both away from Becket House attending to needy parishioners. It was at about 2 AM when Tony was roused from sleep by a banging at the front door. He quickly dressed and opened the door to find a terribly distraught woman in tears, repeating that she wanted to kill herself. He calmly invited her in, made some coffee while continuing to talk to her in a soothing and very adult manner. He sat with her at the kitchen table as she poured out her story of despair while he listened with heart-felt concern for her welfare. At about dawn, Fr. Ron returned from his sick call to find the surprise houseguest and Tony having an animated, but calm conversation in the kitchen. Tony filled him in on what had transpired, gathered up his books and materials and headed off to school, knowing that the uninvited visitor was now in good hands.

On the weekends, Fr. Ron and Fr. Joe took turns assisting and preaching at Masses in the Church of St. Thomas à Becket located right next-door. Fr. Joe also worked with the Catholic Family Movement in the parish, while Fr. Ron worked with the Adult Education Program.

The priests were excited about the project they started and had strong hopes that it would become a model for others to follow. At that time, the Bishops of Quebec were eager that their clergy establish what they had come to call *communautés de base* (community-based groups). These bishops felt that rectory life as it was then experienced in North America and always had been, was not conducive to a family community atmosphere and as such, put the priests too much out of touch with the people they were there to serve. Fr. Ron could easily relate to that feeling when he reflected on the thought that he was just then learning how expensive it was to buy food. He could hardly believe it when he thought back and realized that for the past 15 years or so, someone else had always done his laundry, cleaned house, cooked his meals as well as done the shopping for all the food. This new set-up would be challenging, but he felt that it would be a healthy challenge at that.

However, at the same time that this previously unheard-of idea of priestly community was taking shape, Fr. Ron was discovering that a significant number of young people were conservative in their approach to religion. The guitar and rock and roll Masses were slowly fading away and vestments were "in", especially the Roman collar. The French priests really liked simply wearing lay clothing and the starched Roman collar was not to their liking, but it looked like things were changing. There even was discussion in Fr. Ron's zone that was very much to the point that proper catholic vestments were important. (A "zone" was a grouping of parishes according to district. It would be called a "deanery" in the US.) In fact, there was strong discussion in the zone that the nuns who teach in the area schools assist the priests in bearing external witness by returning to the practice of wearing a religious habit. The sisters in Quebec for the most part had abandoned wearing the habit. It would be interesting to see how all this worked out.

Fr. Ron, always busy, seemed to attract more tasks and assignments. He now represented the Pastoral Zone on the Archdiocesan Christian Education Committee. This was a watchdog group to encourage the teaching of quality Catholic education in the vast system of Catholic schools in Montreal. In just his pastoral zone, for example, there were 10 English Catholic parishes with three English Catholic high schools and seven elementary schools; all of them public institutions. It was a lot of extra work to attend the many meetings and to see to it that the kids would continue to get the best education possible. He never complained about the workload.

As much as the two priests wanted their experiment in priestly community in Becket House to flourish and grow, it did the opposite and foundered, mainly due to lack of adequate finances within the first several months of its brief existence. So, against their wishes, in mid-1976 Fr. Ron and his good friend, Fr. Joe, had to give up the rented house, with each of them moving into a rectory of one of the nearby churches. Fr. Ron was then housed at St. John Fisher Parish in the Montreal suburb of Pointe Claire. Fr. Joe was sent to the Transfiguration Parish in Cartierville as pastor. (A couple of years later, Fr. Ron joined him there.) They both felt that although their whole experiment had failed, they had seriously failed the two young boys who had been invited to live with them and who now had to move in with relatives or make other arrangements. Both young men made out fine in that regard, with Tony moving in with friends for the short amount of time remaining for him in the school system. Pierre had relatives in another part of Canada, where he quickly settled.

The priests held hopes of reorganizing their attempt to create "community" at some future time, but they recognized that it pretty much depended on what the Lord wanted for them and just where they were needed most.

Tony, who has remained in touch with Fr. Ron, reminded him of the episode of the exploding grape juice. Fr. Ron's great farming friends from Middlebury, Albert and Lena Cyr, had delivered two, five-gallon glass jugs of grape juice that they had made. They had heard all about the Becket House setup and wanted to provide a touch of home goodness to be enjoyed by all. However, left unattended in the kitchen, the grape juice slowly began to ferment. One of the bottles simply was not up to the increase in internal pressure and blew up, sending shards of glass everywhere and getting purple grape juice all over the place. The juice stained the kitchen rug and proceeded to seep through the floor where it managed to drip in the only area of the basement where there was laundry hanging on a line. The other bottle of grape juice was quickly uncorked and did no damage; at least almost no damage. Tony, upon returning from Cross-Country practice one day, was beyond thirsty and drank much too much of the stuff. He had diarrhea for days.

Fr. Ron did indeed complete his course of study in the summer of '76 and took his Master's Degree in Education at Boston College. He reflected upon the many courses he had taken and how much he had enjoyed every one of them; from his undergraduate days at Middlebury, through specialized courses in Military Intelligence with the Army, the dual language courses in Oberammergau, the years in the seminaries, and now the Master's at B.C. He would sign up for another course right away if one were needed, or was even offered if it struck his fancy. About the only thing he loved more than people, was constantly learning. He also realized that even though he was approaching his 42nd birthday, and still felt 16, his happiness increased each year. He felt blessed to have the opportunity to work with all these young people. Every morning he would wake up to a new and inspiring challenge for the day, and by day's end would usually feel that he had accomplished something worthwhile.

Although the summer of this year was notable for completing his advanced degree, that highlight paled to insignificance when measured against a once-in-a-lifetime experience that he could never have predicted that he would have. He was asked by the Archbishop to celebrate the Opening Mass in the Olympic Village as part of the Opening Ceremonies on July 17, 1976 for the Games of the XXI Olympiad. Security was extremely strict for all public areas, especially after the tragic Palestinian assassination of a group of Israeli athletes just four years before in Munich, Germany. Every person about to enter any building or access point for this major event was searched very thoroughly and was looked right in the eye by the no-nonsense, well-trained security guards.

The Mass in the Olympic Village was conducted in both English and German and was attended by nearly 500 people, most of them athletes from many different countries. Fr. Ron could easily have conducted the Mass in either of the two languages, but it was concelebrated by Fr. Ron and Fr. Emmett Johns, Pastor of St. John Fisher Church in Pointe Claire. At this time, Fr. Ron was living in the rectory of that church along with Fr. Johns who was six years his senior. The two priests brought the youth choir from St. Thomas High School along with them; a never to be forgotten experience for those fortunate students.

(Fr. Emmett Johns, also known as "Pops" went on to establish a homeless shelter and support group for youths of Montreal who truly needed his professional street ministry. His organization, known as Dans La Rue, was founded in late 1988. He saw to it that street kids and other at-risk youngsters in the Montreal area were provided with food, shelter and, equally important: friendship. His philosophy was to provide "help without judgment". He also worked with the needy youths to help them to get off the streets, educating them about the dangers of such a life. For his outstanding work in this area, he was made a Member of the Order of Canada in 1999, and in 2003, was made a Grand Officer of the National Order of Quebec. These are the most prestigious honors in all of Canada.)

Fr. Ron delivered his homily in both English and German. Preaching in this venue was an experience he would always remember and also one that would most likely never come along again, making it all the more meaningful to him. As he gazed out into the assembled group he could see that the athletes were very serious about being at this special Mass, but he also knew that each of them had a lot on their minds with their principal focus being on their area of competition. As soon as the Mass was completed, all but one person quickly left the Olympic Village and headed to the Stadium to get ready for the Opening Ceremonies and the athletic events to come. This one person who stayed, approached Fr. Ron who must have touched him with his deeply felt celebration of the Mass and his preaching. He was a weight lifter from Kosice in Slovakia. He sheepishly introduced himself and quickly made the request that he would very much like to meet privately, in an area away from the competition and the other athletes. Fr. Ron knew that this young man was in need of his undivided attention and arranged that they meet later in the week there in the Olympic Village. From there, Fr. Ron took him to Notre Dame Basilica in Montreal's Old Town. As the Olympian knelt at the altar praying along with Fr. Ron, he suddenly burst into tears. Fr. Ron's role at that moment was to sympathetically listen and offer whatever the young man needed. It developed that the youth's father was a priest of the Byzantine Rite (Ruthenian) in Slovakia and had been terribly mistreated and abused by the Communist authorities. The young athlete was deeply religious and to avoid persecution of not only him, but his whole family as well, he took his wife and their two little girls to Mass every Sunday by bus to a distant village, making a game of it for his children. Since he was well known in the sports world, there was no doubt that he too would have been abused by the authorities if it were known that he was religious. Fr. Ron's compassionate attitude while listening to the Olympian, and his words of encouragement seemed to lift a weight off his shoulders, an ironic thought considering the athlete's specialty.

(Fr. Ron and the Olympic weight lifter kept in touch by letters and cards over the years so he knew that the Olympian and his wife had settled in Regensburg, Germany. In 1995 Fr. Ron, at Ettal Monastery, celebrated the 25th anniversary of his ordination and was very pleased to greet his Olympian friend there, who was by then a veterinarian with his little girls all grown up and married.)

The Christmas traditions that his high school kids had been involved with continued on as in the past with the only difference being that, if possible, they got even better and more meaningful for all involved. As a special treat at Christmas break time in 1976, Fr. Ron took a group of students with their faculty chaperones to Chamonix in the French Alps for a two-week skiing holiday. As usual, all had a wonderful time and there were very few problems. This time, Fr. Ron did not return to Montreal with the group in early 1977, since he had a few more days in his Christmas break and he wanted to visit some of his friends in Europe.

He traveled to Munich, Germany where he visited a wonderful married couple, Dr. Klaus Remberger and his wife, Monica whom he had met in 1967 when he had been an orderly at the hospital in Prien. They were enjoying reminiscing about the good old days when Fr. Ron had been called Herr Doktor. Suddenly Fr. Ron felt an unbelievably sharp stabbing pain in his lower back, practically bringing him to his knees. His face went white and he thought he might even pass out. His friends at first thought that he may have somehow hurt himself on the ski slopes, but they all knew that was not the cause of his pain. After several minutes, during which he felt fine and wondered what had just happened, the sharp pain returned. Dr. Remberger quickly recognized the symptoms of an attack of kidney stones. What a fortunate place to have such a problem, and how lucky to be in the home of a skilled surgeon who knew the problem and where to go to get it resolved. He was rushed to the hospital in Munich where the doctors found that indeed he did have several large stones in one of his kidneys. There was simply no way that they would pass on their own, so the next thing he knew he was being prepped for surgery. He was in a hospital known as das Krankenhaus der Barmherzigen Brüder (the Hospital of the Brothers of Mercy). It was an up-to-date facility, but was at that time housed in a wing of one of the largest and most beautiful Baroque palaces for many miles around; the Nymphenburg Palace, which had been the summer residence of the rulers of Bavaria from the 18th century. An unusual setting for a hospital, but an impressive place in which to be suffering.

Modern techniques available a few years later, such as ultrasound blasting of large stones while the patient lies on a water-filled cushion (Extracorporeal Shock Wave Lithotripsy), and other high-tech approaches just were not available in 1977. (It is of interest to note that the ESWL technique mentioned above was developed in the early 1980s in Germany.) The surgery that took place in early January was very involved and the recovery period kept him in the hospital for two weeks. As part of the German-based recuperation, his doctors had him drink copious quantities of beer to help flush out remaining bits of gravel. His roommate asked for, but didn't get similar recovery liquids. This young man was undergoing testing via surgery to accurately determine whether he was fertile, since he wanted desperately to be able to father children with his wife, but such was not to be. Fr. Ron was in the room the afternoon when the fellow's doctor came in and informed him that he could not sire any children and that there was nothing medically that could be done to alter that fact. After the doctors left the room, the two patients shared the irony of their different situations. Here were two healthy young men, one who wanted to have his own children but could not, and the other, a priest who maintained a life of celibacy and chose to be a "Father" to many, but never to have any children of his own. The future of Fr. Ron's hospital roommate was interesting, but hauntingly tragic as well. He became the Defense Minister for West Germany and was well liked by many. In some strange episode, he jumped out of an airplane in a skydiving exercise. His chute failed to open and he was killed. There was speculation that this might not have been accidental, but rather a suicide - - or perhaps murder.

The Rembergers, with whom he had only spent a short time, but who were responsible for getting him into the hospital, and who had visited him there, were now travelling so returning to their home for a bit more rest and recuperation was out of the question. Fr. Ron, never without his trusty (and large) address book checked to see what other friends of his might be nearby. The first person in Munich that he called was Tom McCord, from his days in West Berlin. He was Colonel McCord back then and was now retired. Col. McCord had gone on to become the Chief of the Military Liaison Mission to the Soviet Forces in East Germany. Tom and his wife, Danielle, were very happy to be able to provide a little home cookin' and quickly drove to the beautifully unusual hospital to bring Fr. Ron to their home. When they saw the palace where he had been for the past two weeks, they jokingly pointed out that their home was not quite as elegant, but he would just have to do the best he could with what they had.

Ron had met Col. McCord's first wife, Marion, while he was doing his Army Counter-Intelligence work where, regardless of strict chain-of-command, he thought of the Colonel as his boss. He had been saddened to get the news a few years ago of Marion's death in the Potsdam Mission House when Col. McCord was in his advanced rank. He had recently remarried and his second wife, Danielle, was a charming lady of French-Canadian background. She was Catholic, while Tom was not. The three of them shared a lot of stories about faith, and what had happened in their lives over the years, with Tom feeling that it was more than an accident that they should be together now. He expressed the thought that he always knew that 1st Lieutenant Ron Lawson would one day be very involved in helping to do God's work. And would be very good at it too.

The McCords were great hosts to Fr. Ron and saw to it that he was comfortable in their spare room, that he had plenty of nourishing food to eat and that he recuperate fully before being allowed anywhere near a Canada-bound air-craft. Once they were sure he was up to it, they travelled to their condo in, of all places, Oberammergau. They were excited to show off this special place they had where they enjoyed the views, the people, the weather and most of all, the uniqueness of the place itself. Being there again, brought back a flood of warm memories for their houseguest. They surprised him by bringing him to Unterwössen, where he stayed for several days with his good friends the Schweinöster family at their Gasthaus pension. He had last seen them about six and a half years ago during his post-ordination travels with his brother, Sidney. It seemed as though no time had passed, except that the family's youngest child was now 15 while Fr. Ron's lumberjack friend, Tony, was now 30. He was still at his trade as a Holzknecht and had many stories to tell. Everyone at the Gasthaus, except the offspring who had married and moved away, made a point of spending time with their great friend, now a priest.

He spent several days enjoying all of this and feeling nearly fully recuperated and a bit guilty about not being in his office in Quebec. But before he could feel too guilty, the McCords picked him up at the Gasthaus and brought him for a fun afternoon at the Hofbräuhaus in Munich on the way to the airport. They told him that although he most likely no longer needed to keep flushing out his kidneys with beer as he had been instructed to do in the hospital, there wasn't a better place in Germany to follow those doctor's orders. Feeling fully recovered and filled with warm memories of great friends and fabulous places, he boarded his commercial jet for the long ride back home to Montreal. Once he had arrived at Dorval International Airport, Fr. Emmet Johns was there to drive him back to his quarters at St. John Fisher Parish in Pointe Claire.

When Fr. Ron did finally show up back at St. Thomas High, he was 25 pounds lighter than when he left on his special trip. He was good-naturedly teased for days about the length of his Christmas holiday, since by then it was the middle of- February 1977. But he felt strong and healthy and was immersed in his many activities immediately with work at "his" high school being his focal point.

In May of that year nearly 5,000 French and English-speaking students from his School Commission organized a walkathon and raised the outstanding sum of $40,000 for charity, both at home and abroad, with most of it sent to Blessed Mother Theresa. People had been almost conditioned to think "trouble" or even "criminal" when discussing high school kids and the few problem students who unfortunately somehow seemed to get all the press. However, when they saw this marvelous apostolic activity, they soon realized where the hearts of the majority of the students were, especially when they realized that the walkathon was nearly totally the work of the students. Fr. Ron, not at all surprised at what his kids had accomplished, beamed for days any time the event was mentioned.

June of this year was the 25th reunion of the class of '52 from Montpelier High and Fr. Ron wouldn't have missed it for anything short of another massive kidney stone. He had a great time there and got a real kick out of the fact that all his classmates felt 17 years of age too, even if they didn't really look it. He spent some quality time with his folks and attended a few weddings and baptisms of some of his cousins. While he still had a few days before he needed to return to Montreal, Fr. Ron and his younger brother, Sidney, Jr., were off for a brief visit with friends in England and Scotland. They made a point of spending time with his sailing buddies, Robin Plummer and Stephen Finch who regaled Sidney with hilarious anecdotes of the time the three of them had spent in their 30-meter sailboat in the waters around Denmark. Sidney could hardly believe what he was being told, but his brother simply smiled and nodded in agreement. They spent a few days at the home of the Hills, Bill and Diana. Ron had met Bill during their assignment in West Berlin. At that time, Bill had been with the Durham Light infantry; now they shared several adventures, promising to keep in touch. It was only natural that once Fr. Ron had learned that the Hills were living in England that he would visit them whenever possible. Keeping in touch with good friends continued to be a high priority for Fr. Ron who took great pleasure in reliving past times.

At the beginning of September, The Archbishop of Montreal asked Fr. Ron, Fr. Joe Sullivan and Fr. Gerry Westphal to form a team ministry in the parish church of the Transfiguration of Our Lord in the suburb of Cartierville. Each priest was to retain his job as chaplain of their respective high schools; Fr. Ron at St. Thomas, of course, Fr. Joe at Pierrefonds Comprehensive H.S. in Pierrefonds, and Fr. Gerry at St. Pius X high School in Montreal North. Fr. Joe was to continue to serve as Pastor of the parish in Cartierville. All three priests had a great time getting to know and work with a wonderful staff. Their rectory, attached to an 11 year-old church was quite modern and was large enough to house seven guests. This assignment was not the reincarnation of Fr. Ron's attempt to create "community", but was a splendid task nonetheless.

In the first part of 1979 he moved into a men's residence on the MacDonald College campus in Ste-Anne-de-Bellevue as house director and counselor. There he worked with a terrific group of young men, many of whom were engaged in desperate struggles and searches for meaning in their lives. He could often be found conducting rap sessions with these men and finding that the discussions (and arguments) would continue until 3 AM. These sessions proved to be very beneficial, with many of his "students" figuring out for themselves, or so it seemed to them, that copping out of life's responsibilities through alcohol, sex and drugs was not the answer.

The summer of 1979 was a very active one for Fr. Ron without a trip to Europe. He spent several days in Toronto giving a workshop to chaplains-designate of the Toronto Archdiocese on the nature and function of a school chaplain. He was surprised that he was actually able to condense all that such a position involved into the time he had to present it.

Bishop Crowley came to St. Thomas High School again in late May to confirm a group of students in the faith. All of the students really loved it whenever he showed up since he was so inspirational, down-to-earth, hard working, dynamic and personable. What a role model. And how fortunate it was that he was the one who had been so involved in Fr. Ron's development.

In June of 1979, he got a letter, postmarked Prien, Bavaria, the location where he had worked as an orderly in what seemed a lifetime ago. It was from one of the sisters who he had worked with while he was there, Sister Marleni. He hoped that it contained some good news, but had a premonition of just the opposite. Written in German, the short letter informed him that his dear young friend Lorenz (Lenzi) Baumgartner had recently been killed in an automobile accident. He had been a passenger in an auto driven by one of his many friends who had always taken such good care of him. All the others that were in the car, including the driver, were not badly injured. Immediately upon hearing the tragic news, Fr. Ron prayed for Lenzi's soul and celebrated a special requiem Mass for him. He recalled his first encounter in 1967 with the brave, then seven year-old in the district hospital at Prien, Bavaria outside of Unterwössen. It seemed so unfair that Lenzi, now almost 19 and who had overcome so much as he developed through his teens, always relying upon others for his daily needs, but usually sharing his inner light and his easy smile, was suddenly gone. Fr. Ron picked up the beautiful wooden dish that Lenzi had presented him at his special "first Mass" in Unterwössen nine years ago. He could almost see the determined youth holding a pen between his toes as he signed the platter for his special friend whom he always called "Onkel Roni".

If this chaplain ever had any thoughts of slowing down and relaxing for a bit, there always seemed to be another challenge for him to rise to. For example, he was given an expanded job role within the Baldwin-Cartier School Board. He became Coordinator of Pastoral Animation (activities) for 14 elementary and high schools. He felt that this position was an extraordinary challenge, but one that he undertook with seemingly no effort, even if it did keep him wandering like a nomad from school to school.

1980 was a special year for Fr. Ron, since he celebrated Mass in the Cathedral of Mary, Queen of the World in downtown Montreal, for the 10th anniversary of his ordination as a priest. His mother and father traveled up from Vermont for this special occasion and were very proud not only of their son and what he had accomplished, but of the reverence in which he was held by many of the locals. The most influential member of the clergy in all that had transpired, Bishop Crowley, was there, beaming with satisfaction at how his protégé had developed. A large number of people from the Middlebury parish of St. Mary's where he had started his ministry had made the trip to be there, all smiling and wishing him many more years of active work in the service of God. His local ally, Fr. Gerry Westphal, brought along his youth choir, that he had named *Antioch*, from the Transfiguration Parish to perform music that they had composed themselves especially for this event. This group of youngsters was an especially talented ensemble who played a variety of instruments. That music, so beautifully performed, touched the very being of the young priest. The fact that it was composed especially for him was nearly unbelievable. The group, *Antioch*, presented Fr. Ron with a recording of the original music they had just performed, as a 10th anniversary gift. He has kept it with him ever since. After the Mass, a well-attended reception was held at the Royal St. Lawrence Yacht Club in Dorval. Fr. Ron had been an honorary member there since first arriving as high school chaplain in 1972. This was another event that would remain in his memory always.

In July, after he completed his duties at a summer camp that he organized for underprivileged children from his school district, he was off to Oberammergau to see the Passion Play. Once again he found the performance to be very moving, perhaps even more so than when he had enjoyed it the previous two times. He also visited West Berlin, where he had decided to become a priest 20 years previously. He had a wonderful time seeing many of his friends from the times when he walked those streets under an assumed name with his revolver under his jacket. Life had really changed for him and he couldn't be happier.

A change of pace from his many priestly duties came about in June of 1981 in the form of celebrating the 25th reunion of his Middlebury College class of '56. Although the joyous event lasted a whole weekend, it went by much too fast. There was a very good turnout of classmates with participants discovering old friends and making new ones. All the wonderful memories of being between seventeen and twenty-one years of age came flooding back making it easy to realize that they were all pretty much the same persons, even if life experiences in the intervening 25 years had been drastically different from what they had seen in their college days.

In August of 1981 he and another priest colleague, Father Cajetan, were promoted to a senior position in the field of religious education in Quebec. This job was known as *Christian Education Counselor*, and was to be held jointly. In that capacity they were responsible for all aspects of Catholic religious instruction and pastoral activities for 8,000 students in ten elementary schools and three high schools. Fr. Ron was named to a committee in the Ministry of Education for Quebec to represent English-speaking Catholics. His principle job was to develop and document programs in religious education. It was a challenging and heavy responsibility that he, of course, handled with what appeared to be relative ease. The committee members didn't know how hard he had to work to make it look easy.

1981 was memorable for Fr. Ron in another very meaningful way. He and his brothers and his sister-in-law, Corinne, organized a spectacular 50th wedding anniversary for his parents to take place on November 1st.

50th Anniversary

They had reserved a banquet hall at the Brown Derby restaurant in Montpelier where his folks were astounded to greet over 260 relatives and friends at a sumptuous sit-down dinner, complete with a local musician softly playing his acoustic guitar in the background. They all felt that it was a great tribute to their wonderful, supportive parents who enjoyed the event enormously and didn't want it to end.

Fr. Ron realized that without the significant attention to detail provided by Corinne and to a lesser extent, his two brothers, the party may not have been so nearly perfect. His role in planning and providing guest lists, mailing invitations, etc. had to be limited due to the fact that he was far off in Montreal, deeply into his many jobs and simply could not be a "go-to" guy for this special event. He was, however, more than pleased to be in a position to provide a special Papal blessing to the happy couple. As a memento of the day and constant reminder of the Pope's blessing, he presented his folks with a beautiful, certificate, with hand-painted calligraphy on parchment with the Papal seal and signature. The senior Lawsons could not have been more proud of their son, the Catholic priest.

As his years at St. Thomas High School flew by, Fr. Ron continued to be extremely happy with his assignment, knowing that not only was he growing in faith and love, but he was making positive inputs into many people's lives. The Christmas activities continued every year and only got better and more fun with each one. The fact that they did take place was a sort of clock by which he counted the years and rejoiced in their positive effects. He continued to travel to Europe as often as he could during his summers off, meeting up with many people who had been so influential in his life and whom he was bound and determined never to forget. At the top of this European list was Fr. Niegel, or "Franzi", who seemed to never change. Of course, he was constantly in touch with Mother Trapp in Stowe, Vermont who had been his spiritual mentor for so long and would always be special to him. He also marked the passage of time by always writing Christmas letters to his many friends and relatives. He had a truly international mailing list for these summary missives.

High School Chaplain, Fr. Ron

A paragraph from his 1982 Christmas letter captured just how his assignment in Montreal affected him and others. He wrote, in part:

The John F. Kennedy Memorial School in Beaconsfield, Québec, is one of the schools in which I am responsible for the religious education of the children. It has become both a place of solace and a barometer of what has been happening to me all year: solace, because it is a school into which I escape periodically for nourishment and warmth, not as a priest, but just as a person; a barometer, because it is a school for retarded teenagers with whom I have been working for the past four years – young people who are very open about their feelings and who show complete acceptance of me. They call me anything but "Father", usually "Daddy" or "Church-man" or simply "Priest". When I was first faced with the challenge of dealing with the abstract-but-real concepts of God, Jesus, and the Holy Spirit with these youngsters, it didn't take me too long to realize that they can only understand by observing what I am in life. That was only possible when I looked at them as a symbol for the Kingdom of Heaven, and reflected on Jesus' words: that we have to become like little children to enter that kingdom. It involves stripping ourselves of the layers of superficiality with which we wrap ourselves in our approach to other adults. I can't imagine anyone closer to God than 15 year-old Robert who, born with Down syndrome, knows only how to love and accept others; he is a truly innocent child of God. I think we can only become children of God when we do what Robert does: be a friend of Jesus by loving and trusting others with no strings attached.

For several winters, off and on, Fr. Ron had been visiting his former military friends who had by then retired and migrated to the Miami area. (His many and frequent travels were not simply confined to Europe.) In February of 1984 he was at the home of Al Ferris in the city of Miami. Back when Ron was in Hawkins Barracks in Oberammergau in 1959-60, Al had been US Army Captain Alfred Ferris and was in his Polish class. In 1960, at the request of Fr. Pius, Captain Ferris (seventeen years Ron's senior) had accompanied Ron to Munich where he was the sponsor for Ron's confirmation. Originally from New York City, once he had retired he and his wife had settled in Florida enjoying the climate and endless rounds of golf as a civilian. They hadn't been there very long before his dear wife, Kay, had died suddenly of a heart attack while on a beautiful golf course. Several years later, he married a widow and summoned Fr. Ron to fly to Miami to conduct the wedding that was held in the chapel at Homestead Air Force Base. Fr. Ron has stayed in close touch with this good friend who was always such a great guy and who has a wonderful sense of humor.

At this visit at his pal's home, a large number of his military friends were present. Several of them were people he had worked with in West Berlin, while others were from his earlier days in Fort McNair and surrounds. As the evening wore on with cocktails being enjoyed along with the camaraderie, the discussion turned to the serious need for more Army chaplains. Someone made the observation that anyone who had experience as a high school chaplain would be a perfect fit for that critically understaffed position. The group gathered around Fr. Ron and like a school of fish circling some tempting bait, began to work on him, suggesting in progressively more thoughtful statements that he really should rejoin the Army and "move up" from high school.

Fr. Ron tried his best to make them all understand that his career in Montreal was at its peak and that he was very much enjoying his many duties and responsibilities. He had formed a close and unique bond with many people in Quebec and really couldn't imagine being anywhere else. Besides, he knew in his heart that the kids at his high school, including the ones who had graduated, really loved him.

As if to prove the point that Fr. Ron would make an ideal Army chaplain, one of the more outgoing personalities in the gathered bunch picked up the phone and soon had made contact with the Major General in the Pentagon who was the Army's current chief of Chaplains. Fr. Ron could clearly hear not only his name being repeated for clarity, but also quite an impressive resume of his life's work, all the way from Counter Intelligence through the present. He was at first convinced that there was really no one on the other end of the phone and that his friend was simply trying to put one over on him. Suddenly, the telephone was thrust into his hand with the instruction "Here, he wants to talk directly to you." Fr. Ron's smile that said, OK I'll play along, suddenly changed to an embarrassed look of disbelief as he realized that he was indeed speaking with the Chief of Chaplains for the US Army. He verified to the high-ranking officer that he had done the things his buddy had described and was soon given an unexpected invitation. He was told that if he would come right on over to the Pentagon at his earliest convenience, and oh, by the way, with all his expenses paid by the Army, there were a few people who would love to show him why rejoining the Army as a chaplain would be the best move he could make.

After thanking the Chief for the generous offer and telling him he needed to think about it for a few days, but would call him back, he hung up the phone and smiled at his pals who were holding their glasses high in a toast to the future Army Chaplain. He quickly reminded the gang that he would be 50 on his next birthday in ten months, and that 50 was the cut-off age for joining the Army, and what in the world was he thinking about, since he was not as physically fit as he should be, and he was happy just where he was, and continued to ramble on with gradually diminishing objections to the idea.

In parallel with all the verbalizing that was going on, somewhere deep in his heart he was realizing how many times in his life the notion of being an Army chaplain had seemed attractive to him. Father Pius Fisher with whom he had had such a good relationship at Hawkins Barracks in Oberammergau and the monastery at Ettal Abbey, Fr. Rupert Mayer, in whose "cell" Ron had slept for a few days, also at that Abbey, and none other than his principal supporter, Bishop Joyce, had all been Army chaplains at one time. Also, he remembered the not-so-subtle remarks from the chaplains in West Berlin as he was preparing to ship out to become a civilian and to enter the seminary, along the lines of how they had hoped that he just might be back someday to join them. He also knew that he wasn't getting any younger and that he was approaching the cut-off age for joining or rejoining the military. All of these thoughts and ideas swam around in his head for the next several weeks as he continued his duties.

When he had some time off from St. Thomas High the following spring, he did indeed visit the chaplains' offices in the Pentagon. He had a wonderful series of interviews, with each person seeming to impress him even more than the previous one until he agreed to make a serious commitment with the provision that he get written permission from the Archbishop of Montreal. By the time he had returned to

Canada, he was convinced that being a chaplain in the Army was something he was meant to be. He visited Archbishop Paul Grégoire, Archbishop of Montreal (who was to be elevated to Cardinal in four years) to explore the possibility. At first reluctant to lose such a well-loved member of the Montreal priesthood, the Archbishop seemed intuitively to understand that being an Army chaplain would be the correct next move for Fr. Ron for a number of reasons. After a relatively short period of discussion, the Archbishop said. "Why not join the Canadian forces?" Fr. Ron replied with what he thought was obvious; that he couldn't do that since he was an American citizen. The Cardinal sheepishly replied that, by golly, he had forgotten that fact since for the last 12 years, Fr. Ron had seemed like he had been born in Montreal. He granted, in writing as stipulated, his permission for him to leave his jurisdiction and rejoin the US Army, giving Fr. Ron his personal blessing and reminding him that he would be kept in his prayers.

Fr. Ron relayed the permission to the appropriate offices in Washington and was told that he should plan to return to active duty in the Army as a chaplain beginning in June 1984.

With that, his world seemed to turn upside down. All his associates thought he was crazy and had temporarily lost his mind. He was about to turn 50, for heaven's sake, and it was no secret that he was more than a little out of shape. But now that he had come to his decision, it seemed very right to him and he worked hard at getting himself ready for this new chapter in his life. The first thing he did was to quit smoking cigarettes: "cold turkey". He had been a smoker for nearly 30 years, since his college days. Then he hired a personal trainer and immediately got down to the business of working out with dedication. He was soon running two miles (three km) every day and enjoying it, feeling younger and more energetic each day.

When June 1984 rolled around he was ready, even if all those around him still could not believe that they would soon be seeing the last of him as their chaplain. That thought still did weigh heavily on his mind but he consoled himself with the knowledge that many other priests and faculty members were dedicated to the school and would surely carry on his traditionally favorite activities.

A number of farewell parties were organized in his honor. The major one was held at the Royal St. Lawrence Yacht Club in Dorval, with the faculties of several schools and many members of the school board in attendance. He knew that he could never manage to personally say farewell (not goodbye) to all the school kids he had come to know, so he did his best to convey his last message to them in a school publication. Many of those students kept that flyer for years. He was then ready to rejoin the Army.

CHAPTER 20

YOU'RE IN THE ARMY NOW! (AGAIN)
1984 - 1986

The concept of having chaplains serve armed forces all over the globe dates back to the first century. Thousands of men of all faiths have performed that religious duty, often heroically. The US Army Chaplaincy has been in place ever since George Washington, desperately battling the British, set it up in 1775. He wanted his chaplains to be, first and foremost, religious leaders. He knew that they should also provide counseling, visit the wounded, bringing them whatever spiritual nourishment was needed; helping in whatever way their particular faith decreed and also tend to the dead. He expanded their role to include writing letters home for any of the troops who lacked the ability to do so on their own. It would be a significant additional advantage if their discussions of a patriotic nature with the soldiers could help to keep the young, frightened men from deserting.

Since then, chaplains of all faiths have been providing all this and more, such as counseling on what may seem to be mundane things such as staying sober, not cheating at cards and especially not gambling away their meager pay. They provide counseling duties for couples about to be married, religious education and funeral duties. They are also called upon to dialog with persons who may at one time in the past, have professed a particular faith, but for a variety of reason, have lost it and have either become simply "not religious" or in some cases agnostic or atheistic. Cases like that presented real challenges and once in a while, a chaplain would return to his quarters feeling as though he had failed that major test, but knew that he would continue to do his best for his flock. Defined as noncombatants, they rely upon their armed chaplain assistants for protection when they are in active battle areas.

In the middle of June 1984 Father Ron Lawson reported to the Army's Chaplain School at Fort Monmouth, New Jersey and, now a Captain was soon deeply into basic training, feeling very pleased that he had worked out so hard to get in shape so that he could keep up with the youngsters all around him. In spite of his prior conditioning, he felt the tiring effects of the drills: after all, he was almost 50. He essentially went through a basic training course very similar to what he had experienced at Fort Holabird, Maryland in 1957 when he was a kid. He did endure combat maneuvers, in spite of his status as a noncombatant since he had to be aware of tactics, available weaponry and hand-to-hand combat - - just in case. He enjoyed learning to read field maps again and was happy to know that what he had learned over a quarter of a century ago still applied. Part of this training had him become acquainted with a variety of vehicles. He enjoyed driving rapidly and roughly around in a Jeep and was proud to demonstrate a high level of skill as a truck driver. He wondered if he might be ordered to drive visiting dignitaries around, the way Private Elvis Presley did in 1959 while he served with the Army in Germany.

This school included a complete orientation for personnel of many faiths and religious beliefs who made up the different denominations represented in the Chaplain Corps. These would be the people with whom he would be working closely, especially the chaplain assistants who would be setting up services and providing security for him. He soon learned that chaplain assistants were not matched to a particular chaplain by denomination. Most of his assistants were of one Protestant denomination or another, but all were well trained in how to set up for a service of any particular faith: Protestant, Catholic, Jewish or other. Included in this basic training for them were the specifics of how money collected in chapels is handled, the details of creating a budget and how to create an inventory of chapel furnishings.

In September 1984 Chaplain Lawson was allowed to take a few days leave so that he could travel to Montreal to be there for the visit of Pope John Paul II to the Archdiocese. It was September 9 when the Holy Father kissed the tarmac in Quebec City to kick off the first ever Papal visit to Canada, one of the biggest events in Canadian history. Over 7,000 letters from the young people of Quebec had been mailed to him in Rome in anticipation of his visit. A near-capacity crowd of 55,000 young people, many of them in their teens, assembled in Montreal's Olympic Stadium where he spoke in response to many of those letters with uplifting words that were well received. The Pope, with his charisma and popularity, was able to bridge the gap between those who had mixed feelings regarding his favorite themes, and those who were his loyal followers. Several thousand clergy, including Fr. Ron, were present at St. Joseph's Oratory on the northern slope of Mount Royal when the Pope visited this largest of all the churches in Canada. It was a never-to-be-forgotten highlight for Fr. Ron and his religious comrades.

The new Army Chaplain hurried back to Fort Monmouth to join up with a gathering of newly commissioned Catholic chaplains who were on their way to attend a meeting to be held at a retreat center in Larchmont, New York. There, about 20 of these special troops spent about a week together, getting to know one another and discussing a variety of issues of concern to be reviewed with their superior officers when they returned to Fort Monmouth. While in New York, Chaplain Lawson and several others visited the impressive St. Patrick's Cathedral. While the grandeur of the place was surely a memorable sight, what he will no doubt remember for years was getting stuck for half an hour in the rectory elevator with Archbishop John Joseph O'Connor, soon to become Cardinal. The archbishop had the rank of Rear Admiral and was the former Navy Chief of Chaplains. Being stuck like that in a confined space can be upsetting once all conversation is used up, but is even more alarming once most of the oxygen in the air is consumed. When they were finally freed from their imprisonment in the tiny cell, they enjoyed deep breaths of fresh air and then could laugh about their close encounter.

In late September, Chaplain Lawson was sent to Fort Meade in Maryland, just to the south of Baltimore and north of Washington, DC. He was well acquainted with Fort Meade from his time at Fort Holabird back in the late fifties, so he was revisiting old turf and enjoying the memories brought back by seeing familiar areas and buildings. He reported to the HQ Command Battalion, for which he became the Chaplain for the next two years. The commanding officer there was Lt. Col. Bill Parker, with whom this new chaplain soon became fast friends. Later, they ended up in West Berlin together.

After reporting to his immediate superior, Chaplain (Lieutenant Colonel) Dan Kennedy, OMI (Missionary Oblates of Mary Immaculate) who was a native of Boston, Fr. Ron was given his new assignment. He was to spearhead Catholic activities at the Main Post Chapel, taking up duties there and working with a young Southern Baptist Chaplain by the name of Michael Poole. Chaplain Lawson soon discovered that Chaplain Poole was quite a character with a quick wit and a ready smile, always up for some innocent mischief. The two of them got along famously for the next couple of years as they worked together.

Chaplains Lawson and Poole

He often reflected on what may have seemed to some to be his abrupt change in his eventful life, pondering the "why?" of it all. He concluded that the challenge of being a modern 50 year-old priest called for new horizons, new responsibilities, new quests. Since he had changed residences so often in Montreal, suddenly being in yet another new place did not seem strange at all. He soon found that his work in the Army was really not very different from what he had been doing with the teenagers as a high school chaplain, although in this case, a great many of his flock are married. He enjoyed the Army life, finding the work challenging and rewarding. But best of all, he loved the people. His work assignment included a Catholic "parish" of 4000 families on the post. Sometimes he would be "in the field" with the troops. Other times he would be flown around the area in a helicopter to visit units, interacting with the commanders to help spread the word of what he was there to do.

It became immediately apparent that the Main Post Chapel, which provides a wide range of services for Protestants, Catholics, Jews and Muslims was considered a very popular place to get married. This may have been true principally because of its historic background and beautiful interior, and perhaps to a lesser extent because there is no charge for the use of the facility. A donation to the Consolidated Chaplain Fund that was used for various chapel programs was, however, encouraged. There were lots of rules that had to be followed in order for service personnel to be married there. Not the least of these conditions was that the engaged couple must attend a special two or three-day workshop known as the Prevention and Relationship Enhancement Program (PREP) designed to enhance communication and provide techniques to resolve conflicts. The Army has seen ample evidence that couples that attend PREP with open minds do indeed have better, stronger marriages. Other mandates included ensuring that receptions must be held elsewhere, never in the chapel and a strict prohibition against the tossing into the air of any type of confetti: no flower petals, birdseed, rice or anything else that would leave a mess. That rule led to the fact that the wedding couple was responsible to see to it that the chapel was cleaned up and left in at least as good a condition as before their ceremony. In the years that Fr. Ron was an Army Chaplain at Fort Meade, he estimates that he conducted just under a couple of hundred weddings in this Main Post Chapel. He has no data that show what percent are still married, but his guess would be that it is a respectably high fraction.

At Main Post Chapel, 1985

Other than weddings, the chaplain staff handled a lot of counseling sessions with soldiers and their families, Sunday School for both Protestant and Catholic children, and Sunday Masses and services. They arranged it so that in the chapel on Sunday mornings there would be one hour for a Catholic Mass followed by one hour for a Protestant service. On Sunday afternoons there would be a Baptist service that lasted a couple of hours. Since it fell to the chaplain assistants to change the chapel décor as well as make many changes in the set up and arrangement of religious items, an hour and a half was allotted between services so that the hard-working assistants could do their jobs.

Fr. Ron was chaplain to the Headquarters Command Battalion and the US Army Intelligence Corps Command, known as the CONUS MI Group. As such, he was very busy interacting with the soldiers of various faiths who were assigned to these units. Having been an officer in Army Counter Intelligence, he could relate on a personal level with them. He was kept busy providing counseling on a wide variety of subjects. He had seen and heard pretty much the same types of issues in his high school chaplaincy as well as in his previous positions. Just as he was about to think to himself that there was nothing new under the sun, one of the enlisted men or an officer would surprise him with a brand new issue. He always treated such problems with the utmost care and respect, consulting whatever additional resources he could find, but never leaving an issue unresolved.

Early in his chaplaincy at the Main Post Chapel, as he was getting ready to conduct a Mass, he found the tabernacle still locked. The tabernacle was one of the many items that the chaplain assistants moved as they would change the set-up for a different service. It was always set aside in a secure place and locked as a matter of course and then brought to the altar along with all the other required items. This time evidently it had simply failed to have been unlocked. Ever resourceful, with no chaplain assistants anywhere in sight, Chaplain Lawson dashed across the street to the Intelligence Command Post and asked if there was a "lock-picker" assigned there for duty. Sure enough, there was. In a matter of minutes, the tabernacle lock was opened, while Chaplain Lawson's helper pointed out that he would prefer to be known as a locksmith rather than a lock-picker. The locksmith, who provided the chaplain with a spare key while he was at it, was Jack Baldwin who at that time was both a retired Marine Corps CIC (Counterintelligence Corps) sergeant and a retired Army Chief Warrant Officer. The two men became great buddies. Over the years, Chaplain Lawson often visited the Baldwin family, Jack and his wife, Peg, who was a schoolteacher on base. They have been stalwart Catholics for years.

In March 1985 he used a few days leave to travel to Houston, Texas to visit a close buddy of his from back in his "spook" days in the early 60s, Bill Tyler, the former aide-de-camp of Major General Polk. He was now a civilian, retiring from the Army with the rank of colonel, doing very well and living in a very nicely appointed home with his wife, the former Baroness Carina von Kuskoll. The two good friends have stayed in touch over the years. His place was clearly a step up from the BOQ at #1 Flanaganstrasse in Berlin. Bill was gladdened to see his great pal again and was very pleased to know that he was deeply into what he was cut out to be as a priest and an Army chaplain. At one point in their short reunion, he disappeared for a minute or two and returned with a late '60s issue of *Playboy* magazine. With a grin from ear to ear he showed the chaplain the photos of the young blonde that 1st lieutenant Ron Lawson had once had a date with in Berlin. They both agreed that they were not surprised by Ms. Elke Sommer's rise to fame in movies and in such a photo-laden magazine. Bill was quick to point out that he only bought that magazine because he enjoyed reading the great stories by Ray Bradbury and other thought-provoking articles.

Chaplain Lawson knew that his assignment would bring about several new and different situations, but he was not at all prepared for what occurred on one otherwise pleasant afternoon in the summer of 1985. On this particular day he was the duty chaplain, making him responsible to deal with any emergencies that involved the chaplain staff, such as the need for one of them to go to the base hospital for a critically ill patient, and any other serious issue where a chaplain would be needed. On this day, he was summoned to the office of the base Military Police and was told once he got there that there had been a murder-suicide involving one of the chaplains. There were about 20 chaplains at Fort Meade and Fr. Ron knew them all. He learned that the Lieutenant Colonel Chaplain (a married man) who was their executive officer had been for some time having an affair with the wife of an Air Force colonel. Investigation would later show that it was their usual routine to spend noon hours at her home while no one else was there. For whatever reason, on this particular day the woman's next-door neighbors heard the loud sound of a gunshot, quickly followed by one more shot. When the MPs arrived at her home, after being summoned by the concerned neighbors, they had to break down the front door to gain entry. The scene that greeted them was tough to witness, even for seasoned police. The chaplain was lying in a pool of blood with a bullet wound in his upper torso. The MPs searched for a pulse and found none. The woman of the house was also dead of what clearly was a self-inflicted bullet wound to her head. Motive for that tragic act was never established, but there was some speculation that the Lt. Col. may have indicated that he wanted to end the affair and go back to his wife and family. His paramour would have none of that. He left a family of five young children and a wife suffering from cancer. The woman involved left her husband and several teenage children. Not only was this event tragically sad, it caused nearly all on the base to discuss it, with many putting their own spin on it and all feeling upset for the ones left behind. It was quite an awakening for Fr. Ron, both as a priest and chaplain. He had never encountered anything like that and prayed for the wisdom and foresight to be able to intervene should he ever be faced with knowing about an illicit affair such as what had been going on there. Both victims were buried from the Main Post Chapel. Shortly after the Lutheran bishop had conducted the funeral, the chaplain staff was summoned to a secret meeting called by the Chief of Chaplains on base, Chaplain (Colonel) Al Forrest. He was a wonderful person and a great friend to Chaplain Lawson. In the meeting, Chaplain Forrest simply stated that if anyone were "playing house" with someone else illegally, he must cease and desist. That was all that was said, but the message was plain enough.

Fr. Kennedy (his immediate superior, Chaplain Lt. Col. Dan Kennedy) and Fr. Ron organized a parish council, whose first president was the Brigadier General (later Major

General) in charge of the office of the Deputy Commander of First US Army at Fort Meade. This was General Patrick Brady, who was a holder of the Medal of Honor for action in the Vietnam War. This parish council was very active, dealing with issues that pertained mainly to the religious education of the children of Fort Meade. Fr. Ron was surprised to discover that he and General Brady had both served as lieutenants in West Berlin in the 1960 time frame, although they had never met there.

In June and July 1985 Chaplain Lawson took a military "hop" out of Dover, Delaware from the Air Force base there, to Europe. He visited Holland, the UK and West Germany. He enjoyed the experience and was delighted to realize that the airfare cost him only $20. Ah, the perks of being in the Army! He spent two carefree weeks renewing acquaintances with many of his pals feeling rejuvenated in the process. Among that group were Stephen Finch and Robin Plummer and their lovely wives. The guys had a great time once again recalling their carefree sail around Denmark for most of the month of July 1960.

When Chaplain Lawson got to Germany, he wasted no time in getting to the monastery at Ettal where he had become a Catholic in 1960. But this visit was of a solemn nature since this time, his main reason for being there was to pray at the grave of Fr. Pius Fischer, who had baptized him and had meant so much to him. He had died a couple of years previously in his late eighties, a remarkable priest, well loved by generations of Army personnel who had been stationed at Oberammergau, and especially by Fr. Ron.

Columbus Day weekend in 1985 found Chaplain Lawson in Montreal as an invited guest at a function celebrating the 20th anniversary of the founding of St. Thomas High School. Although he was still a seminarian when the school saw its first pupils, he had come to feel very close to the institution and especially the students and faculty he had worked, laughed and prayed with during his assignment there. He was very pleased to be invited to this event. Seeing familiar faces from the facility he had left just a year ago, good friends and colleagues, as well as some students, was heart-warming indeed.

Toward the end of Fr. Ron's assignment at Fort Meade, with its large Catholic population, Fr. Dan Kennedy was reassigned to Fort Myer, Virginia as Post Chaplain and was promoted to the rank of Colonel. Fr. Ron then became responsible for all Catholic activities at Fort Meade, with its three chapels (Main Post Chapel, Cavalry Chapel and Argonne Hills Chapel) and the services conducted in them. He did not lack for things to occupy his time.

In the spring of 1986 he was informed that he would be reassigned to the Stuttgart area in Germany and would be departing for that posting in June '86. Did the Army know how much he loved Germany or was this just a random chance to be back in Deutschland? Of course the fact that he was a German linguist may have had something to do with it. Whatever the reason, he looked forward to his next post.

CHAPTER 21

US ARMY - STUTTGART
1986 - 1987

It was a delightful June afternoon in 1986 when Chaplain Lawson arrived at his new assignment at Stuttgart-Pattonville. This very large American housing project, north of the city of Stuttgart, was named after the famous US general George S. Patton. Several thousand soldiers of various branches of the US military and their families lived there in comfortable, neat housing along the easily navigated roads. The central thoroughfare was named John F. Kennedy Allee, while all the other streets were named after various US states. Stuttgart American High School as well as several American elementary schools looked after the educational needs of the youngsters. Physical education for them was not forgotten. A full size athletic field for football was surrounded by a paved track. A baseball field abutted one end of the track, while a couple of tennis courts were located a few streets away. All the school kids were issued metal dog tags with their name, branch of service of their parent(s), and DOD ID number stamped into them. Usually their religious affiliation was also stamped into these dog tags as well.

Chaplain Lawson found the post chapel to be very attractive with its artfully done stained glass windows and a beautiful Blessed Sacrament chapel within for the Catholic population. He celebrated Mass there daily and although the size of the congregation was not impressive at first, once word got around that a new priest chaplain was in town, attendance picked up, especially on Sundays.

Military housing was scarce when he first arrived, so he elected to live locally in German housing and moved into quarters in the small village of Freudental, about 13 miles (22 km) northwest. Fortunately, the two-door 1980 Chevrolet Impala that Chaplain Lawson had purchased in Quebec, had been shipped by the Army from New Jersey to Europe and when it finally arrived, he was able to pick it up in Stuttgart. It made his commute from Freudental to the chapel at Pattonville and back each day a pleasant excursion. Most of his busy days were spent at that chapel unless there were meetings with other chaplains of various faiths at other chapels. And there were indeed a lot of meetings. Among other task forces, he served on the committee that administered the chaplains' funds where he was heavily involved in creating a budget and approving payments and other extra-curricular activities.

The village of Freudental had been settled over 200 years ago by Jewish merchants who served the small castle there belonging to the Wittemberg royal family. At that time, in the 1700s, the castle was the residence of one of the mistresses of the King of Wittemberg. During World War II, most of the Jews in the village of Freudental were moved out to concentration camps by the Nazis. The majority of them did not survive the war, but a few were able to make their way to Israel. After the war was over, the town was settled by Germans who had been forcibly evacuated from the German territories that had been given to Poland in what used to be called West Prussia. So nearly everyone in this village with a population of about 2000, was a refugee. It turned out that Chaplain Lawson was the only American there. It was very fortunate that he was fluent in German, but then again, the Army knew that and it was one of the major factors in assigning him to this post.

The house in which his first floor apartment was located was in the middle of vineyards that stretched out in all directions, nearly as far as the eye could see. There, white grapes from which the famous German Riesling wine was produced grew in abundance. The people of the village were wonderful to the American priest and chaplain. On several occasions, he would find at his doorstep a gift case of white wine that seemed to magically appear. The villagers would sheepishly avoid eye contact as they hustled by with a grin of satisfaction on their faces. He did his best to thank the gentleman, Herr Franz Schlegel, who owned the house where Chaplain Lawson now lived, hoping that he would relay his thanks to the persons responsible for leaving the wine. Not much of a drinker himself, although he enjoyed the occasional glass of good wine, he always shared his gifts of fine Riesling with his associates. Most evenings when he would return from his duties at Pattonville, he would find a cake or some other sweet dessert on his doorstep, left there for him by Frau Schlegel.

It comes as no surprise that Fr. Ron and Herr Schlegel became very good friends. The German showed his tenant all around the area and explained a lot about the history of the region. He led him on some fascinating trips to places ordinary tourists would probably never get to visit. One particularly memorable trip was to the Burg (Castle) Hohenzollern, the ancestral home of the German emperors. It is a stunning sight, located at the peak of Mount Hohenzollern, about 31 miles (50 km) south of Stuttgart. It was originally built in the first part of the 11th century, but was totally destroyed in a 10-month long battle with neighboring imperial cities some 400 years later. A larger, sturdier version of the castle was built on the original site a few years later, but over time it fell into disrepair and all that was left of it was the chapel. The entire castle was lovingly and beautifully rebuilt in the middle of the 19th century and was the stunning place that Fr. Ron and Herr Schlegel now visited. When they made their way into the chapel, they viewed the well-preserved caskets containing two Prussian kings that had been unearthed at the end of World War II. These were the caskets with the bodies of King Friedrich Wilhelm and his son, Frederick the Great (Friedrich Wilhelm II), both of the House of Hohenzollern. Their bodies had been removed at the end of the war and were hidden to prevent the Russians from hauling them off to the Soviet Union to make a mockery of them. Now they were back in their caskets in the castle again. Since Chaplain Lawson's visit to the castle, both bodies have been re-interred in Potsdam, near Berlin at Sanssouci Palace, the beautiful (some have called it the German rival of Versailles) former summer place of Frederick the Great.

On one of his exploratory drives through the village of Freudental with Herr Schlegel, he was shown a restored synagogue in the downtown area. During the infamous Crystal Night or Kristallnacht, that took place during two nights and days in November 1939, Nazi Storm Troopers aided by many teenage German youths, destroyed 1,400 synagogues and 7,000 businesses in various German towns. One hundred Jews were killed and 30,000 were arrested and sent to concentration camps. The synagogue that Chaplain Lawson was shown had, during Kristallnacht, had its fur-nishings set on fire, including the holy objects and most distressing, the scroll containing the Torah, the first five books of the Old Testament, considered the most holy of the sacred writings in Judaism. Most of that horrible deed was done by a local teen-aged German. As Fr. Ron discussed this nearly unbelievable desecration with his landlord, Herr Schlegel told him that he knew the person who had done it. He arranged for that person, now in his seventies, to come to the house for wine and conversation with them both. When he arrived, Fr. Ron met the admitted main culprit of the terrible deed, who told him that in his older years he was full of remorse for what he had done as a hotheaded Nazi youth. With the help of others, some of whom had also taken part in the destruction, he had worked steadily for years at rebuild-ing the synagogue, replacing all the damaged religious articles. His work was so successful that the old synagogue has for years been serving as a Jewish cultural center for visitors, most of whom come from Israel. On New Year's Eve 1987, Chaplain Lawson had as his house guests a young Army chaplain and his wife, both of whom were Jewish. He had arranged for a tour of the restored synagogue for his guests on New Year's Day. The private tour was conducted by none other than the very person who had been the instrument of both the destruction and the restoration of the beautiful holy building. With his voice filled with despair, he told his audience that he prayed daily for God to forgive him for his terrible deed. The visitors, moved with compassion for this troubled man, hugged him, thanking him for his wonderful restoration efforts and offering their own forgiveness for his youthful transgression.

In February 1987 Chaplain Lawson had arranged to take about 50 teenagers and a few adults from the military parish to one of his favorite places in the world, Oberammergau. This was to be a retreat coupled with skiing fun. The excited gang with their bags and skis traveled by train out of Stuttgart to Munich, thence to Murnau and finally, the jewel, Oberammergau. Everyone had a wonderful time at the retreat, staying at the NATO Lodge located on the side of the mountain known as the Laber. This majestic peak was very familiar to a somewhat younger Chaplain Lawson when he was known as 1st Lieutenant Ron Lawson and lived in Hawkins Barracks in O'Gau. The only problem with skiing on this trip was the snow - - or more accurately the complete lack of it. Sidney Lawson traveled from the US, bringing his skis with him to join his brother and to help out with the skiing and to do anything else that might prove to be of use. Sidney quipped that "... once a chaplain assistant, always a chaplain assistant." But, nobody skied. No snow. Anywhere. Sidney and his older brother even went so far as to travel all the way to Kitzbühel, but alas, there was only beautiful but dry scenery in all directions. This was a most unusual circumstance for an Alpine winter and had never been encountered even by natives of the area who were older than the chaplain. In spite of the unusual conditions, all had an enjoyable, if ski-less time at the retreat. When they returned to Pattonville, none of the folks who had remained at home were ever able to correctly guess the depth of the snow the gang encountered.

Shortly after the first of April 1987, Chaplain Lawson got word from his brother, Milan, about one of the most important people in his life. He was told that Maria von Trapp (Mother Trapp to him) had passed away of heart failure on March 28th at the age of 82. Three days prior to her death she had been rushed to a hospital in the nearby small village of Morrisville in Vermont where she had surgery in a vain attempt to save her life. She had outlived her husband, the Baron Georg Ludwig von Trapp, by 40 years and would now be buried next to him in the family cemetery on their Stowe, Vermont property. There was no way that the chaplain could get to Vermont in time for his spiritual mentor's funeral. He felt a deep, nearly overwhelming sorrow as he recalled how, from the time of his first casual meeting with her nearly 20 years ago to see if he could earn a few bucks on her property, she had been so influential in his life and the path he had chosen; a path she had been determined to keep clear and in focus. He wrote a short letter to her youngest son, Johannes, expressing his deepest sympathies, regretting that he could not be there with the rest of the family and pointing out that he would be saying a series of Masses in which she would be solemnly prayed for. Many people who had come into contact with Maria von Trapp, thought of her as strong-willed and domineering, but to the developing Fr. Ron, she had been his beacon, helping to light his way. He would never forget her.

In May 1987, Fr. Ron had some leave time available to him. He had heard that there would be a bus tour to Lourdes for military personnel and their families and that it would be leaving from the Mark Twain Village, a US Army installation in Heidelberg. He had longed to visit Lourdes for years. This was to be his chance. He had found that a pal of his from his days at St. John's Seminary, Fr. Jack Lincoln, a Boston native nearly his own age, was now a well-loved chaplain stationed there in Heidelberg, just an hour and a half away. He would love to make this trip with his buddy. After discussing the tour and making their plans by phone, Fr. Ron drove his Chevy to Fr. Jack's apartment. He left it parked behind the Mark Twain Chapel nearby. After a long evening of reminiscing about the good old days and even the "demonstration", Fr. Ron spent the night in his friend's spare room. Fr. Jack was extremely pleased that his former seminary cohort had managed to stay the course and had indeed become a well-loved priest. In the morning, they were soon aboard the air-conditioned bus full of military personnel and their families, including several youngsters, headed for the very special grotto at Lourdes in southern France. They both hoped that their seats on the crowded bus would be comfortable since they knew that they had to cover nearly 600 miles (960 km) to get to their destination. The ride, in spite of the interesting scenery that was constantly rolling past their window, was a good chance for both priests to catch up on their sleep with the constant chattering of the younger passengers providing almost a white noise background.

A few short pit stops were made that allowed the busload of people to stretch their legs and breathe some real air. The stops were short since all wanted to get to their ultimate destination as soon as possible. The first significant stop on this pilgrimage was at Nevers in central France where the body of St. Bernadette reclines under glass in a small chapel in the convent of the Church of St. Gildard. She had gone to that convent, about 300 miles (480 km) from her home, as a very young woman to get away from the constant interrogations from people who never stopped wanting to question her about her famous visions of "a small young lady" that she encountered in Lourdes when she was a young, unsophisticated girl. The vision was eventually described by her, in her own youthful voice after she had made repeated requests of the lady for her name, as the "Immaculate Conception", although she did not understand the meaning of those words.

After Bernadette's death in 1879 she was buried in a grave on the convent grounds. Subsequently, her body was exhumed three different times over the years. In 1925, her incorrupt body, fully dressed in her habit, was sealed into an ornately decorated clear glass box where she looked for all the world as though she were taking a peaceful nap. The crowd from the bus was silent as they approached the amazing remains of St. Bernadette. The chaplain priests also were moved at the sight in front of them and received permission to borrow vestments and to concelebrate Mass in this chapel for the pilgrims on their bus, as well as other people that happened to be nearby taking advantage of the unexpected ceremony. Both priests felt humbled and privileged to have had the opportunity to say Mass at this holy site.

The busload of tired travelers spent the night in a comfortable hotel nearby and after a hearty breakfast, continued on their way to Lourdes, a few hours away. Many people made it a point to tell both chaplains how fortunate they felt to have been in their company and to be at a Mass in the special chapel.

When the bus finally did pull into its dock at Lourdes in the southernmost portion of France, the tourists and the two priests were in awe of their surroundings. However, the reaction from many of their traveling companions was muted, but still very detectable. They were not pleased to see so many vendors hawking all sorts of overpriced trinkets and souvenirs. The sight and sounds of those shops were unexpected, somewhat jarring, and surely not what they had come to see. However, as they walked down a gradual incline and past all of that, everything changed. The Catholic Church does not allow any vendors or goods for sale in the sanctuary itself. Suddenly they were at the fringes of thousands of people, quietly making their way closer to the grotto with its lifelike statue of *The Immaculate Conception* and the healing water flowing by. It has been reported that over 5 million people make the pilgrimage to Lourdes each year. This was Fr. Ron's first visit and he was uncharacteristically quiet in a crowd as he prayed silently, very moved by the overpowering feeling of being on sacred ground, close to the Virgin Mary. He knew that this particular time had been designated as the annual Military Lourdes Pilgrimage and there were now about 17,000 soldiers from all the NATO countries gathered there. An impressive sight.

The chaplains and the pilgrims from their bus spent the night in a comfortable nearby hotel, with the next day in the area spent taking in all the activities, including speeches and Masses. Among other things, most took the opportunity to go to the famous baths, considered a healing experience, since the water came from the very well that Our Lady had asked St. Bernadette to dig. No one could seem to get enough of the special feeling of just being close to the famous grotto. It was an extraordinary experience for Fr. Ron, and most definitely for everyone else there as well.

During the Saturday night march around the grounds (an area larger than a couple of football fields put together) everyone recited the rosary, following along with a voice emanating from unseen speaker systems as they processed. As darkness fell, everyone in the crowd lit their candles and held them in front of them as they continued slowly walking and audibly praying the rosary. It was an overwhelming experience. Chaplain Lawson was in uniform and was at one point walking along next to a young German soldier who seemed just a little detached from the spectacle. The youth had been talking to Fr. Ron and saying things along the lines of just where his beliefs in what he had been taught were lacking, or at best, confused. At the ripe old age of 18, he was unsure of his commitment to being a Catholic, but expressed the idea that he really didn't know much about the real beliefs of the faith, or for that matter, those of any other religion. He told Fr. Ron that his unit was from Mittenwald, a little border town between Bavaria and Austria, as part of the Mountain Division. He casually mentioned that he was a native of Oberammergau. Fr. Ron's breath was taken away when he heard that, finding it to be a remarkable coincidence that out of the thousands of people to be casually walking next to and feeling the young man's struggle with his faith, they turned out to have a lot in common. The slow, constant movement of the crowd kept these two people moving forward together, although Fr. Ron was briefly unaware of that fact as everything seemed to him to stop for a minute. He turned to the fresh-faced, handsome young man and told him that he had lived in Oberammergau himself while he was in the Army taking specialized courses in German and Polish for upcoming work in counterintelligence. He also pointed out that he had been a Methodist at that time. The German soldier looked at his new walking companion with increasing awe as Fr. Ron explained that he had become a Catholic in O'Gau, and was a priest and now a US Army chaplain because of his extraordinary experiences there with Fr. Pius Fisher and other events that helped to shape his destiny. The chaplain saw a trace of disbelief in the young man's face, so he reached into his pocket and took out a beautiful, hand-carved rosary that he was never without. He told his new friend that he had acquired it in Oberammergau on the occasion of his baptism. He then handed it to him. The young soldier admired it closely saying that it was truly beautiful and that he had seen similar ones in his hometown and then proceeded to hand it back. Fr. Ron closed his hand around the soldier's and told him that it was a gift to him, and said that it was a sign that one can find meaning in life, even in one's hometown. The recipient of this precious gift at first tried to give it back, but when he could see that the chaplain was quite serious about giving it to him, did his best to express his thanks and said that he would keep it with him always and would make it a point to pray the rosary often.

When the crowd, with Fr. Ron and his walking companion still side-by-side, now with night fully upon them, got to the upper esplanade of the Basilica, they looked out below at all the candles being carried by the walkers. What a sight! It looked like a million bright lights. Fr. Ron turned to his companion and said, "Those candles represent not those who have found meaning in life, but those who are looking. Keep on letting the light burn brighter!" It might have been an illusion caused by the surroundings, but as the young man thanked Fr. Ron for the rosary and his words, the chaplain thought he saw a tear slowly rolling down the soldier's face. These two individuals never met again after that fateful encounter, and Fr. Ron has often wondered what has become of the young fellow who is kept in his prayers. Fr. Ron later described the chance encounter and his gift of his rosary to a young man who needed it to Fr. Lincoln, with whom he shared a room in the hotel. The other priest was busy working on his usual routine of calisthenics, but listened very carefully. Although he didn't say much about it as he continued with his workout and as the touching story was being told to him, he beamed with pleasure when he headed to the shower, saying, "Nice job, Ron!"

Since it was the month of May in which this memorable first visit to Lourdes took place (there would be several more for Chaplain Lawson in future years) both chaplains were very aware of one of the Catholic Church's long-standing traditions of a ceremony known as a May Crowning. In this ritual, a likeness of the Blessed Virgin Mary is crowned, usually with flowers, in a brief ceremony as a way to revere her significance as the "Queen of Heaven" as well as the Mother of God.

Chaplain Lincoln had just come out of a lecture hall in a building adjacent to the grounds of the Lourdes sanctuary where he had led a conference during which he explained the significance of the month of May as it pertains to The Virgin Mary. With a broad smile on his face, he announced to his buddy, Chaplain Lawson, that they were going to have a crowning that day in that hall. Further, he assigned Fr. Ron the simple task of finding a suitable statue of Our Lady, since there was none in the hall. Simple task? This was a significant challenge. After no more than the briefest possible interlude, Fr. Ron, dressed in his priestly vestments began strolling along the various streets and checking out the many gift shops to see what could be found. The first ones he stopped at had nothing suitable to his purpose. He visited The Infant Jesus of Prague gift shop and did see a small statue of The Holy Mother, but he felt that it was too small for his purpose. When he entered the St. Laurence O'Toole gift shop, an upscale establishment with very pricey goods on display, he saw at the back of the store just what he wanted; a beautiful, colorful statue of Our Lady, nearly four feet tall with her hands together in prayer and her head slightly tilted downward in reverence. This was definitely what they needed. The price tag, tucked discreetly behind the statue showed the alarming price of $250. This fact did not deter Fr. Ron from proceeding with his plan. He quickly located the proprietor of the shop. Transfixing her with his clear blue eyes, and with his vestments indicating that he was a Catholic priest, he used his best French and simply asked to borrow the statue. The initial reaction was of disbelief. How could she possibly allow anyone, even a man of God such as the sincere person in front of her, to just walk out of her shop with the statue? He understood her dilemma and carefully explained why he was making this unusual request and promised that the statue would be returned unharmed later that very day. Perhaps it was his smile and attitude of reverence, perhaps it was his command of the French language, perhaps it was those penetrating blue eyes, but the shopkeeper agreed to allow him, aided by another priest, Fr. Jerry who had conveniently just dropped in to the shop, to haul it away as she prayed out loud to heaven above that she was doing the right thing.

It took both priests to carefully carry the beautifully painted and very heavy cast plaster statue, which had been protectively wrapped, into the lecture hall where Fr. Lincoln was waiting. He confidently stood there, with a crown made of the flowers he found nearby on the grounds, knowing somehow that Fr. Ron would be successful in his assignment. The room was full of young people and a few adults, all of whom were eager to enact the special crowning ceremony. Most of those young folks were children of the military personnel that had traveled here on the bus from Heidelberg. Although Fr. Lincoln was very impressed that his buddies had brought him such a beautiful statue, he pretended to take it all in stride as though he expected nothing less.

The crowning ceremony, under the careful direction of both chaplains, was a never-to-be-forgotten event, not only for the youngsters and adults who participated, but for the priests as well. As soon as it was over, Fr. Ron and his helper, Fr. Jerry, lugged the heavy statue, all wrapped up again for protection, back to the St. Laurence O'Toole gift shop, where the very grateful proprietor had been anxiously awaiting its return. Her beaming smile upon seeing her valuable statue back in its place, as well as seeing the priests again spoke more than words. As Fr. Ron was preparing to leave the shop, he invoked a special blessing upon the store and its owner. She would remember him in future years when he came back for additional visits to Lourdes.

The next day, the bus with all of its tired, but happy passengers on board headed back to its starting point in Heidelberg, but made a planned stop along the way at a small French town named Ars. The bus pulled in to a parking area just outside a 12th century church next to a basilica, which is the resting place of Catholic Saint John Vianney (St. Jean-Marie Vianney). He had been a parish priest in this remote French hamlet in the 19th century and was famous for, among other things, his ability to perform miracles, "read" souls in the confessional and to predict events that would happen in the future. He was so well known in his time that as many as 300 people visited him daily. He often slept only two hours a night in order to make himself available to all who wished to visit and be blessed by him. He is now known as the patron saint of parish priests.

The Lourdes pilgrims, tired but very interested, were escorted to the Saint's preserved remains. In a similar manner to the body of St. Bernadette, the incorrupt body of St. John Vianney lies under glass where he reclines at a slight angle as though napping, fully dressed in his vestments including his shoes. Fr. Ron and Fr. Jack gathered the crowd from the bus so that they all surrounded the saint's body. Fr. Jack had asked the sacristan (the person in charge of the many items in the sacristy and the chapel) if he might be allowed to use St. Vianney's extra vestments and his actual chalice so that he could celebrate a most meaningful Mass right there. Normally, the use of these holy vestments and the chalice is reserved for newly ordained priests in order to minimize their handling. The vestments were old and fragile. But Fr.

Lincoln's charming sincerity worked to his advantage once more. The Mass next to the body of St. Vianney was, for the folks that had ridden the bus with the chaplains, another very moving experience to add to their memories of their Lourdes pilgrimage. The tired but happy passengers climbed quietly back on board their bus. It was soon headed back on the long journey to its starting point in Heidelberg

When they finally arrived, the two chaplains said their goodbyes and promised to keep in touch and try to get together in the not-too-distant future. Fr. Ron walked around behind the chapel where he had left his car a few days ago. It was still there, but it wasn't until he went to open the trunk to toss his baggage in, that he realized that his license plates were gone - - stolen. He went directly to the base Military Police to report the theft and ask for some temporary plates so he could drive back to Stuttgart. He was casually told to just go ahead and drive the car without plates. He'd be OK and he could get replacement plates once he was back on his own turf. He felt a little uneasy about those instructions, but went along with what he was told. He had no problems getting back home and within a day or two he had his replacement plates.

Four days later, with the memories of the trip to Lourdes and traveling with his wonderful friend from Boston still fresh in his mind, he was given some stunningly bad news. He was told that Chaplain Jack Lincoln had had a heart attack while in the middle of a baseball game with the troops in Heidelberg. He had died at the base hospital shortly after being brought there. Unbelievable. He had seemed so healthy and was so often doing his calisthenics that Fr. Ron thought that the news must be about someone else. But it wasn't. It was discovered later that Fr. Lincoln had had an ongoing heart condition that he hid from the medics, for no apparent reason. Fr. Ron was very troubled that his dear friend, an excellent priest and chaplain, denied himself the opportunity to have his condition improved or fixed completely since the medical community was at that point in time able to successfully deal with a wide variety of heart problems. Fr. Lincoln's body was shipped back to Boston for the funeral. His saddened buddy prayed for the repose of his soul, feeling quite convinced that his good friend was already in heaven.

A few days later, in the springtime of '87, Fr. Ron joined a group of Army chaplains from all over Europe, for an annual retreat. This time, the location for the retreat was the stunningly beautiful municipality of Berchtesgaden located in the German Bavarian Alps, a place Fr. Ron had visited previously and was where he learned to yodel a few years back. The place they occupied for this retreat, the Obersalzberg, was a former Nazi Luftwaffe (Air Force) facility. It was situated about 2 miles (3 km) east of and above the village of Berchtesgaden.

High on this mountainous area was where Adolf Hitler's house had been located along with the houses of several high-ranking Nazis. The facility that was now provided for the chaplains' use featured a series of cabins that had been remodeled to have private rooms and baths. The nicely equipped central dining facility was where the serious-minded chaplains also held their conferences.

After discussing several issues of importance to all in attendance, a problem was brought up that few had really paid much attention to, but all agreed needed some serious thought and an action plan. A few chaplains spoke about the all too-common situation they had witnessed where a number of their senior Catholic chaplains who had recently retired, suddenly quit their priesthood and got married. Many in the group were very surprised to learn of that fact, but all agreed that corrective action was needed. While it was true that they had been serving with a large number of other chaplains of various faiths, many of whom were happily married, all agreed that was not the root of the problem. As the discussion wore on, the attendees realized that the issue of Catholic chaplains suddenly foregoing their vows and becoming husbands was not something that happened overnight. As more discussion flowed from the participants, everyone present realized that these people would get up at

5:00 AM, run with the troops and spend all day doing "military" things having nothing to do with religious responsibilities, and then would flop into bed late at night, totally exhausted. During this routine, not a single devotional prayer would have been uttered, and clearly no Mass was celebrated. The group reasoned that being called to the priesthood and working as a priest was in many ways similar to being a married lay person. If one doesn't work at one's commitments to one's spouse, then the relationship will likely unravel. This type of slow loss of commitment was surely causing many of the priests to lose their calling over a period of time. So the Catholic chaplains took up the challenge to make a firm commitment to get out of bed an hour early from then on, to say the prayers required of a priest by the Divine Office (meaning certain prayers to be recited at fixed hours of the day or night), and to celebrate Mass privately if there were to be no public Mass. Along with getting up an hour earlier, this approach would help to focus one's priorities in religion. Then, other activities (which were not always obligatory) could be set aside allowing time so that the religious activities, as learned so well in the seminary, would become the focal point. It would be difficult to know how much of a difference this commitment would eventually make, but it is helpful to know that Fr. Ron has been faithful to this protocol ever since it was suggested at the retreat.

During this retreat, he visited the Shrine of Our Lady in the very small nearby town of Maria Gern, located about 2 miles (3km) north of Berchtesgaden. It was opposite the large, jagged mountain known as the Watzman. He had climbed that famous peak a few years previously, enjoying every difficult step of it, but mostly savoring the breathtaking views. This time he didn't climb the Watzman, but spent his time at the shrine in the small pilgrimage church. He had recently learned that the Command Chaplain for Catholics in Berlin had been reassigned to Hawaii. The European Command had hinted that perhaps he might be chosen to go to Berlin even though he didn't have the senior rank of colonel, still being a captain. He really would love to be in Berlin again, even if the chance of his actually being sent there was a long shot. So as he prayed to Our Lady at the shrine, he asked her if she would help him to go to the Berlin Command. As he kneeled, deeply concentrating on his prayers, he softly "heard" her saintly response; *You will be going there*. It therefore came as no real surprise to him when he was summoned to his superior officer that summer and told that he was being reassigned to Berlin.

He left Stuttgart- Pattonville and the charming village of Freudental, both of which he had come to love as well as the many friends he had made there, to head for West Berlin in June 1987 for what would be three very exciting years.

CHAPTER 22

BERLIN 1987 – 1990

Chaplain Lawson arrived in West Berlin near the end of June 1987 in his Chevy coupe. He enjoyed the thrill of pushing his seven year-old vehicle along on the autobahn, never before getting it up to such unrestrained highway speeds. Driving on this world-famous highway was new to him since his previous travels to West Berlin had always been by overnight military trains. After a few minutes of feeling like a racecar driver, he slowed down to a more reasonable, if not sedate, speed at which most, but not all, of the other cars on the highway sailed right past him. He knew that the East German police were ever vigilant and watched for drivers who thought they could peg the speedometer on their cars.

He had gotten on the autobahn A115 at the American checkpoint known as Checkpoint Alpha in Helmstedt on the East German border. About 2 miles (3.2 km) or so along the highway he stopped at a Russian checkpoint inside East Germany at Marienborn where his military identification was inspected. He soon continued on the highway that had, in theory at least, a speed limit of 80 mph (130 km/hr) but in reality, had no general speed limit in many sections of it, through another Russian checkpoint and one more American checkpoint right into Berlin. He stopped for inspection at the second Russian gate in Potsdam at the end of the autobahn and finally at Checkpoint Bravo at Wannsee just inside West Berlin. In short order he was on his way to his destination, the US HQ in Dahlem, about 2 miles (3 km) from checkpoint Bravo. He found it with no trouble at all, especially since the surrounding area was so familiar to him from his last assignment in West Berlin.

After checking in at headquarters, he was assigned billets at an apartment building on the Argentinische Allee. He couldn't have gotten much closer to his '60s assignment since this road ran right into the Clay Allee where he had spent so many of his "spook" days over a quarter of a century earlier. In spite of the significant amount of time that had passed since 1st Lieutenant Ron Lawson had carried out his counterespionage activities on these streets, Chaplain Lawson didn't feel a day older. He even convinced himself that he felt younger and in better shape now. He recalled the many meetings with his friends and team members, the under-cover assignments that still could not be freely discussed, the parties and fun times, but what stood out in sharp detail in his mind was the beginning of the construction of the Berlin Wall on August 13, 1961 just as he was getting ready to leave the Army to study for the priesthood. There were momentous changes happening then in the world, especially in Germany, and in his own life as well.

That ugly wall and all it represented was now an even more hideous and repugnant symbol of Communism. The passage of the intervening 26 years did nothing to help it to blend into its surroundings. The fact that nearly 170 persons had been killed attempting to escape from East to West Berlin in that time frame by testing perceived weak points in The Wall also gave it an eerie status as an unwanted memorial to freedom.

Chaplain Lawson's arrival in this vicinity was only a couple of weeks after President Reagan's famous "Tear down this wall!" command to Soviet leader Mikhail Gorbachev in a speech at the Brandenburg Gate. There was strong sentiment throughout the area that the Wall's days were numbered, not necessarily because of the president's speech and command, which likely had little real influence, but due to the feeling that increasing freedom in the Eastern bloc would surely overcome the evil The Wall represented. President John F. Kennedy's 1963 "Ich bin ein Berliner" speech made it clear that the US had strong support for a democratic Germany. Although many more years had transpired than what may have been hoped for, the Wall's demise was sure to occur. About a half a year before President Reagan's speech, the words "The wall will fall. Beliefs become reality." were crudely spray-painted on a West-facing portion of The Wall near the Brandenburg Gate. But The Wall was still standing.

Chaplain Lawson's priorities were focused on his new assignment. He liked the neat and spacious two-bedroom accommodations in his third floor apartment, and knew that once his furnishings that were being trucked from Stuttgart and Freudental showed up, he would have a nice place to live and to entertain friends and colleagues. He also made it a point to quickly locate the impressive American Community Chapel assigned to him. It was located a couple of blocks away from his apartment and was on the Hüttenweg, a boulevard that goes down through Zehlendorf to Wannsee, both suburbs of Berlin in the American Sector. Pleasant walking areas, because being there again was a bit like being back in time, since the Chapel was located right next to his former quarters in 1960 and 1961 on Flanaganstrasse.

As soon as he arrived at the Chapel and was greeted by the senior chaplain, he was given a note left for him by the previous Catholic chaplain who had already departed for his new assignment in Hawaii. The note contained the types of things that his predecessor would have told him in person had that been possible. It was all helpful information and was written in the spirit of making the changing of the guard as smooth as possible. The last bit of advice, really a very strong recommendation, took him by surprise and brought a smile to his face. He was advised that there was one old custom in the Catholic Chapel that he should be sure to continue. At the end of Mass, the priest would always give out a special treat of the famous German gummi-bears to the young children in attendance. Originally known in German as Gummibär (rubber bear) they are gelatin-based candies in the shape of a bear, less than an inch (2 cm) in length and come in a variety of colors and flavors. That they tend to stick to one's teeth only adds to the fun and the longevity of the chewing. Chaplain Lawson found them to be a very popular and more or less harmless event after each Mass and was happy to continue the tradition. He also quickly realized that the adults who had small children were sort of roped into going to Sunday Mass by their little ones who didn't want to miss out on the sweet treats. He would have liked to have believed that the parents would have attended and brought their children without the bribe but why risk it?

Fr. Ron's supervisor was a Colonel, Chaplain Savely. He was a Lutheran, very experienced and capable in his profession and someone who (again, no surprise) became a real friend and an excellent advisor. Not only was Chaplain Savely the Protestant chaplain for the large American Community Chapel (ACC) on the Hüttenweg, he was the senior chaplain for all the chaplains in the command that included the small chapel in the American Military Hospital in Dahlem, the chapel at Andrews Barracks and the chapel at McNair Barracks.

Chaplain Lawson's duties included saying daily Mass in the Blessed Sacrament Chapel within the ACC, and celebrating the Saturday and Sunday liturgies in the large main chapel where at least 500 people could be seated. He also was charged with counseling anyone in need of such help as well as administering the sacraments, such as baptisms and confessions as well as conducting weddings. Although he was prepared to do so, he never had to conduct a funeral in the American Community Chapel. He also visited soldiers at the various commands in Andrews Barracks and McNair Barracks. He estimated that almost half of the soldiers there were Catholic. Unfortunately, but not surprising to him, only a small percentage of them attended Mass. He gave serious thought to what he might do to improve that ratio, but realistically knew that it was a difficult challenge. It was a challenge that he prayerfully took on as another one of his missions in his ministry.

He also inherited the Catholic chaplaincy at Tempelhof Airbase, since the Catholic chaplain who had been there was reassigned elsewhere and was not replaced. As a result, he often said Mass in the Air Force Chapel at the airbase. He was thankful for the dedication and attention to detail demonstrated by the chaplain assistants, who always made it so much easier for him by setting up for chapel services and events.

There was also a Jewish chapel as part of the American Community Chapel. Attached to it was a well-equipped kitchen where the kosher dishes and cooking utensils were kept. Their well-attended services were always on Friday evenings. The rabbi was a person that Chaplain Lawson remembered from his previous assignment in West Berlin in the sixties. He was Rabbi Lou Fisher, married to a German national, and had worked for the Berlin Command since the end of World War II. He was a wonderful personality and was truly popular with everyone.

Chaplain Lawson always paid attention to the faithful as they attended the Masses that he conducted, noticing the fact that each Sunday he could expect to see the same people seated pretty much in the same sections of the chapel, if not in the same pew that they had occupied the previous Sunday; almost as if they had season's tickets. He had observed this curious phenomenon many times before in the various churches in which he had said Mass. Here in the American Community Chapel, he couldn't help but notice a General Officer and a woman, most likely his wife, seated in the front pew every Sunday. At the end of a Mass shortly after the Chaplain's arrival on base, the General introduced himself and his wife to Chaplain Lawson. He was Major General John Mitchell, the US Commander of Berlin. The Major General and his wife, Joan Cameron Mitchell, were both very steadfast Catholics and became a significant help to him in his chaplaincy in West Berlin. They often had dinner together with Fr. Ron, enjoying each other's company. The newly arrived chaplain couldn't help but be overwhelmed with the grandeur of the Mitchell's living quarters. The Army provided them with the use of a 52-room mansion that at one time had been the home of a wealthy Nazi banker. The dining room in that magnificent place had a table that could comfortably seat 22 people. Of course, wait staff was provided, giving the home a truly elegant feeling. At one of their dinner meetings they got into a discussion about the Bishop of Berlin, Cardinal Joachim Meisner, whose responsibilities included all of West Berlin. It was a special status accorded him by the East German government that authorized him (one of the very few) to exercise his office in West Berlin as well as the East German province of Brandenburg. General Mitchell and his wife had gotten to meet the cardinal, and thought of him as a friend. The general, who was not fluent in German, was eager to discuss political affairs with the cardinal and to determine just how the American Command might be of assistance to him. General Mitchell asked Fr. Ron if he could work out a smooth way to accomplish that goal.

Fr. Ron was surprised to discover that the Cardinal was born on Christmas day of 1933 making the Cardinal just one year more senior than he was. For someone to be a Cardinal at such a young age inspired Fr. Ron to dig deeper into his background. It developed that the good Cardinal had been a close friend of Karol Wojtyla, who became Pope John Paul II in October 1978. The new pope appointed Meisner as Bishop of Berlin in 1980.

Adventurous Fr. Ron drove over to East Berlin through Checkpoint Charlie, which was in the middle of the city of Berlin and was adjacent to the infamous wall. The ominous sign at that American checkpoint declared, "You are leaving the American Sector", and did so in English, Russian, French and German. The American guards waved him straight through while the East German guards, who were allowed only to look at the driver's ID card through the car's rolled up window, did the same. He was on his way to introduce himself to Cardinal Meisner's staff.

Fr. Josef Rudolf was the Cardinal's secretary and carried the title of Dom-Vikar (Parochial vicar). Fr. Ron and Fr. Josef formed a fast friendship that would last throughout the chaplain's assignment in West Berlin and beyond. Eventually,

Chaplain Lawson was introduced to the Cardinal. They conversed easily together in German, with the Cardinal making it a point that Fr. Ron be seated in a particular chair next to his. Fr. Ron had the distinct impression, just by the twinkle in the Cardinal's eye, that there was something special about the chair he was directed to. In a few minutes, Cardinal Meisner warmly explained that in the not too distant past, a good friend of his, who then had been known as Karol Wojtyla sat in that very chair. Now look where he is!

Cardinal Meisner with Fr. Ron in "Pope's chair."   Fr. Josef and Fr. Ron

Fr. Ron enjoyed everything about this meeting with the kind-hearted Cardinal and soon got to the point of his visit. On behalf of General Mitchell, he invited the youthful Cardinal to come to dinner at the General's elegant quarters in Berlin-Dahlem. The thought pleased the Cardinal very much and with great sincerity, he stated that it would indeed be a pleasure for him to accept.

Such high-level meetings need to be initiated with all due attention to proper protocol. In that spirit, when Fr. Ron got back to his apartment in West Berlin, he drafted a formal written invitation, brought it to the official protocol office for the Berlin Command where it was carefully processed, signed and sent out from there. The missive invited both the Cardinal and his secretary, Fr. Rudolf, to dinner at the

General's home. Fr. Ron's role in this historic meeting was to be an interpreter, since the General spoke no German and the Cardinal was not fluent in English.

A few weeks later, Cardinal Meisner and Fr. Rudolf arrived in Berlin-Dahlem and were warmly welcomed into the impressive home of General Mitchell and his wife. Chaplain Lawson made the introductions (actually re-introductions, since the cardinal had been there before) translating freely as each person smiled warmly and did his or her best to use the proper body language, even though they all felt really quite at ease with one another right from the start. It was so much nicer to have the very competent linguist right there, ensuring that everyone understood everyone else. Before-dinner cocktails were enjoyed, although the chaplain was so busy translating on a steady basis, that he did little more than have a few sips of his. Eventually all were seated at the enormous dining room table, with Fr. Ron strategically placed at the end of the table while the General and the Cardinal sat opposite one another at the same end of the table as their translator. That arrangement really worked out very well for the principals involved. Fr. Ron was kept so busy translating and being sure not to put his own spin on colloquialisms or in any other way misrepresent anyone, that at the end of the meal, he was still hungry.

The discussion, which was really mainly aimed at getting to know one another better, focused on two general areas; the status of the Church in East Germany (the German Democratic Republic) and the Cardinal's background. As to the state of the East German Church, the Cardinal explained that ever since the Soviet takeover of Eastern Germany, all the churches in that area were under very strict rules. For example, there was to be no teaching of religion outside the church buildings, and all sermons were recorded and/or listened to very carefully by the Communists, as they tried to detect anti-government statements or anything else that might provoke them. Sometimes the clergy were arrested and jailed if their statements sounded even a little like criticism over the regime's attempt to replace the sacrament of confirmation with the activities of the Pioneer Youth Movement, a means of teaching communist principles to all schoolchildren from age six to fourteen. As the discussion continued to focus on the difficulties and problems for the Catholic Church with either a Communist or Nazi regime in power, the Cardinal's views of Christianity began to clarify.

Joachim Meisner had been born in Breslau, in Lower Silesia, which was then part of Germany but now is the Polish city of Wroclaw. During World War II, his family moved into Thuringia in central Germany to its capital city of Erfurt when he was a young boy. It was in that vibrant city that he had his early education and went on to receive his bachelor's and master's degrees in theology. (This was the same city where Martin Luther attended University in the early 16th century.) Joachim and his family managed to escape the massive destruction of so much of his home country during the war years. When the war was over and he grew to young adulthood, he studied for the priesthood at the seminary of Erfurt, earned a doctorate in theology and was ordained a Catholic priest in 1962. He became Bishop of Berlin when Cardinal Bengsch died in 1979, taking up residence in East Berlin. There, he had a small staff of nuns who tended his quarters on the top floor of the high rise next to St. Hedwig's Cathedral, Berlin's oldest Roman Catholic Church. The building he lived in was owned by the church but was located just across the street and facing the Communist Party Headquarters. He pointed out that they all had to be very cautious about what they said in their building since it was suspected that the entire premises were bugged by the feared East German Intelligence Services (the Stasi). That secret police agency was one of the most effective and repressive in the world at that time.

He also explained another fascinating piece of information about his home at St. Hedwig's. He pointed out that back during the infamous Kristallnacht ("Crystal Night") in November of 1938, a certain Bernhard Lichtenberg, who at the time was a canon of the cathedral chapter (a body of clerics) of St. Hedwig, and had been since 1931, prayed publicly for Jews who had suffered unspeakable destruction of their holy places. Upon learning of his praying for the Jews, he was jailed by Nazi soldiers and then hauled off to the concentration camp at Dachau. He died as he was being transported to that horrible place. Since 1965, his remains have been interred in the crypt at St. Hedwig's.

After the fascinating background supplied by the Cardinal, Fr. Ron was kept busy translating into German the dialog from General Mitchell and Joan, as they described their backgrounds.

The Mitchells at Christmas Ball, 1987

The General delineated his own story of his rise through the ranks and his dedication to his post. Joan, who was of Scottish descent, explained that she fell in love with John when he was a handsome young officer and she was a school teacher while they both lived in Colorado. Their marriage produced five children, all boys, of whom three have survived to adulthood; their parents rightfully proud of them. The General happily explained to the assembled group that Joan, in addition to being a wonderful mother to their boys, was also a very accomplished artist, working mainly in watercolors, but other media as well. Her work was in demand by many art lovers. In fact, Fr. Ron purchased two of her marvelous watercolors: one was a close-up portrait of Blessed Mother Theresa, the other a beautiful rendition of Pope John Paul II dressed in his white garments, walking in a Vatican garden. He has treasured those paintings and all who have seen them have remarked at their artistic beauty.

The evening went by quickly with Fr. Ron nearly losing his voice since he was kept so busy translating. The Cardinal was very pleased to be having this get-together and suggested that he would soon host a dinner party in his quarters in East Berlin, so that they might continue their dialog. General Mitchell was very interested in knowing how he might help the Cardinal in his ministry.

In the early spring of 1988, General Mitchell's oversized limousine, which Chaplain Lawson always referred to as "The Houseboat" was used to deliver the General, his wife, Fr. Ron and Brigadier General and Mrs. Glenn Marsh to Cardinal Meisner's quarters in East Berlin. General Marsh was the troop commander for the American forces in Berlin and was also very interested in knowing more about the Cardinal and his concerns. Mrs. (Claire) Marsh, a native of Sherbrooke, Quebec and her husband were also steadfast Catholics and were great supporters of Fr. Ron's chaplaincy.

The dignified group arrived at Cardinal Meisner's quarters in the early evening with a full moon on the horizon and springtime crispness in the air. After a warm welcome by the Cardinal and his staff, introductions of Brigadier General Marsh and his wife were made. Then all were seated at the large dining room table with Fr. Ron happily continuing in his role as interpreter. After a blessing invoked by the Cardinal, they were treated to a delicious, multi-course gourmet meal that was prepared and served by the head chef of one of East Berlin's finest restaurants. A formal menu had even been printed up for the occasion listing in German and English, the dishes to be savored: a nice keepsake memento of the evening. All the guests agreed that there was no doubt that they had never enjoyed a better meal anywhere.

The discussions that went on during dinner were politely light in nature, but once the delightful dessert had been consumed and after-dinner drinks were poured, the Americans began to explore ways in which they could assist the Cardinal's efforts to provide for his flock. They were expecting that there would be some heavy requests forthcoming that most likely would be difficult to implement, but they were determined to do their best to help out. The room went almost silent as the Cardinal tipped his head forward as if in deep thought. When he spoke, it took Chaplain Lawson a couple of extra heartbeats to translate the straightforward issue and the request. It was phrased as an example for his guests to think about rather than as something that he expected action upon right away.

The Cardinal pointed out that there was a large Catholic orphanage housing boys and girls, which was located in the center of East Berlin not far from the Alexanderplatz and the Berlin Cathedral. The operating budget for that institution was quite limited, but they provided the basic necessities as well as loving care for their charges. However, these children had never in their young lives even seen a banana or an orange, or any other fruit, let alone ever eaten any such exotic item. The Cardinal's eyes seemed to shine with an inner light as he related this directly to his translator, who rapidly conveyed the need to the others at the table.

On the ride back to HQ in Dahlem, Chaplain Lawson outlined a plan to help organize an effort to frequently shop for fresh fruits and vegetables and to bring them over to East Berlin to deliver them to the orphanage. American and Allied vehicles were not subject to search, so it was really not difficult to make these special deliveries. As the good people involved in this project found the effort to be truly gratifying, the task extended to supplying personal items for the seminarians at the East German seminary at Schöneiche.

Easter Sunday, April 3rd, 1988 was a very special occasion for Chaplain Lawson. He and a group of Dahlem faithful had gone on a parish trip to Rome and the Vatican. Included in this group were Cardinal Meisner and Bishop Wolfgang Weider, Auxiliary Bishop of Berlin. Easter morning was a beautiful, clear and warm day with Fr. Ron thrilled at simply being in the middle of St. Peter's Square along with countless others, expectantly awaiting Pope John Paul II who, it was reported, would soon be gliding by in his specially constructed, bullet-proof vehicle, referred to as "The Popemobile". It was nearly 9 AM when Fr. Ron managed to get right to the edge of the path cleared for the Holy Father with the narrow passageway roped off from the crowd. He had been holding the hand of Patrick Oakes, the blond-haired, blue-eyed four year-old son of one of the military couples who had traveled with him. Patrick's parents were a few feet behind the Chaplain and the little guy.

Suddenly, the crowd began to cry out in several languages that "Il Papa" was coming! Sure enough, the Popemobile could be seen slowly making its way along the path cleared for it. Not far from where Chaplain Lawson and friends were standing, the Pope got out of his specially built protective conveyance and began "working the crowd" as he blessed the audience and beamed with pleasure as he shook hands with those he could reach. The special guards, a combination of Italian police, Swiss Army Guards dressed in business suits and the Vatican's own police are always on high alert whenever any pope is as close to the public as Pope John Paul II was then. By a stroke of good fortune, Fr. Ron and friends were on the correct side of the ropes and it would soon be possible for him to not only see "Il Papa" up close, but maybe even shake his hand. Little Patrick was tugging on Chaplain Lawson's cassock and repeating, "I can't see! I can't see!" As the Pope got closer, Fr. Ron hoisted Patrick up and held him at his chest. Suddenly, Fr. Ron was face-to-face with the Holy Father and was almost rendered mute. But not for long. He reached out his right hand and the Pope grasped it firmly. Fr. Ron said in Polish, "We are a group of American military from Berlin." The Pope, with a radiant smile, repeated that phrase back to him also in Polish, took young Patrick in his arms, kissed his forehead, then handed the boy back to the Chaplain as he continued on his way. After that encounter, Patrick and Chaplain Lawson, feeling like celebrities, told anyone who would listen about their good fortune. When Cardinal Meisner heard that the handsome youngster had been kissed by the Pope, he picked him up, marched around with him and held him for several photos as they both beamed with pleasure and excitement, although Patrick really wasn't sure what all the fuss was about.

Pope John Paul II and Patrick in crowd. Fr. Ron mostly hidden from view.

With the unbelievable good fortune of actually grasping the Pope's hand and feeling the special blessing that that contact provided continuing to warm his inner being, Fr. Ron knew that this Easter Sunday would truly be one to remember. He, Cardinal Meisner and Bishop Weider would be concelebrating the 11 AM Mass at St. Peter's Basilica; an unbelievable honor he never previously anticipated. To add an additional special solemnity to this Mass was the fact that assembled in that church were approximately 50 young American boys and girls, all decked out in white, eagerly anticipating their First Holy Communion. Their military parents and they had traveled along with Fr. Ron and the others from West Berlin especially for this unique opportunity to receive that wonderful sacrament in a setting that they would never forget.

Fr. Ron, the Cardinal, the Bishop and the Cardinal's secretary, Fr. Rudolf, all assembled near the altar in St. Peter's Basilica and watched the crowd, including the saintly-appearing first communicants with their hands solemnly pressed together in front of them, their finger tips near their lips, processing in. Eventually everyone was seated and Cardinal Meisner began to address the congregation in German. But Fr. Ron was only dimly aware of the Cardinal's voice and absorbed none of what was being said. He was rendered temporarily spellbound by the unexpected sight in front of him. Under the altar within a glass and bronze sarcophagus, for all the faithful to see, was the unbelievably well-preserved body of the saint who had meant so much to Fr. Ron and who had entered his life at many unexpected moments. It was Pope St. Pius X in all his beautiful vestments, resting in this holy place. Fr. Ron's mind was full of memories. It was almost as though he was watching a movie running at high speed, with no external stimulus entering to spoil the show. He recalled kneeling in front of a portrait of St. Pius X on Christmas Eve, 1960 in Kitzbühel, Bavaria while he felt the strong call to Catholicism in a building where he later discovered that no painting had ever been hung. His internal "movie" projected other scenes; the unexpected dropping into his lap of a holy card of the saint while enrolled in St. John's Seminary, and the deep feeling, practically a knowledge, that back then the good saint was trying to get his attention to prod him along on his spiritual journey.

Suddenly, Fr. Ron was roused from his temporary state of near hypnotic trance as he heard the words "Übersetzen Sie bitte" from Cardinal Meisner. The Cardinal was asking him to "Translate, please." Fr. Ron not only didn't hear the Cardinal's words, he hadn't even been aware that he had been speaking. Saving him from total embarrassment, the good secretary, Fr. Rudolf, smoothly and effortlessly provided the translation that had been requested while the Cardinal looked quizzically at the Chaplain, who looked dazed. While Fr. Rudolf spoke, Fr. Ron, who didn't know until that moment that the secretary was fluent in English, snuck sideways glances into the glass encased tomb. He thought he detected a little grin on the deceased Saint's face. Soon, fully recovered and totally focused, Fr. Ron concelebrated the special Easter Mass with the Cardinal and the Bishop. The additional highlight of providing First Holy Communion to the young children provided an altogether memorable experience.

On their way back to Germany by bus the next day, the group stopped over at Luzern, Switzerland where Chaplain Lawson celebrated Mass on the top of a mountain overlooking beautiful Lake Luzern. The Mass was held on a woody knoll with the lake shimmering in the sunshine far below. Knowing, or at least hoping, that he would get a chance to say a Mass during this trip, Fr. Ron brought everything that he would need for such an event along with him on the train and bus. He, like all chaplains had a very compact Mass kit that held everything needed for Mass including vestments, wine, altar breads, chalice and linens. He had been one of the first ones to get off the bus and after searching the nearby grounds soon found a large, nearly flat rock that was about waist high. It made for a perfect altar.

Mass "al fresco"

Many, probably most, of the group had never before experienced a Mass "al fresco" before this and all agreed that it was among the most memorable events they had ever experienced. He overheard one of the men say in a stage whisper, "This is probably as close to heaven as I'll ever get!" The next day, the return trip progressed in the same manner as did most of the other excursions, with their bus continuing to Frank-furt/Main where everyone in the tired group boarded a military train for the overnight trip back to West Berlin.

A little later in the spring of 1988, the group of chaplains at HQ in Dahlem was visited by the Military Archbishop, Joseph T. Ryan, the spiritual leader for more than 2 million Roman Catholics and the first archbishop of the Archdiocese for Military Services. He had been appointed in 1985 by Pope John Paul II to lead that newly formed archdiocese. A native of Albany, New York, he had been ordained a priest in 1939, and served in the Navy Chaplain Corps from 1943 to 1946. He had been cited twice for bravery in action (in spite of having the role of "non-combatant") after taking part in the Marine landing at Okinawa in April 1945. He had done relief work with the Catholic Near East Welfare Association and the Pontifical Mission for Palestine in the late 1950s, based in Beirut, Lebanon. A few years later, he was appointed the first Archbishop of Anchorage, Alaska.

Navy Chaplain Fr. Ed Condon, Archbishop Ryan,
Chaplain Fr. Ron at entrance to American Community Chapel

Now, there in Dahlem, a large reception was held for him during which he was introduced to many officials from both the military and the State Department present in Berlin. An impressive number of Catholic chaplains from USAREUR (the US Army Europe) stationed all over Europe came to Berlin to greet the most impressive Archbishop Ryan. He stayed for about a week. Of all the possible quarters he could have occupied, he chose to stay with Chaplain Lawson whom he had come to like from their first meeting. Fr. Ron found the archbishop to be a most interesting houseguest, since he was not afraid to speak his mind on any topic - - and frequently did just that.

A group of approximately 30 teenagers, sons and daughters of American military personnel had been preparing to receive Confirmation. When the day came for them to receive that sacrament, they were all struck practically speechless (a first for them no doubt) to realize that none other than Archbishop Ryan was to conduct the ceremony. One of the youngsters said, "I surely don't remember my baptism, and I just barely remember my First Holy Communion, but I will never forget my Confirmation!"

A few days later, Chaplain Lawson introduced a special gathering of young soldiers to the Archbishop. This group of about 16 serious-minded, intelligent youths had been meeting every Sunday evening for several weeks for spaghetti dinners with their Chaplain in his quarters. It was more than a little crowded at these dinners, but all agreed that Chaplain Lawson was wonderfully supportive of their goals. They all expressed an interest in exploring the possibility of giving their lives to Christ by way of the priesthood or other religious life. One of the 16 was a female sergeant, who was diligently contacting various religious orders to gather information. The Archbishop was impressed with these young people and gave them his blessing along with wishes for success in their journeys in the future.

At the Easter vigil service, this same special group of young adults gathered around their favorite chaplain as he introduced them to the nearly full house gathered in the American Community Chapel. They were all pleased at his words that reinforced their strong faiths and were only slightly embarrassed at the applause they received when he concluded his overview of their life plans. He did his best to keep up with their progress towards their life's goals, but most of them went their own ways with only a couple of them remaining in contact with him over the years. One young man wound up in California working in security for a gated community. The female sergeant went to work in the United Kingdom for the US Government.

During Archbishop Ryan's stay in Berlin, Fr. Ron escorted him to the Plötzensee Prison outside Berlin city limits. In this horrible place, more than 2,500 people had been executed, including many of those who had been known, or even suspected to have been involved in the 1944 plot against Hitler. There also had been executions of Soviet covert network operatives: radio operators referred to as the *Red Orchestra*. There had been a guillotine in the death room, however most of the prisoners were hanged. The site that the Archbishop was brought to was a garage with a dirt floor and was adjacent to the prison where the condemned had waited in shackles. Archbishop Ryan was stunned at the thought of what had gone on there and was uncharacteristically very quiet. Fr. Ron solemnly stated that they were standing on holy ground. They both knelt and prayed.

In May 1988, a group of nearly 100 Americans in Chaplain Lawson's area was organized for a trip to Lourdes, France as part of the annual military pilgrimage. They traveled for a couple of hours by military train to Helmstedt, through East Germany to Frankfurt where they boarded buses bound for the eight-hour ride to Lourdes. In the evening, the busses stopped at a hotel in southern France for an overnight and then early the next morning, once the bus drivers had rounded up all the stragglers from the breakfast areas, they were on their way again to the holy grounds. Once there, people spread out in all directions, taking in the beauty of the site. Fr. Ron felt as though it was only a few days ago that he and his great friend, Fr. Jack Lincoln, had made this same trip together. He offered prayers for the soul of his special buddy who had died too young.

Chaplain Lawson headed to the St. Laurence O'Toole gift shop where he had borrowed the beautiful statue of Our Lady for use in a crowning ceremony the previous year. Almost as soon as he entered the shop, the proprietor spotted him and hurried to greet him. In her mile-a-minute French she explained that they had recently sold the statue he had borrowed and hoped that he would not be too upset if she could not offer to loan it to him once again. With his genuine smile and excellent French, he let her know that not only was he not looking to borrow anything this year, but also really appreciated her help a year ago in making that ceremony so unforgettable.

The most memorable part of the Lourdes visit this year for Fr. Ron was the impressive Mass that was held in the huge Basilica of St. Pius X, an underground church built to accommodate nearly 25,000 people. Some of the pilgrims who had traveled with Fr. Ron thought it looked like an underground parking garage. Others pointed out that the enormous concrete structure with its low ceiling and with almost no natural light gave the impression of an overturned boat. In spite of the unique architectural style, or perhaps because of it, the acoustically enhanced voices of the celebrants provided a very moving experience for the large, devout audience assembled there.

The group from West Berlin met a large number of soldiers from all over the NATO countries, just as had been the case when Fr. Ron was last there. Whereas last year the weather in Lourdes had been beautiful, this year the atmospheric conditions were more typical of the area. It rained on and off for most of their visit, allowing the many gift shops all around the perimeter to do a great business in the sale of umbrellas. The rainy conditions in no way diminished the beauty of the Saturday night assemblage and slow march of thousands of visitors with their lit candles under their umbrellas. In fact, the sight of the slowly moving crowd and the unusual effect of the shielded candles still shining brightly as they all recited the rosary was somehow even more moving to observe.

One evening, as Chaplain Lawson was slowly walking on the bridge near the grotto with an extraordinary number of people around him, he noticed a young black airman in uniform sitting on a bench smiling at him while pointing at his own nametag. In French, the young man made the observation that they were both named Lawson as he pointed at Fr. Ron's nametag. The conversation, all in French, was fascinating since it turned out that this fellow was from the African country of Senegal and that in his village, everybody had the same last name; Lawson. The handsome young airman explained that the reason for having so many Lawsons in the village was due to the fact that the land had been owned a couple of hundred years ago by a family with the name of Lawson. Fr. Ron laughingly said, "We must be relatives!" as they exchanged nametags from their uniforms. They both thought, that it was an extraordinary coincidence that out of the thousands of people milling about, two with the same last name, both fluent in French (the official language of Senegal and one of Chaplain Lawson's acquired languages) and from worlds apart should bump into one another. Small world.

After attending the closing Mass in one of the Basilicas on Sunday, the group returned to Berlin the same way they had come, with an overnight stay in a roadside hotel in central France. The next morning the busses continued to Frankfurt where the exhausted pilgrims boarded a military train back to West Berlin.

Chaplain Lawson continued to be very busy with his many responsibilities; activities that he enjoyed very much and that had really come to define his life. In spite of his heavy workload, he always managed to squeeze in time for recreation and travel. He had become so well loved by everyone that he interfaced with, even on a casual basis, that opportunities for adventure abounded. In the early summer of '88, one of the military couples that he had come to know well, Hank and Donnita Whittier, both of whom had roots in

Vermont, invited him to join their group tour to Poland. Donnita had taught Russian at Middlebury College in Vermont. (The Whittiers had lived in Middlebury when Fr. Ron was there as a newly ordained priest.) The group, setting off on a Saturday, traveled by train out of West Berlin through East Germany and into Poland, after getting special permission from Berlin Command to travel through the Communist countries. Most of the tourists admitted to being a bit nervous since this was to be their first trip behind the Iron Curtain and they were not convinced that it would be smooth going the whole time.

At the first stops in East Germany the train became over-crowded with Polish natives who worked there as guest workers, invited by the German government to live in temporary quarters for a relatively short period of time. They were able to earn a much better wage there in East Germany than would have been possible in their own cities or villages. Most of these folks, heading home for the weekend, were bringing aboard all sorts of electronic equipment, even including refrigerators, that they had been able to purchase in the East German "paradise". They wedged their merchandise in the aisles, creating a real hazard and making it impossible to leave one's seat, assuming that a seat could be located. The conductors seemed unfazed with all the mess and nothing was said by them.

During a few hours in the packed but otherwise comfort-able train with the many Poles and their merchandise, they traveled through the western portion of Poland, finally arriving in the east central city of Warsaw, Poland's capital. There they were met by a multilingual Polish tour guide who appeared genuinely happy to greet each one of them and quickly directed them to a tour bus that would become familiar surroundings for the next few days. They joked that here, the aisles were clear and the legroom was adequate to house a small refrigerator, but thankfully no one was trans-porting anything like that.

With the tour director describing just about everything that could be seen from the bus windows, they traveled to many of the famous Warsaw sites, beginning with the former Jewish ghetto. When they arrived at what is one of the most heart-breaking reminders of the inhumanity that had been unleashed on other humans, there was not much of it left to see. The tour director explained that the Warsaw ghetto had been the largest of the Jewish confinement areas in occupied Poland during World War II. When it was first set up in October 1940, its population of approximately 400,000 was about one third the population of Warsaw, while the area it covered amounted to less than three percent of the total area of that city. In short order, thousands of additional Polish Jews were rounded up and forcibly brought to this dreadful place by Nazi soldiers. Its population continued to increase even though diseases and malnutrition took a heavy toll. Over 100,000 ghetto dwellers died due to disease or starvation. Many, perhaps over a quarter of a million, were shipped off to extermination camps and murdered there. Somehow, through weak points in the walls surrounding the ghetto, a fairly large concentration of weapons and ammunition was smuggled in. By January 1943 the occupants, weak and sick though they were, managed an uprising and resisted a final expulsion to death camps. The Nazi response was overpowering as they burned and blew up most of the buildings. By mid May, the ghetto was practically totally demolished and the Nazis were proud to have blown up the Great Synagogue of Warsaw, the largest in pre-war Poland and one of the largest in the world. All that the tourists could now see in that area was what was left of a few small buildings that had not been involved in the attempted resistance. The tour guide noted that in the southeastern tip of Warsaw, (away from the old ghetto) where the beautiful Great Synagogue once proudly stood, there is now a large skyscraper surrounded by successful businesses and stores.

The group from West Berlin was delivered by their bus driver to a well-equipped and clean hotel that they could call home and where they could enjoy meals for the rest of the tour. At their first dinner there, with somber feelings resulting from their visit to the remains of the Jewish ghetto, the subdued conversations were centered on the unbelievable horror of that time and place. Eventually, talk switched to looking ahead to the next interesting portions of their tour.

The next morning, the eager group in the bus was headed for the Franciscan monastery at Niepokolanów, which translates to "City of the Immaculate", located just outside Warsaw. The monastery had been founded by Maximilian Kolbe, born in 1894 as Rajmund Kolbe. He had been a Polish Franciscan Friar living in Niepokolanów in the early part of the 20th century. He took his final vows as a friar in 1914 taking the name Maximilian Maria as a special way of showing his devotion to The Virgin Mary. He was ordained a priest four years later. All the travelers in the group were very impressed by knowing a little of the background of this amazing person. They were fascinated by the description of the vision that had come to him while he was still a youth. In that vision, Our Holy Mother stood before him holding two crowns, one white and the other red. She asked him which he would choose to accept; the white one signified a life of celibacy; the red symbolizing martyrdom. He chose both. The group was especially interested in their guided tour through the monastery he had founded, being very impressed with its beauty and astounded by the sheer quantity and quality of printed material about Our Lady that the monks produced. A main mission of this monastery when Fr. Kolbe had it constructed was to print informational material about The Mother of God and to have it distributed all over the world. This included a newspaper and magazines and a seemingly unending supply of booklets, pamphlets, prayer cards and other beautifully crafted printed works extolling Her special role and how She continues to be so important to the Catholic Church. Fr. Maximilian Kolbe saw to the construction of another monastery in the mid- nineteen thirties, but this time in Nagasaki, Japan, where again one of its central purposes was the printing and disseminating of beautiful informational material centered on Our Lady. He served there for several years before returning to Poland.

This monastery also continues to this day as an important part of the Catholic Church in Japan.

In 1941, Fr. Kolbe was rounded up by Nazis along with many other Poles and sent to the concentration camp at Auschwitz in Poland. Shortly after his imprisonment there, one of the inmates in his quarters tried to escape and was shot. As punishment to his group, they were all forced to stand for hours outdoors in the cold, rainy weather. As additional punishment, a dozen from that group were arbitrarily selected by the Commandant to go into a cell where they were to die of starvation. One of those selected cried out about the plight of his family if he were to die. Fr. Kolbe spoke up and announced that he would take this young man's place; a most unusual request that the Commandant accepted without emotion. Fr. Kolbe was the last in his cell to die, the others expiring one by one within a week, having been in very poor shape to begin with. They had managed to keep up their spirits somewhat by singing hymns and praying the rosary, led by Fr. Kolbe. Days after the last of the others were dead and he was still softly saying the rosary while barely breathing, a Nazi nurse came into the cell and gave him a shot of carbolic acid directly into his heart that killed him instantly.

In October 1982, Pope John Paul II canonized Fr. Kolbe as a Saint, one of the Martyrs of the Faith and the Patron Saint of "Our Difficult Century". The tour group was nearly in tears after learning of that holy man's history. As they walked out of the monastery, they were told that when he was ready to build the facility in Nagasaki, he was encouraged to have it constructed on the side of a mountain that, according to folk legend, was the best location for it in order to be in harmony with nature. He followed his own instincts and had it built on the opposite side. As it would later turn out, when the atomic bomb was dropped on Nagasaki, his monastery was saved, since the bomb's blast hit the other side of the mountain. Had he built it on the "preferred" side as advised, it would have been a total loss along with all within.

The next day the tour went on to visit the Monastery of Jasna Góra (Bright Mount), which houses the legendary icon of Our Lady of Częstochowa, sometimes called The Black Madonna of Częstochowa. Many miracles have been attributed to this holiest of icons of the Virgin Mary that is also one of Poland's national symbols and thought to have been painted by St. Luke himself. One of the many legends connected with it explains why it is called the Black Madonna. Back in the 17th century, the church was ravaged by a purposely-set fire. The mere presence of the icon in the building was alleged to have saved the church from being ruined, but the heat of the flames turned the flesh tone pigments to a much darker color.

Black Madonna

The group was honored to be seated in the sanctuary, in this holiest place in Poland, while Fr. Ron concelebrated Mass in Polish with the other priests of the religious community who resided at the famous monastery. This was clearly a never-to-be-forgotten experience for all the tourists, but especially for Fr. Ron who was ever so glad that he had done well in his studies of the Polish language when he was 1st Lieutenant Lawson in Oberammergau.

Upon leaving the monastery, the group visited a community of religious sisters known as the Sisters of Nazareth in Częstochowa. During that visit, the Mother Superior served tea and had the novices come to sing for the Americans from Germany. The voices of the 30 or so young novices were beautiful as they harmonized with the only accompaniment being their wonderful smiles and bright eyes. They were not the least bit shy about performing and would have enjoyed singing all afternoon. Mother Superior, a friend and former classmate of Donnita Whittier's, explained that there were so many novices, all about 18 or 19 years old, that the community simply did not have adequate resources to feed them all properly. She had to explain that issue to the parents of these women and to ask them to please periodically bring in whatever food, bread, eggs, milk, sausages and so forth they could gather. Fr. Ron's reaction was to tell the Superior, "I'd love to arrange to take them all back to the USA!" For quite a while he let that thought percolate but soon realized the impossibility of it. He was sure that eventually they would all do fine in these holy surroundings. Later, as Fr. Ron's group prepared to depart Częstochowa, they put together a well-wrapped package of Polish money and mailed it to the Mother Superior of The Sisters of Nazareth. Some days later they found out that it was a miracle that the sisters received the package since, unknown to the group, it was illegal to send money through the mails.

The tour went on to visit Kraków in southern Poland, a beautiful city that avoided major damage in World War II and was one of the oldest and largest cities in that country. (Before becoming Pope John Paul II, Karol Wojtyla had been the Archbishop of Kraków.) The tour included a leisurely visit to the central city of Wawel. They explored the Royal Castle where the country's rulers (kings) had governed Poland from the 11th through the 16th centuries and the Wawel Cathedral. This cathedral was sometimes known as Poland's national sanctuary and had been the site of the coronation of essentially all of the Polish monarchs. Their tour guide filled them in on many of the legends and much of the folklore of the area as well as factual background of the construction of the cathedral and surroundings. In true tourist tradition, they explored the central city with its many beautiful shops and restaurants, art galleries and churches. Also true to the methodology of tourists, this group purchased souvenirs at various shops, until someone pointed out that if they weren't careful, they too could fill the aisles of the train back to West Berlin.

With more time available before needing to begin the return trip, Chaplain Lawson asked the tour director if it might be possible to visit Zakopane, a popular ski resort in the Tatra mountains, located about two hours due south of Krakow just about at the border. Canadian friends of his who had been living in neighboring Slovakia on the other side of the High Tatra Mountains had raved about the beauty of the place so often that he was eager to see it for himself, but expected to be told that there was no time for such a side trip. The bus driver would be constantly downshifting to navigate the twisting, rising road. To his surprise, after a brief consult with the bus driver, he was given a "thumbs-up" from the director and before he knew it, they were on their way. The impressive Tatra mountain range stretches across the Polish-Slovak border and contains more than 20 peaks with elevations of over 6,500 feet (2,000 meters). This has been the location for countless World Ski Championships for many years and even in this summer trip, it was a beautiful place to see, even if the bus never left Poland and even if it did make for a little longer excursion than planned.

After an overnight stay in a comfortable hotel there, they gathered at their bus for the last time for the ride back to Warsaw where they boarded a train to West Berlin and returned to the responsibilities they all had. Everyone agreed that it had been a memorable trip that most of them would never have imagined taking. Their apprehensions about being behind the Iron Curtain now seemed to have been a waste of time, but some still had reservations about suggesting the same or a similar trip to their friends. Things could still go wrong with the strict Russians and East Germans watching their every move.

Outside Berlin villa: 1990

Upon his return to HQ, he was moved from his apartment building on the Argentinische Allee where he had first settled upon his arrival in West Berlin. A villa located on the Manteuffelstrasse in Lichterfelde West, not very far from Dahlem was provided by the Berlin Command. This lovely part of Berlin has become home to many diplomats and with its 19th century charm, its cobbled and tree-lined streets with working gaslights, is one of the most appealing residential areas in Berlin. In the photo above, Fr. Ron is proudly attired in his BDUs, or Battle-Dress Uniform.

A month later another trip was arranged, this time a weekend jaunt to Budapest, the capital city of Hungary. It is widely thought of as one of the most beautiful cities of Europe, with the Danube River flowing through it. The group made the most of their short time in that fascinating city, eating in famous Hungarian restaurants, sightseeing and, of course, shopping. They all made it a point to attend Sunday Mass in the Cathedral that was conveniently located right next to the Holiday Inn where they stayed. They had to carefully note the address of their hotel, since there seemed to be a Holiday Inn on just about every street in the area.

Chaplain Lawson was attending to his many duties in the vicinity of Dahlem, Germany on July 17, 1988 when he was informed by the Red Cross in West Berlin that his father had passed away. Arrangements had been made by them for him to return to the USA for the funeral to be held in Montpelier, Vermont. The Chaplain knew that his dad had been suffering from emphysema for at least the past two years. He also knew that once diagnosed with that horrible illness that keeps its sufferers from exhaling without lots of effort, his father had finally quit his life-long cigarette smoking habit. But the damage had been done. He was reminded of his own youthful snitching of his father's smokes, pirating them along with brother Milan. He had become a serious smoker himself after college and had only quit the habit when he was preparing to rejoin the Army as a chaplain. He felt physically much better than he had in a long time once he got past the longing for a smoke, especially after a meal or in the company of other smokers.

As Chaplain Lawson packed his bags for his immediate return to Montpelier, his mind was full of memories of growing up with a fire chief dad who was always committed to being prepared to fight any fire or to rescue anyone in distress, whether that distress was brought on by being trapped in a burning building or by falling through thin ice, or any other calamity. He also remembered that long ago, Sidney Lawson, Sr. was in a smoldering industrial plant where he was exposed to phosgene gas. There was little doubt in Fr. Ron's mind that that episode made a bad lung condition worse.

He phoned his mother to let her know that he would be home in time for the funeral. He wanted to be a source of strength for her at this difficult time. She tearfully acknowledged his concern as she pointed out that his dad passed away peacefully in the local hospital where he had often received periodic overnight treatments. She was very appreciative of her second son's effort to get back home quickly for her.

His trip to Vermont was uncomplicated but time consuming. He flew out of Berlin on a Pan Am jet to Frankfurt, then switched to flight 103 going to New York via London. (This was the very same aircraft and flight number that crashed in Lockerbie, Scotland later that year – on his birthday – as a result of a bomb that had been hidden aboard. All 243 passengers and a crew of 16 were killed.) Shortly after his arrival at New York's JFK Airport, he boarded a flight to Burlington Vermont, where his brother, Milan, was waiting for him. He arrived at his parents' home the day before the funeral. He and his brothers as well as his sister-in-law did their best to console his mother and to be of as much help and support to her as they could. The next day, at the funeral service, his parents' pastor led the congregation in prayer at Trinity United Methodist Church. Fr. Ron greeted other relatives and acquaintances, most of whom he had not seen in a long time, accepting their words of sorrow at his loss. He was introduced to and shook hands with several firefighters, many of whom had been his father's second "family" as they also conveyed their sympathy. After the service, his father's casket was carefully placed atop a shiny fire truck by six of his comrades who were in full dress uniform. Relatives' and friends' cars lined up behind it. The special fire engine solemnly paraded the casket the 20 miles from Montpelier to a newly purchased burial plot at a cemetery in Waterbury Center. Chief Lawson was accorded that honor for having served on the Montpelier Fire Department for over 43 years, with many of those years as its Chief. It was an impressive procession, with a variety of people, young and old, standing at the curbsides, hands over hearts or in a salute as the Fire Chief made his final journey past them. The procession stopped in front of the Montpelier Fire

Department where the local firemen, as well as many from nearby communities stood at attention as the station bell was rung in tribute. The Chief's final destination, Waterbury Center, was Fr. Ron's mother's hometown. The cemetery in that small village was where her deceased relatives were buried. Now her husband would rest there.

Within a few hours, Chaplain Lawson was headed back to his duties in West Berlin. As he traveled back, he tried to put the last couple of days in perspective as he prayed for both his parents, especially his mother, as she had to cope with the sudden changes in her life brought about by the loss of her husband of so many years.

About a month later, on August 15th, 1988 on the observance of the Solemnity of the Assumption of the Blessed Virgin Mary, a small group of about 12 people from the Dahlem area visited the Marian Shrine at Medjugorje (pronounced Med- ju- Gore- ia) in Bosnia in the former Yugoslavia. The idea to make this trip originated with a military parish prayer group, many of whom had heard such unbelievable tales about that impressive shrine that they wanted to see it for themselves. Once again, they obtained permission from Berlin Command to travel into communist territory. The trip stalled for a while when they arrived at East Berlin's Schoenefeld Airport due to a connecting flight's delayed arrival. They had no choice but to sit in a very hot and stuffy waiting area with no air conditioning for nearly an hour while boisterous Bulgarians smoked to their heart's content as they swilled mugs of foamy beer, oblivious to the discomfort of the Americans. Eventually, the pilgrims boarded a Yugoslav airliner for their relatively short flight to Sarajevo where they climbed aboard a bus for the ride to Medjugorje in Bosnia-Herzegovina.

They were there for several days of prayer and meditation beginning on the Feast of the Assumption. There were thousands of people roaming about in that small village with such fame as the location of apparitions of the Blessed Virgin Mary. The visions of *Our Lady of Medjugorje* appeared daily to six young Croatian children beginning in

June 1981 on the Feast of John the Baptist and, according to their sworn testimony, have continued every day since then, or at least for many years. The daily clear, distinct visions in which Our Lady appeared, only to the children, were not always at the same physical place or at a specific time, but her messages always stressed the same themes: Peace, Faith, Conversion, Prayer and Fasting. She was described by the youths as incredibly beautiful, always smiling and joyful. Vast crowds eventually followed the youngsters, but no one else actually saw and heard her as the children did so clearly. However, one priest has claimed to have seen her when she appeared at his church. On the sixth day of the children's visions and conversations with Our Lady, a woman doctor, a professed atheist, was following and carefully observing them to deduce proof that the kids were crazy or at least somehow deluded. She snidely told them that she would like to touch "the lady". The innocent children guided her hand to where they could see Our Lady's shoulder was. The doctor quickly pulled her hand back when she felt a strong tingling sensation. She later told the crowd that something strange was indeed happening there. The faithful believe that Our Lady appears to one of the Medjugorje visionaries (Marija) on the 25th of each month with a new message. As of this writing, the Catholic Church has neither denied nor affirmed this strange apparition.

When Fr. Ron was in the vicinity of the Shrine there in Medjugorje, the weather was extremely hot and humid, reminding him of the Carolinas in summertime, but much more crowded. The Masses in the church went on non-stop in many different languages. He concelebrated several of these Masses, seeing about 75 priests in a crowded small sanctuary. There were over 2,000 people stuffed into a church meant for about 500. The visionaries, then in their late teens or so, were in the balcony and each day, usually at 6:40 PM they would see Our Lady and receive her daily prayer. Fr. Ron watched and listened closely through a few days of that, but never saw or felt anything unusual, nor did any of the other priests that were there near him experience anything out of the ordinary.

His impressions were mixed. On the one hand he was impressed with the sheer number of worshipers and their obvious devotion to their faith. On the other however, he had heard many stories of people seeing the sun spinning* or even having their rosaries turned to gold. He experienced none of those phenomena. What he did strongly experience was being called upon to hear confessions for a long line of people standing outside the village church. He heard all their confessions, taking several hours to do so. He found that to be a very moving experience for him. Also while he was there, visions of Our Lady were seen by the young visionaries (and only by them) as they were seated in the choir loft, in full view of the large number of priests standing behind the altar.

(Author's note: Before I began the task of writing this book, my wife had told me about her cousin Peggy's visit to Medjugorje a few years ago along with her sister, Betty, and more than twenty adults from St. Bridget's Church in Maynard, Massachusetts. I had been told that Peggy and the rest of her group saw the sun spinning. As I got to the point in this biography where Chaplain Lawson visited the shrine in Medjugorje, I phoned Peggy and asked her about her first-hand experience. She explained that early one morning near the end of their pilgrimage, one of the persons in her group came excitedly rushing into her room to gather everyone outdoors to see an unbelievable sight. The sun, low on the morning horizon, was rapidly spinning on its axis and shooting out flames as it spun. She said that the display, witnessed by all in her group and others, continued for about five minutes. During that time, they all could look directly at this spinning sun without the need for sunglasses or anything else to protect their eyes. Suddenly, the phenomenon ended, the sun was the old familiar sun again and could not be looked at directly without eye protection as usual. She

went on to point out that one of the women in her party found, when she arrived back home and unpacked, that her black rosary beads had turned a golden color. No one else in the group saw any change in their rosaries.)

At the end of their visit to this most fascinating place, Fr. Ron asked the sister-sacristan if there was anything his Americans could do for their community of sisters. She replied demurely that they needed material from which to make new habits and they really needed new sandals. He enlisted one of the women in his group to obtain a swatch of the habit material and also to make a note of the style of sandals they wore as well as the range of sizes that would be needed. Once they had returned to Berlin, he approached the Sisters of St. Catherine in Dahlem with his request. They immediately provided the names of nearby places to obtain the desired material as well as a few sources for exactly the right style of sandal. The material and a satisfactorily large group of sandals in the specified sizes were purchased by his group and were soon sent to Medjugorje. It wasn't very long before he received a heartfelt letter of thanks along with prayers for continued success in his work for The Lord.

When Chaplain Lawson had been back in West Berlin for a few weeks, he explained his Medjugorje trip from the Chapel pulpit saying that he was not sure just what to think about the experience because nothing unusual had happened to him. Someone in the congregation spoke to him at the end of Mass and wanted to discuss the thought that "nothing unusual had happened". This person made the observation that ever since the Chaplain had returned from that trip, he had been talking a lot about the religious life and had begun gathering groups of soldiers around him to discuss vocations and providing lots of encouragement to the thought of the priesthood as a career path. Perhaps that was a subliminal message from Our Lady. It is of interest to note that as a direct result of that trip, Fr. Ron began the daily recitation of the rosary. He has continued that practice ever since.

In the fall of 1988, Cardinal Meisner, by then very impressed with the abilities demonstrated by Chaplain Lawson, who it seemed to the Cardinal, made everything he did look easy, felt that he wanted this American to see "his" Germany. He felt that Chaplain Lawson could benefit from a trip into East Germany to visit his hometown of Erfurt, the capital city of the Thuringian province. Although the Cardinal was not born in that city, he did go to school there, eventually studying at the seminary of Erfurt where he was ordained into the priesthood. The Cardinal knew that there were lots of places to be seen and experienced in the well-preserved medieval city at the center of Erfurt. Special arrangements were made by Cardinal Meisner and by the East German government for Chaplain Lawson to make this trip. Normally, personnel in the US military were forbidden from traveling through East Germany without such permission. The determined Cardinal also made the required arrangements for Fr. Ron to be received in East Germany by clerics and others.

Fr. Ron, in his dependable Chevy and on his way to Erfurt, traveled first to a priests' luncheon in Potsdam in East Germany. That event was the Berlin diocesan priests' quarterly meeting with lunch provided. He had also needed papers for that visit as well. That permission was included in a visa to Thuringia and back to West Berlin. The visa was granted from the German Democratic Republic, or GDR; known in Germany as DDR or Deutsche Demokratische Republik, referred to in English as East Germany. The visa cost him 100 West Marks, (about $85 American at the time) which he paid at the Eastern border at Wannsee. From there, he drove the short distance to Potsdam for the special luncheon.

After the satisfying meal with much good friendly conversation, he drove onto the East German autobahn, where there was almost no traffic, all the way to Erfurt. Naturally, under the conditions (autobahn and no traffic) the Chevy just had to speed up, almost as if it had a will of its own. As he flew along, he spotted a group of East German police packed into a small sedan parked in the bushes on the side of the road. They must have been on the lookout for a much sportier (probably red) coupe that they could peel out after. Fr. Ron instinctively slowed down, but they paid him no attention. This was the first time that he had traveled alone inside the GDR, other than East Berlin where he had been countless times before, but he was not in the least uncomfortable with this new adventure.

Upon Chaplain Lawson's arrival in Erfurt after nearly three hours on the autobahn, he headed over to the Church of St. Severi, as instructed by Cardinal Meisner and was warmly greeted by a childhood friend of the Cardinal, Fr. Franz-Josef Wokittel. After several minutes of animated conversation, during which time the two men knew that they had a lot in common in their religious zeal and their easy ability to make friends, he was escorted to comfortable quarters in a convent that was attached to the Church of St. Severi.

The next day, Fr. Franz-Josef took Fr. Ron to the Diocesan Seminary in Erfurt where he was introduced to the faculty and students, all of whom were impressed with his credentials and fascinating background. There were about a dozen priests of the faculty and perhaps 20 or so student seminarians in the audience. None of them was shy about asking questions and Fr. Ron was happy to respond unambiguously, feeling that here was a group with strong faith. He sincerely hoped that all of the students would in fact become priests. One of the questions he was asked, as if he somehow knew the answer, had to do with when he thought they could travel freely to West Berlin and to West Germany. He did his best to assure the assembly that the day would come. They all knew that the mere existence of West Berlin was a sore point for the East German government, while West Berlin had its arms wide open, so to speak, for visitors from the East, especially their brothers from East Germany. Yes, he assured them, the day would come. Little did anyone know at the time that almost exactly a year from then, that "the day" would arrive. He also sat in on a parish council meeting. As he listened to the agenda and the discussions that followed, he realized that no matter where one went in the world, it seemed as though the issues that one would address in such meetings were surprisingly similar.

He found the whole area of Erfurt to be beautiful almost beyond description, especially the Gothic style 1200 year-old Catholic Cathedral located on a hillside. Known as St. Mary's Cathedral, its deep-toned bells can be heard several times a day. Very near St. Mary's Cathedral is St. Severi Church, where he had spent the night. It was another Gothic structure, and it too was equipped with marvelous sounding bells. From the gigantic town square below these cathedrals, he had an impressive view of these historic, beautiful structures.

At about midday, Fr. Ron had a strong feeling that he needed to be inside the 12th century St. Severi Cathedral. He found that it was, as per the usual practice then under communist rule, always kept locked. Fr. Franz-Josef loaned him a key, whereupon he let himself in and locked the door behind him. As his eyes adjusted to the darkness and as he felt the chill in the still air within and sensed the unique aroma so specific to catholic cathedrals, he began to appreciate the beauty surrounding him. He saw an incredibly beautiful stone carving of the Madonna and child Jesus on a side altar. He learned later that it had been made in the 12th century, was alarmed against theft and was priceless. He saw many other very valuable works of art and could appreciate why the place was kept locked when not in actual use. He spent at least an hour inside this magnificent place in the quiet semi-darkness, feeling nearly totally removed from any connection with the world outside. It was an awesome experience for him as he knelt in prayer and contemplation. He reflected upon this trip and how he came to be here, and developed themes to use in future homilies as he prayed for continued guidance in his ministry and the good health to continue in the role he knew he was meant to fill.

After returning to the fresh air outdoors, he and Fr. Franz-Josef went casually walking up the hill from St. Severi

Church through the grounds of a former Benedictine Monastery. He somehow felt a little uneasy about the place they were strolling in and he asked his walking companion what the old monastery was now used for. The answer, given in a matter-of-fact delivery, was totally unexpected. "Oh, this is now the headquarters for the Secret Police." Fr. Ron's immediate response was "Let's get out of here!", as they quickly departed the once beautiful area. Fr. Ron wasn't sure if he detected a slight grin on the face of his guide, but was not about to go looking for trouble.

On the 20th of December 1988, he was summoned by General Mitchell who had a special task for him to fulfill. The General asked him to accompany a seriously ill Colonel to Lourdes to pray for healing. The Colonel, suffering from an advanced, aggressive cancer, was the Commanding Officer of the Military Liaison Mission to the Soviet forces in East Germany. The Mission House and HQ where the Colonel was living were located in Potsdam in East Germany, just outside West Berlin's residential district of Wannsee with beautiful old villas and large flower gardens. Also at this location was one of the great recreation areas on and around the two lakes, the Grosser and the Kleiner (Great and Little) Wannsee. The colonel had very much enjoyed the area up until a year or so ago, when he was stricken with cancer. At this time, weakened by his illness, the thought of visiting Lourdes was very appealing to him, especially being escorted by someone with the experiences and strong faith of Chaplain Lawson.

Following the plan conceived by the American Commander, General Mitchell and his French counterpart, General Cann, Fr. Ron and the colonel flew on a French military aircraft to Paris, and from there, after a short pause they continued to the Tarbes-Lourdes-Pyrénées Airport. No sooner had the whine of the jet engines subsided than the aircraft doors were opened and the Colonel was carefully escorted from the plane with Fr. Ron following right behind. They were introduced to a French officer, a Commandant (the equivalent of a Lieutenant Colonel) who escorted them into a waiting, limousine. After stashing the travelers' bags in the spacious trunk, the Commandant saw to it that his passengers were securely and comfortably seated then got behind the wheel and in no time at all was on the road headed for the Pyrenees in southwestern France, driving carefully to Lourdes. The limousine's plush interior and exceptional suspension system made for a very comfortable ride. Although the Colonel was quite ill, he handled the long air trip and the smooth limo ride exceptionally well. Upon their arrival at Lourdes, they checked into the hotel that had been previously booked for the three of them. Fr. Ron couldn't help but notice that it was now December 21st. He could not have planned a better place to be than Lourdes for his 54th birthday.

Unlike his previous visits to this sacred place, the area now was not at all crowded. He found that this was usually the case there around Christmas time. The trio had a very pleasant three-day stay in Lourdes, as they prayed at the Basilica of the Rosary, went to the famous baths, and attended Mass in one of the basilicas. They also enjoyed excellent leisurely meals in the restaurants of the various hotels. They were able to enjoy the renewing feelings brought on by simply being where they were in spite of the fact that the Colonel's condition was grave and it was feared that he could die at any time. But he smiled, glowed really, pretty much the entire time they were there. He took great comfort from Fr. Ron's quiet words to him as the chaplain discussed the meaning of suffering and the call of the Lord to each one of us to join Him when the time came.

After three days at Lourdes, the men were back in the limo and returned to West Berlin the same way they had come, using military aircraft. After a few weeks, the Colonel was sent to Walter Reed Army Medical Center in Washington, DC. His family was moved to the DC area to be near him. He survived there for more than a year, finally passing away in early 1990.

The year 1988 ended with the visits of several friends, some relatively new ones and others whose connection to Fr. Ron went back several years. In that latter group were his great pals from his first priestly assignment in Middlebury,

Vermont, Albert and Lena Cyr, visiting again all the way from Cornwall, Vermont. They had come to think so highly of him and had been so impressed with his development as a priest in Middlebury, then high school chaplain in Montreal and now an Army chaplain, that they had become almost the equivalent of his fan club. Their Vermont farm was small but prosperous and now that they were retired and with no children of their own, they enjoyed visiting him wherever in the world he happened to be. For most of their international travels, they made it a point to request wheelchairs at their airline gates, so that they could essentially be hand-carried to wherever they needed to go in the confusing airports. They had come to see him in Berlin on two previous occasions. He never tired of greeting them and enjoyed their company, even if he was concerned for their own well-being, since by then they were getting on in age. He recalled how generous they had been the first time he met them. They had brought truckloads of vegetables from their productive little farm when they understood that there was a need for fresh food at St. Mary's Church in Middlebury. Now, every time they showed up at any of his apartments, Lena would take over the kitchen, washing everything in sight and tidying up. And Albert would find the Hoover and vacuum the daylights out of all the rugs, as he whistled, a bit off-key, but happily. Of course, the Cyrs now brought a birthday present for him and as they expressed the thought that having a birthday so close to Christmas was surely a bit of a raw deal in terms of getting presents; they handed him a Christmas present as well.

The end of the year was a virtual merry-go-round of activity, with many Christmas and New Year's parties. There were also some very beautifully done Christmas Masses with choirs in fine voice and special homilies meant to remind everyone of the true meaning behind the merriment.

Chaplain Lawson's duties in 1989 were essentially a replay of those in 1988. He continued to minister to the large Catholic population that by then knew him very well and looked forward to his homilies. Of course he continued to look for opportunities to find new and exciting places to visit. One of his many friends once told him that it was a pretty sure bet that, since he was a Sagittarian (just barely, since persons born one day after his birth date were under the sign of Capricorn and supposedly possessed different traits) he was a great traveler. He put no stock in any of the signs of the Zodiac, but had to admit that his friend was right about his love of travel and adventure.

In the early spring, special arrangements were made by Cardinal Meisner for him to accompany the Cardinal's secretary, Fr. Josef Rudolf, on a tour of the northern part of East Germany to visit several churches and religious sites. Fr. Josef was the rector of an East German seminary on the outskirts of East Berlin in the community of Schöneiche in the district of Brandenburg. He lived there in very simple quarters with the seminarians. So, once again Fr. Ron headed east in his Chevy coupe with the special paper work that would permit him to travel behind the Iron Curtain. It was not a very long drive for the experienced traveler and he arrived at the seminary with no issues or challenges. However, he felt that being circumspect was a good plan and so as to not flaunt his presence or in any way go looking for trouble, once he had been greeted by Fr. Josef, he made it a point to park his car with its military plates in the garage on the seminary property, even though he had registered to be there. They both visited with the seminarians and dined with them, with Fr. Ron spending the night in guest quarters there in the simple building.

Early the next morning, the two priests headed north to Neubrandenburg, a community just to the north of East Berlin and not far from the coast of the Baltic Sea. Fr. Josef drove his Wartburg model 353, a dependable if not very sporty four-door sedan manufactured in East Germany. This was Fr. Ron's first ride in a car that boasted having a three-cylinder, two-stroke cycle engine. Fr. Josef explained that the driver of such a vehicle had to always add a can of oil right into the fuel tank along with every fill-up, since that was the only way the engine was properly lubricated. He went on to point out that the engine freewheeled allowing the driver to shift gears without using the clutch (after he was past first gear) but it also provided no engine braking when coasting downhill. He thought it was a lot of fun to drive, even if some (maybe most) of the seminarians had a bawdy nickname for it, since when he first started it up when the engine was cold, it produced a prodigious amount of blue smoke from its exhaust while sounding a bit like a room full of satisfied diners breaking wind. He laughed off the snide remarks and joked about a friend's wife saying that she got terrible gas mileage on her Wartburg and did produce quite a cloud of smoke, but thought that was a small price to pay for the convenience of having that handy little handbag holder sticking out of the dashboard. Once she was told that that was the choke lever and it needed to be pushed back in after a very short time, she no longer clouded the air behind her and became less of a nuisance to her community whenever she went for a drive. He also was very proud of the fact that his vehicle was, in his opinion, far superior to the two-stroke Trabants that could be seen putt-putting all around the vicinity. He knew that there was no truth to the stories that the bodies of those two-cylinder conveyances were made of cardboard. The fact was that its not very stylish outer shell was made of a composite thermosetting plastic. The little (less than 12 feet [3.6meters] long) auto really was a simple machine. The only instrumentation available to the driver was a speedometer, so that, as Fr. Josef put it, "You could tell how slow you were going." The driver had to remember to check the fuel level by opening the hood and measuring the amount of it with a dipstick. When it was time to add more gas, oil needed to be mixed with the fuel at a ratio of 50 to 1. Many filling stations offered premixed gasoline for the popular little car. Fr. Josef could never understand the amazing popularity of those underpowered autos that took what seemed to be forever to get up to highway speeds. They were everywhere.

Fr. Josef pointed out the many beautiful sights in the old community of Neubrandenburg, making special note of the preserved medieval city wall about a mile and a half (2.3

km) in perimeter with its four elegant gates all of which dated back over 500 years. The Wartburg pulled up next to an old church and the driver and his passenger went in to visit its pastor, a good friend of Fr. Josef. The pastor was very hospitable to his unexpected visitors as he showed them around his church. It was obvious that he had his hands full considering the size of the parish, most of which attended Mass every Sunday, while some attended daily. There also was a regular, fairly steady flow of baptisms, marriages, and occasional funerals to attend to along with the mundane day-to-day issues of tending to his flock.

After this short visit, the travelers walked back to Fr. Josef's car. Fr. Ron noticed that his driver had been constantly checking his mirrors and once in a while would make very sudden and unexpected turns into streets that seemed to be headed off in a different direction. Fr. Ron initially thought to himself that perhaps he should take over the driving, but made no comment. They continued their trip northward, visiting people in different cities where Fr. Josef had been stationed prior to his current assignment as secretary to the Bishop. Eventually, after driving over a long bridge, they ended up on the island of Rügen, right on the Baltic Sea just south of Sweden. Fr. Josef's unique driving moves and constant checking of his mirrors had continued during the entire trip. He finally explained to Fr. Ron that he had been very concerned that they were being followed by the Stasi; the East German police. Either his driving skills had resulted in losing the suspected tail, or they really weren't being followed at all. In any event, there had been no confrontation by those very stern police.

The island of Rügen, on which they were now parked, was the largest of Germany's islands, and had been a favorite vacation destination for years. Fr. Ron could easily see why that would be true. It had an awful lot of coastline due to its unique shape with many waterways, coves and other bodies of water inland. Out of its total coastline of 356 miles (574 km), 35 miles (56 km) of it consisted of sandy beaches on the Baltic Sea. Fr. Josef was enthralled to hear of the nearly month-long sailing adventure that Fr. Ron and two of his buddies had enjoyed in waters not that far from where they now were. Just smelling the salt air helped Fr. Ron recall the fun he had back then as he described his adventures in the small sailboat, exaggerating only slightly for effect.

After sightseeing and a quick stop for a bite to eat in a cozy restaurant, Fr. Josef drove back over the bridge and began to introduce Fr. Ron to the many beautiful sights in the city of Stralsund. The Old Market Square with its 13th century Gothic Town Hall was a place where one could spend hours casually exploring its shops and admiring the many old houses built back in different periods that surrounded it. But Fr. Josef hustled his traveling companion directly over to the Gothic style St. Mary's Church (Marienkirche), the largest church in Stralsund that once, a few centuries earlier, had been the tallest building in the world. He had contacted the rector there, another friend of his, and asked if his guest might be permitted to participate in the Sunday Mass. He wanted to introduce Fr. Ron and since this was already Saturday, they had no time to waste.

The visitors were permitted to spend the night in guest quarters in the church rectory where they enjoyed a nice meal and friendly conversation with the others in residence there. The next morning, as promised, Fr. Ron did take part in one of the Masses. He spoke from the pulpit in perfect German outlining his background and delivering a short, but moving homily. When he had completed his portion of the Mass and returned to his seat at the side of the main altar, he noticed that several people in the pews were crying, some dabbing at their eyes with a handkerchief. When the Mass was ended, he approached those who had been upset to ask what it was that caused their sadness, hoping it wasn't anything that he had said. He replayed his words in his mind trying to deduce if he had inadvertently used a phrase or two that could possibly have been misinterpreted. By the time he got up next to his now small audience, he noticed that they all were smiling broadly and were eager to shake his hand. They spoke almost as one as they said that he was the first

American they had ever seen. The fact that he was a US military chaplain from West Berlin made a profound impact upon them. They wanted his thoughts on when the time might come that they could visit West Berlin and their family members who lived on the other side of that awful wall. Fr. Ron did his best to assure them that the time was coming when the Russians would no longer have any more money and then the gates would be opened. He said a silent prayer that his words could somehow become fact. Little did he or anyone else know then in August, that in three months the Berlin Wall would fall.

He had had a very enjoyable and educational trip with Fr. Josef. The smooth-running Wartburg, now being driven very sedately and without its operator constantly checking everywhere for the Stasi, got him easily back to the seminary in Schöneiche. After expressing his thanks to his tour guide he got back into his Chevy and was back in West Berlin in short order.

Fr. Ron's hectic schedule of duties as Chaplain for his 6,000-member parish while being the only American priest in Berlin continued as previously. Having been out of his base area for what had been only a short time while touring with Fr. Josef, he was amazed to find so much to do to catch up. He was well organized and was back to normal quickly and found the next several weeks moving by rapidly. On Thursday, the 9th of November 1989 he went shopping in East Berlin; an activity he did on a regular basis. But this time there was a significant difference. As he was returning to HQ that afternoon, he noticed the gathering of a large number of both East German police and soldiers on the East German side of the Brandenburg Gate. That very afternoon, it was announced everywhere that the East German government had given approval for its citizens to travel freely to West Berlin. This caused a huge pandemonium with the whole population seemingly attempting to come to the West, with most succeeding. Fr. Ron, witnessing this milestone event, initially thought that it was just like Pentecost when all the Lord's followers, gathered in one place, saw fiery tongues settling on each person. During Pentecost, The Holy Spirit took control and people began speaking in whatever language the Spirit allowed. They went out into Jerusalem back then, speaking in many different tongues, allowing people of different areas to hear the word being preached in their own languages, drawing huge crowds. Something like that was happening in front of him now. He saw the crowds of people singing and dancing and kissing and hugging, exchanging flowers and popping open many bottles of champagne. Most of the people in the crowd were crying with joy. West Berlin was suddenly flooded not only with East Germans, but their autos as well. The smoky Trabants were bumper to bumper with their drivers really not caring that they couldn't get very far very fast, but leaning on their horns to increase the sound level and to celebrate this long-awaited day. Large groups of West Berliners lined the top of the wall in front of the Brandenburg Gate on the Western side. The partying and celebrating went on all that night. The 9th of November 1989 would be a date that would never be forgotten. Fr. Ron would frequently attend Fall of The Wall celebrations, as that milestone would be recalled year after year.

Fr. Ron made it back to HQ, forgetting about doing any more shopping, and found the whole area there also in a wild state of excitement. He quickly found his good friends, Hank and Donnita Whittier, and the trio made their way from Dahlem by subway to the station closest to the Brandenburg Gate, as far as the train could get. They walked from there right on into the mêlée and were eventually at the Gate. Thousands of people were gathered there, singing and celebrating. American and other countries' news outlets had set up camera crews and had managed to get a couple of famous news anchors who were doing their best to report over the crowd noises. There was no doubt that this was an event that would be long remembered. Although the actual milestone of German reunification would not be in place for nearly a year (until October 3, 1990) over the next few weeks, parts of the infamous wall would be chipped away by excited souvenir hunters including the local residents. It wasn't very long after this day that heavy industrial machinery was put to good use to knock down that ugly symbol of oppression that had endured for over a quarter of a century. Having been in West Berlin back in August of 1961, when the wall went up, and now being there to see it come down, made the celebration of its demise all the more meaningful for Fr. Ron.

Although Chaplain Lawson only spent about half of the year 1990 in Berlin, his assignment there included some exciting and memorable events. Not the least of these was the fact that in May of that year he celebrated the 20th anniversary of his ordination to the priesthood. He had arranged to say a special Mass in the impressive Cathedral of St. Hedwig in East Berlin. The building right across the street from the cathedral was where his good friend and significant source of strength, Cardinal Meisner, had lived until recently, using St. Hedwig's as his principal place to celebrate Mass and for all his religious duties. Just a few weeks before Fr. Ron's milestone event, Cardinal Meisner had been moved on to Cologne to serve as their new archbishop. Of course Fr. Ron was happy for the Cardinal, since he knew that he would be very effective in his new role, and the people of Cologne would be getting a very good leader of the faith. But he was sad that Cardinal Meisner would not be available to attend his special anniversary celebration. However, Fr. Ron's good friend, Fr. Josef, who had been the Cardinal's secretary, and was now a parish priest in Erkner, Germany a little west of Berlin, was part of the group who concelebrated this special Mass with Fr. Ron. Having this close friend and excellent priest say the Mass along with him made a special occasion even more memorable. Fr. Ron made it a point to be sure to remember to mail some photos of his big day to the Cardinal.

As many times as he had seen the Cathedral of St. Hedwig, he was still in awe of its beauty and its sheer size. Now, thankfully, there was no longer a concern about the Stasi eavesdropping on conversations in the next-door building where the current bishop lived. The new Berlin Bishop was Georg Maximilian Sterzinsky who, surprisingly, was a little more than a year younger than Fr. Ron, having been born in February 1936 in Warlack in German East Prussia. He was ordained a priest in 1960 and appointed Bishop of Berlin in late 1989 and now made his home in St. Hedwig's. (He would be elevated to Cardinal in 1991 and was appointed Archbishop of Berlin in 1994.)

Bishop Sterzinsky had a background eerily similar to the man he replaced. Not only was he quite youthful to have such an exalted position within the Church, but in his early youth, his family (minus his mother who died when he was quite young) moved to Thuringia, where the Meisner family had also lived. Starting in 1948 he went to school in Erfurt and in 1954 he began his studies of philosophy and theology at the seminary of Erfurt, where he was a couple of years behind his predecessor, Cardinal Meisner.

Since the fall of the Berlin Wall six months previously, the borders between east and west were now wide open. Fr. Ron had invited all of his friends from his military parish as well as many from all around the area to his anniversary celebration. With the renewed freedom of travel, a large number of these folks, many from East Germany, were able to attend his event. The interior of the cathedral was packed with all his invited guests plus a few who managed to get to daily Mass there on a regular basis. All were impressed with the beauty of the large church as well as the Mass itself, concelebrated by several American military chaplains as well as German clergy, especially including Fr. Josef. Fr. Ron was eloquent in his homily as he explained how very much the past 20 years had meant to him and how he knew that he had touched many lives; but he was the one who felt blest to have had his own life enhanced by the many people who touched him.

As he greeted many of the invited attendees right after Mass in the Cathedral, he was introduced to Delores Hope, wife of the famous movie star and troop entertainer, Bob Hope. She had accompanied her celebrity husband, who was in West Berlin for another performance, as she had been doing since the 1940s. It had been her custom for years to attend daily Mass and she had asked some of the military people she ran into where she might find a Mass that would be said in English. It turned out that she had addressed her question to someone in Chaplain Lawson's parish who told her about his anniversary Mass at St. Hedwig's. The two of them enjoyed their short discussion and were both amazed to learn that each of them had been well acquainted with the Baroness Maria von Trapp. Mrs. Hope, married to Bob since several months before Fr. Ron was born, was raised in the Bronx, New York City. She had received several significant honors in her lifetime including having a star on the Holly-wood Walk of Fame, had a street named after her in the Bronx, New York and, although Fr. Ron didn't know of it until some time later, she had received the Outstanding Catholic Laywoman Award from Saint Louis University in Missouri. She wished him good health and many more years of continuing to be such a fine priest and fascinating person. He would have loved to have her and her famous husband join in the festivities at the forthcoming reception, but she had already made plans to rejoin "Old Ski Nose" who had a hectic schedule all lined up.

St. Hedwig Cathedral, Berlin

With Delores Hope after Mass

Right after the Mass, nearly the entire congregation of several hundred people joined in the reception that was held for the Chaplain. It was in the nearby American Officers'

Club in the famous West Berlin Harnack Haus. This is one of Germany's most fascinating places, dating back to 1929 and having been visited by Nobel Prize winners, famous artists, ambassadors and industrialists. Many famous scientists were often seen there including such notables as Albert Einstein and Max Plank. It was reported that Einstein presented his Theory of Relativity for the first time there in the Goethe-Saal, a large room that can easily seat 500 people and is still used for lectures. The room that had served as Einstein's office in the Harnack Haus now is used as a museum in his memory. On this special occasion, the large Goethe-Saal was filled with Fr. Ron's celebrants.

Attending spectacular dinner parties on a fairly regular basis was an activity in which the people-person chaplain was always delighted to participate. He enjoyed the social aspects of these events very much, especially since he would so often meet people that he found to be truly fascinating. It was at one such fancy dinner that he had a good opportunity to get to use his knowledge of the Russian language, even if he was a bit rusty at it.

One memorable evening, he attended a Russian-American dinner party held at the US Mission House to the Soviet Forces in Germany. This facility, located in Potsdam, was an extra-territorial property similar to an embassy. At this elegant affair, Fr. Ron was introduced to a Russian officer, Colonel Kuklin, who had been practicing his English, but having a hard time with the strange language. The Colonel brightened up immediately upon hearing his native tongue being assaulted by the charming American chaplain. The two of them had a few laughs over some of the idiosyncrasies of the Russian language being tripped over, but very soon were communicating very nicely. There really was no need to be concerned about language difficulties, since there was an interpreter always nearby, ready to clear up any confusion.

Colonel Kuklin, who was about the same age as Fr. Ron, was the Commander of SERB (Soviet External Relations Bureau), the liaison group which was the official link between allied missions and the Soviet High Command in East Germany.

Joining the Chaplain and the Colonel, a young Orthodox priest by the name of Father Anatoli was soon participating in the good-natured Russian conversation. Fr. Anatoli's role was the near equivalent of a chaplain. The Soviet military had no chaplains per se, and left that discipline to the Political commissar. Fr. Anatoli who was from the Belorussian city of Minsk, had been sent by the Russian Patriarchate to be the priest in a Russian Orthodox church located in the outskirts of Potsdam. The beautiful but small church that he was assigned to had been founded by Catherine the Great in the 18th century. He explained to Fr. Ron that he had been involved for several years in directing a significant restoration of the church and was pleased with the result.

As the announcement was made for all to be seated, since it was time for the dinner to begin, Chaplain Lawson was called upon, as usual at these affairs, to say an opening prayer. The Soviet leadership present, by prior arrangement, had Fr. Anatoli stand up and give a prayer as well. The three new friends sat together and continued their light hearted banter in Russian, thoroughly enjoying the evening

Fr. Ron and Fr. Anatoli became good friends and since the wall was now down, it was easy for the American priest to visit the Russian priest freely. Later, when Fr. Ron left Berlin, he gave his Byzantine rite vestments and implements to Fr. Anatoli, who was pleased at the gesture. In exchange, the American priest was given a beautiful icon of Our Lady of Kazan that had been painted by a priest friend of Fr. Anatoli. Fr. Lawson has it with him to this day.

Colonel Kuklin, who was the Soviet Commandant of the Allied Missions to the Soviet Forces, was a jovial, likeable character who also enjoyed his meetings with this amazing American who could do very well with the Colonel's native language. As a parting gift when Fr. Ron was preparing to leave Berlin, the Colonel presented Fr. Ron with a Russian officer's winter hat. This beautiful fur hat with earflaps was a warm and cozy way to go out into Siberian wind and snow, should he ever find himself in such a climate. It was a memorable gift of a memorable time.

A Russian Colonel, Fr. Anatoli and Fr. Ron

With Colonel Kuklin, Thanksgiving dinner, 1989.

Fr. Ron was also invited on two different occasions to special dinner parties that were hosted by the Berlin Air Safety Center. That organization had the responsibility to oversee all air traffic in and out of Berlin. They took their job seriously but they knew how to party. Always invited to these dinners were representatives from the American, British, French and Russian forces. At the first of these dinner parties, he was introduced to a young, ebullient Russian lieutenant named Sasha; a nickname for Alexander. Sasha very quickly latched on to the American captain chaplain and proudly announced that he would be Fr. Ron's interpreter. Not only did Sasha not know of his new friend's background in languages, including Russian, he was also unaware of the fact that this American quickly suspected that he was assigned to the Russian Army Intelligence Service (GRU). This assumption would soon be shown to be accurate.

Sasha was very entertaining, using elaborate gestures and many belly laughs. His discussions were usually of little real substance and amounted to what Fr. Ron had come to think of as "cocktail Russian". Quick-witted Fr. Ron said to him at one point "You'd better be careful spending so much time with me or you'll have to file a report with your superiors." After a barely noticeable change of expression, Sasha laughed off the remark, replying that there was nothing for him to be concerned about, since he was only an interpreter.

The location for these parties, the Berlin Air Safety Center, was the former Supreme Court Building of Germany. That place was infamous as the location where those involved in the 1944 plot against Hitler were tried and sentenced: all receiving the death penalty. At one of the dinner parties, Sasha assumed an air of self-importance and told his new buddy to follow him, without elaborating on their destination. They took an elevator up two floors and stepped out into a room that had not been altered since 1945. This, he pointed out, was the very place that the many defendants of the 1944 plot were executed; most of them by shooting. Fr. Ron was simultaneously appalled and fascinated by the place.

One of the things that Sasha liked to talk about with Fr. Ron was Perestroika. That concept had been recently introduced by Mikhail Gorbachev as his plan to restructure the Soviet political and economic system. Later that year when Fr. Ron was back in the US and was at the Pentagon, he purchased an English edition of Gorbachev's book, *Perestroika*. When he got back to Berlin, he met up with Sasha and gave him the book. Fr. Ron told his military cohorts, "You'd have thought I gave him a sack of gold!" He was also pretty sure that his gift must have produced a serious official report to the Soviet Intelligence authorities. Fr. Ron couldn't help but wonder how his interpreter would have reacted had he known of his American friend's past Intelligence career.

Fr. Ron had been visiting the Missionaries of Charity located in the Berlin district of Kreuzberg in the city center. He would say Mass there at least once a week. This truly meaningful Society had been founded by Blessed Mother Teresa in Calcutta, India. It has spread to cover nearly the whole globe and is made up of young Sisters whose only purpose is to provide free ministering to the poorest of the poor; working for their salvation, no matter how difficult or challenging such a task may be.

The Sisters Fr. Ron met with really had their hands full, working in the poorest parts of Kreuzberg, but went about their work, no matter how challenging the task, with a smile on their faces and in their hearts. They all knew when they first took their vows that each member of this Society agreed to go wherever she is sent and does not choose the destination, or the type of work. Fr. Ron admired their devotion to their calling and to God. He could see that many of them had been steadily working at their ministering with very little time for them to "recharge their batteries". He felt compassion for them and on the spur of the moment one day after he had said Mass, he suggested that it was time for some of them to take a day off. He offered his villa in Berlin as a place where they could have a mini-retreat to have a little time for themselves. They accepted his invitation and on one occasion a few of them showed up. He turned the place over to them from about noon to 4 PM. He had set up *The Sound of Music* in his VCR for them and left for other assignments.

When he returned, just as they were leaving, they all told him how much they had enjoyed their "day off" and especially how much they loved seeing Julie Andrews singing and dancing with all those kids. He laughingly told them a little about the real Maria von Trapp and how he had come to know her as a powerful influence in his life.

In his many dinner parties, he often spent time chatting with a British officer, Brigadier Richard Powell, the Commander of British troops in Berlin. They hit it off well from their first meeting and always looked forward to their next dinner where they would laugh over the latest gossip and also seriously discuss current events. The two of them were together on New Year's Day, 1989 and toasted the new year as they wished each other the best.

With Brigadier Powell, New Year's Day
1989

Later in May, the military parish once again organized a trip to Lourdes, but this time it was via German military train from Frankfurt/Main all the way to their southern France destination. Along with Fr. Ron on this repeat pilgrimage were his younger brother, Sidney, and the priest's "fan club", Albert and Lena Cyr from Vermont. Sidney had been very helpful to the Cyrs at each of the airports during their trip, watching out for the two old-timers very carefully. All had a wonderful trip to Lourdes and back to West Berlin, providing everyone with fond memories.

In June 1990, Chaplain Lawson's three-year assignment in Berlin was up. It was now time for him to be reassigned somewhere else. The officer, located in the Army Chief of Chaplains Office in the Pentagon, who tracked his career had gotten in touch with him several weeks earlier and outlined his options for his next post. His file was so full of excellent and/or outstanding reports that they knew they really had a keeper and should continue to stretch his potential. He was offered a choice of attending the Command and General Staff College at Fort Leavenworth, Kansas, or entering a Clinical Pastoral Education (CPE) course also held in the US at Fort Benning, Georgia. Most officers would quickly have chosen the CGSC whose mission is to educate and develop leaders in key roles in Army operational requirements. It was emphasized that entering a CPE course would give him the credentials to be a hospital chaplain if he were ever interested in that area in the future. He looked at himself in the mirror and saw that, in spite of feeling as healthy and spry as he was at 25, he was already 55 and his future retirement from the Army was something to think about. Plus the idea of working as a hospital chaplain really appealed to him. He looked into just what a CPE course of study was all about and quickly discovered some very interesting facts.

This form of theological education, begun in 1925, takes place not only in academic classrooms, but also in various clinical settings where care-giving work is carried out. That includes hospitals, clinics for children as well as adults, hospices, psychiatric and substance abuse clinics and many more places where segments of humanity were in need of physical and spiritual care. That appealed to him. He chose to get the training that a CPE course would provide, and then see just how his life would unfold. He would surely miss his many friends and associates in Berlin and felt that he had grown deep roots in that part of the world.

As he was preparing to leave Berlin for the US, he ran across a few pages he had written during his latest assignment. In his own words, here is what he had jotted down in his memoir.

LIFE IN BERLIN

1. *I often visited the gravesite of Blessed Bernhard Lichtenberg, the former Dean of the Cathedral of St. Hedwig. He is buried in the crypt of that church. As Dean of the Cathedral in the days before the Second World War, he often preached against the Nazi treatment of the Jews. He was arrested and hauled off to the concentration camp at Dachau. On the way, the Nazi thugs beat him to death. A martyr to the Faith, he is considered a role model for priests in the interests of truth and honesty.*

2. *Occasionally, I would take friends to the Alt Histo-rischer Weinkeller in Spandau, a 17th century pub on the Havel River, where I used to spend some time in my previous days in Berlin in the early 1960's. It was a fun place, with live music, and a huge "Bolle" or bowl of wine in the middle of which hundreds of candles had melted as they burned.*

3. *Americans love to shop, and East Berlin was no exception. I went to East Berlin a couple of times a week to visit our shopping "haunts", nicknamed the Frame Shop (to look at and purchase paintings), the Basket Shop (a shop full of knick-knacks), and several others which had great popularity for inexpensive shopping for things that the East Germans had no interest in. One could often find something of great sentimental value in one of these shops. We usually stopped at the shopping plaza in the Friedrichstrasse and had to maneuver between the Russian soldiers shopping there as well.*

4. *The Grand Hotel was one of the best places to eat. Newly rebuilt when I was there, I would visit there with British friends. Again, we would bump into young Russian officers, who studiously kept away from us.*

5. *The Sisters of St. Catherine had a convent in Dahlem, not far from our Hüttenweg Chapel. I visited them occasionally and made an effort to get people to go visit them, providing them with items that they needed, whether food or other goods.*

6. *I kept in touch with the School Sisters of Notre Dame, the same community where my erstwhile friend, Sr. Mary Alfonsa Uciecha was stationed. She was the sister I met at our chapel in Berlin when I was there in the early 1960's. She had died of heart problems in 1964.*

7. *In 1990, I had two occasions to attend dinner parties in East Berlin of American diplomats – one at the home of the ambassador's secretary, and another at the American Ambassador's residence at Niederschoenhausen in the northern part of East Berlin. That was a grand affair, attended by several hundred diplomats and American guests from West Berlin.*

8. *I was greatly honored to be present at a number of dinner parties in Potsdam at the American Mission House, which was the HQ of the American mission to the Soviet Forces in East Germany. My knowledge of Russian helped in being able to indulge in small talk with the Russian officers who were present. At my last appearance there in 1990, the Soviet Commander of the Missions from the USA, Great Britain and France presented me with a Russian winter hat of the type the Soviet Forces wore.*

9. *On one occasion in 1990, I celebrated Mass and preached in the French military chapel in the district of Wedding where the French Forces were stationed. It was a French national holiday – I forget which (Bastille Day?). There was a large parade throughout the area by French forces. Very impressive.*

10. *I attended a number of dinner parties at the residence of the Commander of Berlin, especially in the days of General and Mrs. Mitchell, and also his successor. These were special occasions usually to honor someone in the local community. It was always a most interesting gathering of about 12 guests, and featured a gourmet menu of supreme quality.*

After a round of parties to help send him off, he was on his way to Fort Benning, Georgia. After his careful evaluation of this next move, he left Berlin with eagerness, anticipating what his future would hold. It was to be quite exciting, indeed.

CHAPTER 23

FORT BENNING, GEORGIA
AND DESERT STORM
1990 – 1991

The weather at Fort Benning in Columbus, Georgia when Chaplain Lawson arrived after his recent assignment in West Berlin was beyond hot. It was choking hot. After all, it was July and he knew what he would be in for, so he resigned himself to the thought that he would simply have to get used to it. The oppressive conditions wouldn't last forever... would they? The high humidity simply added to the discomfort and tended to make any normal person head for the nearest air-conditioned place whether that happened to be an office, a movie theatre, a barroom; anyplace where one could escape the outside, at least until one had to go home or to one's quarters. He hoped that his living quarters would be equipped with at least some level of air conditioning. He was sure that his new office space would be so equipped.

The Army had shipped his trusty Chevy to his new locale, but it had yet to arrive, so he made do with taxis at first, later borrowing rides with his new acquaintances. And, true to form, he made friends quickly; "effortlessly" might be a better way to phrase his uncanny people skills that allowed him to be accepted at once.

He made his way to HQ and was escorted to his quarters nearby. He was very pleased when he saw that he would be living in a very nice, four bedroom ranch-style home on base. Four bedrooms? He was about to ask why such opulent space, but decided to go with the flow and enjoy the extra space that surely would come in handy when relatives and friends came to visit. Assuming he could furnish the place. And, yes, it had whole-house air conditioning.

Before he knew it, he was driven to the Clinical Pastoral Education Center (CPE) on post in the Custer Terrace Chapel where he was introduced to the CPE Course Commander, Chaplain (Major) Herb Marbury. He was a very experienced United Methodist chaplain who had been involved with CPE for several years and was very good at what he did. Thus began a wonderful and pastoral relationship between the members of this unique course, all of them Army chaplains: Captain Roger Armstead (African Methodist), Major John Bjarnason, (Mormon), Captain Wayne Harris, (Full Gospel), Captain John Houser (Assembly of God) and Captain Ron Lawson, who was the only Catholic chaplain in the group. The Chaplain Assistant for this motley crew was a young black woman, Sergeant Kita Johnson. Fr. Ron, at age 55, was the "old man" of the group with the others in their 30s except for Chaplain Marbury who was in his early 40s. They all hit it off right away as they sat in a group to discuss their backgrounds and experiences as well as their hopes for the near future.

CPE team

There is no question that the military chaplaincy is a diverse and truly ecumenical organization. To underscore that point it is interesting to note that the person who tracked Fr. Ron's career in the Army Chief of Chaplains Office in the Pentagon was a female Lieutenant Colonel who was a Christian Scientist. She was the one who had strongly suggested that he enroll in this CPE course. She knew he'd love it and be a strong advocate for The Lord in the field.

He soon found out that the CPE course had several qualifiers that would have each of the individuals in the new crew rotated to different assignments every three months. Each chaplain was assigned to a particular ministry for three months and would then be rotated to a different one, with each of them eventually working in all the various ministries. The assignments were: Martin Army Hospital to work with patients in a pastoral way; the Army Detention Facility to work with prisoners; the Substance Abuse Unit to work with clients who had alcohol and drug addiction issues; the Family Life Center to work, as the name implied, with family life issues; and finally, pastoral training at Custer Terrace Chapel. On Sundays, each chaplain was to help out or conduct their own particular faith's chapel service. Fr. Ron helped by celebrating Mass and preaching at Fort Benning's Catholic Mass in the main chapel. Occasionally he would do the same thing in troop chapels around the base.

He was more than a little impressed with the turnout at his first Sunday Mass out in the boondocks. There were about 1000 new recruits in attendance. He had rarely, if ever, had such a large group at one of his Masses before that and it gave him a warm feeling to know that there were so many young men and women with such a strong faith. As he described the wonderfully large and attentive audience to Chaplain Marbury, he was soon brought down to earth when it was explained to him that the new recruits had been given a choice on Sunday mornings: Catholics were to attend Mass or perform some kind of clean-up duty around their barracks. For a little while he had thought the great turnout was due to his reputation as a first class preacher.

His first assignment in CPE ministry was at the Substance Abuse Clinic. Although this was not the first time in his 20 years in the priesthood that he had interfaced with a variety of people of all ages who were dealing with substance abuse, this was more intense since it was his principal focus for three months. He did a lot of individual, one-on-one counseling where he helped the clients to ventilate as they told their stories. He couldn't help but see the parallels these discussions had to many he previously had had in confessionals. Of course he could not, in this setting provide sacramental absolution, but surely made the suggestion to the Catholics that he was available in the Confessional box in the chapel on a regular basis. He also attended typical AA meetings with groups of people, some of whom got themselves into the kind of troubles that they were now in partly because of their lack of maturity and being away from home for the first time in their young lives. There were as many different stories as there were individuals at the meetings. He found the whole assignment interesting in a sad way, but truly felt that by the time his rotation in that clinic was up, he had done some good.

In October 1990, he began his three months at Martin Army Hospital, thoroughly enjoying that ministry. He met many of the staff there as well as patients. Several of the Catholic staff members made it a point to seek out his opinions and guidance on the serious subject of how best to deal with end of life issues. He interfaced regularly with the patients, bringing communion to the Catholics and dignity and compassion to all. Many times he would sit and listen to a sick person while offering his own brand of light-hearted monologue. When the patients he interfaced with were simply recovering from surgery, he would do his best to brighten their day.

One afternoon while he was at the hospital, he was approached by a doctor telling him that they had a patient who was dying of full-blown AIDS. His was one of the first cases of this deadly disease, which at that time, was not at all well understood. The patient's wife was constantly at his side and tearfully let it be known that her beloved husband wished to be baptized and to become a Catholic before he died. Chaplain Lawson instinctively was prepared to jump into action to provide the Sacrament. At that time however, it was simply not known just how to handle AIDS patients. What sort of special handling procedures needed to be followed and just how close one could safely get to the afflicted person without contracting or spreading the disease were really unknowns. Fr. Ron had to suit up in a surgical gown, facemask and gloves before he was allowed to deal with the dying man. The good chaplain accomplished everything needed to perform a perfect baptism with little trouble. The new Catholic seemed to brighten up as he made long and appreciative eye contact with his baptizer, whispering his deep-felt and sincere appreciation. Within a few days, the patient died. His wife acknowledged her gratitude to Chaplain Lawson for his unhesitating actions in seeing to it that when her husband passed away, he was in a state of grace. It was not known how this young man came to contract AIDS, except that he had been working in Africa for some months.

Fr. Ron had somehow managed to furnish his temporary quarters in his ranch style house, including all four bedrooms. His timing for getting all that accomplished couldn't have been better, since he had several friends and relatives drop in to visit him for the upcoming holidays. A few of his cousins from Florida, whom he had not seen in a while, dropped in to visit as they were on their way north; then visited again as they headed back to the warmer climate they had moved to Florida for in the first place. Between Thanksgiving and Christmas he was visited by guests from Vermont. They filled his place for a couple of days with everyone enjoying their time together. Also dropping in to see him was a soldier he had known from Berlin: Loran Walsh who back then had been assigned to the Military Police. Loran was one of the group of 16 who used to meet with him on a regular basis to discuss vocations. He was a remarkable young man who was still trying to get a handle on his future since he continued to relate so strongly to Fr. Ron and his messages relating to vocations.

The CPE class sessions were really done very professionally and were helpful in not only allowing the various chaplains to get to know one another better, but also through casual group discussions, firming up just where each individual's real interests were strongest. In relatively short order, Chaplain Lawson and Chaplain Wayne Harris became fast friends. Often they would go "shopping" at the Ranger Joe's fully equipped military supply store a short drive from their classroom buildings. The two of them would gawk at the unbelievable assortment of military clothes, field equipment, tactical gear, uniforms and accessories of all types. It became something they looked forward to doing on weekends, finding it great fun and interesting as well. They never bothered going in to check out the various tattoos available at reasonable rates at Tommy's Tattoo next door. And they avoided getting their hair cut in the barbershop on the premises. Looking like a new recruit was not part of their plan.

At about Christmas time, everyone was discussing Operation Desert Shield, which had been going on out of Saudi Arabia, targeting Iraq because of its invasion and plan for ultimate take-over of the desert kingdom of Kuwait. His entire group, as well as all the other CPE groups, was trained in mass-casualty ministry. That particular training was disliked by all, but everyone understood its significance, hoping and praying that they would never be called upon to utilize any of it. They had no idea of actually becoming involved in what was happening a half-world away. In late January 1991, just as his group had come to the conclusion that they would most likely escape being involved in the newly named Desert Storm, involving the invasion of Iraq out of Saudi Arabia, they were informed that they would be participating and should prepare to deploy within a week. They knew that they would be part of a United Nations sanctioned coalition force from 34 nations against Iraq. The chances of having to make use of some of their training in mass casualty ministry would be high.

All in his CPE group, except for Chaplain John Houser who was not able to go due to family reasons, left in early February for Dhahran, Saudi Arabia. The excitement in this group was high as they all felt that they would soon be in a position to perhaps make a real difference in the lives of our troops in what would surely be a significant campaign. Of course, before leaving they all had to put several things in order. Not the least of these preparations involved making out a Last Will and Testament and filing it at the Base Judge Advocate's office. They also needed to make arrangements for their mail delivery and to work out a plan for dealing with all their financial matters while they would be overseas. Most of them had spouses and family at Fort Benning, so they simply left those matters in good hands. Fr. Ron got in touch with his kid brother, Sidney, and had him come down to Fort Benning for a day to relieve him of his checkbook and credit cards. He had his mail forwarded to Sidney and trusted him completely to take care of any bills that would come due, assuring him that this desert war would be over quickly. He made arrangements with one of his many friends on the base, Father Mike, who was a Franciscan priest on the post, to look after his house, keeping an eye on his beloved Chevy as well as the overall condition of his place. Fr. Mike was even willing to cut the grass on a regular basis and water the flowers and shrubs, helping to give the place, if not a lived-in look, then at least keeping it from looking abandoned.

They flew from Fort Benning along with a large contingent of troops, in a military transport to Bath, Maine, stopping there just long enough to refuel then abruptly continued on to Belgium, where they refueled again. They were never allowed off the crowded, but strangely subdued plane. It was on February 3rd, 1991 after the long and tiring flight, that they finally landed in Dhahran. This hilly and rocky city, built on a patch of desert was famous for its many oil wells with their pumps constantly bringing up the precious fluid. Those symbols of oil supremacy seemed to be everywhere.

Each of the chaplains was assigned to a different unit in the Saudi desert, all of which were getting ready to invade Iraq. All of the chaplains' initial movements were in the dark, mostly by bus, but occasionally in troop carriers. They stayed overnight in tents, not having a clue as to their actual location. Slipping out of the tent at night to get to the latrine was done quietly and quickly. Eventually they were all in place. Fr. Ron was assigned to a medical hospital unit of some 500 personnel that was located at Rafha, close to the Iraqi border. It was known as the 93rd Evacuation Hospital and was some 400 miles west of Dhahran, along the oil pipeline from Kuwait in the direction of Jordan.

At oil pipeline.

Fr. Ron was quartered in the Chaplains' tent with two other chaplains, a Presbyterian and an Episcopalian. Within a couple of days, the Episcopalian chaplain was sent to a helicopter unit. Fr. Ron and his remaining new tent-mate, Chaplain Goodwill, spent the next couple of months conducting ministry mainly within the confines of the hospital. Fr. Ron's ministry consisted mostly of hearing confessions in the unit's chapel tent, visiting the staff as well as the hospital patients, listening to all of them and doing his best to provide what he thought they needed most. He looked after the spiritual needs of captured prisoners as well as coalition forces.

As Chaplain Lawson unpacked his heavy duffel bag, he brought out one item that got a laugh out of his new pals. Just before their deployment to this war zone, he and Chaplain Wayne Harris had made one last visit to Ranger Joe's incredibly well stocked store. They knew that they would be going somewhere in Saudi Arabia but had no real idea of the specifics. Thinking that they may very well be at the edge of the ocean in Kuwait, Fr. Ron, in a temporary loss of good judgment, thought it would be fun to catch some fish. He purchased a nylon monofilament fishing line and a small collection of lures and a few lead shot sinkers. Here in the middle of the hot desert, the sight of him and his fishing equipment provided a little unplanned comic relief. He kept that gear with him all through his tour in the Gulf and well beyond, keeping it in his bag of mementos of that difficult time and place.

Fr. Ron was surprised to find that a great buddy of his, a fellow about a dozen or so years younger, named Chaplain Sam Boone, was currently right in this same desert. Sam and he had trained together back in 1984 at Ft. Monmouth, New Jersey and had found that they had many interests in common. They hit it off right from the start. What were the odds that they would meet up again in such a place and under such harsh conditions? They hung out together as much as possible and ate their dinners with each other as often as they could.

Chaplain Boone, who was a direct descendant of Daniel Boone (and who pumped that heritage for all it was worth) hailed from Tennessee and with his near-constant smile, usually won over any new acquaintance with his "good ol' boy" charm. His ministry was with The Disciples of Christ Church. Although these two buddies were not assigned together, they were both in Rahfa in the same theatre in this war and palled around as much as they could.

It would develop that Chaplain Boone would stay with the Army, spending many years in Korea as Command Chaplain, finally retiring in May 2010 as a full colonel, Chief of the Chaplain School at Fort Jackson, South Carolina.

Chaplains Boone and Lawson at Rahfa

Fr. Ron's first Mass in a potential battle zone was on Ash Wednesday, February 13, 1991. Anticipating that such might be the case before he actually deployed, he had brought along a large bag of palm ashes from the chapel at Fort Benning. He used those ashes, invoking a special blessing and making the sign of the Cross with his thumb that he had pressed into the ashes, on the foreheads of as many Roman Catholic GIs as he could locate. The ashes were put to good use all over the desert battle preparation area, since when other Catholic chaplains heard that he had blessed ashes with him, they sent some of their troops over to visit him and "while they were at it" they were to pick up a supply. The many soldiers who had their foreheads lightly blackened, just the way they would have if they had been at home on Ash Wednesday, were in this way reminded of the closeness of their chaplains and by extension, of their Lord and Savior.

There was a French Foreign Legion unit "next door" and when Chaplain Lawson had a little free time and while things seemed to be relatively quiet, he made a visit to the French post. He soon located the chaplain there, a very interesting and high-spirited gentleman who hailed from the French Mediterranean island of Corsica. His name was Father Olivet. The two chaplains, both in such a dangerous place and both new to the type of ministry the situation demanded, hit it off right away. They entertained each other in French for a while, describing their unique, but similar backgrounds, then proceeded to wonder about what the immediate future had in store for them. While Fr. Olivet was still laughing heartily about something that Fr. Ron had said, he opened up a small cabinet and took out a bottle of fine cognac and two glasses. Fr. Ron (and most likely Fr. Olivet as well) knew that the US forces were forbidden to have alcoholic beverages in their possession, with the exception of the wine used by the Catholic clergy for the celebration of Mass. But the French were another national force in the coalition and they, at least Fr. Olivet, ignored the rule. The two priests toasted to what they prayed would be their mutual success with one glass each of darned fine cognac.

Frs. Ron and Olivet would meet several times in the course of this war. (And they would meet at Lourdes in 1992.) One memorable meeting was in the Foreign Legion chapel where they both took part in the baptism of a young French soldier who had just recently converted to the Catholic Faith. Fr. Olivet quickly realized that they had everything they needed for the baptism except a godmother. Fr. Ron, ever resourceful, described their requirement to his unit's female sergeant major whom he had often seen at Mass. He was sure that she would be happy to fill the needed role. He was right. She was thrilled to have the invitation.

A great deal of Chaplain Lawson's ministry was by helicopter as he was ferried all around the battle zones in southern Iraq. Never having previously traveled in the noisy and seemingly quite vulnerable flying contraptions, he was initially marginally terrified, but soon got over his dislike of the aircraft and began to enjoy this quick way to get around. He always ducked his head much farther down than actually required whenever boarding or getting out of a chopper with its blades whirring overhead.

Chaplain Lawson and his favorite mode
of transportation: Huey helicopter.

At one of his many stops in the desert, the gathered crowd of troops seemed to him to number at least 5,000. He did his best to say a quick Mass, but he had no real idea how many of them received Holy Communion. He recalled the part of his CPE training that drove home the point that you just have to do your best out there.

He was kept well supplied with whatever items he required for his work. The Army furnished each chaplain with a kit that was shipped in especially for them. The kit contained everything needed by each denomination. For example, the kit for Catholics contained missalettes, small bottles of altar wine, unleavened wafers for Communion, altar linens and occasionally some handy collapsible furniture. The bottles of altar wine were labeled "Mass wine - - For Liturgical Use". Different shipments included different types of wine; white, red or rose, but always, as was standard practice, it had no sediment.

Fr. Ron celebrated Mass every day in the unit's chapel tent, located right next to the hospital, with an average of about 25 troops attending and receiving Communion. He kept his preaching very short and to the point. His Masses only required about 20 minutes from beginning to end, but he sensed that those in the tent took great comfort from them. On Sundays after Mass in the unit chapel tent, he would often be called upon to celebrate Mass elsewhere, especially at the HQ and at the nearby Rafha Airbase for the Catholic members of the staff. He usually had an average of about 50 soldiers and officers present. Frequently, he celebrated Mass for various units that were spread out across the desert. He was chauffeured to the distant ones by the Army or Marine helicopter that he had come to think of as a pretty neat way to get where he was needed.

One episode that took place in one of those remote locations will stay with him forever. He heard confessions and celebrated Mass for a unit of combat engineers who were about to head over the border in the invasion of Iraq. Several of these kids came up to him before Mass for confession, and after the short Mass they shook his hand, some of them hugging him, as they thanked him for being there for them. They then headed for an Iraqi airbase that was known only as *Target White*. Later that very day, nine body bags containing the remains of seven officers and soldiers from that same unit were brought into the Hospital in Rafha to be received and identified by a graves registration sergeant as Fr. Ron, ashen-faced, stood nearby. With a heavy heart he prayed over the remains and provided the best blessing he could for their immortal souls, feeling the direct impact of that war. All the brave men were much too young to die. They had their whole lives ahead of them. Fr. Ron to this day still sees their faces in his mind and continues to pray for Captain

Everado, Lieutenant Funk, and Sergeants Russell, Jones, Smith, Scott and White.

With that tragic event fresh in his mind, Fr. Ron was in the Iraqi desert at a Logistics Base (usually referred to in typical military fashion as a Log Base) and had just celebrated Mass for several hundred soldiers. He boarded a Huey Helicopter with a group of others for the quick trip back to his HQ. Within minutes after taking off and reaching their cruising altitude, they were engulfed in a sandstorm, not only reducing visibility to nearly zero, but also clogging the chopper's engine. The Huey descended rapidly and with no way to judge their altitude with the sand swirling around, it seemed certain that the outcome would be disastrous. Suddenly (and Fr. Ron could have sworn that he heard a choir of angels) they blew out of the storm into clear air with the pilot regaining control, as his craft was about three feet above the hard ground. He looped up to get a good fix on their location and announced that they would be at HQ soon and asked if his passengers enjoyed his special effects. During this frightening near crash, Fr. Ron realized that there was nothing more important in his life than God; not family, position, money, power, influence - - <u>nothing but God.</u> Although he was already very devout and God was central to his being, he still felt that this experience changed his whole life in an instant. He prayed that that sort of event would be something that visits everyone as a means of strengthening his or her faith.

A few evenings later, back at the desert hospital, Chaplain Lawson and his tent mate, Chaplain Goodwill were relaxing in their tent, getting a little drowsy and were just about ready to call it a day. It was cold in their shelter, with the outside temperature falling to near freezing. And they were in the desert: of all places to feel so cold. All of a sudden an alert was sounded that signaled a biological and/or chemical attack was about to take place in their area. They were both instantly wide-awake and rummaged through the tent to locate their MOPP (Mission Oriented Protective Posture) gear. They had practiced with the bulky special protective clothing and equipment, including state-of-the art gas masks, but never expected to actually need all that specialized equipment. (They both had the unshakeable feeling that nothing bad would happen to them.) The alarm they clearly heard was for what was known as MOPP Level 4, in which it was required that, remaining in their tents, they don their special overgarments: field gear and foot wear covers, gas masks and gloves. It didn't take long at all for the two very concerned chaplains to get all their equipment on and ready. They were fully suited within a few minutes, and would stay fully prepared until the alert was over.

They both sat quietly on the benches in the tent, trying feebly to cheer each other up, but both trying to guess at what was the cause of this serious alert. After several minutes, they agreed that they wished that they had had a chance to visit the latrine before jumping into their bulky gear. They waited for what they hoped would be the "all clear" signal. They continued to wait in the tent as their discomfort level increased.

This Chemical Protective Equipment carried the same acronym of CPE that they had been so involved in, Clinical Pastoral Education. But this had a whole new meaning behind the letters. Fr. Ron knew that US forces had not faced confirmed nuclear/biological/chemical attacks since the gas attacks during World War I. This Gulf War was the first time that the MOPP gear would be tested in actual combat situations. He was not eager to be one of the first men to prove its effectiveness.

After what seemed to be forever, Fr. Ron went over to the tent flap and cautiously opened it so that he could see what might be going on around them. He was not at all prepared for what was out there. Not 25 feet away, calmly smoking a cigarette while sitting on a crate was one of our soldiers. He wore no MOPP equipment. Chaplain Lawson, turned to his tent mate, removed his gas mask and said, "I think we've been had! This whole exercise was never meant for us. This is a drill for the French Foreign Legion." The GI sitting on the crate nearly fell off his perch laughing when the two chaplains stepped out of their tent wearing the bulky specialized clothing. No amount of fast-talking on their part could convince him that this is how the modern Army Chaplain now dresses for very special occasions.

Serving together in a war zone has always resulted in mere acquaintances becoming close friends, or at least being very receptive to each other's concerns. This situation was no different in that regard. One of the Protestant chaplains, who had been deployed to this desert along with Chaplain Lawson, had come to the Lawson/Goodwill tent and had been making small talk for several minutes. He asked Fr. Ron to take a walk with him. As they walked around the perimeter of the hospital grounds, with the setting sun making a slow but glorious disappearance, the other chaplain began a serious discussion. He gradually unloaded some personal concerns and by the end of their walk, felt much better for having had the opportunity to vent his issues to the receptive and caring persona of the much-admired Chaplain Lawson. They both realized by the time they returned to the tent, that what had just occurred was nearly the equivalent of what often takes place in a confessional; with the Protestant chaplain assuming that to be the case, while Fr. Ron knew it to be so.

Ever since he had arrived, he had been living under the constant threat of SCUD missile attacks with the possibility of chemical or biological weapons detonating nearby at any time. There was a constant stench as a result of distant explosions in oil fields, reminding him of one of the reasons this operation was going on. In spite of all of that, he and his fellow chaplains were confident of both their own safety and of Allied victory. It was a monumental experience of faith and trust in God's providence. In spite of that, it would take a long time to readjust to normalcy once his tasks in this desert were finished.

By Palm Sunday, March 24, the Gulf War was over. Chaplain Lawson and his associates who were scattered in the recesses of the desert were slowly called back to Dhahran to prepare for their return to the States. They dismantled their tents and gave several to the Saudi National Guard in the area. The previous evening was the end of the Muslim feast of Ramadan. The US chaplains were surprised when a Saudi National Guard pick-up truck arrived on the base. In its open back were a number of lambs, a baby camel and a few goats. All of Fr. Ron's associates, especially the women, were enchanted by the baby animals. Finally, someone who knew the local language asked what they were going to do with them. The gleeful response was "That is our supper to commemorate the end of Ramadan!" The American women were horrified, even though they understood that sacrifices of young animals had been a tradition in that part of the world at that holy event for Muslims for centuries.

Within a couple of days, in the early morning, a convoy of vehicles formed up with all of Chaplain Lawson's associates and other military personnel aboard, making a long line down the pipeline road toward Kuwait with Dhahran as their destination. He was comfortably seated in the back of an Army sedan, one of thousands of Toyotas given by Japan to this war effort. Many hours later, during which time he catnapped with snippets of memories of the past weeks involuntarily being recalled, his sedan arrived in Dhahran. At that point, he left the group after shaking hands with as many of his cohorts as possible and saying his farewells all around. He was picked up by one of the senior chaplains, an Orthodox priest who was part of the main American HQ.

Initially he was housed in the famous Khobar Towers high-rise housing complex built by the Saudis in 1979. It had been essentially unoccupied until this Gulf War. This eight-story structure was originally meant to serve as residential apartments for the Bedouins, who traditionally lived in tents in the desert. The strong beliefs and backgrounds of this Arab ethnic group kept them from wanting to have anything to do with such a building, but rather strongly wished to keep to their old tribal lifestyles. So the place was left vacant until the Allies arrived for Desert Storm. When Fr. Ron arrived, he found that there were several thousand members of the coalition forces housed there, including service members from Saudi Arabia, France, the UK as well as the US. He ran into one of his chaplain assistants from Berlin, a native of Puerto Rico, named Alejandro Rodriguez whose unit was quartered in apartments near his. Fr. Ron was housed with a mixed group of officers from various units. All had stories to tell; very few were happy stories.

After a few days of uncomfortable living in the Towers, he was moved to Log Base Dragon to prepare for shipment out to the US. In the Towers there was no running water, no showers, no furniture. The place was equipped however with stained, thin wall-to-wall carpeting over cement floors. Sleeping bags were minimally comfortable when spread on sand or grass, but the concrete under the half-inch of carpeting made for many sore and aching backs. Log Base Dragon was another tent-equipped facility, but this time adjacent to tennis courts and a clubhouse that served as quarters for parts of the US Headquarters Staff. With the Army's famous mandate to "hurry up and wait" he lived there in a tent on the grass of the clubhouse grounds for almost a week, doing OK and clearly not missing the discomfort of the previous few days. Not very distant from this little tent city was a mosque with its elaborate dome and minarets where Muslims came together for prayer, and occasionally, to resolve disputes. They were called to prayer five times a day: before sunrise, around noontime, mid-day, at sunset and at night. They were not the least bit shy about the sound levels of the music they used for their calls to prayer. Fr. Ron, whose background had always included a love of music was fascinated one evening to recognize that the loud music he was hearing was actually a piece of Gregorian Chant from the Latin Mass; in fact it was the Kyrie. He found that to be of real interest and wondered how its use for Muslims came about. He assumed that someone in that particular mosque must have been fascinated by its quality. Hearing it, even at its raucous sound level and in this totally unexpected setting, reminded him of his younger days in the seminaries as he learned many of the beautiful Gregorian Chants. He had come a long way since those days, figuratively and literally.

A couple of days later, on Friday, March 29, which was Good Friday, a large group including Chaplain Lawson boarded a military aircraft for the initial leg on their journey home to the US. They stopped at Frankfurt, Germany where they were met by a large contingent of volunteer American military wives who had set up a feast for them. As great as that reception was, what truly made it "over the top" was that there were shower and clean-up facilities that they flocked to. What a luxury a hot shower with plenty of soap could be! Once they had digested the great food that was presented to them, and were feeling almost squeaky clean, they were soon back on their aircraft, excited to be back on their way home.

They landed at JFK International Airport in New York for refueling and were soon on their way to Fort Bragg, North Carolina, known as the Home of the Airborne and Special Operations Forces, for a major reception for all onboard. The majority of the personnel in this aircraft, troops, officers and a few chaplains, had been originally stationed at Fort Bragg, so the welcoming crowd included many familiar faces for a large portion of the passengers. Fr. Ron was one of the few who weren't home quite yet. His final destination of course was Fort Benning, Georgia that he would head for the next day.

Chaplain Lawson stayed overnight in base housing along with a colonel who had served as battalion commander and had been on his plane. Coincidently, that officer had been with him during his second assignment in Berlin. A few years later, the colonel made major general.

The next day the exhausted chaplain was in a small airplane with about 20 other people on his way back to his Fort, thinking how good it would be to return to some semblance of normalcy. He was comfortably strapped into his seat for the relatively short trip. Before very long he realized that they were entering a thunderstorm, but thought to himself that he'd been through storms before. As the shaking, pitching and yawing quickly became very violent with bright flashes of lightning thrown in for good measure, he soon began to wonder if this small aircraft was up to the challenge. Very rapid movements up, down and sideways did nothing to relieve his concern. He took his rosary beads out of his pocket and prayed for nearly the whole hour and a half duration of the flight, pausing frequently to wonder if after having survived Desert Storm, he was going to crash in a plane after all. As the aircraft descended to its landing strip at the Lawson Army Airfield at Fort Benning, they glided out of the storm and into relatively calmer, though still bumpy air, landing safely. A spontaneous cheer went up from all the passengers for the flight crew who had managed to get them home in one piece. The fact that their landing destination contained his last name also had somehow helped Chaplain Lawson to know that their landing would be a good one. He knew that he was not related to the highly decorated World War I veteran, Captain Walter Lawson, a Georgia native who had been killed in an air accident and for whom the airfield had been named.

Chaplain Lawson discovered that the others in his CPE group had arrived back several days earlier. Everyone was soon telling their Gulf War stories in CPE classes. All were glad that this was safely in the past and hoped that would be the end of such insanity.

CHAPTER 24

HEIDELBERG
1991 – 1992

Chaplain Lawson arrived safely back at Fort Benning just in time for Easter of 1991. He had been anticipating what traditionally is the most important liturgical event of the Church year: the Vigil Mass of Easter to be held after sunset on Holy Saturday at Fort Benning's main chapel. After just having been in a war zone and experiencing the ugliness of it, he was truly looking forward to the lengthy and beautiful service. He knew that this Vigil Mass would begin with the service of light in the darkness, a theme of his own spiritual growth. The Easter candle would be blessed and lit. It would be the source of candle flame, as those in the darkened chapel closest to the center aisle would tip their candle into the processing Easter candle. Everyone in the church would hold a small candle, each of which would be lit by touching its wick to its neighboring small candle and passing that small flame along the row from person to person. Finally, the darkened interior of the chapel would glow with the light from the many small candles. While each individual flame would be miniscule, when summed together, the effect would be marvelous, signifying Christ risen from the grave. The *Exultet* (sometimes known as the Easter Proclamation) would be sung by the priests and deacons in Gregorian chant after the procession with the Paschal Candle. He knew that there would be lengthy Scripture readings that would emphasize Salvation History. These readings, usually seven in number, would relate Catholic religious roots stemming from the Jews, the history of the Jewish Passover, and the 40 years of wandering in the desert before entering the Promised Land, as well as tracing Christian history down through the early Scriptures.

Fr. Ron also knew there would be blessing of the new Easter water and fully expected that there would be baptisms and confirmations of both children and adults. Usually at the Easter Vigil, adults are received into the Catholic Church as converts. After the lengthy ceremonies have been solemnly carried out, the Mass would continue as usual, culminating with the reception of Holy Communion. He knew all this, and eagerly looked forward to the solemnity of it all.

Seated in the pews with the capacity crowd, he was not prepared for the terrible disappointment visited on the entire congregation by the main celebrant of the liturgy, the senior Catholic chaplain there at Fort Benning who held the rank of colonel. There was no blessing of the Easter candle; the long *Exultet* which, when properly sung takes several minutes, was rushed through leaving much of it out; the rapidly delivered liturgies were glossed over with the readings reduced from the usual seven to two and there were no baptisms. The celebrant explained that he had baptized a couple of converts in private that afternoon. Fr. Ron felt that the whole event had been an abomination and at the end of the service, he let the Colonel chaplain know his feelings eyeball-to-eyeball, in no uncertain terms, telling him that having come home from the Gulf War, he was not prepared for what he experienced that night and was greatly disappointed. He expressed the thought to the chaplain that, "It feels to me as though the most important liturgy of the year has just been reduced to ashes." There was very little response from the Colonel who lowered his eyes but astonishingly did not seem repentant.

Not long after the poorly done Easter Vigil, the Colonel chaplain left the priesthood to get married. Upon hearing of that, Fr. Ron knew that the ex-priest had "lost it" and had let his spirituality and commitment to the priesthood fall apart. He likened it to what happens in marriages that end in divorce. He vowed never to let that experience befall him, thus cheating the people he was meant to serve. He was not the only one shocked and disappointed by the ex-chaplain's performance at the Easter Vigil and his sudden departure from the Church since several parishioners sought out Fr. Ron's views on the matter.

During the spring of '91 Chaplain Lawson's group finished up their work in ACPE (the Association for Clinical Pastoral Education) by writing and then presenting lengthy reflections on their experiences in the Gulf War. This was a difficult assignment for some in the group, but the ever-inventive Fr. Ron put together a meditation based upon the format of the Stations of the Cross. This was an exceptionally creative way to delineate significant things that happened to him in the desert in 1991.

(*See the Afterword for the details of this meditation and reflection.*)

In May, everyone in his group was given their new assignments. All of them had been anxiously awaiting their new postings, with some hoping for certain destinations, but knowing that trying to guess where they might be headed was like trying to predict the stopping point of a spinning prize wheel. They all knew however, that there would be no "Lose a Turn" on this wheel.

Chaplain Lawson was told that he would be assigned to Korea. That thought really excited him, since he had never been to the Far East and that world of different cultures and traditions. He wondered if he might have even half a chance of learning to speak some of the Korean language or to read any of it before heading there. He wanted to be able to properly minister to whomever he would be associated with in that assignment. He was assured that he would be interacting mostly with American troops stationed there, but wanted to be able to deal with the locals as well. But, after about a week of devouring books on Korean history, culture and language, he was informed that the Pentagon had changed its mind, a not unexpected turn of events. A more pressing need, from the Army's perspective, was for a chaplain at a hospital in Heidelberg, Germany. So much for learning a new language. The familiar old routine of getting ready to ship out and saying farewell to his current batch of friends and cohorts was completed once again, with exchanges of addresses and promises to keep in touch.

He arrived in Heidelberg in June 1991, reporting in at the US Army Command at Campbell Barracks, adjacent to the housing quarters that would be his living accommodations. This apartment building in Mark Twain Village, was right next to the one in which his good friend from Boston, Fr. Jack Lincoln had lived. He remembered that a few years previously he had left his car parked in the chapel parking lot not far from Fr. Jack's apartment while the two of them headed off to Lourdes. When he got back he discovered that his number plates had been stolen. He wondered if he would need to find a garage for his Chevy. Thinking about that dependable car, still en route, he figured that it probably had accumulated more shipboard miles than many people do in the course of their travels. He hoped it would arrive soon. Also, thinking about Fr. Jack and his untimely death of a heart condition after having spent such a meaningful time with him at Lourdes, reminded him of life's uncertainties.

He was assigned to the 130th Station Hospital on base and knew that it was the very one where Fr. Jack had died four years previously. It was more famously known by many as the hospital where General George Patton had died at the end of World War II. Once Fr. Ron made his way into the hospital command, he found that his office was located in the sacristy of the chapel building inside the hospital compound. He was soon introduced to Frau Ehrentraud Mueller who would be his secretary. She turned out to be a blessing in more ways than he could imagine. Fluent in English, very polished in her demeanor, and an exceptional secretary who had been at this hospital for a number of years, she became his eyes and ears on what was happening in the hospital itself. He had learned from his CPE studies at Fort Benning that it is difficult to minister effectively to hospital patients if one's office is not inside the hospital itself. In his usual friendly way, he discussed this issue with the hospital administration; smoothly pointing out the many benefits to all concerned if his office could be moved to one inside the hospital. His request was quickly granted, either due to his eloquent presentation or simply that there currently happened to be an unused office. In any event he and Frau Mueller moved his office out of the chapel sacristy and into a neat office on the second floor of the hospital, a location that was acceptably close to nearly all the patients. He said Mass daily in the chapel for a few days. Soon, Fr. Ron noticed that there was a storage room located across the hall from his new office. When he checked out its contents, it seemed obvious to him that it wouldn't take much effort to clear all the accumulated junk out of it, disposing of much and relocating the rest to another storage room in the basement. In an effort very reminiscent of what he had done nearly 20 years previously at St. Thomas High School in Pointe Claire, Quebec, within a few days Fr. Ron and Frau Mueller had created space for a small chapel. They then brought in a table that would become his altar, as many chairs as they could scrounge, as well as a few rarely used items from the main chapel, such as a crucifix, a tabernacle, some candles and other appropriate items.

Fr. Ron celebrated daily Mass in his new chapel with an average of about 20 people (mostly staff, but a few patients) in attendance. He had never had that many when celebrating Mass in the chapel building. That fact drove home the point that with a chapel much more conveniently located, there would be a more significant turnout.

The hospital had a small maternity wing so from time to time there were several new mothers, and their husbands, whom he saw every day for the few days they were there. Each of the young mothers had produced a beautiful baby and he enjoyed blessing the new lives as he prayed that their futures would be peaceful.

There were never more than 50 patients in the hospital, including the maternity ward. Some were in for various levels and types of surgery, some of those having long recuperation periods. There was also a psychiatric ward. Fortunately its population was never very large, but its occupants were always a challenge. Some in that section of the hospital were suffering with Post Traumatic Stress Disorder after having served in the Gulf in Operation Desert Storm. He did his best to get to know those patients and to offer whatever help he could, since he really related to them at a "gut" level as he felt the beginnings of PTSD himself, wondering how long it would take him to get bad memories out of his dreams and occasional daytime flashbacks of wartime out of his mind.

He made it a point to try to get to see each hospital patient several times a week, if not every day and to provide counsel when needed, a hearty laugh at any attempt at humor by a patient, or a special blessing in more serious cases as may be required. It wasn't very long before he was well known by all the staff members: doctors, orderlies, nurses and administrative personnel. He was never really surprised to find that some of the staff would occasionally want to chat with him and the little conversation would develop into a serious discussion of a deeply personal nature. He was always pleased to see these folks at one or another of his daily Masses in his newly acquired chapel.

He always celebrated Sunday Masses in the Mark Twain Chapel across the street from his quarters near Campbell Barracks. He would offer one Mass at 9 AM there and a second one at 11AM at Patrick Henry Chapel. Both were well attended, although he never had many customers in the confessionals on Saturdays. He gave some serious thought to that problem and worked the issue into his homilies, but the situation hardly changed.

Chaplain Lawson had a very special houseguest at Christmas time. Bishop John Nolan, Auxiliary Bishop of the Military Archdiocese, had come from his residence in Bonn about 150 miles (240 km) away, to be the main celebrant for the Christmas liturgies at both the Mark Twain Chapel and the Patrick Henry Chapel nearby. Bishop Nolan was no shrinking violet. Now at age 67, he was in the habit of making the rounds of installations all over Europe and usually showing up unannounced. He and Fr. Ron had met some time ago at a chaplains' conference and they discussed the Bishop's upcoming travel plans. Fr. Ron suggested that it would be great if the Bishop could manage to show up in Heidelberg for Christmas some year. With that conversation almost forgotten, Fr. Ron was pleasantly surprised in mid-December when he got a phone call from the Bishop indicating that he would indeed like to visit Heidelberg that Christmas. Of course Chaplain Lawson replied that that would be wonderful and that he would be honored to have the Bishop as his houseguest for the duration of his visit. As soon as Fr. Ron was aware that the Bishop was on his turf, he welcomed this fascinating person, showing him around the facility and bringing him to reside with him for as long as he wished. They both enjoyed learning more about each other's backgrounds during the Bishop's stay.

It was a special delight for the parishioners to speak with the Bishop after Mass where they learned a little about some of his background. Before becoming a bishop, Fr. John Nolan had spent years in the Catholic Near East Welfare Association, working out of Beirut, Lebanon. The CNEWA had been founded in 1926 by Pope Pius XI to support the pastoral mission of the Eastern Catholic Churches. One of the most significant things the Bishop had done, which could easily be thought of as "beyond the call of duty" was to visit the Americans being held prisoner in their own embassy in Tehran, Iran. That hostage crisis made headlines around the world for the 444 days of its duration. It began in November 1979 when 53 Americans were imprisoned there by a group of Islamic students and militants who took over the American Embassy in support of the Iranian Revolution. Bishop Nolan carried a Vatican passport that allowed him to get right into the sealed-off embassy. He visited the frightened detainees several times, mainly as a way to boost their morale, to pray with them for a peaceful resolution to the crisis and to hear confessions of any of the Catholics who wished to avail themselves of that sacrament.

A very meaningful and personal Christmas gift from Bishop Nolan to Fr. Ron was a Papal Blessing. This beautiful document certified that the Holy Father had bestowed his apostolic blessing on Father Ron Lawson. He was very touched by the gesture and was appreciative of that special gift.

Shortly after Christmas, the Pastor of the Catholic community's main chapel, Fr. Jerry Haddad, a chaplain-lieutenant colonel, retired from the Army. Since his actual replacement was not due to arrive for quite some time, Chaplain Lawson was asked to look after Fr. Haddad's parish functions. This required that he spend time in the parish offices at both Patrick Henry Chapel and Mark Twain Chapel a couple of days a week to keep track of Catholic military parish activities. Fortunately, Fr. Ron was well-organized and kept careful notes of what appeared to be the most critical data. This extra assignment was not too much of a burden and he handled it well. About a month later, in February of 1992, the US Army Europe (USAREUR) Senior Catholic Chaplain also retired. Of course, Chaplain Lawson was then asked to take over his desk also a couple of days a week in addition to his already overloaded schedule. This added workload placed a considerable hardship on him, but he handled it well. Fortunately, the very efficient Frau Mueller kept him fully apprised of his responsibilities in the hospital, even if he had significantly less time to be there and some of the patients didn't get to see him as often as they would have liked. Luckily, a contract chaplain was available to celebrate Mass in the hospital.

He found himself being pulled even farther from what he had come to think of as his primary business at the hospital when in March, covering for the USAREUR Chaplain's responsibilities, he accompanied a group of senior staff in a tour of the location of the famous World War II Battle of the Bulge in Belgium and Luxembourg. That battle, planned in secret by the Germans and launched in the mountains in the deep winter of '44 and '45 with terrible weather conditions, was meant to split the British and American allied line in half. The "bulge" referred to the initial incursion the Germans put into the Allies' line of advance as seen on a map at the time. It was the single largest and bloodiest battle that the American forces had encountered in the war to that point with over 19,000 American lives lost. However, the allied forces prevailed. Fr. Ron found the tour of the area to be of genuine but solemn interest and could picture in his mind the horrible scenes of human destruction that had taken place there.

No sooner had he gotten back to his duties in Heidelberg, than he was required to join a committee planning the annual Lourdes Military Pilgrimage that would be taking place, as usual, in May. He attended a meeting of that committee in Luxembourg where he met the many NATO representatives who were organizing their own national participation. His previous experiences at Lourdes helped him to provide high quality and well thought-out inputs to the group.

He might have thought that he would now settle back in at the hospital, at least until the May Lourdes pilgrimage, but since he was so good at arranging trips, he was asked to help organize a trip to Israel. This very special journey was for about 20 people, all either actively in the military or in some way closely connected to it. This adventure was to take place just before the Lourdes trip and would last 10 days. All who made this trip would later agree that 10 days was just barely enough.

Father Peter Vasko, a Franciscan priest stationed in Jerusalem and working for the Custos of the Holy Land, gave the tour. (A Custos is a superior officer in the Franciscan Order; usually one who is tasked with the responsibility of seeing to it that pilgrims who visit the Holy Land are directed to the appropriate shrines, and even to ensure that they are properly housed while there.) Fr. Ron found this to be perhaps the most meaningful trip he had ever taken, since during his ten days there he visited all the major shrines in the Holy Land, including: the Nativity at Bethlehem, The Shepherd's Fields (the site where Shepherds kept watch on that night when Christ was born), Capernaum, or Capharnaum (the small village near Nazareth that for a time became the "home town" of Jesus), Mount Tabor (the scene of Christ's Transfiguration), the Nazareth site of the Annunciation, The Holy Cenacle (the site of the Last supper), Dominus Flevit (where the Lord wept), the Tomb of Mary, the memorial of Moses, the Way of the Cross (the road followed by Jesus on the day of his crucifixion, although the current buildings and shops make it very different now), the Basilica of Gethsemane (the site where Jesus had prayed and was subsequently arrested), the Kidron Valley, located on the eastern edge of Jerusalem and where many important events of biblical history took place, and the Shrine at Bethany.

Of all the those wonderful places he visited, the most impressive and deeply moving moment for him was having the opportunity to celebrate Mass at the Tomb of Our Lord in the Holy Sepulchre at 5 AM one day.

Celebrating Mass at Tomb of Holy Sepulchre, Jerusalem.

That very special site, where Jesus rose from death, lies among the many buildings of the Old city of Jerusalem where it is obvious that the ages have taken their toll on them. Fr. Ron had fully studied the history and significance of this area, but to actually have an opportunity to celebrate a Mass at the tomb was an overpowering privilege and an unexpected honor. As he studied the monument to the burial of The Lord, he could understand why so many pilgrims to this location had such a difficult time visualizing how it must have looked nearly 2000 years previously. So many monuments and structures have been built there, that what had been the bare area outside the city walls of first century

Jerusalem was nearly impossible to imagine. Fr. Ron was in no hurry to end this trip, but duty called back in Heidelberg.

The staff and patients in his hospital did not have him in their midst again for very long before he was off again, this time on his way to Lourdes for what would be his fourth pilgrimage. The travel to and from the southern France destination was facilitated in a much more efficient manner this time, as the Heidelberg Americans were flown in a special military aircraft. Even though he had been there three previous times, Fr. Ron found the sanctity of that special place to be every bit as meaningful and spiritually fulfilling as ever.

In mid autumn of 1992, Chaplain Lawson was given the opportunity to leave the Army at age 58, nearly the mandatory retirement point. Even though he still felt that he had much work to do as an Army chaplain, a health scare prompted his superiors to have him consider the option of mustering out. He was on leave and had been visiting his family in Vermont for a brief vacation.

Mom and her three boys at Nelson Pond.
1992

He was really enjoying his visit, bringing the folks up to date on his latest escapades and admiring the showy fall displays that the oaks, maples and other colorful trees were putting on for him. One afternoon while eating an apple and talking to his mother, he felt a strong tingling sensation throughout his whole right side, from his shoulder and arm, right down to his right foot. At first he thought he had accidently come into contact with a live electrical wire, but the fact that he was nowhere near any such wire made him realize that the unusual feeling was caused by something else. He tried to not let his mom notice that he had just experienced something unusual, but with her strong maternal instinct for trouble for her boy, she pressured him to seek medical attention. Partly to satisfy her wishes and partly to get to the bottom of the strange sensation, he drove himself to the Central Vermont Hospital, about a ten-minute drive away.

Once there, and after a relatively short wait in the Emergency Room, he was seen by a doctor. After hearing the symptoms, doing some preliminary testing and understanding Fr. Ron's participation in the Gulf War, the doctor felt that in spite of the fact that his patient "felt fine", a CAT scan of his brain should be done right away. Fr. Ron thought that this was overkill but felt that he had no choice but to submit to the procedure.

Much to the chaplain's surprise, the doctor told him that the results of the imaging showed clearly that a blood vessel had burst in the left side of his brain and he had experienced what the experts called a Transient Ischemic Attack or TIA, sometimes referred to as a mini-stroke. Such a warning stroke with its short duration of symptoms almost always results in no permanent brain injury. To be on the safe side, the doctor suggested that an MRI be performed on his brain to better evaluate the scope of what they were dealing with. The patient clearly showed that he was in full control of his faculties, so it was agreed that it would be OK for him to get himself to an Army hospital facility for the testing.

Fr. Ron thanked the doctor for his diagnostic efforts and drove back to his mother's home where he packed his bags. He had a hearty supper and a good night's rest. Early the next morning he kissed his mom goodbye after breakfast, and headed south for the 12-hour drive to Walter Reed Army Medical Center in Washington, DC. He convinced himself that he still felt fine and wondered if perhaps he was over-reacting to a little tingling sensation, even if that odd feeling was still with him. He also realized that the mini-stroke he had experienced was perhaps a warning sign. He kept his mind off himself on the long drive as he paid attention to the road, stopping for rest and food along the way.

After arriving at the world-renowned hospital, where he had phoned in advance to let them know that he was on his way, he went through the typical Army bundle of paperwork and was processed in. He felt a little foolish about all the fuss being made over him since he felt basically OK. Once he was in that large and famous facility, his first instinct was to begin to minister to the patients. It was hard for him to accept the fact that *he* was now a patient and had to allow the staff to do their thing. He brought the CAT scan that had been done by the Vermont hospital with him and handed it to the doctor who was assigned to him. He was quickly prepped for a brain MRI. The result of that imaging test confirmed what the CAT scan had shown. He had suffered a very mild TIA as a result of a ruptured blood vessel in his brain. The doctors at Walter Reed came to his room individually and in groups over the next couple of days, all interested in learning more about his symptoms and also about his fascinating background, especially his service in Desert Storm. They ordered blood work and constantly tracked his vital signs, while he was hooked up to an array of heart monitoring sensors. They prescribed an unappetizing menu, at least for the next few days. They were all pleased to confirm that there were no debilitating effects of the warning stroke.

In about a week he was discharged from Walter Reed and told that he could continue on with his life, but should seriously consider toning his level of activity down a notch while simultaneously increasing his level of physical fitness: eat a little less, control high blood pressure, stick to a low cholesterol diet, get the proper exercise and be sure to get an adequate amount of sleep. The doctors at this first-class hospital had detected what appeared to be signs of Sleep Apnea, a condition in which he would actually stop breathing for what might be several seconds at a time several times during the night. He was advised to have that potentially very serious problem evaluated by a sleep study and if it was found that he indeed had the condition, he would need to take a proactive approach and obtain the correct treatment. They also detected pre-diabetes and gave him plenty of good advice as to how to prevent that from becoming full-blown.

The staff at Walter Reed could detect the signs of not only Post Traumatic Stress Disorder (PTSD) but also, more specifically what had come to be called the Gulf War Syndrome, a condition that was not well understood. He thought he had kept secret from the various doctors that had seen him that it was a rare night that his sleep would not be disturbed by nightmares, some so strong as to cause him to thrash about so violently as to kick his blankets right off his bed. But they were aware of his demons. None of the medical staff could state with any certainty if his TIA was in any way connected with his service in the Gulf. It was however, strongly suggested that he should consider retiring from the Army.

By November 1, 1992, he was a civilian again; no longer an Army chaplain, but as always, a Roman Catholic priest on a mission. He would continue his unquenchable thirst for travel, friendship and most of all, bringing his light to people everywhere, as he would continue his ministry.

CHAPTER 25

A VETERAN MINISTERING TO VETERANS

Getting used to life as a civilian would surely take some time. Fr. Ron contemplated his options while being mindful of his medical and stress-related issues. There was little doubt that his body and mind had suffered more than he was willing to accept during the relatively short time he spent in Operation Desert Storm. He had always been able to pick up and go whenever and wherever the situation presented itself while still fulfilling his responsibilities. Most of the time, he felt just fine and would be able to continue as always, even if he was nearly 58.

He had moved back into his mother's house as soon as he left the Army, making her very happy that her boy was there. This was not the same place that he and his brothers had grown up in, since his folks had downsized as soon as their kids were on their own. Also, with his father's passing a few years ago, it felt a little strange being there, even though this was his home state of Vermont. He had plenty of space for the many items he had accumulated over the years. Even he was amazed at just how much he had managed to acquire. Every item had a story behind it, and every one was precious.

He made himself helpful to his mom and was happy to be able to do so. In spite of that, the early winter of 1992 was grey and gloomy, or perhaps just seemed that way to Fr. Ron as he recalled the snowy winters of the past when he would be on the ski slopes with bunches of friends and students, enjoying the icy snowflakes on his tongue as he laughed into the wind. He knew that he was not old, but now that his career with the Army was over, he felt a bit down as he contemplated his next move in his career path. He would always be a Catholic priest and knew that he was meant to continue in the vocation that he loved and that had brought him (and many others) so much joy over the years.

In December, he got a call from the Military Archbishop, Joseph Dimino, a former Navy chaplain residing in Washington, DC who suggested that he apply for employment with the US Department of Veterans Affairs. That call broke right through his temporary melancholy and he got right to it. He discovered that there was a position open at the V.A. Medical Facility in Bedford, Massachusetts for a Catholic Chaplain. He quickly applied for that spot and with his impressive background and experience; he was interviewed immediately and just as quickly was on the job.

One of his first cousins, Richard Marchant, known to Fr. Ron always as "Rich", and his family lived in Arlington, a Massachusetts town just east of Lexington and therefore not far from Bedford. Rich's mother was Fr. Ron's aunt, his father's sister. Back in the good old days as a youth growing up in Montpelier, Ronnie and the Marchant children had shared many good times on the farm, playing all sorts of kid's games, swimming in the nearby ponds and, occasionally, getting into a bit of mischief. Rich was the youngest of his siblings and although with the 20-year age gap between them, he and Ronnie didn't play together back then, they became great friends as adults. Fr. Ron had conducted Rich's wedding in 1973 to the delightful Janice Byrne. Rich and Jan went on to have four children, with Fr. Ron performing the baptisms of each of them. As soon as they heard that he had retired from the Army and would be working nearby in Bedford, they suggested that he come to stay with them. He was very happy with the offer and settled into their spare room. He enjoyed their company, reminiscing about family memories that really didn't seem very distant at all. They had plenty of space for him and all his priceless "stuff". He would frequently offer to cook a special meal for them based upon his learning experiences from his time as a 2nd lieutenant in the Washington DC area. After a few attempts, during which he realized how much he had forgotten about preparing a meal, he was happy to simply enjoy the food prepared by Jan. Although the Marchants would have loved to have him as their houseguest indefinitely, he stayed at their place for only a few weeks.

For the next six years he was the go-to chaplain in the sprawling V.A. facility in the small town of Bedford, with Hanscom Air Force Base nearby, and with its next-door town of Lexington, famous for its Minutemen in Revolutionary days. Bedford was only 15 miles (24 km) northwest of Boston and all that the city had to offer, and had provided to him in the past. He was made for this job.

The year 1993 was the beginning of what would be six years of Fr. Ron's work at the Bedford facility. Much of his time was spent in the clinic for those veterans, many of whom had served heroically in Vietnam, who were now in treatment for substance abuse (alcohol and drug addiction). There were also a few patients who had served in his Gulf War. He had received excellent training in his CPE courses at Fort Benning as an addiction therapist and had dealt with some very difficult cases there. He saw much of the same behavior here in this suburban town with veterans from miles away. Although he was not surprised, it bothered him to realize that those problems were so pervasive.

In addition to his work with the veterans in the substance abuse clinic, he also took on a position in the clinic for the homeless. This was known as the Domiciliary and focused on those who needed training in new job situations as well as those who needed legal advice and educational skill updates. Altogether, these positions were very challenging and interesting to him, absorbing him fully. He enjoyed the work it sometimes took to talk about spiritual issues with people who haven't had contact with God in a long time, yet so desperately need Him. He found this assignment very demanding, as he counseled people who have suffered not only from addiction, but also from many losses in life: loss of family, dignity, self-esteem, faith, meaning in life as well as hope. He really had no idea of how effective he was being with them, but realized that the importance of his role there was to show the concern of another human being for someone who has nowhere else to go but up.

In his work there at the V.A. facility, he networked with many experienced and talented individuals, none more helpful to him and the vets than Katherine F. (Kay) Arnold, a volunteer patient advocate. She was the widow of Bill Arnold who had been a young officer with the elite Special Operations Forces of the Army Rangers and who had seen significant service in World War II. He had been captured and held as a Prisoner of War in Germany for nearly two years. By the time Chaplain Lawson arrived on the scene, Kay's many years of experience in helping veterans with legal issues and with making helpful contacts with the outside world for them once they were to be released from programming, was of monumental value to him in assisting veterans to once again become good citizens in the community.

Chaplain Lawson celebrated Mass in the nondenominational chapel on a regular basis. Many of the veterans who attended his Masses would frequently approach him once the service was complete and exchange war stories. Many of these young people had seen and experienced things they had never previously openly discussed. He wound up doing a lot of counseling in his time at this V.A. facility; not all of it in a neat office, but whenever and wherever it was needed.

Although he enjoyed the hospitality shown to him by his cousin's family, and they enjoyed his company in their home, after a few weeks with them, Fr. Ron thought it would be a good idea for him to find a nearby apartment. Rich's wife, Jan, recalled seeing a sign on the lawn of a nice house nearby indicating that there was a furnished apartment for rent within. It was conveniently located on Fessenden Road in Arlington, right off Massachusetts Avenue, which was the main route out of Arlington, through Lexington and into Bedford and the V.A. facility. They drove over to see the place and meet the homeowners who lived upstairs over the vacant first floor apartment. Fr. Ron, always an excellent judge of character, took a liking to the elderly couple right away; and they to him. As he was being shown around the property, he spotted a statue of the Blessed Virgin Mary out in the back yard. He signed up for the apartment on the spot. Rich, Jan and the kids helped Fr. Ron move his belongings into his new place and reminded him that they were not very far and hoped that he would continue to join them for dinners, at least once in a while. In spite of the fact that this apartment was neat and clean, was convenient to his work at the V.A. and that he enjoyed chatting with the home owners whenever he saw them, he would call this apartment home for only a few months; from late December 1992 to mid spring of 1993. It was fortunate that he had not been required to sign a long lease.

For pretty much his whole career as a priest he had always lived in a church rectory. After a few months at the Bedford V.A. facility, he was invited to live in such a setting once again. Home for him then shifted to a very comfortable room in the rectory of Saint Agnes Church, also in Arlington, along with six other priests. He very quickly bonded with his new housemates and enjoyed their company. They could never get enough of the stories of his travels and experiences. The other six ranged in age and experience from one young new priest to an 80 year-old Senior Priest in Residence, who had seen it all and enjoyed regaling the others with his memories, even if his memories may not have been crystal clear and even if he happened to tell the same story over and over. Three of the priests were parochial vicars for the parish, while one was working for Catholic Charities while he was in residence at this rectory. The other, Fr. Brian Flatley, was the pastor of St. Agnes Church. Fr. Ron would live in this setting for several years until a calamity forced all the residents out.

In August of '93 Fr. Ron managed to get away to Germany to visit Oberammergau and Unterwössen, two of his all-time favorite places in the world. He then traveled on to Ireland, a country he had not visited before, but always knew that he would. While in the Emerald Isle he had a wonderful reunion with a young Irish rock band he had met while he was in the Berlin Military Chapel back in 1987. He could hardly believe that this unusual rock band was still together and really doing quite well. He remembered his first impressions when he encountered them in Berlin six years previously. At one of his Masses then, as he was delivering his homily in his usual method of walking up and down the center aisle and talking from his heart to the congregation, he nearly lost his train of thought. There, several rows from the altar were seated three pretty young girls and one handsome young boy. The group had their hair spiked and, most arrestingly, painted a very vivid tone of green. It was no doubt that they were trying to make a statement. Just what that statement might be, was lost on the priest. They all smiled at him as he obviously was momentarily distracted by their appearance. As he quickly resumed his preaching, he remembered the sage advice about never judging a book by its cover. At the end of that Mass, the green-haired young folks came up to meet him as they politely commented on how much they enjoyed his homily. Finally, one of them, with a mischievous grin explained that they were an Irish rock band on tour, and that they called themselves *Who's Eddy*. Fr. Ron, with a wink in his eye, looked at the only male member of the group and said, "I'm betting that you're Eddy." It turned out that they were three sisters and a brother of the Molloy family: Dara, Jacqui, Orla and Keith from Dundalk, Ireland. It was good that Fr. Ron had not put any money on his bet that the only male in the quartet was Eddy. Their parents, Nualla and Ollie Molloy, who were about the same age as Fr. Ron, had come along with the young musicians on this tour enjoying the whole adventure and surreptitiously acting as chaperones for their kids.

Fr. Ron recalled that this group had been a big hit with the youngsters of his West Berlin parish back in '87, especially the ones preparing for their confirmation. The icing on the cake for the parish youth was a pre-confirmation concert for them by this rock band. It was held at the residence of

Brigadier General Marsh in the presence of Cardinal Meisner, the Bishop of Berlin at the time. Prior to that concert, they had washed the green out of their hair in deference to their audience and looked quite presentable. Their singing, with their strong backing band, had everyone in attendance, including the General and the Cardinal, smiling and rocking to the beat. Their performance included a powerful live act in which they mixed dance with disco, soul and great vocals. As they left General Marsh's residence, Dara expressed her appreciation to Fr. Ron for setting up their concert and, shaking his hand, made a comment to the effect that she and her group would someday see him again. Who could have predicted that not only would that youthful group stay together for six whole years and more, but also that they and Fr. Ron actually would meet once more? You never know.

Meeting this highly successful foursome again, but now near their home base, was not only a welcome surprise, but a chance to hear more of their unique, good-time musical blending of pop and mainstream dance and their own compositions. They presented Fr. Ron with a couple of their latest CDs; one was called *Right Now* and the other was labeled *Take Me Up*. They both contained the type of music that makes young people everywhere want to get up and dance to the pulsating percussion beat, special keyboard effects as well as the strong vocals. Very powerfully entertaining.

One of the most lasting and meaningful things Fr. Ron picked up while in Ireland was the tradition of saying the *Hail Mary* during Mass at the *Prayer of the Faithful*. Our Holy Mother was always of singular importance to him ever since he was first called to Catholicism over 30 years previously. Weaving that special prayer into his Masses became practically a trademark of his.

The year 1995 was a milestone year for Fr. Ron, since in May of that year he would celebrate the 25th anniversary of his ordination to the Roman Catholic priesthood. And celebrate he did. Even though he was beginning to feel the effects more strongly of his Gulf War illness, he refused to let that slow him down. His celebrations began in May with an anniversary Mass at St. Agnes, where he had been living for the past several years. One of his great buddies from his days back in the Army chaplaincy, Sam Boone, a Protestant chaplain currently stationed at Fort Jackson, South Carolina, was one of the speakers. Fr. Ron felt greatly honored by the fact that his pal took the time to be there and that Chaplain Boone's message left everyone in attendance with the clear knowledge that Fr. Ron had been well loved in his days with the Army Chaplain Corps. A few days later, he was back in his hometown of Montpelier, Vermont. There, he celebrated a Mass in St. Augustine's Parish Church where he had been ordained. Many people from his past; high school and college classmates and an array of relatives, both young and old were in attendance and all spoke highly of him, proud of what he had accomplished: none more so than his family.

The three amigos

The following week he was at St. Patrick's Basilica in Montreal to share his anniversary with friends and former students living in Canada. There was a well-attended reception for him at St. John Fisher Parish in Pointe Claire.

Not content to simply travel relatively locally, he had arranged a magnificent celebration back where it had really started for him: Bavaria. He celebrated Mass in the beautiful

Monastery at Ettal, the place where he, as a young Army officer, had entered the Catholic Church back in 1960. Just seeing the amazingly beautiful statue of Our Lady of Ettal over the main altar once again, rocked him to the core. In honor of his 25th anniversary, he was authorized to pick up the heavy and unique marble statue as he gave a brief blessing with it to the people assembled there. The monastery Mass was followed by the Sunday Liturgy at the village church in Oberammergau. Ascension Thursday Mass was held at the Romanesque pilgrimage church at Raiten, on the border of the Austrian Tyrol and only about a mile and a half (2.5 km) west of Unterwössen where he had spent so many wonderful days. What made this particular Mass extra special for him was that he concelebrated it with his dear friend, Father Franz Niegel, known to him as Franzi during the restorative eight months while he lived there in late 1967 and early 1968, regaining his call to the priesthood.

Fr. Ron with Franzi in the sacristy
of St. Martin Church

He saw a lot of familiar faces and enjoyed laughing over tales from the more carefree days back then. The last celebration before returning to the US was with some of his favorite people – the mountain people of the Chiemgau at the 8th century chapel in Streichen, high up on the side of an Alpine mountain. The German-Austrian border runs right through the middle of this old chapel, but the truly memorable part of this trip was that his rugged friends spent the entire afternoon with him, making music on their traditional instruments and singing as only they could.

As he flew back home, his aching joints and tired bones spoke to him in ways they never had before. Although he refused to allow the effects of his time in the Gulf to be obvious to other people, he knew that he was not as strong as he felt that he should be. And he realized that in spite of his efforts to mask it, others did notice his pain. While he was in Heidelberg after his return from the desert war, he had developed a sudden loss of cartilage in both knees, making walking very painful. His chronic edema of both ankles that really affected his entire lower legs, was hidden from view by his clothing, unless he wanted to wear shorts or a bathing suit. Most people did not see that swelling, but noticed that his gait was off as he walked. There was no question that he suffered post traumatic stress disorder as a result of having to deal with dead bodies in combat as well as the constant threat of attack with all manner of weaponry, even if he had convinced himself that he was immune from any real danger. The anxiety disorder, PTSD, is known to be a severe and ongoing emotional reaction to an extreme psychological trauma. Many veterans of Desert Storm were told that they had Gulf War Syndrome, a condition whose symptoms for some time were controversial. Nearly identical illnesses in previous years had gone under the heading of "shell shock", "battle fatigue" and "traumatic war neurosis". Whatever it would be called, some early medical tests were done to try to get to the root of the problems. This included checking to determine if he was harboring a parasite, or whether he had unknowingly inhaled poisonous gases. Those tests, along with the evaluation of why he should experience the sudden loss of knee cartilage and equally sudden swelling of his lower legs, were never really conclusive. His frequent nightmares and daytime flashbacks of stressful situations continued.

During his six years at the Bedford facility he conducted research on nearly 2000 patients. He had organized a format for interviewing patients to determine what their real needs were. The patients and the staff collaborated on this project. After a few years, Fr. Ron realized that he had assembled an impressive amount of data. With the significant help of a researcher on the staff, the material became a published paper. At the urging of the staff researcher, Dr. Charles Drebing, and others, Fr. Ron wrote to the American Psychological Association in Chicago asking if he might present this paper documenting the results of his research to that august group. In relatively short order, the APA got back to him with a form for him to fill out and return. He couldn't help but think that they were almost as bad as the Army when it came to paperwork.

Eventually, in the fall of 1997, he was invited to deliver his paper, *The Long Term Impact of Child Abuse on Religious Behavior and Spirituality in Men*, before the American Psychological Association in Chicago.

He delivered a second paper to the same organization in San Francisco in 1998: *The Spiritual Injury Scale: Validity and Reliability*. Both papers were well received by the APA. Chaplain Lawson enjoyed the lively discussions that followed each presentation.

All of the data in both these papers was quite complicated and had required a significant input from the V.A. researchers, Dr. Drebing and his staff, to steer Fr. Ron through the content format. Although the papers were indeed presented successfully, they were never implemented as such. However, Fr. Ron was hailed as one of the few V.A. chaplains who had published something of note.

On a Friday afternoon in May 1997 the Rectory at St. Agnes Church burned to the ground. All seven of the priests who had been living there lost essentially everything, but fortunately no one was injured in the conflagration. Somehow, a fire had started in the wall behind the kitchen stove on the first floor and flared out into the rectory on the third floor. Fire departments from Arlington and a few surrounding towns were quickly summoned and had the blaze under control shortly, but not before the Rectory was a total loss. Fr. Ron had been at work at the Bedford V.A. and knew nothing about the inferno until he headed back to the Rectory and saw the fire apparatus blocking access to his home. He was stunned, but grateful to realize that no one had been physically hurt by the flames. The diocesan newspaper, *The Pilot*, showed a front-page photo of Fr. Ron holding the tabernacle that had been rescued from his room, with Cardinal Bernard Law and a fireman looking on. With the fire doing so much damage, it was surely a miracle that the private tabernacle escaped harm.

Cardinal Law amazed at
condition of Tabernacle.

Photo © Lisa Kessler

Fr. Ron had a close priest friend, Fr. Jim DiPerri, who had, just a few years earlier, been a parochial vicar at St. Agnes and had lived there in the Rectory. Once he heard about the St. Agnes blaze, Fr. Jim offered the suddenly homeless priest the opportunity to reside with him in the Rectory of St. Catherine of Siena in Charlestown, Massachusetts. This church was close to the Boston Harbor waterfront, but still not that far from the V.A. Hospital in Bedford. Fr. Ron really loved his new home in Charlestown since once he had arrived on the scene, he was constantly interfacing with younger clergy and seminarians that were working with the poor in the inner city. As Fr. Ron, aided by Fr. Jim and other helping hands, moved what was left of Fr. Ron's possessions into his new quarters, realizing how intense the fire had been, all were amazed to discover how relatively unharmed was Fr. Ron's ordination gift from Mother Trapp. That colorful hand-carved wooden statue of Our Lady had suffered only slight smoke stains which, with a bit of effort, were banished from view. Also, his beautiful wooden plate signed by his young friend, Lenzi, was unharmed.

In the spring of 1998, Fr. Ron had the opportunity to apply for an opening in the National office of the Chaplain Service located in Virginia. This would be a very interesting promotion for him and he knew it was something that would continue to stretch his intellect while still keeping him at his life's work in the priesthood. Once again, he rounded up his local friends to say farewell as he prepared to head south. He always felt that he personally had gained something from each and every one of his assignments and the many people he had come to know. This one in Bedford had been no different.

Once he got to his southern destination, he got right to work at the National Headquarters of the Chaplain Service of the US Department of Veterans Affairs in Hampton, Virginia. Within a year he was promoted to the position of Associate Director of the National V. A. Chaplain Service. In that role he represented the interests of the chaplain staffs in the 40 or more V.A. medical centers located on the US East Coast, all the way from Maine to West Virginia. He also served as senior Roman Catholic priest in the V.A. and chief consultant to the more than 300 priests who were employed then in the 172 V.A. medical centers across the United States. He also served as the National Secretary of the V.A. Catholic Chaplains organization. As might be expected, fulfilling these duties involved a significant amount of travel as well as public speaking engagements all over the country. Of course he had always enjoyed being on stage and speaking before large audiences, as he thought back on the great times he had had in his high school performances in *The Mikado* and other fun plays. However, these current performances were not choreographed affairs, but required a significant amount of on-the-spot problem solving and, occasionally what he would refer to as fence mending. He loved leading the many conferences, running workshops and doing a fair amount of recruiting as well. By special arrangement with the Military Archdiocese, Fr. Ron was given the designation, *Special Liaison of the Archdiocese for the Military Services to the Department of Veterans Affairs.*

Once again, his home-away-from-home was in a Rectory of a Catholic church, this time in the Hampton Roads area in Norfolk, Virginia. This particular church captivated him from the moment he first saw it. It was bound to happen sooner or later, but it still caused an almost electric feeling when he realized that it was the parish of St. Pius X. It seemed that this special saint was continuing to keep an eye on him. He couldn't help but notice that the altar in this church of St. Pius X did not have a relic in the altar stone as had been customary since the earliest of times, but was now no longer a requirement. A "relic" would be a tiny portion of a saint's body, such as a bone or even a bone chip. Fr. Ron had a first class relic of St. Pius X. A first class relic is the physical remains of a saint, such as a bone, or a hair. A second-class relic would be something that a saint wore or used, while a third class relic, usually a piece of cloth, would be something that touched a first or second class relic. He had been carrying this very precious bone fragment from his favorite saint around with him ever since a chance meeting with a priest in Montreal at the church of St. Thomas Aquinas. At that location, there was a fairly large collection of such relics as well as a broken chalice that the priest was about to dispose of. Fr. Ron rescued the relic of St. Pius X, along with papers documenting its authenticity. He saw to it that the small portion of the Saint's remains was implanted into the altar stone, where it remains to this day.

Fr. Ron was duly impressed by the geographical area he was then living in. "Hampton Roads" describes both a body of water and the significant amount of land area that surrounds it. A prominent feature in that locale is known as "The Harbor" and is one of the world's biggest natural harbors, while its land area includes dozens of cities and towns. Military facilities nearly overwhelm the harbor, while still leaving room for shipyards, coal piers and hundreds of miles of waterfront properties and beaches.

He was kept very busy with his duties in the chaplain service, but also celebrated Mass and preached to a large congregation every Sunday. He also served as Chaplain at nearby Langley Air Force Base for the four years he would serve in this assignment.

In March of 1999, Fr. Ron got a phone call from both his brothers who told him that their mother had passed away suddenly at the age of 87. He quickly packed a few things and was on the next jet to Burlington, Vermont where Sidney met him. He knew that his mom had been in failing health for several months. A hospital bed had been set up in her living room where she could be reasonably comfortable while being looked after by a combination of Visiting Nurses and her local sons and her daughter-in-law, Corinne. Osteoporosis, mostly affecting her hip and spine had led to small fractures of her spine, and eventually a fractured hip. This led to a pulmonary embolism, causing her death.

On Thursday, March 4, 1999 at eleven in the morning, there was a *Celebration of the Life of Ruth E. Lawson, age 87,* held in the Waterbury Center Community Church in Vermont. This old Methodist church, built in the early 1800s, had been where Fr. Ron's mother had worshipped as a youngster and had been thought of by her as her home church. She had expressed her wish to be buried from that church when her time came. For several years she had been an active member of the Trinity Methodist Church of Montpelier near her adult

410

home, where young Ronnie attended services and where he sang in the teen choir. Now he was back in Vermont as a Roman Catholic priest to conduct his mother's funeral.

He wore an alb (similar to a tunic) under a white stole, which was a long scarf of embroidered linen that he wore over both shoulders. He could sense her supportive presence as he joined with the congregation in singing the Opening Hymn, *Amazing Grace*. This was followed by his scripture reading from Thessalonians, after which the congregation, including Fr. Ron, sang the traditional hymn *The Old Rugged Cross*. After leading the Responsive Reading of *The Consolation of Isaiah*, Fr. Ron read a passage from Matthew, one his favorite Gospel readings. The congregation was seated and silently wept as he delivered a heart-felt remembrance of the life of his mother. He then invited comments from the congregation and was comforted to witness several people stand up and give short presentations about his mom, each of them praising her virtues. All stood as he led them in the recitation of *The Lord's Prayer* and then gave the Closing Blessing after which the congregation sang the old hymn *Softly and Tenderly*.

Built 1832-1833
Waterbury Center Community Church
Waterbury Center, Vermont

Fr. Ron and his family invited everyone present to join them in the downstairs dining room where he greeted many people he had not seen in years as well as some he had never met. All of his mother's living relatives and many of her friends were present, including her 90 year-old childhood friend, Alice Sweet, a cousin. It was comforting to hear so many people say so many positive and, in many ways, remarkable, things about his dear mother. It was pointed out that before she was married, Ruth Ella Russell had been trained as a teacher in what was then known as Montpelier Seminary (now part of Norwich University) graduating with the class of 1931. She had been so proficient in French that she had been exempt from having to study that language. Her father had died at a young age, leaving her with only her mother and several close-knit siblings. She had had to work for her room and board while she was in training but always had done so cheerfully. Although she must have been disappointed to discover after she married later in 1931, that it was against Vermont law for a married woman to teach in public schools, she greatly enjoyed her family, giving her three boys and her Fire Chief husband total devotion.

Fr. Ron received many words of praise for the sensitive and faith-filled ceremony he had conducted. He accepted all these compliments graciously, but deep in his heart he had longed for the opportunity to provide the blessed Eucharist, as had been his privilege for nearly the past 30 years. His mother's casket was then taken to the nearby cemetery and solemnly buried next to her husband.

One of Fr. Ron's closest relatives whom he had not seen in quite a while was his nephew, Dan Lawson, son of Milan and Corinne. Dan, born in July 1964, was a sturdily built young man now and the two of them enjoyed talking about one of Dan's passions in life, football. Dan's great grandfather, Ira Warner Lawson excelled at football back in 1898 when he was a student at Goddard College located in rural Vermont. Dan believes that he has inherited "football genes" from great-grandpa Lawson and continues to play at a high level of proficiency in an adult league. It is his house painting business however that helps him pay his bills. Dan enjoyed his chat with his uncle, impressed with the fascinating adventures that have come his way as a Catholic priest. When they parted, they promised each other that they would stay in touch.

Nephew Dan

May 18, 2000 found the intrepid traveling priest back in Oberammergau, Bavaria. He was there, at the special invitation of the pastor of its parish church, to attend the opening of the Passion Play. He was very moved by the thoughtfulness of that pastor and even more so by the splendor of that decade's opening presentation of the world-famous play. This performance seemed to be more awe-inspiring than any of the previous ones he had seen. He also took advantage of this locale and timing to celebrate 30 years of his ordination into the priesthood. He made a silent pledge to himself that he would repeat the celebration again at the next decade's presentation in 2010.

In early September 2001, Fr. Ron traveled from Virginia to Washington, DC with a group of Catholic chaplains from the Military Archdiocese to attend a retreat run by the Sisters of the Atonement at the Franciscan Retreat Center located adjacent to the National Shrine of the Immaculate Conception. Early in the morning of September 11, Fr. Ron was up early and prayed the prayers of the Divine Office, as had been his routine for many years. At this location, the other chaplains and two bishops who were in attendance joined him in those early morning special prayers. He and the other military and V.A. chaplains had been on this retreat for three days now and he was enjoying the experience. After a hearty breakfast with his comrades, he strolled around the outdoor garden areas within the Retreat Center. He gazed up at one of the clearest blue skies he had seen in a while, thinking to himself how beautiful were God's creations. The crisp fall air added to his feelings of calmness and well-being. As he was enjoying the morning and looking forward to the next portion of the retreat, one of his chaplain friends approached him looking pale and shaken. What Fr. Ron was then being told was not believable. The news his friend was bringing him could not possibly be accurate. They quickly got to a TV set and saw that the World Trade Center buildings in New York City had been flown into by what appeared to be hijacked passenger jets. No one had any real idea of what was happening or what was about to happen, but everyone was stunned. The first airliner that flew into one of the Twin Towers did so at 8:45 AM, just as Fr. Ron had been enjoying the beautiful and peaceful morning. The second one crashed into the other tower at just after 9 AM. The group of chaplains and the Sisters were glued to the television as were pretty much the rest of the people of the world, with no one understanding this unbelievable horror. Shortly, at nearly quarter of ten, American Airlines flight 77 crashed into the Pentagon, sending up huge plumes of smoke and triggering immediate evacuation. By 10:10 AM, portions of the Pentagon collapsed while at that same moment, United Airlines flight 93 crashed into a field in Somerset County, Pennsylvania; southeast of Pittsburgh. It was later determined that that aircraft was headed for the Capitol or perhaps the White House, but the bravery and heroic action of passengers prevented it from completing its plan as they overtook the hijackers and caused this plane to crash into a field.

All the chaplains at the retreat with Fr. Ron who were associated with the Pentagon, only a little over seven miles southwest of where the retreat was being held, were called back immediately to aid in whatever way they could at the smoky, unprecedented scene of destruction of a part of that famous building. Other chaplains headed off quickly for New York City to help out there, but were soon caught up in snarled traffic on the highways and rail lines. The FAA had shut down all New York City airports by 9:17 AM and by 9:40 AM they had taken the unprecedented action of halting all flight operations at all US airports. The gridlock that brought nearly all street traffic in DC to a virtual stop made it practically impossible to even consider trying to get anywhere in that area. It was much later, in the early evening, before Fr. Ron was able to get over to the Pentagon to see if there was any way he could be of aid. The fires in that portion of the building were still burning well into the evening and were reported to be "…contained, but not under control." He could see for himself the damage that was done to that building, wondering how many lives had been lost in the attack and if there were people in there even then that may be trapped. He would never forget the smell of that unbelievable smoke and seeing the nightmarish ruined building side while feeling helpless to do anything about it. He was fully prepared to give any kind of aid to anyone that he might come across in the ruins, or if God willed it, to provide a Final Blessing. He always carried the Holy Oils with him in his car, so as to be prepared to provide the sacrament of Extreme Unction should such a need arise anywhere. However, he was not called upon to provide this final blessing on this never-to-be-forgotten day.

It was discovered a few days later, that the very spot where the hijacked airliner had hit the Pentagon was where the office of the Chief of Army Chaplains had been located. This had been the place where Fr. Ron had been interviewed just prior to his rejoining the Army as a chaplain in 1984. The office and all its contents had been relocated to another part of the building, quite a distance away in order to clear space for some building reconstruction that had not yet been completed when the attack took place.

Fr. Ron returned to his duties with the V.A. in Norfolk, Virginia but felt himself slowing down a bit and tiring out a little sooner in the day than he used to. Although work went on pretty much as usual, there was a heightened level of security throughout the area. He was living among a large number of military installations where it was obvious that nothing was taken for granted with regard to any type of potential terrorist attack from any quarter. Most of his parishioners at St. Pius X Church were military. There was a constant awareness of personal security for all of them and their families. Nothing would be the same after the horrific events that still seemed somehow unreal.

As part of his duties, Fr. Ron spent a few days at the Manhattan V. A. offices where the smoke and rubble every-where were constant reminders of what had seemed to be starting out as a beautiful day, but turned so tragic. He also was on the move nearly every day as he traveled for the V.A. to interface with chaplains at the various installations over which he had responsibility. He went to California to visit with the Catholic chaplains there to help them cope with whatever problems they may be having in carrying out their specific ministry. He also bounced from hospital to hospital along the East Coast to conduct similar interviews with several chaplains: some very junior and inexperienced and others very familiar with their roles and missions, but who were still pleased to get his inputs and support.

He was glad that he had made a wise choice in finally trading in his old Chevy with which he had traveled around so much of Germany. He had done his best to keep it well maintained, but it was becoming worn out. He traded it in for a new, 2001 Chevy Blazer SUV. That vehicle suited him much better now that he was finding getting into and out of the old car a bit of a hassle. The SUV provided him with great legroom and he really liked the better view of the road he had from the driver's seat. There was a lot he liked about his new wheels.

In late October 2002 as he was approaching his 69th birthday, he thought that it may be time to retire from government service. He was clearly eligible for such a change in status and knew he was getting a bit older. The concept of retirement did not come easily to the normally very active and outgoing priest, but he knew that he would always be involved in one way or another with parish life and with ministering to its flock.

It was time once again to say good-bye to close friends and to pack his belongings for yet another move. Instead of returning to the greater Boston area directly, this time he planned to drive further north to Montpelier, Vermont and his family home.

CHAPTER 26

"RETIREMENT"

Fr. Ron took his time driving north, enjoying the scenery, but not the heavy traffic, along the way. There was little doubt that the traffic had gotten progressively worse over the years and it seemed to him that more drivers were blowing right by him as he tried to keep his speed to no more than about 5 or 10 miles an hour above the posted speed limit. It had been a little over two years since he had spent much time at his family home in Montpelier. The last time he was there was when he had come up from Norfolk, Virginia to conduct his dear mother's funeral service in March 1999. Sidney, Jr. had been living there since before their mom passed away, the homestead then having been passed along in joint ownership to Ron and Sidney.

Fr. Ron was pleased at the way his kid brother had been maintaining the property. He had almost forgotten how beautiful the leaves on the many trees in the area could be at this time of year. As he gazed at them, he was for no apparent reason, reminded of his strange episode while out for a run one beautiful fall day in 1969 at the Seminary of Our Lady of Angels in New York. He hadn't thought about that "uplifting" experience in a long time and wondered again at its significance. The men brought each other up to speed on happenings in their lives with Sidney noticing that his brother clearly was in a lot of pain much of the time, but that he still managed to do whatever he wanted and to travel to whichever destination called to him. Fr. Ron pointed out that he expected that soon, perhaps right after the first of the year, he would be heading off to somewhere in the greater Boston area so that he could get much-needed medical treatment for his conditions. Sidney voiced the thought that it was good that Ron had retired: enough already!

Even though he had retired from government work with the Department of Veterans Affairs, he knew that as long as he maintained his intellect, which showed no signs of diminishing in the slightest, and was in good enough health to get around, even if it involved some pain; maybe even a lot of pain, and the use of a cane, he would never retire from the Roman Catholic priesthood. In fact, the whole concept of retirement did not sit well with the active and alert Fr. Ron.

After a couple of weeks at home in Montpelier, he got a phone call from the Catholic chaplain in Heidelberg who had successfully tracked him down. The chaplain asked him if he would be willing to come back to help out under contract. Many, in fact nearly all, of the priest-chaplains who had been providing their ministry there were now off to Iraq, Kuwait and Afghanistan. The proposal was very appealing to Fr. Ron who then drove to Canada to consult with his bishop, Cardinal Jean-Claude Turcotte of Montreal, to obtain official approval for this unprecedented move.

With Cardinal Turcotte at Montreal's
Grand Seminary

Cardinal Turcotte, about a year and a half younger than Fr. Ron, had been appointed Archbishop of Montreal in 1990. Among many other noteworthy episodes in that cardinal's past included the significant role he played in organizing all that needed to be done to host the historic visit to Canada of Pope John Paul II in 1984. Many highly placed individuals in the Catholic Church had expressed the thought that Cardinal Turcotte would make an excellent pope. Fr. Ron always addressed this pillar of the Church as "Monseigneur" when referring to him as Archbishop or "Your Eminence" as Cardinal and was pleased at how well this Bishop always treated him.

After they reviewed the work that Fr. Ron had done since rejoining the Army as a chaplain back in 1984 and everything he had accomplished since he left the Army in November 1992, they then consulted with the Military Archbishop (MilArch) in Washington, and a decision was made. At the strong suggestion of the MilArch, Fr. Ron was indeed assigned to work, as a civilian, on an eleven-month contract with the US Army in the Heidelberg military community, beginning in January 2003. He was very happy with the assignment and eagerly looked forward to again being in a part of the world that he had come to know and love.

Fr. Ron knew that when he returned to the US after his new assignment was up, he would want to locate to the Greater Boston area, near the V.A. medical facilities. He drove to the restored rectory at St. Agnes Church where he knew that he could spend at least a weekend while he made plans for his return in about a year. From that rectory he phoned a priest friend from his earlier time at St Catherine of Sienna in Charlestown, Fr. Jim DiPerri. Fr. Jim, who at that time was on the faculty of Pope John XXIII National Seminary in Weston and had other assignments as well, had a brief opening in his schedule and drove over to St. Agnes to see Fr. Ron with a potential solution to his friend's housing needs in mind. Once they had caught up on old times and brought each other up to date on the more recent activities in each other's lives, Fr. Jim drove him over to Winchester.

There, he introduced Fr. Ron to Fr. Tom Foley, pastor at Immaculate Conception Church in that relatively small but prosperous town. Fr. Tom, like so many others before him, took an instant liking to Fr. Ron and after learning about his fascinating background with more than a lifetime of experiences around the world, was happy to offer him the opportunity to join his parish as "Senior Priest in Residence" whenever he returned from his contract assignment in Germany. Fr. Tom showed him the room in the rectory that he would stake out for him and suggested that once he was ready to head across the ocean, that he drive to this Winchester church and leave his car in their garage until he got back and was ready to settle down again. Problem solved.

For a while there, at the end of 2002, it had looked as though the entire Lawson family of Milan, Ron and Sidney, Jr. would all be retired. Both of Fr. Ron's brothers had retired from their jobs with the State of Vermont in the spring of that year. While both Milan and Sidney had eagerly anticipated their retirements and had a string of activities that they were looking forward to, Fr. Ron had been uneasy about the concept of retirement. But now, with the MilArch's great plan, he was chomping at the bit to get back into the business of doing what he was meant to do and feeling younger by the minute. He looked forward to being reunited with some of his military pals and also getting back in contact with his many German friends as he packed his essentials for his upcoming transatlantic flight. He couldn't remember just how many times he had flown that route, but he had surely accumulated a bunch of frequent flier miles.

Fr. Ron spent most of 2003 serving as a civilian with the US Army in the area of Heidelberg, celebrating Masses and being available for confessions or simply consultation as may be needed. He was housed in an apartment building adjacent to Mark Twain Chapel. This was just across the street from where he had lived when he was last stationed in this beautiful city in the southwestern portion of Germany, back in 1991. More than 3 million tourists visit the romantic town of Heidelberg each year. Several special events are hosted there to help increase the tourist trade. A Classical Music Festival is held each spring. Every summer one of the featured events is the Castle Festival during which performances of plays such as *The Student Prince* are well attended. Illumination of the castle and the old bridge with strings of lights and fireworks adds to the festive atmosphere. Fr. Ron had not had much extra time to take in these and other special events in his previous time in this city, but even though his duties kept him more than busy, he was able to enjoy most of the charming activities this time while there as a civilian.

He met many young soldiers in the hospital and had the opportunity to get to know them. They were extraordinary young people whom he felt honored to serve. Having been in the first Gulf War in 1991 in Saudi Arabia and Iraq, he was in a unique position to empathize with the circumstances these troops were facing. The fact that he was now a civilian, but was doing practically the same things on a day-to-day basis as he did when he was a military chaplain just made him smile all the more often. He knew that he was doing God's work and enjoyed the interaction with troops and civilians alike. No uniform or rank needed.

His contract with the Army in Heidelberg, which was for nearly a full year, seemed to fly by and before he knew it, it was late in 2003 and time to head back to the Boston area. The plan that he and Fr. Tom Foley had worked out nearly a year previously was still good. Upon his arrival in Boston, Fr. Ron made his way to Winchester and the Immaculate Conception Church. It didn't take long to shake off the effects of jet lag and to once again get right into being active with another parish. It really came as no surprise that he blended in very smoothly as Senior Priest in Residence there, soon becoming a favorite of many parishioners.

In his new assignment he had time to ease back a bit and reflect on his life and the society around him. Between assisting in this parish ministry, catching up on his reading, and immersing himself once again in his family's genealogical research, his days flew by. Of course, he was still in serious and fairly constant need of medical treatment that he continued to get at nearby veterans' hospitals. With his 2001 SUV at his disposal, he was able to drive himself to medical appointments as necessary and not be a burden on anyone else in the rectory in that regard.

It was true that he really found getting to places he wanted to be was more difficult these days and had recently begun treatment on a regular basis at the Veterans hospital system for his severe osteoarthritis, mainly in his legs as well as stenosis-induced nerve problems, also affecting his legs. Adding to his difficulties was the loss of cartilage in both his knees, making walking painfully difficult. Twice a week he would spend up to a couple of hours pushing himself hard at physical therapy in a local gym. He made it a challenge to try to go a little longer each time as he worked out on their state-of-the-art treadmills and elliptical machines. His physical therapists were always impressed at his determination to regain strength, but it was clear that he was in pain more frequently these days. Working out in the heated pool, doing aerobic exercises, was the closest thing to fun that he did while being supervised by a therapist. But when all the formal routines were done for the day, he would simply enjoy swimming and recalling his many days teaching that wonderful sport to so many kids. But with his current physical limitations, even that once-so-natural and carefree activity was a challenge.

A few of Fr. Ron's friends had made the strong suggestion to him that he seek out a highly skilled local chiropractor. Some of those friends, or their acquaintances had seen phenomenal results with all manner of back problems at the hands of such practitioners. It didn't happen overnight for them, but after a few months of careful physical manipulation of individual vertebrae along with readjustment of the spine and other specialized hands-on procedures, many of these friends had begun to experience significant relief from their pain. Fr. Ron, after listening to the many success stories, was convinced that there would be a very good chance that his spinal stenosis could be greatly improved and that the pain in his legs would be relieved. He visited a well-known and highly recommended chiropractor for nearly two years. He always left the office feeling that the man had really done a great job of moving parts of his skeletal structure around to perhaps where they ought to be. However, he never got any relief from the pains in his legs and eventually gave up on what had at first looked like a promising treatment.

Unlike some of the other people he would chat with at the gyms or that he might come into contact with in the parishes he served, he did not let any of his aches and pains stop him from doing the things that mattered in his life nor would he let them hold him back from traveling whenever and wherever the opportunity presented itself.

There was the distinct possibility that he might move back to Quebec to serve once again in the Archdiocese of Montreal. That thought was very interesting to him, but as he had learned to do over the years, he was waiting for God to point the way. Fr. Ron visited Montreal to discuss options with the head of the pastoral office that dealt with English language parish affairs. He was indeed offered a position as a pastor in one of Montreal's West Island's churches. The thought really appealed to him and he knew that he would truly enjoy such an assignment. With his significant background and experience in many levels of Roman Catholic priesthood as well as the administrative work that went with it, he knew that he would make a fine pastor. However, as he prayed over the choice offered to him, it was soon apparent that there were many obstacles to such a move. For one, he would need to become a Canadian resident once again. Although that thought was appealing enough, he was very concerned that his need for medical treatment would not be fulfilled as effectively in Quebec as it would surely be done in the greater Boston V.A. system with its nine campuses and their talented staffs located within a 40-mile radius of Boston.

Official papers were drawn up and signed by the Canadian cardinal granting him permission to reside in Boston and environs for as long as he wished. This written permission from the Montreal cardinal was a requirement, since back in 1977 he was legally incardinated in the Montreal Archdiocese. From that time on, the Montreal Archbishop has controlled his destiny. Anywhere Fr. Ron wanted to reside, or to work, even to re-join the Army, required his written permission, which he always readily granted. Incardination of priests in the Catholic Church, a process required of every priest in the world, ensures that a clear ecclesiastical superior is "in the loop". Fr. Ron continues to remain under the jurisdiction of the Montreal Archbishop who has always been more than satisfied with his priestly career.

He continued to live with Fr. Tom Foley in Winchester, enjoying that community for nearly the entire year of 2004, until it was announced that this was one of the churches in the Boston Archdiocese to be closed. Fr. Foley moved on to become pastor at St. Ann's Church in Dorchester in September. Fr. Ron stayed on in the rectory of Immaculate Conception Church in Winchester until October when the parish officially closed, breaking the hearts of many parishioners who had known no other church. Fr. Foley asked Fr. Ron to come and reside with him at St. Ann's. He remained there, ministering to that parish and easily working his way into the hearts of yet another group of Catholics for the next four years.

St. Ann Church in Dorchester is located about a half a mile (3/4 km) from Dorchester Bay, which leads out to the Atlantic and is a few miles south of Logan International Airport. The friendly residents of that area of Dorchester, most of whom were parishioners at St. Ann Church hailed mainly from Irish or Italian roots. They had lots of little kids; about 300 of them were in the parish school where they learned the basics of the Catholic faith, leading towards their first Holy Communion. Fr. Ron enjoyed their bright-eyed enthusiasm and their open-minded approach to learning the basic beliefs being presented by their teachers, some of whom were nuns, while many others were lay people from the parish.

In the spring of 2005, Fr. Ron once again traveled to Germany where he spent precious time in Oberammergau, revisiting some of his favorite places. He then went on to Heidelberg to spend some time with friends who lived in St. Leon-Rot, a suburb about 10 miles (16 km) south of that beautiful city. These folks were a devout Catholic married couple, Dan and Theresa. Dan was a civilian working for the US Army under contract with the Department of Defense. Fr. Ron had met them just two years previously while he was on his contract assignment there. After Dan and Fr. Ron reminisced about their common backgrounds, the three of them set off for an excursion that would have them visiting Fatima in Portugal and, in about another month or so, exploring Naples, Italy.

Although the small group had visited the little village of Fatima previously, they wanted to go there again for no special reason other than to be close to Our Lady. They all knew the details of the fantastic story that had made the very name "Fatima" evoke strong prayerful emotions. It was in a field outside that little town, about 90 miles (145 km) north of Lisbon, that The Blessed Virgin Mary appeared six times to three very young shepherd children over a period of five months in 1917. The fact that Our Lady gave three messages ("secrets") to the children and hence, to the world, is widely known. The continuing concern that remained for quite some time over the "third secret of Fatima" made the miraculous encounter with The Blessed Virgin all the more mysteriously fascinating since its message was not disclosed at the time the first two were. That secret had been revealed to the Vatican shortly after the first two by Blessed Lucia, who was ten-year old Lucia in 1917, to be the vision of a man dressed in white being shot. This was understood to be a reference to the 1981 attempted assassination of Pope John Paul II in St. Peter's Square although the secret was not disclosed by the Vatican until May 2000.

While the group was attending a Mass being said in Polish in the open-air worship site surrounding the spot where the Blessed Virgin had appeared to the three visionaries, the priest solemnly announced that Pope John Paul II had just died. Everyone at that Mass was stunned and stayed there as the priest led the congregation in prayer. They then quickly scurried to their nearby hotels and watched TV with sorrow to understand what was going on in Rome. They knew that the funeral would take place six days later and then be followed by the traditional nine days of mourning, known as the *novemdiales* devotional, with the Pope's body lying in state in the Vatican.

While in Portugal, but with heavy hearts due to the loss of the much-loved Pope, Fr. Ron and his friends visited briefly in the Lisbon area as was their initial plan, and made it a point to go to the famous shrine at Santarém in The Church of The Holy Miracle. This is one of the most-visited pilgrimage sites in Portugal. In the thirteenth century, when it was known as the Church of St. Stephen, a Catholic woman with a philandering husband had made a pact with a sorceress whose price for "correcting" him was a consecrated Eucharistic host. After receiving communion at Mass, the woman surreptitiously removed the wafer from her mouth and hid it under a cloth as she attempted to rush out of the church with it to deliver her payment to the sorceress. The host immediately began to bleed, causing others in the church to think she had cut herself as they rushed to try to help her. She managed to get to her home where the frightened woman hid the bloody host in a trunk. She and her husband both confessed her sacrilegious behavior to the priest who immediately came to their home to retrieve The Blessed Sacrament and brought it back to his church. The liquefied host can be viewed to this day in its special mounting in a silver monstrance.

After visiting the shrine, the travelers spent the night in Lisbon, flying back to Heidelberg where they, along with many others, watched the papal funeral on television. What they observed with great sorrow was the largest single gathering of Christianity in history. Many kings, queens, presidents and prime ministers made their way to Rome to show their love and respect for the great man who was well loved throughout the world. It was estimated that four million mourners had made the trip and had solemnly walked by the pontiff's body to pay their last respects.

About a month later, the same group that had traveled together to visit Fatima traveled off to Naples, Italy. This was a pre-planned visit to get together with Army friends who were then stationed at the Naples Naval base on the west coast of Italy at the waters of the Tyrrhenian Sea. They spent a fun-filled week renewing old friendships and touring all around that beautiful oldest city in Italy. With views of Mount Vesuvius, which was not very distant, they enjoyed pizza Margherita in the local pizzerias, being surprised to learn that pizza actually originated in Naples. It was a relaxing visit during which they all enjoyed the crowded streets that offered views of beautiful old architecture including some marvelous churches.

It was soon time for Fr. Ron to say his farewells to his traveling companions and return to Dorchester and his residence at St. Ann Church. Shortly after settling back in there, he reflected on his understanding that the best way to be happy is to forget one's own sorrows and reach out to others. Also, he knew that prayer is always comforting, especially when it involves concern for others. He implemented that philosophy in a unique way. As his own gift to all of our soldiers who have died in Iraq and Afghanistan he began to celebrate a Mass in each one's memory, one-by-one. He started doing this in Germany while under contract with the Army in 2003 and knows that it will take several more years to complete. He has all the deceased soldiers' photos; their names and rank and their hometown information, obtained from *The Army Times* publication, and has it all stored in a computer file. It is unfortunate that he finds the need to increase the size of the list faster than he can say the individual Masses. This is something he is committed to doing until the task is complete; however long that may take.

In November of 2006, Fr. Ron was invited to a special wreath-laying ceremony at the Tomb of the Unknowns in Arlington Cemetery in Washington D.C. He met there for this solemn ceremony with his veterans group, the formal name of which is the Army Counter-Intelligence Corps Veterans or ACICV, people with whom he served while he was in Army Counter Intelligence in the 1950s and '60s. The vets honored him by making him their National Chaplain. He relished his meetings with friends that he had not seen in all those years, everyone reminiscing about things they had done and seen which, until recently, could not be openly discussed. He was saddened each time a name from that era was mentioned when it was discovered that that person had passed away. He confided to a few of his closest pals that he had made arrangements to be buried there in Arlington, in this most meaningful place when his time came. Since that meeting in 2006, it has been their plan to meet each year around Veteran's Day in November for the visit to the military cemetery and to share lunch and memories at the Army base at Fort Myer, Virginia.

While he was still in Washington, the day after the wreath-laying ceremony, the German Embassy hosted the 17th annual *Fall of the Wall* dinner party. Invited to this event were all those military personnel who had been stationed in Berlin in 1989 when the famous wall came down. Not only was Fr. Ron invited by the German Embassy to attend this annual celebration, but he was also asked to be a speaker before the dinner. Having been in West Berlin in 1961, when the Wall was first erected, and having also been there when it came down, made his presentation doubly interesting for the large audience. The *Fall of the Wall* party was great fun for everyone present and lasted until well after midnight.

In early December 2006, as he was heading back to the rectory of St. Ann Church after having just celebrated Mass, he stopped, as was his usual custom, to chat briefly with some of the parishioners who were on their way home. One of these smiling people handed him a note that made such an impression on him that he included it in his Christmas letter for that year. The following is a direct quote from that letter.

A couple of weeks ago, a parishioner gave me a note that made me smile rather broadly, and I have shared the message contained therein with various groups and from the pulpit. The message read: "GOOD MORNING! THIS IS GOD. I will be handling all of your problems today. I will not need your help! So, relax and have a great day!" With all the frustrations and problems we all face, what a refreshing message to contemplate! It is absolutely true that when faced with the impossible (serious illness, financial disaster, a break-up in relationships, a death in the family), we are often left helpless in knowing what to do. And so....putting everything consciously into God's Hands is the best solution to all problems in life. We mostly can't do anything about most problems anyway, so why not? My wish for you this Christmas is to leave everything in God's Hands and let Him direct the traffic in your life.

As Christmas 2006 approached, Fr. Ron was busy packing for yet another visit to Oberammergau, Bavaria. He spent the entire Christmas season and into the beginning of 2007 traveling around that intriguing Alpine region and being continually amazed that for the first time that he could remember, there was no snow on the ground at this usually snowy time of year. Regardless of the lack of snow, he enjoyed being with some of his favorite people and was particularly impressed with the beautiful midnight Mass liturgy in the unheated village church. Fr. Ron concelebrated that special Christmas Mass with the pastor, Father Peter. These two priests had met some time in 2002 when the young Fr. Peter had first arrived on the scene. This 18th century village church, known as the Church of St. Peter and St. Paul, was a charming building constructed in a striking Rococo style, but without a dependable source of heat. The interior of this frigid church glowed brightly from the many lit candles. An orchestra accompanied by an adult choir of mixed voices provided a beautiful medley of perfectly selected holy German Christmas music. The joyful sounds they made reverberated throughout the packed church. It was so cold inside the beautiful building that the worshipers could see their breath as they sang out, following along with the choir. Fr. Ron knew from past experience that it could very well be nearly as cold in the church as it was outside, so he had brought a warm set of long-johns with him and was glad that he had the foresight to wear them.

As Fr. Ron's assignment at St. Ann's continued, he found himself recalling many of the excursions he had been on, with each one of them having special meaning for him and, although perhaps not clear at the time of the trip, each one having an underlying reason for becoming important in his life. He especially remembered the first time Fr. Bill Carroll, with whom he had worked at St. Agnes before the fire, introduced him to a relatively newly ordained priest back in 1994, Fr. Steve Donohoe.

"Boston Priests" at shrine of St. John Vianney in Ars, France.
Recently ordained Fr. Steve Donohoe 2nd from right.

At the time, Fr. Donohoe was parochial vicar at St. Patrick Church in Lawrence, Massachusetts. The introduction was on a trip somewhere, but there had been so many similar trips that he wasn't really sure of just where in the world it was. At any rate, he recalled that he took an instant liking to the young Fr. Donohoe, ordained by Cardinal Bernard Law in 1992 after having completed his seminary training at St. John's in Brighton. That was a place he remembered well, even if he had been expelled in that earlier unbelievable misunderstanding. Fr. Ron and Fr. Donohoe would over the years, travel together with several other priests to a variety of different places, such as France; to visit all kinds of shrines and spiritually meaningful places, including Omaha Beach; to Ireland at least three times on retreat to Dublin with the well known and well-loved Sister Briege McKenna; to Italy, Spain and Portugal.

From his 1994 introduction to Fr. Donohoe, Fr. Ron had witnessed the young priest mature and grow in his devotion to the Church as well as to his country. He may have seen a bit of a younger version of himself in Fr. Donohoe who had been a Navy chaplain for four years from 1997 to 2001. During their many trips together, Fr. Ron and Fr. Donohoe discussed much of their own different backgrounds with each having a common view of life and ministry. Fr. Donohoe loved to travel almost as much as the priest that he no doubt thought of as "the old-timer" did.

After completing his work as a chaplain, Fr. Donohoe became parochial vicar at St. Patrick Church in Natick, Massachusetts. Fr. Ron was only marginally surprised to see his friend appointed in 2004 by Archbishop Sean O'Malley to the faculty of the archdiocesan seminary. Fr. Donohoe truly preferred being out in a parish setting, interfacing with the people whom he so enjoyed serving. On June 1st, 2007 he was appointed pastor of St. Mary Church in Chelmsford, Massachusetts and was immediately welcomed by the parishioners. All during the time that these two priests knew each other, from their first meeting in 1994, they found it easy to talk about all manner of things with the older, more experienced priest occasionally learning something new. Fr. Ron shared his thoughts with Fr. Donohoe about just where this senior priest should wind up living, asking if someday it might be possible for him to join the younger priest, wherever that may be.

After about four years at St. Ann Church, for a variety of reasons, Fr. Ron began to feel that he needed to move on and that it was time to have a change of venue. So, in November 2008, he made one phone call and asked if there just might be a place for him at St. Mary rectory in Chelmsford. Fr. Donohoe was delighted to be able to help out his fellow priest friend and was more than thrilled to have him move in.

Shortly before Thanksgiving of 2008, nearly a month before his 74th birthday, Father Ron Lawson arrived at St. Mary Parish in Chelmsford and was warmly welcomed by the parishioners as their Senior Priest in Residence. On his first Sunday in that new location, at the 11 AM Mass, he slowly made his way to the left side of the altar, using his cane for stability. He sat quietly while one of the parish priests said Mass. When it was finished he rose from his seat and made his way to the lectern. He immediately captivated yet another group of Catholics, young and old, as he introduced himself and gave a fascinating account of his basic story. As the faithful gradually came to know him, there was much after-Mass talk that centered around the thought that he was "very nice" and seemed quite "real" as he radiated his obvious devotion to his life's calling. Everyone was sure that he must have had many positive and even heart-warming experiences in his travels before arriving here. As an example that illustrates how people in his earlier assignments had been moved by his unique personality and strong faith, consider the following. Mary Catherine Rolston, who had been at St. Thomas High School 35 years previously when he was a chaplain there, recently wrote the poem below. She composed the moving tribute and mailed it to him as a birthday present in 2008. She and her husband have kept in touch with him over the years and are proud of the fact that he is Godfather to their eldest son, Matthew.

Father Ron

Burly with roots that run deep and wide
Standing tall with limbs that extend, protect and guide
Flexible and able to withstand storms, wars and time
His age means nothing as he forever seems like he is in his prime
Like the Angel Oak shelters, and endures
Listening, counseling, praying for God's mercy and cures
His piercing deep set eyes, jolly laugh have mesmerized many
youth
Challenging them to seek out spirituality, love and Christian truth.
His sermons have inspired, lingering with viscosity
Dynamic determination, humility and adventurous curiosity
Propelled to climb mountains, ski and hike during his favorite
season of snow
Shattering any winter negativity, fanning burning coals of optim-
ism to a glow
Drawn to the outdoors where his favorite color blue paints the
infinite skies, simple tastes, spaghetti and meatballs are always a
welcome surprise
This man of the cloth, rescuer of souls, dreams of covering skies
like a superhero desiring to fly
Charismatic, yet, humble,
surrenders to our Savior,
showing how in living we
must allow our egos to die.

When he first began celebrating Masses at St. Mary
Church in Chelmsford, he always made his way to the altar
with a sturdy cane at his right side. Climbing the few steps
behind the raised altar seemed a real challenge. In short
order, new railings were installed on either side and he
gratefully used them as he made his way to and from the
place that he was meant to be and was totally at home once
there. His voice was always strong and resonant as he said
the Mass. He was the first priest that any of the parishioners
had encountered who introduced the *Hail Mary* into the
Mass and everyone followed along in reverence. His homilies were always short and to the point; often educational,
sometimes with an amusing introduction, always inspiring

and frequently ending with the admonition to "Think about it."

He vanished from sight for a few weeks in July 2009 causing many regulars at the 11 AM Mass that he so often said, to wonder about his absence. He had gone into a local V.A. hospital to have both his knees totally replaced. They were done within a week of each other. He was back in the rectory in about a week and it wasn't very long before he came slowly walking up the center aisle, trusty old cane at his right side one Sunday at 11AM and upon reaching his destination behind the altar announced, "I'm baaack!" A round of applause followed that triumphal greeting, although most in the crowd really didn't know that he had gone to have the serious and usually quite painful knee replacement surgery.

Within six months after his surgery and with his new knees working so well, he was seen to come smoothly walking up that center aisle with a broad smile and swinging his arms. No cane needed. Once in place behind the altar, even though he still needed the help of the railings, he announced that "This is my maiden voyage - - without a cane!" Another round of applause. He honestly seems to be getting younger and has lost none of his vitality and Joie d'Vivre, with his people skills very much intact as he plans the 40th anniversary celebration of his ordination. That will take place, of course, in Oberammergau in June 2010.

Fr. Ron has touched the lives of so many and in return has been blessed by the many friendships he has made on his journeys. Now he has become a well-loved persona as Senior Priest in Residence in this new home he has made as he continues bringing his unique brand of spirituality and down-home goodness to yet another group of appreciative parishioners.

AFTERWORD
By Father Ron

SPIRITUALITY ON THE JOURNEY

My spiritual journey has included a number of different happenings that have served to increase the depth of my spiritual personhood. An example of that is my almost daily experiencing of the "sparks of light" for 50 years. In my travels to Ireland between 1995 and 2007 to spend time on retreat at All Hallows Seminary in Dublin, I had occasion to speak any number of times with the retreat director, Sister Briege McKenna, a Poor Clare nun famous for her healing ministry. Twice in my conferences with her, she explained something to me that she saw in my heart: that I stand spiritually in the presence of the Transfiguration event on Mt. Tabor; she saw light shining right through me onto the Blessed Sacrament, Who is, of course, Jesus the Lord. Sister said this in conference at least a couple of years apart, in reference to what was going on in my soul.

Father Arthur MacKay, in a paper on one of the Eastern Fathers, Gregory Palamas, in which St. Gregory discusses "Uncreated Light", he calls the light of the Transfiguration by that title, "Uncreated Light", generated by God out of nothingness. I feel that the sparks of light I have experienced over the years, and the revelation by Sister Briege are related to Uncreated Light. In a way, these are mystical responses to my request all those years ago in that Austrian chapel, to let me be a light.

And how has "Light" manifested itself?

Experiencing the "hug" of the Holy Spirit on the seminary grounds in Albany, in the fall of 1969 while running in the woods. I felt lifted up high in the air by someone who was hugging me. For about 3 months, whenever I opened the Tabernacle in the seminary chapel to distribute Holy Communion, I sensed that arms extended out from that Tabernacle to embrace me. It was an incredible sensation, a gift from the Holy Spirit for fidelity, I feel. Although the sensation did not last longer than a couple of months, the memory is still with me.

Jesus has appeared to me twice: once as a street beggar who came to the door of the Rectory on Green Street in Albany as I worked there during my time as a deacon. The church of St. John served as a social service center at the time, and as I ushered the man into the rectory to feed him, or whatever, once I got past the smell of alcohol, and the stink of the streets, I knew he was Jesus. It was in his eyes and made all the difference in the world as to how I treated him. Just as Blessed Mother Theresa of Calcutta has said, once one gets through His distressful disguise, one sees Who it is, in His eyes. The second time I saw Him was in Heidelberg in 2003 at the Post Exchange (like a military mall). He was walking across my path, appearing to me as a 20-year-old soldier in battle dress uniform. He turned briefly and looked at me, and then I knew Who it was. Both of these appearances were gifts to me.

In 1995 I received a phone call from Doug in Montreal, a friend whom I had not seen or been in touch with for a number of years. He simply wanted to tell me how much our friendship had made a difference in his life, that I had helped him survive his raucous and depressing youth. He said he needed to tell me that and thanked me profusely.

While stationed in Heidelberg as hospital chaplain, I received an anonymous note from someone who had been a parishioner in the military parish. The individual wanted to thank me for bringing him/her back to a belief in Jesus Christ. It was a simple and meaningful expression of gratitude.

A former student of mine from St. Thomas High School in Pointe Claire, Quebec, recently wrote:

"The reason I am writing…is to thank you from the bottom of my heart. You see, I was a very quiet, shy teenage girl – even as an adult, I'm not much of a conversationalist. But, I have been blessed with the gift of faith in Jesus from the time I was a young child preparing for my 1st Confession and 1st Holy Communion. You nourished that faith immensely during my high school years, and I want you to know just how much you impacted me spiritually. I will always remember that when I spoke to you, you gave me your undivided attention, and I noticed you did that with everyone – that kind of respect comes from recognizing the other as a child of God. However, I am most in debt to you for sharing your love and devotion to the Blessed Sacrament with us, by the way you offered up the Mass. You held the consecrated Host and chalice up with a beautiful reverence, and explained to us why. I used to attend Mass before classes started in the morning….and it was a very special time for me. Recently I have been preparing to do the "Mass Talk" on a retreat weekend, and I got to thinking about how I have grown in faith over a lifetime of attending Mass. I just wanted to "thank you" for your part in that. Your example and love rooted me deeply in a relationship with Jesus that I cherish. May God bless you always, Fr. Lawson."

In July of 1993 I was a houseguest at the home of Berlin military friends, John and Joan Mitchell, who were then living in Colorado Springs, Colorado, and continue to reside there. They took me to Boulder, CO to attend an apparition of Our Lady at the shrine of Mother Cabrini – outside on the hilltop in cool early morning weather. The "seer", Veronica Garcia, had been having these visitations from Our Blessed Mother ever since she had returned from a retreat in Medjugorje. I knelt next to Veronica on the grassy slope and during the apparition, Veronica was in ecstasy, her head thrown back and looking straight up. She said that she sees and listens to words from both Our Lady and Jesus Himself. She was in this position for about 5 minutes, during which I felt very warm and had to remove my jacket. I smelled the beautiful smell of roses and the rosary in my hand turned golden; even the black wooden beads had a golden hue. I had asked Veronica to ask Our Lady what my future would be like. She told me that Our Lady's message to me was that I would find out when I returned to Boston, where I was working at the V. A. Medical Center in Bedford. I had the Blessed Sacrament with me in a pyx at the Mitchells' home, and smelled roses every day in my guest room while there. Joan Mitchell saw the sun spinning there, in Colorado, and I saw cloud formations of religious themes: 2 angels holding the Sacred Heart of Jesus and the Immaculate Heart of Mary, a fish, a cross, etc.

On a trip to France in 1994 with a group of priest friends, we went to the American cemetery at Omaha Beach. I discovered where all the chaplains of various faiths were buried, and I said a rosary over each of their graves. It was a very meaningful experience, as was the Mass celebrated by Fr. Steve Donohoe to commemorate the 2nd anniversary of his ordination at the altar in the Convent at Lisieux that used to be cleaned every day by St. Therese of the Child Jesus, the "Little Flower". We could feel her presence.

On another trip to Italy, we spent some time at the mountain where St. Francis of Assisi received the "stigmata". It was cold and rainy, somewhat snowy as well, and we could just imagine what kind of discomfort St. Francis was put through.

At the Shrine of Knock in Ireland, Sr. Briege told the story of how a young priest dying of cancer, sat in a wheelchair before the exposed Blessed Sacrament. In an instant, he was completely healed.

In Ukraine, on another trip, we visited a shrine to Our Lady at Hrushev, a small wooden church which covered over a well of holy water since the 16th century when Our Lady appeared there. It had been closed all during the communist era – some 50 years. A young teenage girl spotted a woman on the upper balcony of the closed church one day in the late 1980's and the woman identified herself as Our Lady. This led to thousands of people coming to visit the church, but no one was allowed inside. The police tried to force the people away – this was in the countryside, in a farming community. This led to the conversion to Catholicism of the entire Orthodox parish. We met the young priest who was pastor of the church and celebrated Mass there. It was very moving to hear of the story and how the people were able to re-open their parish church.

In Vilnius, Lithuania, I was shown a Greek Catholic Church, built in the 17th century, which was being restored, having been used all during the communist era as a public toilet. The young Basilian monk in charge showed me how they had discovered the bodies of martyred priests and nuns, buried underneath the floor of the church foyer, and underneath the area near the altar behind the iconostasis. I remarked that we are standing on holy ground, and that their blood would ensure a renewal of the faith of the people.

A group of priests and I travelled to Poland in the late 1990's, one of the stops having been the Franciscan monastery outside Warsaw, built by St. Maximilian Kolbe in the first part of the 20th century. The story of St. Maximilian Kolbe is well described by the author of this book, in Chapter 22. When I visited what had been his room back at the monastery, I found a guest book on the desk. I wrote my name in it, and then wrote, "Son of the Eucharist". I was amazed at having written that, but realized that it identified me rather completely: it revealed to me my true role as priest. And how did this happen? I was reflecting early one morning in the Lourdes grotto on the grounds of Niepokolanów about where we had just been visiting, namely in Vilnius, Lithuania. We were staying with a Jesuit community, which was rebuilding a church that under the Communists had been preserved as a museum of atheism (!). At dinner one evening, a guest was the Archbishop of Kaunas, Sigitis Tamkevicius, with whom I could only communicate in Russian. As a young priest in the early 1980's, he had been imprisoned in a gulag in the Soviet Far North for using an illegal printing press to print religious information. He said he had spent 5 years in solitary confinement. When asked how he survived that, he simply said that he had taken the Lord Jesus with him and spent the whole time on retreat. One could tell by looking in his eyes what that had done to him. His eyes were aglow with the blessings of the Spirit. What a beautiful person! What a beautiful testimony to Jesus in the Blessed Sacrament! I knew that I belonged in that company, that my mission was to promote Jesus in the True Presence, that I was a Son of the Eucharist.

I have been saying a Requiem Mass for each soldier, sailor, marine or coastguardsman who has died in the wars in Iraq and Afghanistan. I began at the beginning of the Iraqi conflict in 2003 while under contract with the Army as a chaplain in Heidelberg. As of Easter 2010 I have completed over 2500 such Masses. That means I will need another 6 years to complete the project! It is a wonderful way for me to exercise my priesthood.

I have embraced three saintly figures as role models for my life, my priesthood:

Blessed Rupert Mayer, SJ, who was a chaplain in the German Army in WWI, lost a leg in battle in Rumania, came to Munich after the war to be pastor at the Buergersaalkirche. It was there before WWII that he preached against the Nazi treatment of the Jews. For that he was to be sent to a concentration camp, but instead ended up spending the war years under house arrest at the Benedictine monastery of Ettal in Bavaria. The Hitler government gave him this reprieve because Fr. Mayer held the very same medal for bravery in war as did Hitler – the Iron Cross (Eisenkreuz). Rupert Mayer died at the end of the war, and is considered a martyr of the Faith. It was in his bed at Ettal where I slept the week after Christmas 1959 while in search of life's meaning. Little did I know at the time that I would become an Army chaplain!

Blessed Kaspar Stangassinger of Berchtesgaden, a Redemptorist priest from the Monastery of Gars. He died young at age 28 from tuberculosis. I admire his background because his ministry was to the youth. That is essentially what I did at Middlebury VT, and all those years in Montreal.

Blessed Pier Giorgio Frassati, an Italian from Turino, who died at age 25, having spent his youth in working with young people, serving the poor in particular.

At one point in my early priesthood, I came into possession of a dozen or more religious relics, that is, traditional relics, 1st class, of the bone of a saint. I had been visiting a priest friend at the parish of St. Thomas Aquinas in Montreal, only to discover him cleaning out his sacristy. We were just making casual conversation when I realized that he had thrown a bunch of relics into a nearby trashcan, along with a broken chalice. I asked him about them, and he said he was throwing them away because they were of no further use. I found the conversation strange, but asked if I might have them, and he said I could. Later I took them, cleaned them up. They were indeed 1st class relics of the saints and blessed of Montreal: St. Marguerite Bourgeois, St. Marguerite d'Youville, Bl. Andre Bessette and a host of others. After mounting them in a reliquary for display, I used them as a teaching tool for our youngsters at St. Thomas High School, concerning the blood-soaked and holy soil we were walking on. I would introduce the subject by talking about the nuns who had a small convent on the land at the water's edge in my parish of Corpus Christi in Senneville/Ste. Anne de Bellevue, Quebec. They had been missionary sisters from France who settled in our territory back in the 1600's and were murdered by marauding Iroquois Indians. The broken chalice turned out to be an antique, and when repaired/restored by the religious goods people, Desmarais & Robitaille, I presented it to Bishop Crowley for use at a high school Mass. He recognized it, because his first assignment as a priest was at St. Thomas Aquinas. That chalice was given to a newly ordained priest in 2005, a graduate of the Seminary of Blessed John XXIII. And why was I chosen to come across these relics and that chalice? The Holy Spirit.

Within days it was discovered that the priest who had given them to me had left the priesthood and married. You never know.

While meditating in front of the exposed Blessed Sacrament, especially if the monstrance/ostensarium is at the same level as my eyes, I have come to realize a theological truth: namely, that as I see Jesus in the Consecrated Bread with my face superimposed, it works in reverse: Jesus is looking at me into my eyes & soul. As I am in Him, He is in me.

A LENTEN PILGRIMAGE TO THE DESERT

Introduction

Iraq had invaded Kuwait in August 1990. That very month many thousands of American military were sent to the Persian Gulf region to confront aggression. From August until January 1991, there was a wait-and-see attitude, but we all knew that, sooner or later, we would have to move against the Iraqis in order to expel them from Kuwait.

The air war began on January 16th, and most of us watched television news in our spare time, to keep track of events on the other side of the world, not knowing whether we would ever be involved. A number of troops and their chaplains from Fort Benning had already deployed for Saudi Arabia. I had just entered the third quarter of residency in Clinical Pastoral Education at Fort Benning, when we were informed that – according to some master plan in the Pentagon – the five of us would have to put aside our studies and go on to minister in Saudi Arabia. We were to be replacements for casualties that were assumed would take place as the war progressed. My initial reaction was relief that the wondering was over: wondering whether or not I would be called to the battle zone. Secondly, I knew in my heart that nothing would happen to me, and so I was somewhat eager to participate in the events in Southwest Asia. With Lent about to start some two weeks hence, I knew that the experience could be spiritually uplifting, if I let God lead me through the "desert experience."

My mission was in the field of pastoral care to soldiers, so I decided that my coming experience in the Middle East would be an application of my residency in pastoral education training: nourishing soldiers through effective religious ministry, counseling and spiritual guidance. To help me along in my mission, I kept a journal of events and my reactions to them. When I realized that the events took place all during the Lenten season of 1991, I decided to relate them in the form of a Lenten meditation, which, theologically, would reflect the Paschal Mystery: the Passover of the ancient Jews into the Promised Land; the Passion, Death and Resurrection of Jesus, and the theology of baptism, or the dying of the old self to sin, and the rising from the cleansing waters to new personhood. The experience in the desert was just that for me: a renewal of spirit in the Lord. I had gone into the desert where the ancient Church Fathers had gone to purify themselves, and – like them – came out of the experience refreshed and invigorated.

The form of the meditation is that of the ancient Catholic devotion, the Way of the Cross. In the Middle Ages, pilgrimages to the Holy Land emphasized visiting and celebrating the Eucharist at holy sites; from this practice arose the devotion of the Way of the Cross. People started at the Garden of Gethsemane and stopped to meditate at from 9 to 18 different places, ending at the tomb in what is now the Holy Sepulchre in Jerusalem. The Way of the Cross spread to Europe during the 16th and 17th centuries. In relating one's own sufferings to those of Jesus on His way to Calvary, we give up our sufferings to Jesus, Who takes them on Himself and frees us from fear, pain and depression.

FIRST STATION

JESUS IS CONDEMNED TO DEATH

We adore You, O Christ, and we praise You, because by Your holy Cross You have redeemed the world.

Wisdom 3: 1-8

"But the souls of the just are in the hand of God, and no torment shall touch them. They seemed, in the view of the foolish, to be dead; and their passing away was thought an affliction and their going forth from us, utter destruction. But they are in peace. For if before men, indeed, they be punished, yet is their hope full of immortality; chastised a little, they shall be greatly blessed, because God tried them and found them worthy of himself. As gold in the furnace, he proved them, and as sacrificial offerings he took them to himself. In the time of their visitation they shall shine, and shall dart about as sparks through stubble; they shall judge nations and rule over peoples, and the Lord shall be their King forever."

Reflection:

It took us nearly 24 hours to get to Saudi Arabia, and once there, we spent several days being shunted from place to place, always in the dark, under cover of night, with little sleep, sometimes a cold shower to relieve the heat and shed the crud. I never knew where I was; we were like insects, numberless, nameless, disoriented. We were getting angry, and were helping others to spill out their anxieties and anger. We began to help one another, to smile, to find ridiculous situations and places very amusing...the doctor who refused to use the latrines at a Saudi military installation known as King Khalid Military City (KKM) because of the filth, but finally had to give in…getting lost in the compound of an unknown unit in an unknown location in the middle of the night…worrying about snakes and scorpions but not being able to keep from falling asleep. I was angry at the US Government for compromising our value-system, at first not allowing chaplains to wear branch insignia (the cross), so as not to offend people who basically hate us anyway, because we are non-believers! I found this un-American; I refused to observe this and wore my crosses everywhere. The people around me appreciated that. Those of us with crosses became folk heroes! The Saudis were never offended, and the one person who recognized the significance (the Hospital's commanding Officer) thought it was appropriate.

Prayer:

Father in heaven, Jesus was condemned to death because he was an affront to sinners. Help me in my struggle in life, not to let darkness overwhelm me or the forces of evil divert me on my pilgrimage. Lord, be my guide. Amen.

SECOND STATION

JESUS TAKES HIS CROSS

We adore You O Christ, and we praise You, because by Your holy Cross You have redeemed the world.

Isaiah 53: 4-7.

"Yet it was our infirmities that he bore, our sufferings that he endured, while we thought of him as stricken, as one smitten by God and afflicted. But he was pierced for our offenses, crushed for our sins, upon him was the chastisement that makes us whole, by his stripes we were healed. We had all gone astray like sheep, each following his own way; but the Lord laid upon him the guilt of us all. Though he was harshly treated, he submitted and opened not his mouth; like a lamb led to the slaughter or a sheep before the shearers, he was silent and opened not his mouth."

Reflection:

Kuwait had been badly damaged and looted, the people raped and traumatized. I had visions of being sent to Kuwait to help the people to restore their sanity, once the country was liberated. I had even joked about having an eventual apartment on the sea in Kuwait City. It was not to be. I was still in transit along with hundreds of others, to a destination I knew not where. The soldiers had left their families behind in the States and began to miss loved ones, as tiredness seeped in, and as disorientation caused by moving around in the nighttime, took over. We were all soon to be arriving at our units and settling in – at least having a hole in the ground or a tent to call our own. We had moved from Dhahran to King Khalid Military City, squeezed into a C-130 with all our equipment. I thought, "What do we do if there's an emergency?" None of us were able to move at all in the plane. We unloaded on tarmac and waited around for further transportation for that night's lodging in some tent. There were more of us to accommodate than there was room. I remember a colonel in the middle of the night looking for a place to sleep, and he ended up sleeping outside on the ground! We tried hard to look after each other, to be of help, and – indeed – the mood was catching. We were so tired, the lack of amenities didn't really matter. I just remember how helpful everyone was toward each other, and how we went out of our ways to be kind, to get equipment squared away, to store things away, to put up bunks, to share food. I knew I was going to like THIS Army!

Prayer:

Father in heaven, Isaac once carried wood on his shoulders for a sacrifice intended to be his own; Jesus willingly bore the wood of the Cross to take away our sins. Help me carry my brothers' burdens as we struggle together in the darkness. Amen.

THIRD STATION

JESUS FALLS THE FIRST TIME

We adore You, O Christ, and we praise you, because by Your holy Cross You have redeemed the world.

Isaiah 1: 16-19.

"Wash yourselves clean! Put away your misdeeds from before my eyes; cease doing evil; learn to do good. Make justice your aim; redress the wronged, hear the orphan's plea, defend the widow. Come now, let us set things right, says the Lord; though your sins be like scarlet, they may become white as snow; though they be crimson red, they may become white as wool. If you are willing, and obey, you shall eat the good things of the land."

Reflection:

I remember at one point being herded with a group of officers just after arrival in Dhahran, getting ready to move out to Cement City in the dark. I ran after the others toward a bus and fell flat on my face, having stumbled over a guy wire holding down a tent. I narrowly missed being impaled on the tent peg. How would the military explain my injuries to my family? We all became very careful about night movements after that. In fact, the lava rocks all over the desert floor made it impossible to move about even in daylight without watching where you were stepping. It was awful; it was tiresome!

Here we were in the holy land of Islam. The Saudis did not want us to shovel the sacred soil into sand bags to protect our tents (they finally relented). I couldn't figure out for the life of me why – if the land was so sacred – the place was trashed everywhere? There was garbage everywhere you went in Saudi Arabia, alongside the roads. Every now then you'd see a sheep or camel carcass, for good measure! The desert was littered with auto wrecks. I still haven't figured out the dichotomy in Arab thinking.

I was at the 93rd Evacuation Hospital in Rafha, up north on the Iraqi border…far enough from the action not to be too worried, yet near enough to house lots of Iraqi prisoners who needed desperate medical treatment. These poor guys had been abandoned by their officers and made to stay in their bunkers without food or water for many days. They were in terrible shape, and their wounds had been left to fester. I couldn't figure out why Arabs would treat brother Arabs the way they do…not just the rich Kuwaitis (Jealousy? Revenge?)…but their own soldiers!

Prayer:

Father in heaven, the sons of Jacob once sold their brother Joseph for a pitiful 20 pieces of silver. Judas sold out Jesus for 30. Let my ministry to others who suffer never include a price tag. Amen.

FOURTH STATION

JESUS MEETS HIS MOTHER

We adore You, O Christ, and we praise You, because by Your holy Cross You have redeemed the world.

Luke 2: 33-35:

"The child's father and mother were amazed at what was said about him; and Simeon blessed them and said to Mary his mother, 'Behold, this child is destined for the fall and rise

450

of many in Israel, and to be a sign that will be contradicted (and you yourself a sword will pierce) so that the thoughts of many hearts may be revealed.'"

Reflection:

Just as the mother of Tobias suffered grief when her son went off into a foreign land, so Mary's heart is pierced by a sword as she encounters her suffering Son. Her pain is softened by her trust in God's providence.

The rabbi came visiting us in Rafha, and was of great comfort to the Jewish personnel present in the compound. We later found out that he personally called each of their wives to let their families know they were all right. It was a strange situation in our modern world, having Jewish personnel in the Saudi desert with us, and knowing that the rabbi was not far away! (Only in America....).

As I visited the various brigades in the area to celebrate Mass and hear confessions, I never seemed to have enough Bibles or religious items on hand. Even every Baptist in sight was wearing a Rosary around his neck! I carried over my heart a small book of the New Testament and Psalms that had been carried by my great-great grandfather Ira Tompkins in the Civil War. He was a soldier with Vermont Volunteers and was killed in action at Cedar Creek, VA in October 1864. I took great comfort in reading over Scripture that he had read over 127 years ago. I wonder what he felt in battle. Did he have the same feelings I was experiencing? Was he afraid? Our soldiers all carried a copy of Psalm 91 as an assurance that God would protect them. And so He did! Wherever I celebrated Mass, whenever I recited the Rosary with the soldiers, we prayed fervently for peace. God answered our prayers. There were to be no casualties during the war weekend for soldiers in our XVIII Airborne Corps area. We were awed.

My first Mass with the engineers brought many of these burly, tough soldiers to tears. Afterwards, one of them told me that it was the first Mass they were able to attend in over

451

seven months. That made me angry. There was no excuse for their being denied the right to have Mass. I saw a lot of tears from time to time as we prayed the ancient prayers of faith.

Prayer:

Father in heaven, comfort us as we face uncertainty and peril. Give us strength and trust to march forward with faith in your goodness and providence to keep us safe! Amen.

FIFTH STATION

SIMON OF CYRENE

We adore You, O Christ, and we praise You, because by Your holy Cross You have redeemed the world.

Luke 9: 23-25:

"Then he said to all, 'If anyone wishes to come after me, he must deny himself and take up his cross daily and follow me. For whoever wishes to save his life will lose it, but whoever loses his life for my sake will save it. What profit is there for one to gain the whole world yet lose or forfeit himself?'"

Reflection:

While celebrating Mass at the Headquarters of the XVIII Airborne Corps at Rafha, I bumped into two very good friends whom I had known in Berlin Brigade. What a surprise! We got together on Sunday evenings for MRE's-by-candlelight! (MRE, as anyone who has ever served in our armed forces knows, is short for *Meals Ready to Eat*.) As I had been their pastor in Berlin, they were eager to help me anyway they could. Thus my visits to brigades in Iraq were made easier by helicopter. I am very grateful. Lots of time & energy were saved.

I heard a story later in Dhahran about a young priest up on the frontlines, who spent considerable effort erecting a Catholic chapel made out of spare wood from equipment crates. The soldiers were fantastic about this project; it had everything in it that a Catholic church would, including an altar and tabernacle. It was so well done, that it was carefully dismantled, upon redeployment, and has been sent to the Museum at the Chaplain's School at Ft. Jackson, SC. That was making good, constructive use of nervous energy for a project that has done a lot of good. Another way people were always helpful – covering for each other in duty, going the extra mile.

When it came time to give recommendations for awards in the combat zone, I felt that there were four people in the unit who deserved the most credit: the mess sergeant, who tirelessly worked at providing quality meals; the sergeant in charge of the laundry & showers, both of which were dependant on temperamental generators & equipment; the private from the motor pool, who was in charge of fixing the ever-breaking-down generators, thus providing us with critical electricity; and the mail clerks, who boosted troop morale fantastically by their driving a long ways to pick up and distribute mail. To these men and women we owe a debt of gratitude for making our pilgrimage in the desert less painful.

Prayer:

Father in heaven, let me be an example of love and care to your people. Grace me with those moments when I can be of service in Your name and thereby further the Kingdom. Amen.

SIXTH STATION

ST. VERONICA AND THE FACE OF JESUS

We adore You, O Christ, and we praise You, because by Your holy Cross You have redeemed the world.

Matthew 17: 1-3:

"After six days Jesus took Peter, James, and John his brother, and led them up a high mountain by themselves. And he was transfigured before them; his face shone like the sun and his clothes became white as light. And behold, Moses and Elijah appeared to them conversing with him."

Reflection:

In 1 Kings 22: 1-36 we can read the account of how Micaiah is slapped in the face for revealing the truth to Ahab, the King. Likewise, Jesus is struck in the face, spit upon and scourged.

I recall several visitors to my tent at Rafha, all of whom were chaplains and chaplain assistants on their way out of the Iraqi desert, heading into a holding area in the Saudi desert before redeployment back to the States. Every one of them had faces covered with a fine layer of desert dust, and it made them surreal. One African American and I had a good laugh, because when he looked in the mirror, all he saw was a reflection of one of those African faces that are often painted in different colored powders. It took us all a long while to get used to the blowing dust and sand storms. The dust simply covered everything, no matter how covered things were. One minute the sun would be shining on a beautiful morning in the desert. When that happened, we all did our laundry, hanging things out to dry. Within minutes, the sand storms would begin, covering everything in fine dust. Even our operating rooms in the hospital – designed to be airtight, fell victim to the blowing dust. It was awful. In the middle of the night, with the wind kicking up, we would have to get up in the freezing cold of the desert night to prevent the tent from being blown down. Goggles and neckerchiefs over the nose were often the order of the day!

Seeing soldiers who cried when I said Mass, because they had missed their religious practices so much, was very touching. Tough, dirty, young faces crying during Holy Communion: an image I will not forget.

Iraqi prisoners who were lying in bed, waiting for their wounds to be tended to, at first showed great fear, because they had been told we would execute them. (At the enemy prisoner of war compound at Log Base Romeo in Iraq, the Iraqis at first wouldn't go to the latrines, because they were afraid that was the place they were to be shot.) When I approached any of them with a chocolate bar or gum, saying, "Salaam aleikum", their faces would brighten up with a sudden smile, knowing that I meant what I said in Arabic, "Peace be with you."

Prayer:

Father in heaven, may I see the face of your Son Jesus in those I minister to – extending the same care and reverence I would to the Sacred Host. Amen.

SEVENTH STATION

JESUS FALLS THE SECOND TIME

We adore You, O Christ, and we praise You, because by Your holy Cross You have redeemed the world.

Matthew 5: 1-12:

"When he saw the crowds, he went up the mountain, and after he had sat down, his disciples came to him. He began to teach them, saying: 'Blessed are the poor in spirit, for theirs is the kingdom of heaven. Blessed are they who mourn, for they will be comforted. Blessed are the meek, for they will inherit the land. Blessed are they who hunger and thirst for righteousness, for they will be satisfied. Blessed are the merciful, for they will be shown mercy. Blessed are the clean of heart, for they will see God. Blessed are the peacemakers, for they will be called children of God. Blessed are they who are persecuted for the sake of righteousness, for theirs is the kingdom of heaven. Blessed are you when they insult you and persecute you and utter every kind of evil against you falsely because of me. Rejoice and be glad for your reward will be great in heaven. Thus they persecuted the prophets who were before you.'"

Reflection:

People have sometimes asked me how I can serve a war machine as a priest. My reaction? First of all, I serve with the Army in order to permit our soldiers to exercise their option of freedom to express their religious beliefs. Secondly, our soldiers are the only ones in our country who swear to give their lives for others in defense of freedom – a clear analogy to Christ's sacrifice.

What were we doing in the Persian Gulf area, assisting people who hate us because we don't believe in their brand of religion? "Blessed are those who are persecuted in the cause of right, for theirs is the kingdom of heaven." It is clear to me that we are the ones who win out, because of our openness, because of our non-judgmental nature. The Saudis and other wealthy Arabs amazed us for their obvious lack of willingness to do hard work. They always have some poor Pakistani or Filipino doing their work for them. There are third world people everywhere, though, trying to escape the clutches of poverty and hunger and disease. I think of the plight of the Kurdish refugees, and the disasters that visit the Bangladeshis with great regularity, and the immense problems faced by east Africans in the struggle against famine.

In Genesis 3: 17-19, we read how Adam is condemned to eat bread by the sweat of his brow. And we reflect on how Jesus struggled on toward Calvary in a stream of bloody sweat.

Prayer:

Father in heaven, let me not be afraid to do my share in alleviating the sufferings of others. Strengthen my resolve to be true to my convictions, and let them be reflected in my actions. Amen.

EIGHTH STATION

THE WOMEN OF JERUSALEM

We adore You, O Christ, and we praise You, because by Your holy Cross You have redeemed the world.

Luke 23: 27-31:

"A large crowd of people followed Jesus, including many women who mourned and lamented him. Jesus turned to them and said, "Daughters of Jerusalem, do not weep for me; weep instead for yourselves and for your children, for indeed, the days are coming when people will say, 'Blessed are the barren, the wombs that never bore and the breasts that never nursed.' At that time people will say to the mountains, 'Fall upon us!' and to the hills, 'Cover us!' for if these things are done when the wood is green what will happen when it is dry?'"

Reflection:

The surprising factor in the Iraqi war zone was the large number of women in uniform. Our problem with that fact had nothing to do with combat, but rather with the living arrangements in close quarters. It worked out for most people. Those who were uncomfortable soon got over it when one was forced by circumstances to ignore modesty and much privacy. Our women were highly respected and I never once noted a problem based on sexual difference. Having many women around provided, in fact, for a more normal atmosphere. There were a few emotional conflicts; some couples fell in love and that had to be dealt with. But, for the most part, women in the combat zone worked out just fine. Our French neighbors in the nearby French hospital compound, wasted no time or effort in getting to know our female soldiers!

I flew up to Iraq, as my pilgrimage progressed, and was met by a Military Police captain (who happened to be a female) whose troops were in charge of the prisoner of war compound up there. At Mass there were a lot of female soldiers, several of whom identified themselves as graduates of West Point. The Army was never like this! This was all in contrast to the way Saudi women are treated: the local Arab women were covered in black from head-to-toe, and were seldom seen in public. I got the impression they have the status of cattle. How degrading. Our own women did not experience difficulty in local towns while shopping, because the Saudis rationalized – as only they can – that a female soldier is not a woman. She is a soldier. Therefore, the problem of mixing with men and wearing a uniform doesn't matter. The same applies, I am told, to Saudi female teachers and doctors. One woman in Rafha, dressed all in black, approached me in a store and told me in perfect English, "I want you to know, you are welcome here." Curious…..

Prayer:

Father in heaven, help me to uphold the dignity of woman; help me to promote the welfare and equality of women through prayer and example. Amen.

NINTH STATION

JESUS FALLS THE THIRD TIME

We adore You, O Christ, and we praise You, because by Your holy Cross You have redeemed the world.

Ephesians 6: 10-17:

"Finally, draw your strength from the Lord and from his mighty power. Put on the armor of God so that you may be able to stand firm against the tactics of the devil. For our struggle is not with flesh and blood but with the principalities, with the powers, with the world rulers of this present darkness, with the evil spirits in the heavens. Therefore, put on the armor of God, that you may be able to resist on the evil day and, having done everything, to hold your ground. So stand fast with your loins girded in truth, clothed with righteousness as a breastplate, and your feet shod in readiness for the gospel of peace. In all circumstances, hold faith as a shield, to quench all the flaming arrows of the evil one. And take the helmet of salvation and the sword of the Spirit, which is the word of God. "

Reflection:

I was standing outside the 93rd Evacuation Hospital waiting for a real exercise in mass casualties. Seven dead soldiers were brought in helicopters and one lone survivor. American engineers were clearing unexploded bombs from the Iraqi airport at Target White, when a bomb went off. Seven were killed. The survivor, the XO of that particular company, was a young first lieutenant, who had a shrapnel wound that needed tending to. Most important of all, though, was that he wanted, he needed to talk with a priest. In the next several hours, I help him debrief. The people who were killed were his friends. One of them had been his roommate back in the States. It was tough having to process through one's feelings about this event. The lieutenant read at Mass the next day, which I held in memory of his fallen comrades. A lot of people attended. He put himself together and went back to Iraq to help the other men deal with the pain, the anger, the guilt.

This was the same group of combat engineers for whom I had celebrated Mass the very morning of their death at Target White. They had all gone to confession; they were all serious about their faith; the seven came back to the compound in nine body bags. I realized what a role I had played that day. It was daunting; it was crushing.

One priest who had spent quite a long time in Iraq mentioned that, thanks to God, he didn't have to anoint a single soldier. I thought about that and realized how much God had listened to our prayers and petitions for peace, for safety. Most of us were most fortunate. The Iraqis didn't fare as well. The only person I anointed was a soldier who had accidentally set off a grenade, wounding himself severely in the backside. But he was young and tough, and he survived, although he faces much reconstructive surgery. I still pray for Kevin and trust the Lord will be a strong part of his recovery.

Prayer:

Father in heaven, we thank You for Your providence in guiding us through the darkness and forces of evil that surround us. Continue to be our light and assurance in times of trouble; give us courage; keep us safe. Amen.

TENTH STATION

JESUS IS STRIPPED OF HIS CLOTHES

We adore You, O Christ, and we praise You, because by Your holy Cross You have redeemed the world.

Ephesians 4: 23-26:

"Be renewed in the spirit of your minds, and put on the new self, created in God's way of righteousness and holiness of truth. Therefore, putting away falsehood, speak the truth, each one to his neighbor, for we are members one of another. Be angry but do not sin; do not let the sun set on your anger."

Reflection:

It was difficult to keep one's clothes clean, because of the blowing sand and dust. And, as one chaplain observed to me, the only water he had to drink and clean with was in his canteen. It was worse for the Iraqis, who had had no food or water for days when we picked them up. They were lice-ridden, and we had to burn their clothes to prevent disease! What a place!

A number of patients came into our hospital complex, their skin covered with blank charcoal from wearing the clothing designed to protect against chemical and biological weapons. We often had to don these awkward suits and boots, as well as the ever-present masks; one never knew if a SCUD was about to land, whether the alert was for real, whether this was the time we'd be attacked. I was fortunate.

Not so some of our National Guardsmen & women in Dhahran. We could only pray and trust in God. We were clothed in grace…I was living between two generators that effectively drowned out any outside sound (like compound announcements, "Attention on the compound! Attention on the compound! – just like in the movie, MASH). I was always worried that we would miss an alarm or alert because of the stereo noise of the generators. One morning at 0430, my tent-mate woke me up, saying there was an alert. We donned gas masks, and waited for further instructions or an "all clear". After sitting in the dark for a half-hour, I peeked outside and saw someone sitting not 25 feet away smoking a cigarette! I told my tent-mate that I think we were mistaken.

(It turned out that he had heard a practice alert for the French Foreign Legion next door to us.) We were always worried about whether we were properly dressed: gas mask, Kevlar helmet. etc. During the day it became so very hot, we had to peel down to something comfortable. At night it was very cold in the desert, and so winter clothing was the norm. It was crazy. And when it came time to turn in our equipment later at Ft. Benning, I bumped into a soldier who had slept in his sleeping bag every night for eight months, without being able to clean it! It stood alone by itself. And I thought my sleeping bag was bad after 60 days....

Prayer:

Father in heaven, let me be stripped of all sin in my life; clothe me with refreshing grace as I go about doing your work on my Lenten pilgrimage. Amen.

ELEVENTH STATION

JESUS IS NAILED TO THE CROSS

We adore You, O Christ, and we praise You, because by Your holy Cross You have redeemed the world.

John 3: 14-17:

"And just as Moses lifted up the serpent in the desert, so must the Son of Man be lifted up, so that everyone who believes in him may have eternal life. For God so loved the world that he gave his only Son, so that everyone who believes in him might not perish but might have eternal life. For God did not send his Son into the world to condemn the world, but that the world might be saved through him."

Reflection:

From the very first in Saudi Arabia, we were all warned about the snakes and scorpions in the desert, and to be careful about where we put our hands in our tents. We all chilled to this news, and were cautious. Up in Rafha, I soon realized that the time of year was not right for the appearance of snakes and insects. The nights were freezing cold, and until the weather permitted, no insects would show their faces in the wilderness. So much for snakes. The snake, though, became the instrument of God's providence with Moses, when the Israelis – desperately thirsty in their desert wanderings – begged for water. Moses, with God's prompting, lifted the serpent and it became a stick with which Moses then struck water in the desert. Being with a medical command whose symbol is that very healing serpent of Moses, helped me connect the symbol: a symbol on the one hand of evil (referring to the Genesis account of the role of the serpent and Eve, relating to original sin); and a symbol on the other of salvation (the serpent-stick of Moses bringing forth water for a thirsty people).

The Cross is both an instrument of horror, of trauma, of death; and it is an instrument of salvation. It became an altar of sacrifice, in the Jewish understanding of sacrifice, upon which the blood of an Innocent, Spotless Lamb was shed for our sins. This is a difficult concept to understand; once one understands the meaning of the lamb of sacrifice in the Jewish usage, then one begins to understand the correlation of what is meant by Jesus as Lamb of God & taking away our sins forever. The whole idea of Jesus, as God-in-the-flesh, going through this whole exercise in order to both get the attention of the people of God (the Jews), and also to be THE instrument of salvation for mankind, is mind-boggling. We believe it because He said so, and because He rose from the dead to prove the point.

I wonder how many of us are able to relate our sufferings to those of Jesus. Salvation through death and resurrection is powerful. But to become a new person in the Lord, we have

463

to allow our old selves to suffer and die and then rise through the baptismal waters.

Prayer:

Father in heaven, let me be lifted up with the Lord in a renewal of my dedication to You. Amen.

TWELFTH STATION

JESUS DIES ON THE CROSS

We adore You, O Christ, and we praise You, because by Your holy Cross You have redeemed the world.

Romans 6: 3-11.

"Or are you unaware that we who were baptized into Christ Jesus were baptized into his death? We were indeed buried with him through baptism into death, so that, just as Christ was raised from the dead by the glory of the Father, we too might live in newness of life. For if we have grown into union with him through a death like his, we shall also be united with him in the resurrection. We know that our old self was crucified with him, so that our sinful body might be done away with, that we might no longer be in slavery to sin. For a dead person has been absolved from sin. If, then, we have died with Christ, we believe that we shall also live with him. We know that Christ, raised from the dead, dies no more; death no longer has power over him. As to his death, he died to sin once and for all; as to his life, he lives for God. Consequently, you too must think of yourselves as being dead to sin and living for God in Christ Jesus."

Reflection:

Flying over the battlefield in Iraq, I noted the total destruction of the Iraqi tanks and equipment. Any dead personnel were long since buried or carted away. Some of our chaplains in the front lines during the action, saw bodies strewn about, but not in the numbers that suggest wanton destruction. The battlefield area was mainly open desert, and didn't really involve villages and civilian populations, as far as I could tell. We landed once to refuel, and as we pulled up afterward, the helicopter got caught in a sandstorm that created zero visibility and downdraft. We quickly settled again on the ground; it was the only time I felt any kind of fear, but knowing instantly that there is nothing, no one more important than GOD. We had been saved in an instant when we could have been destroyed. Only God did that. So, neither power, money, family, or friends have any meaning, other than GOD. I became convinced of that.

A young officer who had flown part-way with us wanted to explore one of the destroyed tanks; coming back to the helicopter, he tried to board with some unexpended rounds of Iraqi ammunition! The pilot quickly ordered him to cease and desist! I was surprised at that young officer's thoughtless, reckless behavior. I commented on the solders in our hospital at Rafha who had suffered severe injuries from such foolhardy attempts to bring back "souvenirs". The tragedy behind many injuries and deaths suffered in the desert was that they were the result of exploring destroyed Iraqi equipment, and not paying attention to the possibility of mines. Our hospital was not overwhelmed by this kind of injury, but one suspects that much of this could have been avoided.

Prayer:

Father in heaven, let me turn my fear over to You, so that wherever I go, whatever happens, I will be in Your hands. Amen

THIRTEENTH STATION

JESUS IS TAKEN FROM THE CROSS

We adore You, O Christ, and we praise You, because by
Your holy Cross You have redeemed the world.

Luke 2:46-50.

"After three days they found him in the temple, sitting in the
midst of the teachers, listening to them and asking them
questions, and all who heard him were astounded at his
understanding and his answers. When his parents saw him,
they were astonished, and his mother said to him, 'Son, why
have you done this to us? Your father and I have been
looking for you with great anxiety.' And he said to them,
'Why were you looking for me? Did you not know that I
must be in my Father's house?' But they did not understand
what he said to them. He went down with them and came to
Nazareth, and was obedient to them; and his mother kept all
these things in her heart."

Reflection:

Most of the chaplains I knew were on duty 24 hours a
day; at Rafha we were busy well into the night quite often,
listening to soldiers, visiting the sick, helping with problem-
solving in the unit. Most problems centered around the lack
of mail for very long periods of time. Yet the system was
inundated with mail of all kinds from very well-intentioned
people, who sent boxes and boxes of cookies and candy and
mail addressed to "any soldier" – all this was backed up on
the runways in Dhahran and KKMC. Eventually, it all found
its way to the soldiers and were they ever glad!

Another problem had to do with what we call "priest-
coverage." So many units didn't have Catholic chaplains,
and that meant that – unless there was a visiting priest, or a
soldier designated as Eucharistic Minister, soldiers would go

without Catholic ministry for long periods. I travelled across endless miles of bumpy desert to visit soldiers in five different brigades. In Iraq I was able to travel by helicopter, but that was the rare exception!

I met many wonderful people in my journey, not the least of whom were other priests and chaplains whom I had known elsewhere. It made for a super reunion, to get together with the brothers and share experiences, troubles, joys and good fellowship. The other chaplains were so very supportive, it made my ministry easy.

As we began to tear down the hospital compound, once clearance had been given and we were scheduled to move down to the Persian Gulf area in preparation for the trip back to the US, I noticed how everyone pitched in, regardless of rank, to make the work so much easier. Taking down the tents and trying to clean the desert off them, and then to empty the sand bags was fairly strenuous work...not as difficult as putting them up, but nonetheless tough work.

Prayer.

Father in heaven, as I go about being Your instrument in the salvation of others, let my hands be Your hands in molding and smoothing and healing. Amen.

FOURTEENTH STATION

JESUS IS LAID IN THE TOMB

We adore You, O Christ, and we praise You, because by Your holy Cross You have redeemed the world.

John 12: 24-26.

"Amen, amen, I say to you, unless a grain of wheat falls to the ground and dies, it remains just a grain of wheat; but if it dies, it produces much fruit. Whoever loves his life loses it, and whoever hates his life in this world will preserve it for eternal life. Whoever serves me must follow me, and where I am, there also will my servant be. The Father will honor whoever serves me."

Reflection.

I don't know why I should suddenly think of all those flies. There were flies everywhere in the desert. We often wondered where they all came from and what they subsisted on (us!). The desert was absolutely barren; there was no vegetation or water in any direction. There was nothing living either. No bugs, no animals, Nothing. But there were flies everywhere. I wonder what God had in mind making flies?

And then suddenly, driving down the oil pipeline in those last days, I looked out and saw as many as 5000 camels grazing in the desert! What in the world were they eating? Sand? Rocks? We stopped and looked. There were tiny green shoots of grass growing everywhere on the desert floor. We just hadn't noticed. It happened overnight. And the Bedouins were feeding this meager ration to their camels.

I thought of the ancient Israelis, traveling all those many years over the nearby desert to find the promised land. They experienced so much death and hunger and thirst in their quest. God was with them, though. I thought of them one morning when I saw a bird. A bird! Here in the desert! And the bird was skittering around from rock to rock. I took a closer look with my binoculars and saw that it was a quail. A quail in this desert – a descendant of one of the quails God provided the ancient Jews with, when they begged for meat. It was a sign of new life …new growth. The desert was not completely like the moon, after all. It contained the seeds of new life. And then I thought, I am on my way home, on my way to Easter – not a week away!

We convoyed in sections some 500 miles to Dhahran, taking 23 hours over 2 days. It was a long haul, but we knew the worst was behind us. When we got to the Persian Gulf, I left the unit and settled in first at Dragon Base, in preparation for deployment back to the States; then I was off to stay at the famous Khobar Towers – new high-rises built for the Bedouins, who had refused to move in! So my last view of Dhahran was from a Bedouin high-rise, entombed...waiting...with thousands of other soldiers, nowhere to go, but home..

Prayer.

Father in heaven, I thank You for guiding all of us through a difficult journey, and for hearing our prayers for peace and confident hope in the future. Amen.

FIFTEENTH STATION

JESUS' RESURRECTION

We adore You, O Christ, and we praise You, because by Your holy Cross You have redeemed the world.

Colossians 3: 1-4.

"If then you were raised with Christ, seek what is above, where Christ is seated at the right hand of God. Think of what is above, not of what is on earth. For you have died, and your life is hidden with Christ in God. When Christ your life appears, then you too will appear with him in glory."

Reflection.

When I think of the Resurrection and the Easter events, I recall being startled during Holy Week, and spotting first one, and then several butterflies. I also remember noting that this was a sign of new life in the desert – Easter in the wastes of Islam. And the birds! Suddenly there were the birds chirping. And the flowers and grass in Dhahran! I stopped in stupefaction at a simple flower. I had not seen much of any growing thing for long time. I knew all was well. God was with us still.

Many confessions and conversions took place in the desert. I wonder what the Saudis would think if they knew the extent of Christian (and Jewish, for that matter) witness in their holy desert? We made it holy. It had been made holy many hundreds of years ago by our Christian forefathers; it was made holy thousands of years ago by Jewish tribes, escaping the slavery of Egypt. New young men came forward, wanting to give their lives to Christ, and asking for information about how to become an Army priest. All these signs of grace...the baptisms...the reception of Holy Communion...the call to grace.

And we sanctified the Arabian desert by leaving some of our blood there; blood which will nourish the seed of pride of duty, of honor, of country, of our value system in Christ. Anyone who has died for this just cause, has certainly not died in vain. Desert Storm created a storm, with a residual calm thereafter: the calm of the beginning of lasting peace, of changed lives, of renewed dedication on the part of our nation, of a turning to God.

I think of the messages of Our Lady at Medjugorje, which emphasize fasting, prayer, repentance & peace; these things happened in Desert Storm.

Prayer.

Father in heaven, as I go forward from the pilgrimage in the desert, continue to guide me during the Easter of my life, to renewed commitment to a life in Christ: to feed the hungry, clothe the naked, comfort the sick, assist the poor. Let me, too, pray for the welfare of the Iraqi nation, and other Arabs as well, that they come to know Your blessings through peace. Amen.

On the Meaning of Light in My Spiritual Life

From *A Treatise on John by St. Augustine:*

We Christians are the light, at least by comparison with unbelievers. Thus the Apostle says: *For once you were darkness, but now you are light in the Lord; walk then as sons of the light.* And elsewhere he says: *The night is far spent, the day is drawing near. Let us therefore lay aside the works of darkness and put on the armor of light; let us walk uprightly as in the day.*

Nevertheless, since the days in which we are now living are still dark compared to the light which we shall see, hear what the apostle Peter says. He speaks of a voice that came from the Supreme Glory and said to the Lord Christ: *You are my beloved Son in whom I am well pleased. This voice, he says, we heard coming from heaven, when we were with him on the holy mountain.* Because we ourselves were not present there and did not hear that voice from heaven, Peter says to us: *And we possess a more certain prophetic word to which you do well to attend, as to a lamp shining in a dark place, until the day dawns and the morning star rises in your hearts.*

When, therefore, our Lord Jesus Christ shall come and, as the apostle Paul says, *bring to light things hidden in darkness and make plain the secrets of the heart, so that everyone may receive his commendation from God,* then lamps will no longer be needed. When that day is at hand, the prophet will not be read to us, the book of the Apostle will not be opened, we shall not require the testimony of John, we shall have no need of the Gospel itself. Therefore all Scriptures will be taken away from us, those Scriptures which in the night of this world burned like lamps so that we might not remain in darkness.

When all these things are removed as no longer necessary for our illumination, and when the men of God by whom they were ministered to us shall themselves together with us behold the true and dear light without such aids, what shall we see? With what shall our minds be nourished? What will give joy to our gaze? Where will that gladness come from *which eye has not seen, and ear has not heard, which has not even been conceived by the heart of man?* What shall we see?

I implore you to love with me and, by believing, to run with me; let us long for our heavenly country, let us sigh for our heavenly home, let us truly feel that here we are strangers. What shall we then see? Let the gospel tell us: *In the beginning was the Word and the Word was with God and the Word was God.* You will come to the fountain, with whose dew you have already been sprinkled. Instead of the ray of light which was sent through slanting and winding ways into the heart of your darkness, you will see the light itself in all its purity and brightness. It is to see and experience this light that you are now being cleansed. *Dearly beloved,* John himself says, *we are the sons of God, and it has not yet been disclosed what we shall be; but we know that when he appears we shall be like him, because we shall see him as he is.*

I feel that your spirits are being raised up with mine to the heavens above; but the *body, which is corruptible, weighs down the soul, and this earthly tent burdens the thoughtful mind.* I am about to lay aside this book, and you are soon going away, each to his own business. It has been good for us to share the common light, good to have enjoyed ourselves, good to have been glad together. When we part from one another, let us not depart from Him.

ACKNOWLEDGMENTS

This book could not have come to life if it were not for the astounding memory and recall of names and places possessed by Father Ron Lawson. It has been my privilege to work closely with him for the many months it took to capture his fascinating faith journey. His great knowledge of all aspects of the Catholic faith and of scripture has helped to keep the account of his life and travels in proper focus. He guided me through the complex spellings of the names of some German towns and customs, pointing out when and where to insert an umlaut or other grammatical symbols. He also has a keen eye for proper grammar and misspelled words, and even making note of mysteriously missing periods at the end of an occasional sentence. He has been a joy to work with.

I also owe a debt of gratitude to my wife, Pat, who not only has been supportive all during the time it has taken for this project to come to completion, but has read all of it as it was being born. Her many helpful suggestions to straighten out my sometimes twisted grammar and unusual sentence structure were much appreciated.

Sidney Lawson, Jr. provided a great deal of valuable input that covered several key aspects of the book. His help is gratefully acknowledged.

The cover artwork was generated by my close friend, Lawrence Pumfrey. Working from a rough idea of mine, he created the simple, yet meaningful design. His wife, Judy, also a gifted artist, had insights into the cover design that she shared with him. They have a website where their work can be seen. Visit http://www.pumfreygallery.com/

I also had help in researching the details of the Navy dive-bomber that was the taxi for Ron to get home for

Thanksgiving in 1958. My close friend from my childhood days, Fred Bortolussi, contacted friends of his who are knowledgeable in that field. Through the efforts of Fred and his friend Larry Trollen, I was able to correctly identify and describe the Douglass AD-5 Skyraider. Another friend from my high school days, Mel Foster, who had been a pilot in the Strategic Air Command, verified my description of some of its key details. Many thanks to them for their efforts on my behalf.

Whatever errors of fact, or of any other type that may remain, are solely my responsibility.

Richard L. Rotelli

Made in the USA
Lexington, KY
15 September 2017